BUDDHISM IN ASIA

Buddhism in Asia

REVIVAL AND REINVENTION

Edited by

NAYANJOT LAHIRI
UPINDER SINGH

ICCR

ISEAS YUSOF ISHAK INSTITUTE

MANOHAR
2016

First published 2016

ISBN 978-93-5098-116-0

Published by
Ajay Kumar Jain *for*
Manohar Publishers & Distributors
4753/23 Ansari Road, Daryaganj
New Delhi 110 002

Printed at
Salasar Imaging Systems
Delhi 110 035

For our Teachers

P.S. Dwivedi

and

D.E.U. Baker

Contents

Introduction

NAYANJOT LAHIRI AND UPINDER SINGH

THIS VOLUME EXAMINES the many manifestations of the Buddhist revival in Asia. This revival is among the most striking pan-Asian cultural phenomena of modern times, stretching from India and Sri Lanka, across Myanmar and Thailand, to China and Japan. While 'revival' is usually understood as a restoration of what had declined or disappeared to its original form, it is used here in a broader sense. 'Revival', as deployed here, describes the varied developments and changes that took place in the practice and propagation of Buddhism, and the expansion in the religion's contours and popularity during the nineteenth and twentieth centuries, in ways that have continued well into the present. This led to the creation of a new kind of Buddhism which, instead of being derived from traditional forms, was explicitly modernistic in its formulations and practices. The term 'reinvention' draws attention to this phenomenon.

The contributions that make up this volume were first presented at a conference on 'The Buddhist Revival in Asia' held in Singapore in December 2010. The Indian High Commissioner of Singapore at the time, T.C.A. Raghavan, took the initiative of shepherding the conference, under the joint auspices of the Indian Council for Cultural Relations (New Delhi, India) and the Nalanda-Sriwijaya Centre at the Institute of Southeast Asian Studies (Singapore). The presence of some delegates was facilitated by the Max Planck Institute (Gottingen, Germany) and the Nalanda University (Bihar, India). This finally made possible a meeting of scholars from India, Sri Lanka, Nepal, Singapore, Hong Kong, Germany and the United States of America.

Asia is a vast landmass and a large part of it gets geographic coverage in this volume, from the coastline of Taiwan on the east to the western fringe of India. There are three segments of Asia that figure prominently here and, for this reason, the book's parts are organized around them, i.e. India, Sri Lanka and China (with Taiwan figuring in relation to its Buddhist interface with the Peoples' Republic of China). Each of these parts has its own distinct flavour. In the case of India, the modern histories of iconic monuments and sites associated with early Buddhism – ranging from Sarnath and Sanchi to Nagarjunakonda and Amaravati – figure prominently. On the other hand, the Sri Lankan section focuses on the changing trajectory of modern Buddhist manuals, as also on those involved in the revival there, from Anagarika Dharmapala to an all-monk party, Jathika Hela Urumaya, which contested the 2004 parliamentary elections. In the case of China, the many forms of Buddhist revival are specifically assessed, qualitatively and statistically, to highlight the ways in which these were tempered by the broader political realities from the nineteenth century till the present.

At the same time, common themes and issues cut across the parts. There are several essays that examine the impact of political shifts on Buddhism's presence and profile. The trajectory of Nagarjunakonda in Andhra Pradesh in India is an example of this, a historic landscape whose dramatically diverse religious landscape came to be compromised as it was increasingly projected as a monochromatic Buddhist site, in consonance with the ideas of an influential section of the political leadership of post-Independence India. The political leadership of the People's Republic of China, on the other hand, has had a more ambivalent relationship with Buddhism. While, initially, it was supported by the Communist regime, during the 1960s and 1970s, the active hostility of the state, as seen in the Cultural Revolution, dramatically reduced the presence of temples and monasteries there.

The individuals that figure in this book – extraordinary ones who became monks (Dharmanand Kosambi in India and Taixu in China), reformer-nationalists who became icons of Buddhism (B.R. Ambedkar in India and Anagarika Dharmapala in Sri Lanka) and the creators of texts (Mohottivate Gunanda who compiled a Buddhist manual and Liang Qichao's political fiction that promoted a socially-engaged Buddhism) – may have led dissimilar lives. However, as various papers emphasize, there is, in each instance, a kind of cross-fertilization between Buddhism and contemporary discourses which makes them unambiguously modern. That their own lives and movements were aided by quicker modes of travel, publishing houses, Buddhist clubs and associations in what has been described as a 'Pan-Asian axis' among Buddhist adherents and sympathizers is also clearly highlighted. This was a time of rapid transformation, from South Asia to China, and the interactions among individuals, institutional interventions and agendas of reform produced a Buddhism that was both hybrid and modern. Notwithstanding efforts to provide ancient lineages to their programmes, as with attempts to re-sacralize Buddhist relics in India, or in the distinctly antique flavour invoked in restablishing China's cultural relations with other nations, it is its hybrid form that emerged from its encounter with modernism, which stands out in the story of the Buddhist revival in Asia.[1]

What does this mean for the term 'revival'? Can it be considered an appropriate term for the resurgence of Buddhism in modern Asia? Was Buddhism across Asia in a state of decay? How does the great variety in the modern forms of Buddhism compare with earlier counterparts? In view of the creative religious innovations and changes in some regions, does 'reinvention' capture the character of modern Buddhism better than 'revival'? Readers will find that several of the essays in this book have engaged with the question of terminology and the nature of changes that Buddhism underwent in various national contexts. In a few nation states, 'revival' has meant the re-invigoration of Buddhism following some centuries of decline, while in other instances, it implies the resurgence of a religion that was under threat because of the policies of the political leadership. There are others where there was no marked decline prior to a Buddhist resurgence from the nineteenth century onwards. Again, in several instances, the new kinds of Buddhist formulations and sensibilities in Asia need to be seen as 'reinvented' avatars since instead of negotiating with traditional forms, these essentially represent attempts to 're-conceive Buddhism in modern terms'.[2] Above all, what emerges from the themes explored here is that a comparative perspective provides a meaningful way to revisit the revival and reinvention of Buddhism in Asia.

I. BUDDHISM IN INDIA: THE INTERFACE BETWEEN THE ANCIENT AND THE MODERN

Before discussing the Buddhist revival in Asia, the process of its decline in its homeland, India, needs to be touched upon. It is clear that Buddhism did not completely disappear from the subcontinent. Several monastic centres such as Sanchi, Amaravati and Nalanda survived into medieval times, and there is a much longer, continuous and continuing Buddhist tradition in the western Himalayas, especially in the areas of Ladakh, Lahaul and Spiti. Yet there is no doubt that compared to its strong, visible and widespread presence and influence in the early historic period, Buddhism did witness a discernible marginalization in the subcontinent from the seventh century onwards. The idealization of Buddhism, which is a feature of many writings, right from the Western 'discovery' of Buddhism onwards, is implicit in some of the suggestions that have been put forward for its decline, such as the hypothesis that it was 'corrupted' by internal developments or tantric influence. Decline in royal patronage can only be a part of the explanation and a rupture in the sangha-laity bonds must have lain at the heart of the phenomenon.

While the decline of Buddhism in India during the medieval period is still inadequately understood, its revival is much better documented, and this forms the subject of the first part of this book. The essays here deal with various aspects of Buddhism in India between the nineteenth and twenty-first centuries, including local and international Buddhist revivalist organizations and movements, and the intersection of the revival with the histories of archaeology and Buddhist sites. They also deal with Buddhist relics, an issue where archaeology, religious sentiment and international diplomacy converged. Some of the contributors have used hitherto untapped archival material to reconstruct the details of stories that are only sketchily known through published sources. Taken together, the essays reveal the intersection of the personal and the political, as well as the academic and the devotional understanding of Buddhism. They also reveal elements of continuity and change in the understanding of Buddhist sites and in the activities that coalesced around them over two centuries.

Meera Kosambi ('The Buddhist Imprint of Twentieth-century

Western India: The Contribution of Dharmanand Kosambi and B.R. Ambedkar') focuses on the lives and thoughts of two individuals who played an important role in the Buddhist revival in India – Dharmanand Kosambi and B.R. Ambedkar. While Ambedkar might have read Dharmanand's writings, it is curious that the two stalwarts never seem to have met. As Kosambi states, 'Buddhism was the site at which their life trajectories almost intersected'. These two men belonged to the western state of Maharashtra and played a major role in making the twentieth century, as Meera Kosambi describes it, a 'Buddhist century'. They came from different poles of the caste spectrum – one was a Gaud Saraswat Brahmin; the other, a Mahar 'untouchable'. Both turned to Buddhism at a critical juncture in their lives but their understanding of the religion and the ways in which they internalized and propagated it were radically different. Kosambi discusses all this against the larger background of the social inequities in Maharashtra at the time, the movements for social reform, and the very different responses that Dharmanand and Ambedkar had towards Gandhian nationalism.

While Ambedkar is well known as the iconic political leader of the Dalits, Dharmanand's life and thought have received the importance they deserve only recently, through the writings of Meera Kosambi.[3] At the turn of the nineteenth century, Dharmanand turned his back on worldly life and became a Buddhist monk, travelling extensively in his quest to 'find' Buddhism. It was a lonely journey marked by physical and emotional hardship and deprivation, one that led him to travel the length and breadth of India, as well as to Nepal, Sri Lanka and Burma. Along the way, Dharmanand became a Buddhist scholar, eventually translating Buddhaghosha's *Visuddhimagga* and contributing towards establishing Pali as part of the curriculum of Bombay University and the Fergusson College in Poona.

Ambedkar's was a very different trajectory. Trained as a lawyer and with direct, bitter experience of caste oppression, he devoted his life to the upliftment of India's oppressed 'untouchables'. Ambedkar was aware of the enormous impact of symbolic acts, as is evident from his public burning of a copy of the *Manusmriti* in 1927. He was directly involved in political movements, disagreed radically with Mahatma Gandhi on the issue of how to solve the problem of untouchability, and went on to form his own political party, the Independent Labour Party. Kosambi discusses why Ambedkar turned to religion, specifically Buddhism, in order to change the fortunes of India's Dalits. She suggests that while Dharmanand's was a discovery of the 'original' core of Buddhism, Ambedkar's was more of a reinvention, reflected in his explicit assertion that the Buddhism he was espousing was Navayana (the new vehicle). But in an important sense, both Dharmanand and Ambedkar had an idealized understanding of Buddhism, connecting it with social justice and equality in different ways. Dharmanand linked it with socialism, while Ambedkar saw in it a panacea for centuries of caste oppression.

The Buddhist places of pilgrimage were important, not only for Dharmanand and Ambedkar but for all those who sought to rediscover or reinvent Buddhism in the nineteenth and twentieth centuries, whether in India or elsewhere. The next four essays in this part turn our attention towards important Buddhist sites in India, discussing how they figured the Buddhist revival movement, and how issues of archaeology, conservation and relic diplomacy became intertwined with the process. Nayanjot Lahiri's essay ('Buddhist Revival and the Restoration of Sanchi') deals with two issues – the first is the Buddhist revival in Asia during the nineteenth and early twentieth centuries, and the second highlights the goings-on at Sanchi, the site of an ancient Buddhist monastic site in central India. In fact, the essay draws attention to the close connections between the restoration of Sanchi, Buddhist revivalism and the policies of the colonial state. Further, Lahiri points out that the nineteenth-century Buddhist revival in India cannot be seen as an isolated phenomenon and that it shared certain marked similarities with contemporary developments in South Asian Islam, Hinduism and Sikhism. Across the board, we witness a reduction of religious heterogeneity and diversity, and attempts to forge greater uniformity and monolithic religious identities. The specific kinds of redefinition and reinvention that occurred varied considerably, and were strongly influenced by the other traditions with which these religions interacted. However, there were differences as well. The Buddhist revival in India did not stem from its Indian adherents, neither a numerically large nor influential group, but from a rapidly evolving and growing internationalism for which India, the

Buddhist homeland, was an important symbolic centre. The ancient Buddhist sites, often in an abandoned and derelict state, took on great importance in this process. For their part, British explorers, archaeologists and policy makers saw themselves as guardians of the Indian Buddhist heritage. It is, therefore, not surprising that many of them focused on this heritage and disapproved of the religious plurality that marked activities at many sites that they identified as primarily 'Buddhist'.

The second part of Lahiri's essay focuses on the conservation work at Sanchi against the background of the Buddhist revival, and the attitudes and interventions of the colonial state. Starting the story from the discovery of the site in 1818, Lahiri sketches the history of its subsequent documentation and destruction at the hands of archaeologists, and the conservation work conducted there during John Marshall's tenure as Director-General of the Archaeological Survey of India (hereafter, ASI) and George Nathaniel Curzon's viceroyalty. In contrast to the usual lack of scholarly acknowledgement of the role of the princely states in archaeological and conservation projects, Lahiri emphasizes the interest and initiatives of the Bhopal durbar in general, and of Sultan Jahan Begum, in particular. Not only did the Bhopal durbar finance the publication of Marshall's volumes on Sanchi, the restoration work that was undertaken at the site and the building of the site museum, it was also involved in a prolonged wrangle with the Maha Bodhi Society over custodianship of the relics. These and other significant details emerge from Lahiri's examination of the archival sources.

What we see at Sanchi is the relationship between a Muslim ruling house and a Buddhist monument. The initiatives of the Bhopal durbar belied the necessary connection that the British assumed between the religious affiliation of an ancient monument and its modern custodians, an idea reflected, among other things, in the provisions of the Ancient Monuments Preservation Act of 1904. But this was not only a British prejudice. The role of the Bhopal durbar was under-acknowledged in Prime Minister Jawaharlal Nehru's speech on the occasion when the relics were supposedly restored to Sanchi, indicating the carryover of colonial attitudes into independent India. Even more ironic is the fact that the photographic exhibition mounted in the Sanchi site museum as recently as in 2006 made no mention whatsoever of the patronage of Sanchi by the Bhopal durbar.

Upinder Singh's essay ('Buddhism, Archaeology and the Nation: Nagarjunakonda, 1926-2006') draws attention to the Western discovery and privileging of Indian Buddhism in colonial times, and to the enormous symbolic importance of Buddhism in modern India, exemplified in the choice of the wheel and the Sarnath capital as national emblems. Singh shows how such understandings of the Indian past had an important influence on the trajectories of archaeological interpretations, research and conservation. She does so by using new archival material in order to trace the long-term history of an important archaeological site – Nagarjunakonda in modern Andhra Pradesh – bringing the story close to the immediate present.

Singh's essay highlights different stages in the exploration, excavation and interpretation of the remains at Nagarjunakonda, and identifies the various issues that came to the fore at different points of time. The archival material enabled her to identify and document the behind-the-scenes tensions and debates that underlay official announcements and enactments, the conservation work and the relocation of the recovered artefacts here. In the early twentieth century, the issues that arose included the clash between a British superior and his Indian subordinate in the Southern circle of the ASI, over who should get credit for the important discoveries. Relics were identified as qualitatively different from other artefacts and there was a difference of opinion over the manner in which their discovery was to be announced to the world. The discovery of the Indus civilization was announced by Marshall in 1924 through *The Illustrated London News*[4] but just a few years later, this was considered an inappropriate publication for the announcement of the relic finds at Nagarjunakonda. Where the relics were to be housed was another major issue, and the various claimants such as a Ceylonese vihara and the Maha Bodhi Society had to contend with Hindu, Andhra and nationalist sentiments, in this regard. Singh discusses the agenda of the Maha Bodhi Society vis-à-vis the ancient Buddhist places and especially their interest in collecting relics. The presentation of the relics to the Mulagandhakuti Vihara in Sarnath in 1932 was an impressive event, and the display of a high degree of internationalism on this occasion, in fact, marks an important aspect of the twentieth century Buddhist revival in Asia.

The second moment in the history of Nagarjunakonda documented by Singh is very different. It is a well-known fact that the building of the Nagarjunasagar dam in the 1950s led to the permanent submergence of the site in the waters of the Krishna river. What is less known are the details revealed in archival sources about the prolonged discussions, negotiations and disagreements, which pitched the proponents of development and historical heritage against each other. There was strong parliamentary concern about the issue and Prime Minister Nehru took a special personal interest in it. The ASI's operations at Nagarjunakonda were unprecedented from several points of view: they involved a massive excavation project, a unique collaboration between archaeologists and hydraulic engineers, and the actual physical transplantation of certain structures. All these features make this site extremely important in the history of archaeology and heritage policy.

While the two moments in the history of Nagarjunakonda – one located in colonial India and the other in independent India – seem very different, there are also threads of continuity. One is the tendency to privilege the early historic Buddhist antecedents of what is clearly a multi-period and multi-religious site. Relic diplomacy, too, continues to be important across the two periods. Further, the larger issues of the intersection of archaeology and religious sentiment, and the conflict between heritage and development, are of continuing importance in contemporary times as well.

Sonali Dhingra ('Archaeology, Pilgrimage and Heritage: Modern Amaravati, 1900-2011') discusses the long-term history of another important Buddhist site of Andhra – Amaravati. The first part of the story is one which has received considerable scholarly attention, namely, the discovery of the site, its changing interpretation and the dispersal of its sculptures.[5] However, Dhingra moves further on in time, raising a number of interesting issues in the process. Unlike Nagarjunakonda, where both sculptures and relics attracted interest, the reputation of Amaravati has, over the decades since its discovery, rested on its sculptures, despite the discovery of relics at the site. From this follows an intriguing question: why is it that the Maha Bodhi

Society, which was so keen to collect relics from all the major sites in the country, showed no interest in the relics discovered at Amaravati? Dhingra suggests that the lack of authentication of the relics via inscriptions and the derelict nature of the site were two important reasons for this.

Dhingra draws attention to the close connection between scholarly work on Buddhist sites and the development of pilgrimage circuits. She examines the stark contrast between the largely denuded archaeological site and the beautiful 'fantasy stupa' that has become so emblematic of Amaravati. New Buddhist architecture and images, including a colossal Dhyana Buddha complex, have dramatically altered the site's landscape in recent times. Amaravati has a place in Tibetan legend as well, which was recently affirmed by the holding of an important ceremonial, the Kālacakra initiation, in 2006. Yet, according to Dhingra, this well-publicized ceremonial has not had a major long-term impact on the nature or volume of pilgrim traffic there. We should also note that an exclusive focus on Buddhist connections here is limiting, as Amaravati has been a multi-religious site from at least the early medieval times, the Buddhist establishment sharing space with the Śaiva Amareśvara temple nearby. This is an important point to keep in mind, as studies of Buddhism tend to isolate it from its larger, interactional religious context.[6]

In recent times, the convergence between the aspirations and activities of Dalit Buddhists and Tibetan Buddhists, the interests of the central and state governments in India to generate revenue through the promotion of spiritual tourism, and international funding for Buddhist sites and pilgrimage places has led to the revitalization of many ancient Indian Buddhist sites.[7] While the activities of Anagarika Dharmapala and the Maha Bodhi Society as agents of Buddhist revival have attracted a great deal of attention, Dhingra looks at another organization – the Ananda Buddha Vihara Society, active in Andhra, discussing the architecture of the monastery in Hyderabad, its revivalist agenda and activities, its sources of patronage and its links with international Buddhist organizations. The fact that Amaravati is a source of inspiration for the devout within this Buddhist community shows the potent symbolic significance of an almost vanished ancient monument. The prominence given to Amaravati in Andhra school textbooks, as Dhingra points out, shows that this religious symbol has also become a symbol of regional pride.

Sraman Mukherjee ('Relics, Ruins and Temple-building: Archaeological Heritage and the Construction of the Dharmarajika Vihara, Calcutta') focuses on the history of the relic found at Bhattiprolu (in present-day Andhra Pradesh), from the time of its discovery in 1892 to its ceremonial presentation for enshrinement at the opening ceremony of 'the first new Buddhist temple of colonial India', the Dharmarajika Vihara in Calcutta in 1921. While narrating the bid for the relics made by Buddhist associations such as the Maha Bodhi Society and the Bengal Buddhist Society, Mukherjee looks closely at the different connotations and meanings associated with Buddhist relics and ruins. He also examines how the contending claims of 'secularization' and 'sacralization' unfolded in the context of these two kinds of remains.

Relics and ruins were ultimately assigned two different domains – one religious, the other secular – and two different kinds of appropriate custodians and abodes – the temple and the museum. However, Mukherjee's analysis shows that we are not looking at a static attitude or policy towards them; further, that relics found at various Buddhist sites did not all share the same fate. Following in the wake of the enthusiastic relic-hunters of the nineteenth century, the early twentieth century saw a significant change from the earlier policy of packing off relic caskets along with their relics to museums abroad: the ASI started differentiating between the two and actively engaged in a series of negotiations and activities involving the 're-sacralization' of relics. This new policy emerged as the result of the ASI's engagement with the Buddhist revivalist movement and the pressures from Buddhist associations based in India to keep relics within India. The Maha Bodhi Society's aggressive engagement with the physicality of Buddhist sacred places (such as in the famous case of Bodh Gaya) involved laying claims to fresh relics being unearthed from time to time by archaeologists. Mukherjee looks at the Society's sources of patronage, and its connections with other Hindu, Buddhist and political associations. He also examines the activities of the more locally-oriented Bengal Buddhist Society.

Against the background of the implications of the Ancient

Monuments Preservation Act of 1904, the vision of Curzon and Marshall, and the new conservation agenda, Mukherjee discusses how relics became part of 'relic diplomacy'. In the process, relics sometimes got separated from their reliquaries but the latter, especially inscribed ones, were understood as having an important authenticating function. The making of duplicate relic caskets for religious institutions emerged as a solution that sought to keep everyone happy. Mukherjee points out that while getting embroiled with such issues, the ASI also became involved in negotiations and adjudication over issues that did not, strictly speaking, lie within its purview, such as the design of the Dharmarajika Vihara in Calcutta. Other issues that are raised in the essay and which merit further examination are the activities of the Burma Circle of the Archaeological Survey, and the important long-term connections of pilgrimage and patronage between Burmese Buddhists and Bodh Gaya.

The different trajectories of the stories of Sanchi, Amaravati, Nagarjunakonda and the Bhattiprolu relic indicate the many variables that were involved in the complex life histories of sites, monuments and relics, and the negotiations that took place with the aspirations and demands of different kinds of local, national and trans-national institutions. In recent years, there has been a very visible strengthening of international connectivities of various kinds at ancient Indian Buddhist sites. But museum practices do vary. While sacred relics are sometimes displayed for the devout in relic galleries in museums far removed from the sites where they were found (for instance, in the Holy Relics Gallery in Hyderabad), there are also plans to send museumized relics back to their original sites (as for instance, with the Vaishali relic, which is currently housed in the Patna museum).

II. TEXTS, POLITICS AND THE SANGHA IN SRI LANKA

The second part of this book shifts the focus to Sri Lanka. Kitsiri Malalgoda ('New Manuals for New Times: A Comparative History of *Buddha Ädahilla* and *A Buddhist Catechism*') examines the different and yet entangled histories of two influential nineteenth-century Buddhist tracts. In tracing these histories, Malalgoda brings alive the complexities of Sri Lankan Buddhism. The first text in question is

Buddha Ädahilla, compiled as a text for the Buddhist laity by a local monk named Mohottivatte Gunananda and (as Malalagoda argues persuasively) published in about 1872. The second is *A Buddhist Catechism*, written as a textbook for newly-established Buddhist schools by the famous Theosophist-Buddhist, Henry Steele Olcott; this was published in 1881 and endorsed by a leading monk, Hikkaduve Sumangala. The contents of the first edition of *Buddha Ädahilla*, some of whose verses go back to very early times, are, in fact, known only from the summary provided in *A Buddhist Catechism*. The difficulties of using the labels 'old Buddhism' and 'new Buddhism', respectively, for these two texts emerge clearly from Malalgoda's discussion. Although they differ in terms of authorship, content and audience, and can be seen as two distinct types of religious literature – one that looked back to an older tradition and the other that tried to squarely answer the questions of the present – both shared a common historical context. Malalgoda outlines some of the key features of this larger context, including the modern transformations that were making their impact on the island, in general, and on Colombo, in particular. The railways, the steam engine, the printing press, the plantation economy, migration and the secularization of education were some of the major agents of transformation. Colombo emerged by the late eighteeenth century both as an important colonial port city and as a premier centre of Buddhism in Ceylon, with an altered and distinctly multi-ethnic and multi-religious demographic profile.

Malalgoda's discussion touches on many important issues concerning the relationship between Sri Lankan Buddhism and colonial modernity. Among these is Buddhism's relationship with the Theosophists. *Buddha Ädahilla* was published before the formation of the Theosophical Society in 1875. *A Buddhist Catechism*, on the other hand, belongs to the honeymoon period between Theosophy and Buddhism, although decisions about its contents involved delicate negotiations between Olcott and the Buddhist monks on key doctrinal issues, such as the definition of *nirvāṇa*. We also see multiple religious identities gradually making way for more clearly-defined and hardened, exclusivist ones. Buddhism has always had a close, sometimes conflict-driven, relationship with the state and Malalgoda delineates the relationship between Buddhism and British colonialism, showing how the sangha quickly adapted to new, non-Buddhist political masters. Further, although certain Buddhist practices become interiorized and confined to the domestic spheres, the British were prone to imitate the practices of the pre-colonial rulers when it came to public ceremonial, much to the chagrin of the Christian missionaries.

While all this is specific to Sri Lanka, certain aspects of Malalgoda's discussion connect well with issues relevant to the Buddhist revival in India, discussed in the first part of this book. For instance, in tracing how Colombo eventually took over from Kelaniya and Kotte as a religious centre, our attention is drawn to the important role played over the centuries by the old (mostly destroyed) temples and how they became potent, visible symbols around which the Buddhist revival – or reinvention – tended to coalesce. The second common feature is that of internationalism, visible in both areas. While *Buddha Ädahilla*'s popularity was largely confined to Sri Lanka, *A Buddhist Catechism* attracted international circulation and appeal, going through several editions and translations. It should be noted that the Buddhist revival in Sri Lanka was marked by an awareness of and a feeling of affinity with the Buddhist lands of Southeast Asia. Third, Malalgoda's essay discusses the eclipse of older organizations like the Buddhist Theosophical Society by the Maha Bodhi Society. The interest of such groups in the appropriation and revival of the old Buddhist sites and the acquisition of relics ties up with some of the issues discussed in the first part of this volume.

H.L. Seneviratne ('The Buddhist Utopia: An Aspect of the Buddhist Revival in Sri Lanka') highlights the complex nature of the Buddhist revival in Sri Lanka and takes a critical look at its long-term impact. Beginning with an assessment of the ideas and activities of Anagarika Dharmapala, Seneviratne argues that the he contributed both to a cultural regeneration, as well as to a persisting cultural malaise that was rooted in this very regeneration process. His main critique is Dharmapala's inability to move beyond a narrow ethno-religious nationalism, which, it is argued, was incapable of addressing the long-term multi-ethnic and multi-religious realities of Sri Lanka.

The primary aim of Seneviratne's essay is to examine the elements that constituted Dharmapala's construction of a Buddhist utopia, located in an imagined pure Buddhism of the ancient past and based on the virtues of the Middle Path. Dharmapala attributed the end of this utopia to the corruption of the religion by Western impact during colonial rule, and the replacement of the original ethical ideals by ritual and false beliefs. Seneviratne argues that the elements condemned for falling under the latter rubric were the very ones that had, in earlier times, been integral to the transformation of Buddhism into a syncretistic, cultural religion with mass popular appeal. The three overlapping strategies that were used to reclaim this utopia by Dharmapala and his young, energetic monk-soldiers (fresh products of the new Buddhist educational institutions) included a programme of rural development and awareness, the invention of a new Buddhist sermon to replace the traditional one, and the use of the printed word. The idea of a new sermon betrays the Christian impact on the Buddhist revival and the emergence of a 'new scripturalism'; Dharmapala saw it as a potent instrument for recreating a utopian moral society, and his ideas coalesced with the needs and aspirations of the new urban laity as well as the monks. Seneviratne goes on to look at how a series of pamphlets written by the scholar-monk, Walpola Rahula, published in 1933-4, represented a strong and irreverent attack against popular beliefs and rituals, accompanied by an emphasis on Buddhist ethics.

Civilizational identities were central to the politics of independent Sri Lanka, in terms of election slogans and programmes, as well as in the constitutional provisions of the nation state. Seneviratne's main argument is that the ideas and activities of the Buddhist revival in Sri Lanka had a long-term negative impact. As agendas became increasingly narrow and identified with Sinhala Buddhists and the interests of elite groups, they encouraged a Sinhala Buddhist cultural nationalism that rejected cultural pluralism and gave a long-term fillip to majoritarianism.

One of the specific consequences of the encounter between Buddhism and modernity has been the striking visibility of Buddhist monks in the sphere of politics. This is especially so in Sri Lanka where the protestant nature of the Buddhist revival in the late nineteenth century was a response to colonial oppression and against the cultural challenge that its adherents faced as a consequence of the colonial state's support of Christian missionary activities. The outcome of the confrontation was the emulation of the model of Protestant Christianity by the Sri Lankan Buddhists, a phenomenon that has been widely highlighted. However, as the third essay in this part, which is by Anuruddha Pradeep ('The Political Dimension of Buddhism in Sri Lanka') highlights, after Independence, the relationship between monks and politics has continued to grow there. In fact, its latest avatar is a twenty-first century direct parliamentary intervention, emanating from a decision of an all-monk party called Jathika Hela Urumaya to contest the 2004 parliamentary elections. Pradeep takes this intervention – frequently decried by both supporters and critics of Sinhala Buddhist politics – as the starting point for scrutinizing the claim that there was no tradition of bhikshu politics.

Offering a *longue durée* perspective, Pradeep suggests that monks have usually come forward to safeguard the community whenever it faced a threat, an early manifestation of which he traces back to ancient times and to the role of bhikshus in the *Mahāvaṁsa* story of King Dutugemunu's war against the invader king, Elara. Through a discussion of this war, he also raises the question of the relationship of Buddhism and violence. Notwithstanding the centrality of non-violence within Buddhism, the paper distinguishes between ideals and realities and argues that while 'Buddhists act according to Buddhist principles in ordinary situations', in the face of an invasion, they would act as any other social group. It was a similar issue of survival that was central to the war of Sinhala bhikshus against the LTTE in recent times.

In this journey from the late centuries BCE to the present, Pradeep examines the ways in which Buddhists resisted their British rulers in the nineteenth century and the changing contours of bhikshu politics in that phase, the role of Vidyalankara monks (especially Walpola Rahula Thero) after Independence, and the fraught relationship of Sinhala Buddhists with Tamil nationalists. It is against this background that the establishment of the Jathika Hela Urumaya is situated, as one event in a longer process. If a modern form of Buddhism emerged in response to the colonial challenge, the advent of an all-monk party has to be understood, as the paper highlights, against the ideological challenge of political separatism.

III. THE REVIVAL OF BUDDHISM IN CHINA

The four papers in this part critically examine some aspects of the Buddhist revival in mainland China and Hong Kong where the intersection of different forms of the religion with the challenges and opportunities created by contemporary realities – whether in the form of historical figures pushing social and political reform or through practices that are Theravada-based or Taiwanese-inspired – are mapped in many different ways.

That the Buddhist revival frequently drew upon ancient cultural links in order to reanimate interactions between China and India in the twentieth century is central to Tansen Sen's essay ('Taixu's Goodwill Mission to India: Reviving the Buddhist Links between China and India'). The paper's focus is the Chinese reformist monk, Taixu (1889-1947) and his 'Goodwill Mission' to India in 1940. Taixu is widely recognized as a central figure in the revival of Buddhism in modern China. Hailing from a poor bricklayer's family in south-eastern Zheijiang Province, this individual, whose family name was Lu and given name Ganlin, became a monk due to his poor health which prevented him from undertaking physical work. Upon his entry into the Order, he was given the Buddhist name Taixu.[8] He then went on to become revolutionary, although Sen's paper is more concerned with his later work, especially his critique of the Buddhist clergy and his efforts in overcoming their shortcomings. Through the microcosm of this monk-intellectual, the manner in which the internal dynamics of reforming Buddhism within China dovetailed with the external realities of the Guomindang government's need to garner support for their war against Japan in the 1930s is highlighted.

In order to provide a context to Taixu's 'Goodwill Mission', Sen paints a large canvas which, on the one hand, moves from the political upheavals that provide a backdrop to Taixu's critique of and attempts to reform the Buddhist community in China to his advocacy for the participation of monks in the war against Japan. On the other hand, Sen explores the interactions between India and China from the late eighteenth century onwards: the spread of the Chinese diaspora in India; the role of Tan Yunshan, the first director of Cheena Bhavana established at Visva Bharati in Santiniketan in 1937; the discourse in China about the reasons for the collapse of India in the face of British colonization; and the ideals of Asianism advocated in the early part of the twentieth century.

The idea of reviving Buddhist interactions, as Sen points out, was part of a wider initiative on the part of intellectuals and politicians, ranging from Rabindranath Tagore to Liang Qichao, to foreground the idea of Asian unity. At the same time, these engagements were also sometimes problematic, as is evident in the mixed reception that Tagore's visit to China in 1924 received, where his 'praise of Oriental civilization' was seen as oddly traditionalist by the radical intellectuals there.[9] Moreover, the idea of Asian unity itself could become vulnerable in situations of military conflict. In 1940, for instance, there was a significant threat to the idea of pan-Asianism because of the Japanese invasion of China in the 1930s. The varying attitudes of Chinese Buddhists and Japanese Buddhists to the Sino-Japanese war have been examined elsewhere in some detail, but a major reason for Taixu's visit to India was to garner support for China's anti-Japanese war.[10]

Due to the war, Taixu's mission was as much a political mission as a religious one, tellingly summed up in Sen's description of the event as a 'political pilgrimage'. For this reason, while undertaking a tour of Buddhist pilgrimage sites, Taixu met leaders of the Indian National Congress, including Jawaharlal Nehru, about which the government back home was constantly informed. That such politico-religious missions followed the form of what were perceived to be the ancient relations between India and China in many ways was highlighted by Taixu, who, in his address at the Ashoka Day celebrations in Banaras and in his lecture at the Banaras Hindu University, expressed the hope that in the near future, 'the cultural relations existing between India and China in the days of Xuanzang will be re-established between these two countries'.

The foremost Chinese intellectual who propagated the idea of the revival of Asian Buddhist interactions was a predecessor of Taixu – the scholar-activist, Liang Qichao (1873-1929). Unlike Taixu who was a monk, Liang was a lay practitioner of Buddhism. He was an acclaimed journalist, philosopher and reformer, and forms the subject of Dan Smyer Yu's paper in this volume ('Ensouling the Nation through Fiction: Liang Qichao's Applied Buddhism'). The scholarship of Liang, especially as a journalist and as the author of works on the history of China as also on Buddhism, is widely acknowledged. His critique of the weaknesses of his country after its defeat in 1895 by Japan is also well known: the phrase 'Sick Man of Asia' was coined by him to describe China's vulnerable state. His novels and poems, though, have attracted far less attention. Of these, what is described by Smyer Yu as political fiction – evidently a literary genre that was politically charged – is the primary subject of analysis here. Through an inter-textual reading of Liang's writings, the essay highlights his promotion of a socially-engaged Buddhism in order to raise public consciousness towards the building of a new, modern China.

The ideas of Liang Qichao were deeply influenced by European Enlightenment philosophers and thus, were very much a product of the encounter of Buddhism and Western modernist discourses. The genre of political fiction itself, as Liang readily admitted, originated from Europeans who infused their political ideals into their writings and such works, he believed, were critical in changing public opinion. Equally, that fiction came to be seen as a powerful tool for raising awareness and furthering reform had a great deal to do with the model that the Meiji Japanese political novel provided.[11] In the case of China, Liang believed that it would help in remaking the nation and bring political salvation. The task that he set himself was to use political fiction for political reformation. Importantly, the idea of reformation in and a renewal of China, in his political fiction, was grounded in the religious principles of Buddhism. To put it in another way, Buddhist ideals were seen as having the capacity to awaken and liberate the Chinese people. Liang was deeply conscious of the need to heighten the Chinese national consciousness, pointing to the fact that the people had failed to even give a name to their own country. The word 'China' ('Zhongguo'), as he put it, 'is what people of other races call us. It is not a name the people of this country have selected for themselves.'[12]

According to Smyer Yu, Liang advocated the acceptance of 'applied Buddhism' – a socially-engaged Buddhism that was a blend of Western modern practices and Eastern Buddhist spiritual and moral sources. This had emerged out of his wide travels in Europe, North America and Japan, as also his engagement with ideas of Western rationalism and science. There was no conflict in Liang's writings between modern phenomena such as a nationalist renaissance and ancient Buddhist values. Like Taixu, Liang represented an attempt within modernist Chinese Buddhism to establish the compatibility of the religion's psychological and civilizational values with the issues and challenges pertaining to the creation and sustenance of modern nation states.

The connections between Liang's ideas and Buddhism are explored by Smyer Yu in some detail. Thus, for example, his utopian ideas are shown as having a Buddhist basis, especially when he used his mentor, Kang Youwei's concept of the great commonwealth. This was the idea that all sentient beings had the same nature and came from the same womb. It 'was intended to be a common thread to sew together the collective mind of the whole nation and was meant to be enshrined in the individual souls of the population through the words of ideals uttered from realistically portrayed fictional characters'. This idea had a strong Buddhist orientation and was borrowed from Mahayana Buddhism.

From papers that examine the Buddhist revival in China to the ideas and agendas of individual reformers, this part of the book moves on to look at the religion's modern trajectory in China in broader terms. Bill M. Mak's contribution ('Theravada Buddhism as Part of the Buddhist Revivial in Mainland China and Hong Kong: Two Paradigms') explores the development of Theravada Buddhism within the modern revival of Buddhism by juxtaposing two regions, that of Mainland China and Hong Kong. These, while sharing a common religious heritage, have had entirely different political systems since the middle of the twentieth century. The political and cultural developments and differences are explored, among other things, through quantitative data, which are cited to understand the changing pattern of modern Buddhism in these two areas. In the case of China, as the statistics relating to Buddhist monastics and temples reveal, there was a decline in their numbers in Communist China, especially as a consequence of the Cultural Revolution. While there has been a revival in the last few years, these institutions have still not reached their pre-1949 strength. This is evident in the fact that there were 100,000 monastics in 2006 as compared to 500,000 in 1940. This striking decline and resurgence, however, was not experienced in Hong Kong where British rule for a hundred and fifty odd years did not adversely impact the adherents of the religion. In fact, apart from anything else, Hong Kong became a refuge for the thousands of Buddhist monks who fled China from the 1940s till the 1960s.

Beyond quantitative data, the paper highlights the different milestones that signal the changing pattern of state engagement with Buddhism. In the case of the People's Republic of China, to begin with, the government was keenly interested in continuing with the initiatives to use Buddhism as a part of diplomatic policy, which had begun in the Republican era. An important reason for the establishment of the Buddhist Association of China in 1953 was to further such diplomatic initiatives. However, in the 1960s and the 1970s, Buddhist monastics and temples shrunk to an all-time low, because of state-supported campaigns against them. Since then, the government engagement has been more positive and, most recently, has returned to the old policy of integrating Buddhism into foreign policy initiatives. Ironically, though, even while Buddhism has been given a very high profile in government initiatives, Theravada Buddhism is considered an alien form of the religion and suffers from various government restrictions imposed upon it. Theravada teachings and practices are only allowed in indigenous Theravada temples or in Mahayana Buddhist temples with whom some form of cooperation is established. Consequently, as before, the majority of Theravada monasteries and temples remain concentrated in the south-western part of China, centring on the Yunnan province.

Theravada Buddhism in Hong Kong, on the other hand, is more globalized and forms a study in contrast with Mainland China. A number of Theravada temples associated with the Thai tradition were set up there in the 1980s and 1990s, while the growing number of meditation centres have multiple lineages – Burmese, Sri Lankan and Thai. Alongside, vipassana meditation is also offered in many institutions with Mahayana affiliation. The public profile of Theravada Buddhism has also been helped by regular public talks about it and novitiate programmes which allow members of the public to experience the life of a Theravada monk. As a result, Theravada Buddhism has not remained confined to the traditional temple culture. Instead, the great variety in its activities reflects the openness offered by Hong Kong. In fact, it appears to have grown steadily because its activities are open to the larger public and not just to the local Buddhists. This is qualitatively different from the situation in Mainland China, where the government policy towards religious practices is restrictive.

If the new forms of an explicitly modern engagement with the religion are seen as a significant reason for the expansion of Theravada Buddhism in Hong Kong, the lexicon of modernity is even more striking in Weishan Huang's contribution on Shanghai ('Sustainable Development and Karma Logistics: The Moral Discourse of Reformed Buddhism and Capital-linked Business Professionals in Shanghai'). In her essay, the author examines the incorporation of a new moral discourse emanating from Taiwan into Shanghai, carried by trans-national Taiwanese merchants and incorporated into their business practices in the early 1990s. The Chinese economy began opening up from the 1990s and, by 2000, foreign companies gained permission to establish wholly foreign-owned enterprises without joint state ownership there. Taiwanese migrants were among those who took advantage of this economic shift, moving their businesses to China to avoid costs and enhance quality. While the economic dimensions of this migration have been studied by several scholars, the different ways in which it has changed the religious landscape is little known.

In Shanghai, the changes have emanated from Taiwanese entrepreneurs with trans-national links with the Buddhist Tzu Chi Foundation based in Hualien in Taiwan. Its founder, Master Cheng Yen, became a Buddhist nun in 1963 and since then, she has expanded the social work of Tzu Chi across the world through trained commissioners and Faith Corps members who are lay leaders. Tzu Chi of Shanghai is said to be directly under the supervision of the founder herself. The person who brought Tzu Chi to Shanghai is also a woman – Sister Yufen Chiou, who transplanted her manufacturing company from Taiwan to Shanghai.

The ways in which Tzu Chi has been integrated into business management practices is evident from the case studies cited in the paper. While Huang emphasizes that such practices are visible in private, not public, spaces as a consequence of government restrictions, some of the examples she cites suggest that these Buddhist-inspired

beliefs have a resonance in the public domain as well. One example is that of the Ting Hsin International group, the largest instant noodle maker in China, which has fifty-two units all over the country. The influence of Tzu Chi teachings on the corporate culture there is evident from the emphasis on vegetarianism, recycling and on saving energy. In fact, the necessity of carbon emissions reduction is very central to Ting Hsin's mode of functioning. Such beliefs and practices represent an innovative and Buddhist modernism whose core is a kind of environmentally proactive humanism concerning sustainable development. There is nothing traditional about its protocol, nor is its concern inspired by an interest in reclaiming an orthodox form of Buddhism. The pivot for expanding the Tzu Chi network are business people in Mainland China. The Buddhist-inspired beliefs of Taiwanese-origin entrepreneurs have both expanded the reach of Tzu Chi teaching and changed the culture of the business establishments that they run in China. The links with Taiwan are also constantly renewed. Annually, in the month of May, Tzu Chi commissioners from Shanghai, as also commissioners from all over the world, fly back to Hualien to attend the Global Tzu Chi Day on Mother's Day. Among other things, this is an institutional mechanism which has imparted a trans-national dimension to the programme, by ensuring a regular personal flow of religious ideas and interactions among its commissioners and members.

IV. AFTERWORD

The Buddhist revival in Asia, to put it simply, is diverse in its manifestations and encompasses all kinds of modern contexts. This modernity, which was simultaneously trans-national, forms the theme of Peter van der Veer's 'The Construction of World Buddhism'. This essay provides a bird's-eye view of transformations in Buddhism in India, Sri Lanka and China.

That Buddhist 'discovery' and revival unfolded in the era of high imperialism, as the essay suggests, within the apparatus of imperial knowledge – ranging from scholars and missionaries to traders and colonial officers – forms an integral dimension of this phenomenon. The important ways in which developments that were a consequence of colonialism came to structure certain facets of Buddhism can clearly be seen in the case of Sri Lanka. The character of Buddhism there was influenced by the publication of Buddhist texts by the Pali Text Society, as also the knowledge that emerged from archaeological excavations at Anuradhapura. Subsequently, it was reconfigured as an integral element in the religious nationalism of the Sinhalese people. The links between national reform agendas and Buddhism can also be seen in the case of China, especially from the career of Liang Qichao who believed that his nation should adopt Western materialism based on science in order to overcome its backwardness. This was to be combined with a moral foundation that was based in the spiritual East.

In India, as in Sri Lanka, textual research and archaeological fieldwork combined to give a visibility to the presence of early Buddhism. At the same time, as van der Veer points out, within the consolidation of such knowledge, there was an unease about the presence of other religions in spaces that were sacred to Buddhism in ancient India. The paper, for instance, points to the discovery of Buddhist Sarnath, which came to be seen a symbol of 'timeless Buddhist spirituality', where, simultaneously, the presence of other religions, including Jainism which was older than the Buddhist faith, was ignored. Later, it was Buddhism's anti-Brahmanical origin and character which became central to the expansion of its support base, as seen in the conversion of B.R. Ambedkar and lakhs of Hindu 'untouchables' to Buddhism.

Van der Veer's contribution underscores another integral part of the understanding of Buddhism in the nineteenth century related to the recognition of its presence in multiple nations. Its visibility in many parts of Asia meant that the West 'discovered' that like Christianity, Buddhism was a world religion. Like Christianity, it was also considered to be a religion that occupied a high ethical plane. This was fundamentally different from the hostility that was frequently present in colonial perceptions of Islam and Hinduism. Finally, the trans-national character of modern Buddhism is highlighted by the careers of some Buddhist reformers. Anagarika Dharmapala is one such individual. His life and career unfolded across several continents as he travelled from Ceylon to India, the United States of America,

Europe, China, Japan, Chicago, London and many other places. Again, the knowledge of the presence of Buddhism across nations got wide publicity as a consequence of events that were on a global scale, such as the World Parliament of Religions in Chicago, where the spiritual merits of Asian religious traditions were highlighted by delegates from many Asian nations.

* * *

The essays in this book shows how the experiences of imperialism, nationalism and globalization have left a deep imprint on the Buddhist resurgence in various parts of Asia. They also show how this resurgence assumed a great variety of forms depending on the specificities of the historical and cultural context, including Buddhism's encounter with other religious traditions. Continuities with the past are not absent, and revivalist movements have been characterized and propelled by a strong sense of history. Although they have often presented themselves as a reform, revival or reinvigoration of an older tradition, this, in effect, involved crafting new interpretations of a distant past, and the introduction of new ideas and practices. The term 'reinvention' seems to capture this aspect of dynamic change better than 'revival', and does not presume a prior decline. Yet the choice of terms is not as important as tracing the trajectories of the phenomenon and the awareness that its impact extended far beyond the religious domain into many spheres, including those of cultural practice, national identity and international relations.

The revival and reinvention of Buddhism in the countries of Asia over the past two centuries has been and continues to be moulded by a complex of internal factors, as well as by pan-Asian linkages and networks. Although the latter have characterized Buddhism's history from early times, their intensity and range have increased rapidly in the era of globalization. As is the case with other world religions, Buddhism is marked by innumerable sectarian divisions; striking degrees of diversity at the national, regional and local levels; as well as an awareness of an overarching global identity and solidarity. It remains to be seen how the intersection of these aspects will continue to unfold against the background of changes in political regime, the integrative and competitive aspects of the world economy, increased social connectivity and conflict, and the accentuation and erosion of religious identities.

NOTES

1. See MacMahan (2008).
2. MacMahan (2008): 22.
3. See Kosambi transl. and ed. (2010).
4. For a discussion of how the Indus civilization was discovered and its discovery announced to the world, see Lahiri (2005).
5. For details, see Singh (2004), Howes (2010), and Shimada (2013): 1-24.
6. For an examination of Bodh-Gaya on these lines, see Lahiri (1999).
7. See Singh (2010).
8. For Taixu, see Long (2000).
9. These are the words of Mao Dun (or ShenYanbing) which have been quoted by Amartya Sen in his analysis of Tagore's association with China. Sen (2011): 9.
10. See Fumihiko (2010).
11. For the influence of Japan's intellectual milieu on Liang Wichao, see Willcock (1995).
12. Cited in Li Liu and Xingcan Chen (2006): 330.

BIBLIOGRAPHY

Fumihiko, Sueki. 2010. 'Chinese Buddhism and the Anti-Japan War', *Japanese Journal of Religious Studies*. 37/1: 9-20.

Kosambi, Meera, tr. and ed. 2010. *Dharmanand Kosambi: The Essential Writings*. Ranikhet: Permanent Black.

Howes, Jennifer. 2010. *Illustrating India: The Early Colonial Investigations of Colin Mackenzie (1784-1821)*. New Delhi: Oxford University Press.

Lahiri, Nayanjot. 1999. 'Bodh Gaya: An Ancient Buddhist Shrine and its Modern History (1891-1904)', in *Case Studies in Archaeology and World Religion: The Proceedings of the Cambridge Conference*, ed. Timothy Insoll. Oxford: Archaeopress, pp. 33-47.

———. 2010. *Finding Forgotten Cities: How the Indus Civilization was Discovered*. Ranikhet: Permanent Black.

Liu, Li and Xingcan Chen. 2006. 'China' in *Encyclopaedia of Early History & Discoveries*, ed. T. Murray. New Delhi: Pentagon Press, vol. 1, pp. 315-33.

Long, Darui. 2000. 'An Interfaith Dialogue Between the Chinese Buddhist Leader Taixu and Christians', *Buddhist-Christian Studies*, vol. 20, pp. 167-89.

McMahan, David L. 2008. *The Making of Buddhist Modernism*. Oxford: Oxford University Press.

Sen, Amartya. 'Tagore and China', in *Tagore and China*, ed. T. Chung, A. Dev, W. Bangsei and W. Liming. New Delhi: Sage, pp. 3-10.

Shimada, Akira. 2013. *Early Buddhist Architecture in Context: The Great Stūpa at Amarāvatī (ca. 300 BCE-300 CE)*. Leiden: Brill.

Singh, Upinder. 2004. *The Discovery of Ancient India: Early Archaeologists and the Beginnings of Archaeology*. Delhi: Permanent Black.

_______. 2010. 'Exile and Return: The Reinvention of Buddhism and Buddhist Sites in Modern India', *South Asian Studies*. 26, 2, pp. 193-217.

Willcock, Hiroko. 1995. 'Japanese Modernization and the Emergence of New Fiction in Early Twentieth Century China: A Study of Liang Qichao', *Modern Asian Studies*. 29(4), pp. 817-40.

PART I

BUDDHISM IN INDIA: THE INTERFACE BETWEEN THE ANCIENT AND THE MODERN

CHAPTER 1

The Buddhist Imprint on Twentieth-century Western India

The Contribution of Dharmanand Kosambi and B.R. Ambedkar

MEERA KOSAMBI

FOR CENTURIES, BUDDHIST monastic rock-cut caves, splendidly sculpted and sometimes decorated with vividly coloured frescoes, have dotted the mountainous terrain of the state of Maharashtra in western India. They have stood testimony to the presence of a once-vigorous and active religious organization honoured by communities of lay followers whose generous donations have been commemorated in standardized, carved figures accompanied by inscriptions. Also involved in the prosperity of the Buddhist monastic order was the region's mercantile community. For, in an apparent paradox, the cave complexes, situated in serene and sylvan settings on hillsides, conducive to the meditative life of the monks, additionally served as overnight halts for the caravans of wealthy merchants located along the major trade routes.[1] Some of these cave complexes, such as Ajanta and Ellora, have endured as world-famous sites of art. However, they also remained the only vestiges of the region's ancient Buddhist heritage, even as Buddhism itself went into a decline well before the end of the first millennium AD, partly because of the hostility of Hindu kings but also partly because lavish royal and lay patronage had introduced certain practices into the Sangha that diluted its original austerity and moral purpose.[2]

This process of decline was accompanied by a parallel process of the absorption of Buddhism into Hinduism as its minor adjunct in an attempt to neutralize its independent existence and negate its message. This was paradoxical in that Buddhism – along with Jainism – had arisen in the sixth and fifth century BC as a new religious doctrine in north India in opposition to Brahmanism, which rested on a strictly hierarchical caste structure and the supreme importance of rituals performed by the monopolistic Brahmin priesthood. Buddhism preached an ethical philosophy, stressed good actions as the sole means for spiritual salvation, and dispensed with the dominant priesthood as also with the caste hierarchy – maintaining that a high or low caste status should be contingent upon good or bad actions and not ascribed to the accident of birth. Yet the ultimate irony was the manner in which the potent protest posed by Buddhism was nullified by the induction of the figure of the Buddha himself into Hinduism as the ninth of the ten incarnations of Vishnu, the god of preservation, in what is sometimes known as the Hindu trinity of Brahma, Vishnu and Shiva.

It was only in the twentieth century that Buddhism was retrieved from this general amnesia in Maharashtra and revived emphatically enough to make it a 'Buddhist century'. Interestingly, this was not the result of a well-orchestrated movement, or any movement at all, but the outcome of persistent efforts by two remarkable individuals: Professor or 'Acharya' Dharmanand Kosambi (1876-1947) and Dr. B.R. (Babasaheb) Ambedkar (1891-1956), who worked within two entirely separate spheres of activity. In the first half of the twentieth century, Dharmanand, in his quest for spiritual solace, not only converted to Buddhism as a monk but also reinscribed the Buddhist doctrine into the cognitive universe of the educated and liberal reading public through his copious writings, mostly in Marathi.[3] His choice of Marathi, the region's language, was ideological: he wanted to ensure a wide outreach within India. The second half of the century began with Ambedkar leading a mass conversion to Buddhism of the lower castes, then known as 'untouchables' and now as Dalits. This was the climax of his social and political activism to uplift these communities; its long-lasting effect permanently changed both the collective psyche of these communities and the socio-religious composition of the region through the second half of the twentieth century and into the present century. His interpretation of Buddhism is captured almost solely in one English book that was published posthumously as *The Buddha and His Dhamma*.

This paper seeks to outline the life trajectories of these two individuals, the nature of their interest in and understanding of Buddhism, and their methods of propagating it. Dharmanand was a Brahmin and Ambedkar a Dalit, and they approached Buddhism from these opposite extremes of the caste spectrum. Incidentally, they were diametrically opposite in appearance as well. Dharmanand was always simply dressed in white khadi: *dhoti*, *kurta* (traditional loose shirt) and a Gandhi cap – except when he was in Europe or the USA and was required to dress in the European style for climatic and cultural reasons. Ambedkar was always dressed in a good quality suit and tie to reiterate his status acquired by his own efforts and to shows that an educated Dalit could and should be well-dressed. Dharmanand's Buddhist philosophy was a personal statement; Ambedkar's was political. Both understood, interpreted and, thus, 'revived' Buddhism in their own ways. It is these two paths to the discovery, practice and revival of Buddhism in western India that form the substance of this paper.

BUDDHISM AND THE SOCIAL REFORM DISCOURSE

The wider frame for understanding these two socio-religious interventions is the social reform discourse that unfolded in Maharashtra from the mid-nineteenth century onwards under British colonial rule. Initially, the two axes of reform were gender and caste-related injustices. Predictably, the former was the preoccupation of the upper castes, especially Brahmins, whose treatment of women was oppressive (mainly because of customs like child marriage and enforced widowhood), while the latter engaged the attention of the lower castes.[4] In some ways, the two discourses overlapped. This was noticeably so in the case of organizations like the Prarthana Samaj (Prayer Society), which combined social reform with the religious reform of the Hindu practices and, thus, also created a more tolerant religious milieu.

Integral to Hinduism was the form of social stratification known as the caste system related to the traditional fourfold *varna* hierarchy.

The *varna* system had the Brahmin literati and priesthood at its apex, followed by the Kshatriyas or warriors, the Vaishyas or merchants, and, lastly, the Shudras or peasants and menial workers who formed the lowest stratum. This was the hierarchy of the so-called 'caste Hindus'; below and beyond it were the communities earlier generically known as 'outcastes' or 'untouchables' because of the dirty and 'polluting' work (such as scavenging) that they were compelled to do. Although originally based on a social division of labour like a class system, the caste system became rigid over time. The English term 'caste' is also used to denote *jati*, the regionally specific communities that fit only broadly into the *varna* framework; the term is used to indicate *jati* throughout this paper. The entire caste structure was based on strict rules of ritual purity and pollution: inter-caste marriage was forbidden as was inter-dining or eating cooked food in the company of persons belonging to other castes. Besides, any given caste was prohibited from eating food cooked by or drinking water served by a person of a lower caste. The physical touch of the 'untouchables' was considered to be ritually 'polluting' to all caste Hindus.

The rigidification of the caste system meant that an individual was unable to change the caste which was ascribed by birth or leave the traditional occupation associated with it. The most oppressive feature of the system was the humiliation of the 'untouchables': they had to live outside the main settlement of the village or town and keep their distance from others while walking on the streets. They were denied access to the common water source of the village and refused entry into temples. Ancient scriptures, especially the hegemonic socio-legal treatise, the *Manusmriti*, prescribed severe punishment for any transgression of these inhuman conditions.[5] Starting with social reform discourse of the nineteenth century, the term 'untouchable' underwent several changes: first to 'Ati-shudras' (i.e. lower than the Shudras) in the nineteenth century, then the 'depressed classes' in the early twentieth century, 'Harijans' ('God's people', a term coined by Mahatma Gandhi) from about 1920, and, finally, to the currently prevalent 'Dalits' (downtrodden), which is the community's own preferred identificatory label.

The Hindu social reform discourse also resulted in religious reform (while prompting religious revival as well). The upper-caste discourse gave rise to the Prarthana Samaj, a monotheistic socio-religious organization established in 1867, which sought to reshape Hindu society along more liberal lines and remove caste discrimination. Associated with the Prarthana Samaj was the Depressed Classes Mission, which sought to uplift the lowest castes. A parallel, lower-caste reform movement was pioneered by Jotirao Phule who launched the Satyashodhak Samaj ('Truth-seeker's Society', established in 1873). Phule exposed the coercion and exploitation of the lower castes by the hegemonic Brahmin priesthood in rather militant terms, such as 'slavery'.[6] The trope of social slavery and bondage of the lower castes was to endure in the reform discourse which Ambedkar inherited.

Meanwhile, the changing nationalist scenario meant that political priorities sidelined social priorities in the late nineteenth century. In the twentieth century, with Gandhi's ascendance, the freedom struggle assumed the strategy of passive resistance. Dharmanand and Ambedkar responded differently to Gandhi's philosophy and movement, as discussed in greater detail below. Dharmanand felt an affinity with Gandhi's path of truth and non-violence (which were rooted in Buddhism), and he tried to remove caste discrimination in his own solitary way. Ambedkar's clash with Gandhi was political: he openly opposed Gandhi's proposed solution of absorbing Dalits as the fifth – and lowest – *varna* within the Hindu hierarchy and denying them the status of a separate 'minority'. Ambedkar saw such a minority status, along with the related political privileges, as the only guaranteed means of their empowerment.

TWO PATHS TO BUDDHISM

Dharmanand Kosambi (9 October 1876-4 June 1947)

Dharmanand Kosambi's life was plotted along the Buddhist meridian. His personal Buddhist journey was to take on an unexpectedly transnational character and also serve as a detailed commentary on the state of Buddhism in India's South Asian neighbourhood in the nineteenth century.[7]

Dharmanand was born in a rural family of Gaud Saraswat Brahmins in the then Portuguese colony of Goa in coastal western India, south of Maharashtra. The state's vernacular educational infrastructure being inadequate at the time, he was sent to various relatives in and around Goa for his schooling and was eventually compelled to drop out of school despite a good academic performance. (He was not inclined to go to a Portuguese school.) Trapped in a deadening, dull rural routine and married against his wishes at the age of fourteen in accordance with the prevailing custom of child marriage, Dharmanand went into a deep depression, which affected his health. His only solace was reading and with the help of borrowed Marathi books, he began to cultivate his mind considerably. This reading included a short life of the Buddha from which he drew great spiritual comfort. It made such a deep impact on him that he vowed to dedicate his life to the study and propagation of the Buddha's message among his fellow Maharashtrians – a vow he observed throughout his life. (Dharmanand identified with the larger, neighbouring Maharashtrian community because his mother-tongue, Konkani – a spoken language – had not yet developed as a language of knowledge and literature.)

In 1899, at the age of twenty-three, Dharmanand left his home, family and his newborn first child to venture forth on his quest – without any support, money or even a clear plan of action. For months, he travelled by train or, more frequently, by foot. He ran out of his meagre funds, was sometimes befriended by strangers and often had to beg for food. This was to be, periodically, his way of life for the next few years. Soon, he reached Banaras, the premier centre of Sanskrit learning in north India. He had cherished a vague notion that Sanskrit, being an ancient language, would give him access to Buddhist scriptures. For over a year, he studied at Banaras and made great strides in his Sanskrit studies but came no closer to a knowledge of Buddhism. At this time, Dharmanand was compelled to outwardly observe the caste norms of Brahmins but did not do so thereafter; nor did he ever believe in caste discrimination.

Unexpectedly, Dharmanand was able to visit Nepal – regarded as the home of Buddhism – when a Nepali fellow student was to return home. With hardly any money, warm clothes or even shoes, Dharmanand trudged barefoot up the mountains through occasional snow and reached Kathmandu only to find that Buddhism was not a living religion in Nepal at the time and was, in fact, treated with disdain. Disillusioned, he returned to India and went to Bodh Gaya in Bihar, expecting some help to reach his goal. He was told by the solitary Buddhist monk there, who was Burmese by nationality, that the nearest Buddhist centre of learning was Sri Lanka. He also suggested that help could be obtained from the Mahabodhi Sabha of Calcutta (now Kolkata) in eastern India. Dharmanand travelled to Calcutta in his usual physically exhausting fashion and was then planning to walk all the way to Madras (now Chennai), when the Mahabodhi Sabha collected a subscription to buy him a ticket to Colombo via Madras.

In Sri Lanka, Dharmanand was able to study Pali at last in 1902. He mastered it with ease because it is derived from Sanskrit, under the able guidance of Acharya Shri Sumangala, the founder of the Vidyodaya College. He was also initiated into the Buddhist Sangha as a novice monk (*saamaner* in Pali). His studies went well and he achieved fame, but the Sri Lankan food affected his health and he was compelled to return to India. Having landed in Madras, he faced an uncertain future again. But after a few months, he sought help from some Burmese acquaintances to get to Burma (now Myanmar). Here he was ordained as a full-fledged monk (*bhikkhu* in Pali). However, after a year or so, the old difficulty with the local diet cropped up again and he was compelled to return to India – this time to Calcutta in 1906. He then went on a pilgrimage to the Buddhist holy sites in north India and, subsequently, made another visit to Burma to learn and practise meditation in a remote set of caves. Later, he was to pay two more visits to Burma.

His return to Calcutta was another defining moment in Dharmanand's life as he was now drawn into the orbit of academia – first, national and then, international. He taught Pali and Buddhism at Calcutta University, having introduced the subject in the curriculum. Now he gave up monkhood after the appropriate rites, knowing that it would be difficult to practise it in the absence of a Sangha. He was also reunited with his wife and family after six years. During his two years in Calcutta, Dharmanand visited Sikkim to study the state of Buddhism there and found it in decline, as in Nepal.

Dharmanand left his well-paying university job in Calcutta in 1908 and came to Mumbai (formerly Bombay) to live with his wife and children on a small stipend offered by Sayajirao Gaikwad, chief of the princely state of Baroda in Gujarat, north of Maharashtra. The stipend was to offer him time and leisure to study Buddhist texts, and to lecture and write books about Buddhism. At this point, his life trajectory was to change yet again. He happened to teach Pali to a Harvard professor of Sanskrit who was visiting Mumbai and a year later, he was invited to Harvard University to assist another professor in editing the iconic Buddhist text, Buddhaghoshacharya's *Visuddhimagga*, for the Harvard Oriental Series. His two-year stint at Harvard (1910-12) was insufficient for the task, so he made three more trips, spending a total of eight years there. The text was finally ready in 1927 but was, for some reason, published only in 1950, three years after his death.[8]

Back in India, Dharmanand introduced Pali into the curriculum of Bombay University and taught the language for six years (1912-18) at Fergusson College in Pune (formerly Poona; the college was then affiliated to Bombay University). Later, he also taught it at Mahatma Gandhi's Gujarat Vidyapeeth at Ahmedabad for three years, from 1923 to 1926. He produced an able batch of students who took over the task of teaching Pali in the colleges and universities in and around Maharashtra, and they, in turn, continued the tradition after Dharmanand.

At this time, Dharmanand had already been drawn into Gandhi's orbit and promoted the ideology of satyagraha (or non-violent resistance) in various ways, which included a walking tour of the villages of Pune district. He also participated in Gandhi's Salt Satyagraha in 1930 and was subsequently jailed for several months. In 1931, he went to Russia for a year to teach Pali and Buddhism at the Leningrad Academy of Sciences. He spent his later years editing the oldest, original Buddhist texts and guiding students (including Dalits) informally in their studies. In 1936, Dharmanand built, with generous donations from philanthropists, a Buddhist vihara in Parel, the textile mill district of Mumbai, and tried to eradicate caste discrimination and untouchability among the mill workers. He was able to keep his early vow and spread the message of Buddhism through the Marathi-speaking region of western India by writing twenty-two books and various articles in Marathi from 1910 to 1947.

Some of these were translated into other Indian languages. He also wrote occasionally in English.[9]

Never the quintessential family man, Dharmanand led a peripatetic life once his children had grown up. In 1947, at the age of 70, he found his health declining and his capacity for useful work impaired. Finally, he fasted unto death in the time-honoured Jain fashion at Gandhi's Sevagram Ashram at Wardha. After a month, he breathed his last on 4 June 1947, two months before India obtained Independence. During this last month, he received a donation from a philanthropic industrialist, which he turned over to Gandhi to be utilized for sending students to Sri Lanka to study Pali and Buddhism. Such students were, indeed, sent. In life, as in death, Dharmanand propagated the message of Buddhism.

B.R. Ambedkar (14 April 1891-6 December 1956)

Bhimrao Ramji Ambedkar reached Buddhism by a very different path – as the culmination of his lifelong struggle to redress the social disabilities of the Dalits. In fact, the study and propagation of Buddhism occupied only a few short years at the end of his life, although his considerable impact on India today survives mainly through the large body of Dalit Buddhists, many of whom have confidently transcended their erstwhile social and economic handicaps.

Ambedkar was born into the Mahar community, the majority Dalit community in Maharashtra that functioned as hereditary village servants.[10] His father, a retired military man, gave him a good education, first in small town Maharashtra and later, in Parel in Mumbai. Young Bhim's childhood was scarred by the usual forms of humiliating discrimination; even his school in Mumbai barred him from studying Sanskrit, the 'divine' language solely reserved for Brahmins. (He is said to have studied some Sanskrit later in life and was also coached in Pali when he developed an interest in Buddhism.) His bright performance, however, earned encouragement from some liberal teachers.

One of these teachers helped Ambedkar get a scholarship from Sayajirao Gaikwad of Baroda, to study at Mumbai's renowned Elphinstone College. About this time, he was married at sixteen to a nine-year-old girl. After graduating in 1912, he went to the USA on a scholarship, also from Sayajirao Gaikwad to pursue higher studies at Columbia University. Here, he obtained a Master's degree in 1915 and a Ph.D. in 1916, both in economics. He then went to England to study economics at the London School of Economics and law at Grey's Inn because British degrees were valued more in India. However, the scholarship from the state of Baroda ran out and he returned to India. He was later awarded a D.Sc. by the London School of Economics in 1923 and became a barrister in Mumbai in the same year.

Back in India in 1917, Ambedkar was required to serve Baroda State for ten years in return for the State aid. However, his 'untouchability' prevented him from getting lodgings, and elicited contempt from his colleagues and even the office boys. He faced the same discrimination during his subsequent two-year term as a professor of political economy at Sydenham College in Mumbai. In fact, for most of his life he was to struggle against this 'status discrepancy' – a high academic and later political status, coupled with a low ritual status of which he was repeatedly and humiliatingly reminded.

In the 1920s, Ambedkar launched a multi-pronged social and political programme for Dalit empowerment. He popularized his constructive social agenda through innumerable speeches and articles in a series of Marathi newspapers that he started and edited, and tried to inculcate self-respect and a desire for education among the Dalits. He also established educational institutions and students' hostels in many places in Maharashtra. His protest against Hindu caste discrimination took the form of the ceremonial burning of a copy of the *Manusmriti* – the iconic Hindu scripture which sanctioned the oppression of 'untouchables' – at a large meeting in 1927. The symbolic value of the act was enormous. In order to secure the same rights as caste Hindus for the Dalits, Ambedkar launched two famous initiatives: access to the common water tank in the small town of Mahad in 1927 and entry into a Rama temple in the holy town of Nashik in 1930. Such was the resistance of caste Hindus that the two incidents turned into court cases and dragged on for many years to be finally resolved, respectively, in 1937 and 1947.

Ambedkar's early plank for political activism was the eventual enfranchisement of the Dalits. As the unchallenged leader, he earned nomination to the Bombay Legislative Council in 1927 and deputation to the sessions of the Round Table Conference in London in 1930, 1931 and 1932. Dalits comprised about a fifth of the population of British India, amounting to 60 million, and he sought separate electorates, for them along with the two other religious minorities of Muslims and Sikhs. These two communities won the right, but Gandhi opposed this proposed separation of a sizeable segment of the Hindu society and ultimately went on an indefinite fast in 1933 until Ambedkar gave up many of his demands, in what became known as the Poona Pact. Later, Ambedkar established the Independent Labour Party in 1936. (His proposed Republican Party was established after his death and soon split into two factions.) His political success was spectacular. In 1941, he was appointed by the Viceroy to the Executive Council of the Government of India. Ultimately, he was appointed the first Law Minister of Independent India in 1947 and Chairman of the prestigious committee for drafting the country's constitution.

Socially unable to make headway within the caste-ridden Hindu society, Ambedkar decided to opt out of Hinduism altogether. He made a public announcement in 1935 that although he was born a Hindu, he would not die as one. Leaders of all major religious communities in India vied with one another to attract him, impressed by his leadership of the millions of Dalits. Ambedkar considered these religions seriously and ultimately discounted Christianity and Islam as foreign religions to settle in favour of Sikhism, which would not 'denationalize' Dalits. A handful of his followers even converted to Sikhism but he was deterred by the discovery that caste-based inequalities also existed within the Sikh community. Ambedkar did not reveal his final decision on the issue until almost fifteen years later.

From about 1950, Ambedkar started showing an open interest in Buddhism. He saw it as the best option because it was an indigenous Indian religion and would not denationalize its followers. Additionally, its moral appeal was stronger because it enjoyed no national or international patronage.[11] Ambedkar attended Buddhist meetings in India, as well as in Burma, Sri Lanka and Nepal. He wrote rather infrequently on Buddhism, though;[12] his only book on the subject,

The Buddha and His Dhamma, was published posthumously in 1957.[13] He was otherwise a prolific writer and focused mainly on India's economic and political problems, also critiquing various facets of the doctrine and practice of Hinduism – especially the caste system and untouchability – in his books and articles.[14]

Ambedkar converted to Buddhism on 14 October 1956 in Nagpur. An estimated 300,000 of his followers, also converted on the occasion. Ambedkar's second wife also converted to Buddhism along with him. He had married Dr. Savita Kabir in 1948, at the age of 57, many years after the death of his first wife. This Gaud Saraswat Brahmin lady was then his personal physician, treating him for a variety of ailments, including high blood pressure and severe diabetes. The marriage attracted a great deal of notice: *The New York Times* compared it to the marriage of a member of the royalty with a commoner.[15]

However, a hectic schedule of work and travel took their toll. Less than two months later, on the night of 6 December 1956, Ambedkar passed away in Delhi at the age of sixty-five, and was cremated in Bombay on the following day. The occasion was marked by the conversion of 200,000 Dalits to Buddhism in Maharashtra. The momentum gained at the time has since led to the mass conversion of Dalits throughout India.[16]

ANALYSING THE BUDDHIST 'REVIVAL' IN MAHARASHTRA

Although Buddhism was the general religious-ideological site at which the lives of Dharmanand and Ambedkar almost intersected, the paths which led them to it were extremely divergent, as already indicated. Their varied objectives predictably shaped their understanding and explication of the religion.

Given his deeply spiritual quest, Dharmanand sought to understand Buddhism through a clear understanding of its three core elements: the figure of the Buddha, his original doctrine and the structure of the Sangha. His 'revival' of Buddhism, thus, became a retrieval of the original Buddhist doctrine by the weeding out of later accretions (belonging to the Mahayana sect and written mostly in Sanskrit) to reach the pure, unadulterated core texts (belonging to the Theravada or Hinayana sect and written in Pali). The gradual process of identifying the authentic core of Buddhism started with his first Marathi book in 1910 (Dh. Kosambi 1910; M. Kosambi 2010: 243-311). Here, he presents the life of the Buddha, the basic concepts of his doctrine and, additionally, the functioning of the Sangha both as described in ancient texts and as prevalent in twentieth-century Buddhist countries like Sri Lanka and Burma of which he had first-hand experience.

Dharmanand's primary contribution is his understanding of the historical person of the Buddha. This acquired bolder contours in his later books and especially in his best-known book, *Bhagavan Buddha* (Dh. Kosambi 1940-1). This book was regarded as the standard text on the subject and the government of India had it translated into several Indian languages in 1956, on the occasion of the Buddha's 2500th birth anniversary. Dharmanand's constant effort was to free the figure of the Buddha from a web of magic and legend, and portray him as an all-too-human, albeit extraordinary man.

The process reached completion in his posthumously published play, *Bodhisattva*.[17] The reason for putting forth his interpretation of the Buddha's early life and personality in the form of a play rather than a monograph was that despite ample supporting evidence, Dharmanand had to rely partly on his intuition and wanted to claim artistic licence. The essence of the play is that Gautama (or Gotama in Pali) was not a prince but the son of a Shakya oligarch. (Dharmanand explains that 'Siddhartha' was not his true name, but rather a title – 'siddha-artha', or one who has accomplished his aim – bestowed on him at a later date.) From childhood, he was sensitive and meditative; later, he supported caste and class equality, as well as the practice of celibacy until the mid-twenties. Gautama renounced family life not because he happened to see the reality of old age, disease and death for the first time in his late-twenties (as the legend goes), but in order to avert a war with the neighbouring oligarchy of the Koliyas over the distribution of the waters of the river Rohini, which formed the boundary between them. This pacifist attitude antagonized the Shakya council which forced him into exile. He then practised various forms of asceticism, finally gave them up for deep meditation and gained enlightenment. Thus, he was transformed from a Bodhisattva into the Buddha, and the play ends at this climactic point. (Dharmanand understands the term 'Bodhisattva' as referring to the person of Gautama in search of 'bodhi' or enlightenment, who later became the Buddha. He does not subscribe to the notion of several Bodhisattvas as representing the Buddha in his previous births; this idea was interpolated into Buddhist texts later.)

The Buddha's 'enlightenment' was articulated through the religious philosophy or Dhamma known as Buddhism. Its core ingredients were the Four Noble Truths; namely, Suffering as an all-pervasive fact of the human existence; Craving as the source of Suffering; the need for the Extinction of Craving; and the Path to such Extinction. This path is the Noble Eightfold Path: Right Knowledge, Right Resolve, Right Speech, Right Action, Right Living, Right Effort, Right Thought and Right Samadhi (or meditation).

Dharmanand's second important contribution was to establish the 'modernity' of Buddhism as a religious, social and even political ideology, and, thus, its relevance to twentieth-century India and the world. This was done in two ways. First, he linked the principles and functioning of Buddhism to those of socialism. As a member of the Buddhist Sangha for some years, he had seen that it was based on the principle of the collective ownership of all assets and collective decision-making. He made this connection – and wrote about it – practically as soon as he discovered socialism during his first trip to the USA via England in 1910. He was the first author to introduce socialism to Maharashtra – and perhaps to India – through his Marathi writings and speeches from 1910.[18] Second, Dharmanand related the core principles of Buddhism – truth, non-violence and avoidance of possessions – to Gandhi's political ideology of satyagraha, which was based on the same principles. He, thus, established the relevance of ancient Buddhism to India's twentieth-century freedom struggle as well. In fact, his opposition to Hinduism was pivoted on the justification of violence in it, as well as its emphasis on rituals and caste discrimination.

* * *

Ambedkar's understanding of Buddhism was partly derived from Dharmanand's, even while it differed on significant points. In 'reviving'

Buddhism, Ambedkar also reinvented it, as shown by his sole (English) book on the subject, *The Buddha and His Dhamma* which was posthumously published in 1957.[19] Scholars who have worked on Ambedkar term it a 'reconstruction' of Buddhism. On the eve of his conversion, Ambedkar was asked whether his Buddhism belonged to the Hinayana sect (the Lesser Vehicle or the original doctrine also known as Theravada) or the Mahayana sect (a splinter group known as the Greater Vehicle). He is reported to have said that it was 'Navayana': the New Vehicle, also known as Neo-Buddhism.[20] Other Ambedkar scholars also claim that Ambedkar 'made [the] Buddhist tradition critical by offering [a] radical reinterpretation of Buddhism'.[21] In sum, while deploying Buddhism for his social objectives, Ambedkar moulded it to enhance its attractiveness and effectiveness for his followers, and used it as a tool for economic and socio-political restructuring. His reasoning was that: 'The purpose of Religion is to explain the origin of the world. The purpose of Dhamma is to re-construct it.'[22] Some Ambedkarites say that he 'interpreted Buddhism in his own unique way so as to make it more relevant in the context of a contemporary, . . . ever-changing human society'.[23] His compilation of Buddhism has been compared to his drafting of the Indian constitution: both major documents were selectively and carefully reassembled from older ones – ancient Buddhist texts, in one case and American, British; and Indian law, in the other – to shape the religious and political life of Indian society.[24]

The socio-economic context for this exercise is important. The Mahar community of his birth (the largest Dalit community in Maharashtra, as mentioned earlier) did not occupy a special occupational niche in the village economy. Other large Dalit communities, such as the Mangs (or Matangs who worked as rope-makers) and the Chambhars (leather-workers), enjoyed occupational security within the village economy; the Mahars were treated as lowly village servants. Thus, the basis for their conversion was 'material, not spiritual'.[25] The feeling of being generally dispossessed in one's own country comes across poignantly in Ambedkar's complaint to the Mahatma in 1931: 'Gandhiji, I have no homeland'.[26]

Ambedkar had formed his understanding of Buddhism from a number of secondary sources, including Dharmanand's writings. Given that Dharmanand was the only authority on Buddhism to write in Marathi and that he had written steadily from 1910 to 1947, knowledge of at least some of his books can be assumed on the part of a Maharashtrian interested in Buddhism. However, Ambedkar does not acknowledge Dharmanand, or any secondary sources at all, in his book *The Buddha and His Dhamma*. This has been attributed to the fact that the book's introduction was truncated and some material omitted during its posthumous publication – a move regarded by some eminent Dalit scholars as controversial.[27] A supplement to this book, in the form of a list of sources for Ambedkar's book, has been published and includes numerous references to Dharmanand's *Bodhisattva*.[28] However, scholars note of Ambedkar that many references to Dharmanand's *Bhagavan Buddha* have been left out.[29] They also claim that Maharashtrian Buddhists consider the latter book as possessing primary importance and their support has been crucial in it remaining in print.[30]

The issue here is not Ambedkar's extent of borrowing of ideas but of his interpretation of Buddhism. In his introduction to *The Buddha and His Dhamma*, he identifies four core issues relating to Buddhism as being most important. The first is the reason for Gautama's renunciation: here, Dharmanand's influence is evident in that his interpretation has been accepted. The second core issue is the 'Four Aryan [i.e. Noble] Truths' dealing with the existence of suffering and its extinction through the eightfold path. According to Ambedkar, this 'cuts at the root of Buddhism' because the emphasis on sorrow 'makes the gospel of the Buddha a gospel of pessimism'. He, therefore, treats it as 'a later accretion by monks'. However, in the body of his book, Ambedkar does refer repeatedly to the pervasiveness of suffering as part of the human condition. According to scholars of Ambedkar, his objective is not to deny the fact of pervasive suffering but to deny it the status of an eternal truth.[31] The third core issue is the Buddha's denial of the existence of the soul even while affirming the doctrine of karma and rebirth. Ambedkar's explanation is that the Buddha used these words in a different sense from that employed by contemporary Brahmins. Surprisingly, despite his rationalist approach, Ambedkar accepts Gautama's ten previous incarnations as Bodhisattvas. This has been seen by some as an attempt to introduce the factor of moral evolution.[32] The fourth and last core issue relates to the function of the Buddhist monk. Ambedkar sees him as 'a social servant devoting his life to [the] service of the people and being their friend, guide and philosopher', rather than being the 'perfect man'. In his general portrayal of 'Siddharth Gautam' as he calls the Buddha, Ambedkar has retained many of the touches of magic and legend associated with the former's life.

The question arises as to why Ambedkar wrote his famous book in English if his objective was to reach the Dalits who were barely literate in their own mother-tongue. One suggested answer is that he wanted to write a 'Bible of Buddhism' because there was no unified and authoritative statement of the doctrine; such a book in English would enjoy a wide outreach within India and outside. It could later be translated into the Indian languages and would also reach caste Hindus whom he repeatedly challenged.[33] After all, Ambedkar's acceptance of Buddhism was as much a statement of his faith in the doctrine as of his loss of faith in and rejection of Hinduism.

Another of Ambedkar's innovations was a special rite for conversion to Buddhism. Originally, during the Buddha's time and for centuries after, Indian lay followers of Buddhism indicated their adherence to the doctrine by repeating the three 'refuges' (in the Buddha, the Dhamma and the Sangha), accepting the Four Noble Truths, following the Noble Eightfold Path, vowing to follow the basic ethical rules of conduct (to tell the truth, not to steal, etc.), listening to Buddhist sermons, and observing certain holy days (as *uposatha*). There was no ritual conversion for lay followers. Only in the case of novice monks and full-fledged monks was there a specially prescribed rite. But Ambedkar's objective was to make an emphatic social and political statement; a ritual of conversion – especially on a mass scale – was part of his agenda. To this end, he introduced a conversion ritual which included a repetition of the three standard 'refuges'.[33] Additionally, there were 22 'oaths' which he had himself composed to reaffirm faith in the Buddha's teachings as supreme, pledge the observance of the basic rules of ethical conduct and repudiate faith in Hindu deities.[34]

Ambedkar's conversion and Buddhist 'revival' have been variously interpreted. His conversion is seen as 'less a rejection of political solutions than a rewriting of religious and cultural change into a form of political intervention' and providing a new political identity for the Dalits.[35] It has also provided them with a new social identity in terms of self-respect and educational opportunities. Ambedkar's 'new Buddhism' introduced 'independent thinking' and a surge in creative writing 'to such a degree that it literally changed the face of Marathi literature'.[36] It provided the impulse to the Dalit community to make its presence felt.

Finally, one more commonality between Ambedkar and Dharmanand was their comparison between Buddhism and Marxism, though with divergent conclusions. Ambedkar's essay 'Buddha and Marx', posthumously compiled from three different typed copies, concludes that the Buddha can give the modern world liberty, equality and fraternity, whereas Marx can only provide equality.[37] The divergence can be explained by the fact that Ambedkar based his view of Marxism and Buddhism on the two doctrines; Dharmanand relied upon the functioning of the Buddhist Sangha of which he had a first-hand experience.

CONCLUSION

That twentieth-century Maharashtra suddenly rediscovered Buddhism after many centuries of amnesia was to the credit of Dharmanand Kosambi and B.R. Ambedkar. Buddhism was the site at which their life trajectories almost intersected within the larger social, religious and political reform movement in the region. Strangely, there is no record of their ever having met. Some think that Dharmanand's Gandhian affiliation may have prevented direct contact.[38]

All the same, both men converted to Buddhism and propagated it to achieve their own varied objectives. Both supported it in preference to and as a rejection of Hinduism, thus approximating the original purpose of the doctrine when the Buddha first expounded it more than two millennia ago.

To Dharmanand, Buddhism promised salvation through ethical conduct; to Ambedkar, it promised social equality for the Dalits through a release from upper-caste oppression. Dharmanand was a solitary thinker, while Ambedkar was essentially a 'political man' and a social leader. Yet importantly, both tried to relate this ancient doctrine to the twentieth-century social and political conditions to make it a living religion. Their efforts, whether as personal or political statements, took divergent forms. But both firmly reinscribed Buddhism on Maharashtra's social map in the twentieth century.

ACKNOWLEDGEMENTS

I would like to thank Dr. M.G. Dhadphale, former Professor and Head of the Department of Sanskrit and Pali, Fergusson College, Pune; Dr Mahesh Deokar, Professor and Head of the Department of Pali at the University of Pune; and Dr. Pradeep Gokhale, formerly of the Department of Philosophy, University of Pune, for their help through discussions of certain points related to this paper.

NOTES

1. D.D. Kosambi (1985): 266-78.
2. Dh. Kosambi (1935): 97-9, 296-7; D.D. Kosambi (1957): 63-6.
3. Dharmanand Kosambi is referred to as 'Dharmanand' rather than 'Kosambi' in this paper because his surname is usually associated with his son, the internationally renowned mathematician and Indologist, D.D. Kosambi. Dharmanand's Marathi writings were put on a website (www.dharmanandkosambi.com) by Yashwantrao Chavan Pratishthan of Mumbai in November 2011.
4. M. Kosambi (2007): 15-23.
5. Doniger and Smith (1991).
6. Keer and Malshe (1969): 68. Jotirao Phule dedicated his famous Marathi booklet on this subject, *Gulamgiri* ('Slavery,' first published in 1873), to the Americans who had struggled to end slavery in the United States.
7. M. Kosambi (2010).
8. Warren (1950).
9. A chronological bibliography of Dharmanand's writings in Marathi, English and other languages is given in M. Kosambi (2010): 414-17.
10. Keer (2010); Rodrigues (2009): 6-17. Rodrigues has included in his selection Ambedkar's writings on economics, politics and law as well as religion, caste, and untouchability, but not Buddhism.
11. Guru (2008): 320.
12. In an incomplete manuscript discovered after Ambedkar's death and published under the rubric 'Revolution and Counter-Revolution', there are some translations of Pali *suttas* (sets of verses) (Ambedkar, vol. 3: 95-439).

One of his manuscripts was published posthumously under the rubric of a 'Pali-English Dictionary' (Ambedkar, vol. 16). This is more in the nature of an extended glossary probably meant for personal use; personal communication from Dr. Mahesh Deokar.

13. A new edition of *The Buddha and His Dhamma* has been brought out by Rathore and Verma (2011), correcting the numerous misprints in the original and incorporating Moon's references, among other things.
14. Ambedkar's writings and speeches have been posthumously published in a set of 16 volumes (Ambedkar, 1979-98). They cover the period from 1916 to his death; some of the material was incomplete and otherwise unpublished.
15. Keer (2010): 404. Ambedkar's view of inter-caste marriage was complex. He claimed that inter-caste marriage was the only effective solution to the abolition of the caste system (Mungekar, 2010: 14). But he also advised young, educated Dalit women against marrying upper-caste men (Keer 2010: 353). His own rationale for marrying a Brahmin woman was that he wanted 'an educated lady who knew cooking and was a medical practitioner' and such a lady was impossible to find among the Dalits (Keer 2010: 403).
16. A good example of such conversion is that of a community of leather-workers of Agra in north India, ably discussed in the anthropological study by Lynch, 1969.
17. Dh. Kosambi (1949); M. Kosambi (2010): 358-408.
18. M. Kosambi (2010): 14-16.
19. Ambedkar (1992).
20. Gokhale (2008): 109, 135.
21. Guru (2008): 320.
22. Cited in Gokhale (2008): 139.
23. Mungekar (2010): 24.
24. Cited in Viswanathan (1998): 228.
25. Guru (2008): 316-19, 323.
26. Cited in Keer (2010): 166.
27. Personal communication from Dr. Raosaheb Kasbe, then holder of the Dr. Ambedkar Chair, University of Pune, July 2010.
28. Moon (1995).
29. Personal communication from Dr Mahesh Deokar.
30. Zelliot (2008): 99.
31. In an incomplete manuscript discovered after Ambedkar's death and published under the rubric 'Revolution and Counter-Revolution', there are some translations of Pali *suttas* (sets of verses) (Ambedkar, vol. 3: 95-439). One of his manuscripts was published posthumously under the rubric of a 'Pali-English Dictionary' (Ambedkar, vol. 16). This is more in the nature of an extended glossary probably meant for personal use; personal communication from Dr. Mahesh Deokar.

32. Personal communication from Dr. Pradeep Gokhale. Marathi and Hindi translations of the book are known to have appeared.
33. During his lifetime, Ambedkar's followers added a fourth 'refuge' in his name (*Bhimam saranam gachchhaami*), but he discouraged this personality cult at once. Personal information from Dr. Mahesh Deokar and Dr. Gopal Guru.
34. These 'oaths' are listed in Zelliot (2008): 103.
35. Viswanathan (1998): 212.
36. Zelliot (2008): 95, 105.
37. Ambedkar, vol. 3: 462.
38. Zelliot (2008): 99.

BIBLIOGRAPHY

Ambedkar, B.R. 1992. *The Buddha and His Dhamma* (*Dr. Babasaheb Ambedkar: Writings and Speeches*, vol. 11). Bombay: Government of Maharashtra, Education Department.

———. 1979-98. *Dr. Babasaheb Ambedkar: Writings and Speeches*, 16 vols. Mumbai: Education Department, Government of Maharashtra.

Doniger, Wendy and Brian K Smith, trs. 1991. *The Laws of Manu*. New Delhi: Penguin Books India.

Gokhale, Pradeep. 2008. 'Dr. Ambedkar's Interpretation of Buddhism', in *The Philosophy of Dr. B.R. Ambedkar*, ed. Pradeep Gokhale. Pune: Sugava Prakashan, pp. 109-52.

Guru, Gopal. 2008. 'Mukati Kon Pathe: Emancipation, Which Way?', in *Marga: Ways of Liberation, Empowerment, and Social Change in Maharashtra*, ed. M. Naito, I. Shima, and H. Kotani. Delhi: Manohar, pp. 313-27.

Keer, Dhananjay. 2010. *Dr. Babasaheb Ambedkar: Life and Mission*. Bombay: Popular Prakashan, 4th edn., rpt. (1st pub. 1954).

Keer, Dhananjay and S.G. Malshe, eds. 1969. *Mahatma Phule: Samagra Vangmaya* (*The Complete Works of Mahatma Phule*). Mumbai: Maharashtra Rajya Sahityaani Sanskriti Mandal.

Kosambi, D.D. 1957. 'The Decline of Buddhism in India', *Exasperating Essays: Exercises in the Dialectical Method*. Poona: People's Book House.

———. 1985. *An Introduction to the Study of Indian History*. Bombay: Popular Prakashan, rev. 2nd edn., rpt. (1st pub. 1956).

Kosambi, Dharmanand. 1910. *Buddha, Dharma ani Sangha*. Mumbai: Nirnayasagar Press.

———. 1935. *Hindi Sanskritiani Ahimsa* (*Indian Civilization and Non-Violence*). Mumbai: Dharmanand Kosambi.

———. 1940-1. *Bhagavan Buddha*, Parts 1 and 2. Nagpur and Pune: Suvichar Prakashan Mandal.

———.1949. *Bodhisattva: Natak* (*Bodhisattva: A Play*). Mumbai: Dharmanand Smarak Trust.

Kosambi, Meera. 2007. *Crossing Thresholds: Feminist Essays in Social History*. Ranikhet: Permanent Black.

———. tr. and ed. 2010. *Dharmanand Kosambi: The Essential Writings*. Ranikhet: Permanent Black.

Lynch, Owen. 1969. *The Politics of Untouchability*. New York and London: Columbia University Press.

Moon, Vasant. 1995. *Pali and Other Sources of The Buddha and His Dhamma with an Index* (Supplement to vol. 11 of *Dr Babasaheb Ambedkar: Writings and Speeches*). Bombay: Education Department, Government of Maharashtra.

Mungekar, B.L. 2010. *Dr. Ambedkar's Approach to Buddhism: Towards a Socio-Cultural and Democratic Revolution*. New Delhi: Northern Book Centre.

Rodrigues, Valerian, ed. 2009. *The Essential Writings of B.R. Ambedkar*. New Delhi: Oxford University Press (1st pub. 2002).

Rathore, Akashsingh and Ajay Verma, eds. 2011. *B.R. Ambedkar: The Buddha and His Dhamma: A Critical Edition*. Delhi: Oxford University Press.

Viswanathan, Gauri. 1998. 'Conversion to Equality', in *Outside the Fold: Conversion, Modernity, and Belief*. Delhi: Oxford University Press, pp. 211-39.

Warren, H.C., ed., rev. Dharmananda Kosambi, [*sic*]. 1950. *Visuddhimagga of Buddhaghosacariya*. Cambridge, Mass.: Harvard University Press (Harvard Oriental Series).

Zelliot, Eleanor. 2008. 'Dr. Ambedkar's Path to Buddhism: A Marg to Navayana?', in *Marga: Ways of Liberation, Empowerment, and Social Change in Maharashtra* ed. M. Naito, I. Shima, and H. Kotani. Delhi: Manohar, pp. 95-110.

CHAPTER 2

Buddhist Revival and the Restoration of Sanchi

NAYANJOT LAHIRI

THE ARCHAEOLOGICAL RECOVERY of Buddhist sites, and the manifestation of this phenomenon in the revival and redefinition of Buddhism in colonial India evokes images of many different places, persons and events. Images of the Sanchi Stupa, of the discovery and documentation of Buddhist monuments scattered across the landscape of Taxila, of the temple at Mahabodhi and of the ancient Buddhist centre of learning at Nalanda are now as familiar to interested scholars as are the names of those archaeologists who frequently dug these ruins out of oblivion and wrote about them. That some of those sites became iconic in the revival of Buddhism is also well known. The movement to reclaim the Mahabodhi temple at Bodh Gaya for the Buddhists that began soon after its archaeological documentation and restoration in the latter part of the nineteenth century is the best-known example of this. It is also one which highlights the persona of Anagarika Dharmapala, the founder of the Maha Bodhi Society and a religious crusader, whose aim to reify Mahabodhi as an exclusively Buddhist place of worship was in the mould of what became emblematic of Buddhist revivalism.

This paper, though, is not about modern religious crusaders of the Buddhist faith nor about the institutions they founded. Instead, it seeks to draw attention to the restoration of Sanchi against the backdrop of the revival of Buddhism. This is because the conservation and guardianship of monuments associated with Buddhism, including Sanchi, were framed, in a manner of speaking, by this revival. The first section examines this revival but instead of summarizing what is known about it from the many available monographs on modern Buddhism, it sees it as part of a wider redefinition that was taking place in the world of South Asian religions in British India. In fact, as the first section argues, the vocabulary used by Hindu, Islamic and Sikh reformers appears to be very similar to what was encountered within Buddhist revivalism. The image that the British created of themselves as the guardians of Buddhism and the ways in which their vision coincided with the ideas of Buddhist revivalists is also discussed.

The second section is primarily concerned with the princely state of Bhopal in whose principality Sanchi, the best preserved of all the Buddhist monuments in India, was located. Bhopal's ruling house was neither Buddhist nor a self-proclaimed saviour of Buddhism, and yet was crucial in the modern revival and restoration of Sanchi. This is a little-known story and is worth retelling because, among other things, the outstanding restoration work undertaken there with the Bhopal Durbar's support in the early twentieth century ensured that Sanchi became, and continues to be, the modern icon of ancient India's Buddhist past. If, on the one hand, it was a model of the Sanchi Stupa which was prominently displayed on the dais when B.R. Ambedkar took his Buddhist vows on 14 October 1956, on the other hand, it was the same stupa which had provided the inspiration for the dome of the Viceregal House (now Rashtrapati Bhawan) in New Delhi.[1] Many decades later, on 29 May 2010, India's president, Pratibha Patil, dedicated a life-size replica of the Sanchi Stupa, costing some four million dollars, to China at the ancient Buddhist monastic site of Luoyang in central China.[2]

The eventful modern history of ancient Sanchi, especially the metamorphosis of its damaged and vandalized structures to the beautifully conserved monuments that we now see and which are widely recognized as emblematic of early Indian Buddhism, is well known. The technicalities of the impressive architectural restoration undertaken there in the early twentieth century by John Marshall, Director-General of the Archaeological Survey of British India, are described in his own definitive volumes on Sanchi. However, it is through the archives that the other characters in the conservation and restoration of Sanchi become visible, especially the rulers of the

Bhopal Durbar. This requires reiteration since the durbar which supported Sanchi was a Muslim ruling house and such shrine guardians hardly figure in narratives on the restoration of Buddhist sites, itself an important strand in the story of the modern revival of Buddhism. As the paper demonstrates, in post-Independence India, too, due credit has not been given to the erstwhile rulers of Bhopal in the re-enshrinement of the relics at Sanchi, even in the speeches and writings of Prime Minister Jawaharlal Nehru who was present at Sanchi when these were brought there in November 1956.

SOUTH ASIAN RELIGIONS, REFORMIST MOVEMENTS AND THE BUDDHIST REVIVAL

A marked feature of modern India (and, no doubt, of earlier periods as well, which, however, are beyond the scope of this paper) has been the presence of heterogeneities within the major religious traditions, which militate against present-day ideas of pure or universal religious communities, as the categories of Hindu, Muslim, Buddhist and Sikh would tend to suggest. This was well summed-up by Shail Mayaram who, in her description of the 'complex ethnic universe' of South Asia, pointed to the phenomenon of communities which had dual or triple religious affiliations, a phenomenon which also figured in many a census report where there are Hindus who appear to be animists, Buddhists who are also shamanistic, and 'Muhammadans' who are Hindus.[3] It is for the same reason that the distinguished historian of Sikhism, Harjot Oberoi, is known to have commented that 'it is all very well for historians of religion to think, speak and write about Islam, Hinduism and Sikhism, but they rarely pause to consider if such clear-cut categories actually found expression in the consciousness, actions and cultural performances of the human actors they describe'.[4]

What is striking, however, is that while many South Asian religions were marked by an untidy blend of diverse practices, from the nineteenth century onwards, one can also observe a marked consolidation of groups that strongly and self-consciously attempted to return to a more monolithic, or what they considered to be the original 'true' forms of those traditions.

So, for instance, in the case of Hinduism, the much-cited description offered by Alfred Lyall in 1884, based on his observations and experience in the Indian province of Berar – where the worship of 'mere stocks and stones and of local configurations, which are unusual or grotesque in size, shape or position' coexisted quite happily with the 'supreme gods of Hinduism, and of their ancient incarnations and personifications, handed down by the Brahmanic scriptures' – highlights the religion's diverse strands.[5] Around the time that Lyall was writing, these appear to be the very diversities that were sought to be ironed out by the Arya Samaj. Founded in 1875 by Swami Dayanand Saraswati, the Arya Samaj version of Hinduism, with an emphasis on the infallibility of the Vedas, rejected idol worship, and the worship of multiple gods and goddesses, as also all Hindu avataras.[6]

Similarly, among Muslims in South Asia, there appear to have been multiple strands of thought and practice. There was, on the one hand, a reinvigoration of the Chishti Sufis and Shi'a efflorescences in Awadh and Bengal, along with the visibility of Muslim communities whose 'Hindu' practices are well-documented, such as the Meos who composed the Mewati *Mahabharata* in the early eighteenth century and the Muslims of the Santhal Parganas who were known to carry sacred water to the shrine of Baidyanath.[7] On the other hand, the nineteenth century was marked by Islamic reform and revival movements that positioned themselves as movements that sought to return to 'true' Islam. This was, as Barbara Metcalf noted, evident is the eschewing of customary practices and in the tendency 'to be "scripturalist" in returning to the written records of the Koran and the traditions of the Prophet'.[8] In many instances, such movements targeted saints and apostles, especially the *pirs* of Sufi shrines, as also practices like pilgrimages and prostration before them.[9]

In the case of Sikhism, too, Oberoi's work has shown that Sikhs could belong to many different traditions. He mentioned a variety of these: Udasi, Nirmala, Khalsa, Nanak-panthi, Ram Raia, Baba Gurditta, Baba Jawahir Singh, Guru Bhag Singh, Nihang, Kalu Panthi, Ram Dasi, Nirankari, Kuka and Sarvaria. He also pointed out that 'many of these Sikhs shaved their heads, some smoked tobacco, others were not particular about maintaining the five external symbols of the faith'.[10] It was from the late nineteenth century onwards, however, that Sikhs in growing numbers took part in campaigns to 'purge' their religion of this diversity and what were viewed as Hindu accretions. By the beginning of the twentieth century, this new identity came to be known as 'Tat Khalsa'.

The nineteenth-century revival of Buddhism shared many of these elements. For one, it was marked by attempts to bring the religion into conformity with its early doctrines and this redefinition encompassed various parts of Asia, from Ceylon to Burma and Siam. In Burma, for instance, the Buddhist religion of the bulk of the province was described in the 1891 Census Report as 'a thin veneer of philosophy laid over the main structure of Shamanistic belief' to which the 1901 Census Report added that Buddhism was the 'superficial polish' while animism supplied the 'solid constituents that hold the faith together'. During the reign of King Mindon (1852-78), however, royal Buddhism became the patron and promoter of Pali orthodoxy.[11] In Ceylon as well, there were various Buddhist fraternities that prescribed adherence to the religion's early principles and doctrines. In this case, the protestant nature of the reforms owed a great deal to the challenge that Christian missions posed. Kitsiri Malalgoda has demonstrated that the Buddhist response to Christianity assumed a coherent form only in the latter half of the nineteenth century and that the outcome of the confrontation was the emulation of the model of Protestant Christianity by Buddhists:

> Noteworthy among the resultant changes were the imitation by the Buddhists of the organizational forms, tactics and expedients of Christian missionary bodies, as also the acquisition of a new militancy, which had more in common with the spirit of Christian missionaries of the time than with their own more traditional attitudes towards other religions. In keeping with the same developments were also the process of laicization, or the involvement of laymen in roles of religious leadership, and its concomitant, the displacement of monks from some of their traditional positions of leadership.[12]

The point here is that the Buddhist revival in India and attempts to re-establish a 'pure' Buddhism need to be understood against the background of similar reforms that were underway in other parts of Asia.

In relation to reform movements within other South Asian religions, a basic difference, however, needs to be remembered. The visibility of the Buddhist revival did not really come from its practising adherents in India. The number of Buddhists in India were few but not as few as is generally believed. In the 1901 census, for example, the Buddhists in Bengal were said to be 237,893 while there were 35,000 in Kashmir, roughly 7,000 in Spiti, Lahaul and Kinnaur (which then formed part of Punjab), some 9,000 in Assam and a small colony of 1,000 Buddhists called Saraks in the Tributary States of Orissa. In terms of numbers, they were far more numerous than the census-enumerated Hindu reformist groups like the Arya Samaj (whose adherents were about 92,419) and the Brahmo Samaj (with 4,050 adherents), even if they did not enjoy the same visibility. The varieties of Buddhism that were practised by most of these communities, in fact, have not been closely studied but whatever is available in the official publications of British India suggests that these were not closely related to the ancient canon. An instance in point is that of the Orissa Saraks – a name which is said to be derived from Sravaka (a hearer) – who worshipped Chaturbhuja.[13] Usually, Chaturbhuja is applied to Vishnu but was said to be identified by the Saraks with the Buddha. There were also heterogeneous social practices in the monastic community within one region as, for example, in Spiti (then in Punjab and now in Himachal Pradesh) where, at one end of the spectrum was the celibate Gelukpa sect to which the principal and richest monastery at Ki belonged and, at the other, was the Dukhpa sect which permitted its monks to marry. Buddhist revivalism does not appear to have taken root in such Indian communities.[14]

Instead, several of the key figures in this revival were influenced by and operated in a pan-Asian and, on occasion, what can be described as a global scenario. Various nationalities, in fact, are represented in this revival. The American Colonel Henry Steel Olcott and the Russian Helena Petrovna Blavatsky, for example, founded the Theosophical Society in New York in 1875 and soon established contacts with Asian Buddhists, especially those in Ceylon. It was a Ceylonese member of the Theosophical Society, David Hewavitarne, who, in the 1890s, as Anagarika Dharmapala, became the best-known religious leader of Buddhist revivalism. Due to strides in communication, Dharmapala could, with relative ease, make Mahabodhi's restoration to the

Buddhist community the subject of his speeches to gatherings not only in Ceylon and India but also in London, Tokyo and Chicago. Part of Dharmapala's appeal, as at the 1893 World's Parliament of Religions, was rooted in the fact that the form of Buddhism that he presented was a system of ethics and philosophy that was in sync with the 'emerging global ecumene' rather than the diverse practices of Buddhist adherents in different parts of Asia.[15] It was also one which, like nineteenth-century Oriental scholarship, regarded real Buddhism as being located in ancient texts, while local practices which had evolved over the centuries were viewed as degenerate forms.[16]

The same ease of communication which facilitated Dharmapala's travels also facilitated the movement of others. Mahavira or Mahavir Svami, the first Hindu in modern times to have become a Buddhist monk, initially became interested in Buddhism when he went to Ceylon to take part in wrestling matches. There, he studied Pali and, in 1890, was ordained as a monk. It was Mahavira Svami who made Kasia or Kusinagara, an important early Buddhist archaeological site, his permanent abode where he got constructed a dharmashala in 1901 with funds from Burmese Buddhists, especially Maung Khee Zarhee (also called Khezari Babu).[17] It was, incidentally, a monk of Burmese origin, U. Chandramani, who not only carried forward Mahavira Svami's work at Kusinagara but also extended his activities to other sacred places with early archaeological Buddhist relics: Sravasti, where he got a Buddha vihara constructed; Lumbini, where a similar vihara was made; and Sarnath, where a Dharmashala was constructed for Burmese pilgrims.[18] It was U. Chandramani who was the Dhamma-guru of B.R. Ambedkar and the man who ordained him in 1956. Not all Asian Buddhists who came to India's Buddhist sites, however, were of a spiritual bent. Count Kozui Otani, for instance, who was the head of the Nishi Honganji sub-sect of the Jodo Shinshu Buddhism in Kyoto, sought permission in 1902 to explore and excavate in the Patna and Gaya districts. It is another matter that this was denied to him but his aim there must have been to combine archaeological work with rifling through treasures in much the same way that he had done along the Silk Route.[19]

Along with the revivalist movement, Buddhism's visibility was also the result of what Philip Almond has described as the 'British discovery of Buddhism'. The various phases in this discovery during the nineteenth century have been mapped out by him, from understanding its presence as a living religion in various parts of Asia to one that came to be defined through the 'progressive collection, translation, and publication of its textual past'.[20] There were many milestones in this process of textualization in which a vast number of Buddhist manuscripts and texts were collected, edited, translated, and published by Western and Indian scholars. Simultaneously (and this has not been described by Almond), what gave this religion a striking visibility was the archaeological discovery of Buddhism. More than any other person, it was Alexander Cunningham who, with the Chinese Buddhist pilgrims' travelogues in hand, documented and excavated a very large number of sites from those in the Northwest Frontier Province and Punjab to the monuments of central India – including those at Taxila, Sanchi, Bharhut, Mahabodhi, Nalanda and Rajgir. As a consequence of his work, the archaeological bearings of Buddhism were mapped out on a massive scale. Later as well, in the early phase of John Marshall's tenure as Director-General of the Archaeological Survey of India (1902-28), a conscious strategy to re-examine Buddhist sites, ranging from Charsada and Vaisali to Kasia and Amaravati, was evolved.

Such work also came to be deployed to create an image of British colonials as guardians and saviours of Buddhism. This is palpably evident in all kinds of publications, as also in archival notings and forgotten letters. An early example is a poem composed by Alexander Cunningham and published in *The Bhilsa Topes* in 1854:[21]

Nought but the Topes themselves remain to mock
Time's ceaseless efforts; yet they proudly stand
Silent and lasting upon their parent rock,
And still as cities under magic's wand;
Till curious Saxons, from a distant land,
Unlock'd the treasure of two thousand years,
And the lone scene is peopled. . . .

That British explorers held the keys to unlocking India's history shines through this poem. Incidentally, a very different leitmotif was used by Cunningham for representing indigenous people. One encounters 'bigoted Musalmans', 'avaricious zamindars' and destructively rancorous 'fiery Saivas', and they are all represented as vandals.

More than fifty years later, a letter written by D.B. Spooner, an Archaeological Survey of India officer, to his uncle in the United States of America captures this identification in an even more direct way. Spooner was the officer who carried what were presumed to be the Buddha's relics from the Kanishka Stupa in the North-West Frontier Province to Calcutta. He wrote to his uncle about

> . . . the splendid time I had in Calcutta. The Bones of the Buddha were fastened around me and I set off from Peshawar with an armed guard, (one of my chaprassis in red and gold) who sat up 3 nights to guard the Relics. Then the Dalai Lama of Tibet, the 'living Buddha,' came for private worship of them, and officially acknowledged them to be Bones of himself 2500 years ago! The group was photographed and I will send you a copy, but the Government has forbidden its publication, so please do not give it to the papers. The Dalai Lama – the last man in the world I ever expected to see – is the small bear headed man in the centre. He is holding the Relics in his hand in the new golden casket. The ancient casket of King Kanishka in which I found them is on the table. Then came the very impressive ceremony in Government House Calcutta when Lord Minto the Viceroy presented the Relics to the Prince of Burma. The function took place in the Throne Room, and the whole Government of India was present in full uniform and about 200 of the great personages of the land, including the Prince of Orleans. It was a splendid blaze of colour and quite the finest thing I have ever seen. But almost the best part of it was the long marble hallway approaching the Throne Room. This has a long row of stately columns on either side, and between these columns stood tall and stately Sikh lancers in uniform, who presented arms as each person came up the hall. It was perfectly splendid. I have never seen anything approaching it, outside a theatre.[22]

Surprisingly, nobody seems to have found anything incongruent in armed soldiers being an integral part of a ceremonial occasion centred around the bones of the most peace-loving South Asian who ever lived.[23] From the end of the nineteenth century, as known from the example of the Piprahwa Stupa relics which were given to the King of Thailand, Buddhist relics had become instruments of diplomatic goodwill.[24] That the use of such relics continued to bolster the image of the British as guardians of Buddhism well into the twentieth century is evident from Spooner's candid account.

If British colonials saw themselves as saviours of Buddhism, there was also an impatience and disapproval with regard to any kind of hybridity or heterogeneity around its sites of worship. An example of this is the dispute around Mahabodhi, a site which Viceroy George Nathaniel Curzon regarded as only a Buddhist shrine, a view that was premised on a classification in which religious complexes were perceived as belonging to one religion and its community of believers – the religion of the founders of the shrine. In the seventy-two letters and enclosures, covering 120 closely-printed pages that were included by him in *Indian Archaeology 1899-1905*, nowhere is there any reference to features connected with Mahabodhi's archaeology and history, highlighted in 1892 by Cunningham's own work on the shrine, or to the fact that these attested to the antiquity of its mixed pilgrim traffic.[25] Curzon's view that other ritual practices were either acts of usurpation or defilement, incidentally, also coincided with the ideas of Buddhist revivalists. This is a view that has been articulated by later scholars of religion as well. An example is Benoy Gopal Ray's uneasiness with the 'cobwebs of Hinduism' in places like Chittagong where, in spite of the reformist movement, there were Buddhists who offered *pindas* to their ancestors.[26]

Curzon's monument conservation policy also came to be premised on this assumption and in the view that came to be formalized, it was underlined that apart from the government, religious monuments and shrines could be safeguarded only by co-religionists. This is evident from the provisions of the Ancient Monuments Preservation Act of 1904. One of its clauses stipulated that in the case of religious monuments, only those owners could enter into an agreement with the government who were followers of the religion to which the monument belonged.[27] As Clause 6.3 of the act put it, 'Nothing in the section shall be deemed to empower any person not being of the same religion as the persons on whose behalf he is acting to make or execute an agreement relating to a protected monument which or any part of which is periodically used for the religious worship or observances of that religion.' It is this religious frame of reference which would become crucial in the case of the conservation of Sanchi and the question of its guardianship, as will soon be evident.

MAPPING THE MODERN HISTORY OF ANCIENT SANCHI

Destruction and Excavation

Why was large-scale architectural restoration required at Sanchi? This ancient complex needed urgent and extensive repair because although its monuments had been in a remarkably good state of preservation when it was discovered in 1818, as these came to be dug and documented by British treasure hunters and archaeologists, they were substantially disfigured by the means and circumstances of the latters' work.[28] The stupas were first opened up in 1822 by T.H. Maddock, the political agent at Bhopal, and his assistant, Captain Johnson.[29] In their search for hidden antiquities, Maddock and Johnson succeeded in destroying substantial parts of the old monuments, including the great stupa (or Stupa 1). Similarly, Alexander Cunningham and F.C. Maisey combined their great discoveries at Sanchi with inflicting great damage there. Their excavations yielded relic boxes, caskets and the relics of monks, including those of the Buddha's foremost disciplines, Sariputta and Mahamogallana.[30] However, like the first excavators, neither Cunningham nor Maisey thought it necessary to repair the structural breaches that their shafting of the stupas created. The extent of the damage must have been considerable because thirty years later, their own countryman, Lepel Griffin, was to angrily note that 'a thousand years of time and weather have not done so much injury to the invaluable Topes at Sanchi as was caused by the action of Major-General Cunningham . . . who years ago, mined deep into the Topes in the vain search for coins or inscriptions, and never filled in these excavations.'[31]

Griffin was then serving as Agent to the Governor-General in central India and it was he who, in the early 1880s, persuaded the imperial government to spend several thousand rupees on repair work at Sanchi. As a consequence, the enormous breach in the face of the great stupa was built with dry masonry and its two gateways, which had earlier collapsed, re-erected. The gateway of Stupa 3 (Fig. 2.1)

FIGURE 2.1: THE GATEWAY OF STUPA 3 WHICH WAS RE-ERECTED IN THE 1880s

was also re-erected, the sculpture was cleaned and the approach road on the northern side of the hill, along with the ancient causeway which led to Stupa 2, improved and restored. In subsequent years, although one does not hear of major conservation at Sanchi, some minor repairs did continue. The pace of work in the 1890s must have been slow because money allocated by the imperial government for archaeology was severely slashed. By 1898, Viceroy Victor Bruce Elgin was even uncertain whether archaeological work in India required any state assistance. While the reasons for this state of affairs need not detain us here, what appears to be reasonably clear is that it is only with the arrival of Curzon in 1899 that a singularly bleak era of desultory archaeological work came to an end.

Sultan Jahan Begum and Sanchi: An Inauspicious Beginning

The ruler of Bhopal during the viceroyalty of Curzon was Nawab Sultan Jahan Begum (1858-1930; Fig. 2.2), the last in a dynasty of

FIGURE 2.2: SULTAN JAHAN BEGUM WITH HER GRANDDAUGHTER

women rulers of that princely state. She is generally remembered for her pioneering work in education and on women's emancipation. She presided over the All Women's Conference on Educational Reform and was the first Chancellor of the Aligarh Muslim University. Sultan Jahan's life and work, along with that of the earlier women rulers of Bhopal, has been discussed at length in Shaharyar Khan's *The Begums of Bhopal*. But what does not find mention there is the stellar role of the Begum in the architectural restoration of Sanchi in the early twentieth century.

The story of Sultan Jahan's engagement with Sanchi began a few years after she took over the reins of the state of Bhopal, in 1901. This was just after Sanchi was visited by Curzon. From the beginning of his viceroyalty, buildings and their restoration were a high priority for the Viceroy. In fact, he visited Sanchi during the first year of his viceroyalty in November 1899 and, as with other monuments that he visited, he left a list of instructions on the repairs to be undertaken there.

As a consequence of Curzon's note, repairs were started in 1904 by H.B. Cook, the state engineer of Bhopal. Cook's manner of execution proved alarmingly destructive. Officials charged with such work usually try to conserve all the old relics in ancient monuments – broken and half-decayed though they may be – because their value and authenticity depends upon the preservation of their ancient fabric. Yet Cook, instead of repairing old structural elements, decided to remove them. Several old railing pieces, coping stones and pillars from the main stupa's balustrade were taken out by him and replaced with new stones.[32] What also seems amazing is that John Marshall was completely unaware that repairs of this kind had been undertaken at Sanchi. He was to visit it shortly afterwards, by which time, he reported, it was too late to rectify Cook's 'restoration'.

Cook's faulty restoration soon became the occasion for a larger dialogue within the portals of the colonial government on ways to conserve Sanchi. From the correspondence, it seems that in addition to poor restoration work, the caretaker arrangements with regard to the hundreds of sculptural relics that were lying around came to be viewed as highly unsatisfactory. Marshall was to recommend the creation of a museum to ensure their safe custody and this is where the ruling house of Bhopal comes in. Interestingly, while the poor restoration was explained away by Marshall as an aberration that had resulted from personal injuries that the British state engineer had suffered, the religious affiliation of the chowkidars now came to be blamed for the state of Sanchi. Marshall made it clear that he considered Muslim chowkidars inherently incapable of looking after Buddhist monuments. These, he suggested, required to be tended by 'devoted hands', those of Buddhist chowkidars whose services, he believed, could be arranged through the Maha Bodhi Society.[33]

In making this suggestion, the Director-General had evidently not bargained for Nawab Sultan Jahan Begum. She would later become Marshall's main benefactor and his Sanchi volumes, in fact, are dedicated to her memory. However, the relationship did not begin on an optimistic note. Sultan Jahan was a 'hands-on' Begum and was known to personally examine each file, inspect the treasury, look through the registers and even appoint estate employees herself. Quite naturally, Marshall's letter with his suggestion of replacing Muslim caretakers at Sanchi with Buddhist ones was referred to her. Almost immediately, she conveyed her distaste of and opposition to such a proposal.

Some of this opposition apparently stemmed from the well-known 'trouble maker' reputation of the Maha Bodhi Society's founder.[34] Anagarika Dharmapala, by then, was a widely-recognized figure in India whose founding of the society was known to be closely connected with his perception of the Mahabodhi Temple at Bodh Gaya. By the time he came to Bodh Gaya, he had preached in large parts of his country, raised funds for his faith and propagated his religious agenda through pamphlets and periodicals. For a religious crusader of this mould, a shrine where both Hindus and Buddhists worshipped was abhorrent, as was the presence of a Hindu legal proprietor. Consequently, the main object of the Maha Bodhi Society had been to 'reclaim' the temple at Bodh Gaya for the Buddhists. No legal proprietor, especially someone like the mahant of Bodh Gaya, whose preceptors had enjoyed the fruits of religious patronage there for a hundred and fifty years or so, was likely to give in to such demands without a serious fight. Thus, a massive dispute came to develop around this shrine in the late nineteenth century, one that made national headlines and went on to become the subject of a spate of litigation.

The Begum must have known about this and was also probably aware of the parallels between her situation and that of the legal proprietor of Mahabodhi. Her personal faith, like that of the mahant, was not Buddhist. So she probably anticipated that if the help of the Maha Bodhi Society was sought for the superintendence of the Buddhist monuments in her principality, Dharmapala would, sooner or later, make a claim for taking over Sanchi as well. Yet the Begum was also incensed by Marshall's suggestion as it effectively meant that her capacity to look after Bhopal's monuments was being doubted. As she put it, Marshall's action was calculated to cast a slur on her administration which was not deserved. Marshall, on the other hand, (mis)understood her resistance to the appointment of Buddhist watchmen as relating to her personal religion and this soon came to be presented by him as a disinclination to preserve Sanchi itself. Hence, he seriously mooted the possibility of 'relieving' her of Sanchi by arranging for the imperial government to take over its custody.[35] The endeavour here, as in the case of the caretakers, was to exclude the local princely family from a monument in its own principality because of their personal religion. Fortunately, this was not to happen due to the Begum's resistance but, obviously, Marshall's interaction with Sanchi and the Begum of Bhopal began on a sour note.

Restoring Sanchi

However, many years later, the relationship of Sultan Jahan Begum with John Marshall would take an entirely different and altogether more cordial turn. This was in the summer of 1912 when the Begum let it be known that she was anxious to procure some monographs on the Sanchi Stupa. There is nothing in the official records that can thrown light on the timing of her request. We do, however, learn from her autobiography that Sanchi had figured in her public life on many occasions. Over the years, she had hosted viceroys, military commanders and the members of Indian princely families there. Furthermore her son, Hamidullah Khan, and his bride were first brought here before being taken to Bhopal. This was in 1905 when the bridal couple's wedding party returned from Peshawar and was received by the Begum with pomp and presents at Sanchi's 'Dak' bungalow. But it must have been her latest visit that was still fresh in her memory.[36] In November 1911, when she returned from Europe, Sultan Jahan had stayed at Sanchi because of an outbreak of plague at Bhopal and it was from here that she had proceeded to Delhi to attend the Durbar of George V. It is possible that this last sojourn rekindled her desire to know more about the splendid Buddhist remains in whose vicinity she had so recently camped.

When Marshall heard from private sources that the Begum was trying to acquire available publications on Sanchi, he decided to take the initiative and offered her pertinent volumes in his library. Apparently, at some point in the recent past, she had personally mentioned to Marshall that she was interested in getting a complete monograph published on Sanchi. Hence, he also used this as an opportunity to remind the Begum that the publications available on Sanchi were outdated and inaccurate. They ought to be replaced, as he put it, with a monograph more worthy of the famous monument and one that was financed by the Bhopal Durbar.[37]

To Marshall's surprise and delight, the Begum responded generously and enthusiastically. As authoring such a monograph required that the Director-General stay at Sanchi, she offered him all the necessary logistical and financial support. This included reserving a bungalow for his wife, children and their governess; arranging cows for his camp; paying a handsome honorarium to Alfred Foucher (a French scholar and an acknowledged authority on Buddhist iconography) for his collaboration; and providing the labour that was required for the actual survey work.[38]

At Sanchi, although Marshall had visualized his work only as a prelude to the preparation of a monograph, he realized, soon after arriving there, that before this could be prepared, the site would need to be extensively excavated and its monuments repaired. The work was eventually spread over several years with different historic monuments and areas being simultaneously excavated and repaired. There is little doubt that the large exposed and conserved monuments that we see in Sanchi were largely the result of Marshall's massive programme, which was finally completed around 1919.

What is not as well known is that the very persons whom he had viewed with such grave suspicion played a crucial role in Sanchi's restoration. Ironically, there is nothing even at the museum which stands at the foot of the Sanchi hill to remind visitors of the Begum's contribution. In the photo exhibition displayed there in 2006, while the 'remembered' ranged from Cunningham to Marshall, there was no mention of Sultan Jahan Begum's proactive patronage of Sanchi: this in spite of her having been the main benefactor of Sanchi's modern restoration programme. The cost of that work, as also that of the construction of the Sanchi museum and the publication of Marshall's definitive volumes on Sanchi, had been entirely financed by the Bhopal Durbar. Most strikingly, in sharp contrast to what Marshall had to say in 1905 about the unreliability of Muslims, including those that he had employed in the Archaeological Survey, a Muslim, Munshi Ghulam Qadir, was his excavation assistant and right-hand man at Sanchi. Marshall's preface to the Sanchi volumes acknowledges that Qadir 'did yeoman's service in the task of excavating and restoring its monuments' and, in fact, a whole paragraph is devoted to his contribution.[39] Incidentally, it was the same Ghulam Qadir to whom Marshall had also entrusted the excavation of the Dharmarajika Stupa at Taxila.

Return of the Relics

This story, however, does not end with the completion of Marshall's restoration programme. There is another element in Sanchi's modern history that is relevant from the perspective of Buddhist revivalism and which concerns the return of what were believed to be some of its relics.

Antiquities from Sanchi and other Buddhist sites of central India, including the corporeal relics of the Buddha's direct disciples and later Buddhist teachers, along with the caskets in which they had been placed, had been taken away by Cunningham and Maisey who had excavated the stupas. Most of what they found eventually reached two London museums, the British Museum and the Victoria and Albert Museum. But what is little known is that once Marshall's conservation work was over, the Bhopal Durbar made a serious move to get the British Museum to return its share of the Sanchi antiquities. Today, there is a large public debate about the movement of cultural treasure and the necessity of its 'return' in situations where it was not acquired legitimately. There is also a legal framework within which objects of various kinds have, in fact, been returned to their homelands. However, such cases were relatively rare in the early part of the twentieth century when the demand for Sanchi's relics were first made by the Bhopal ruling family.

The Bhopal Durbar first discussed the possibility of bringing back the relics with John Marshall in or around 1919. Marshall had spent the summer of that year in England and during that time, he made a list of antiquities from Sanchi present in the British Museum. He also asked for casts of these objects to be made and despatched to Bhopal. This must also have been the occasion for considering the possibility of bringing back the originals from Sanchi. Marshall's opinion was that even though Sanchi was the rightful and appropriate place to preserve the relics and caskets, it was unlikely that the British Museum could be prevailed upon to return them.[40] The matter of repatriating the objects was then dropped.

However, it was to resurface after a lapse of several years in the 1930s and this time, it would eventually lead to the transfer of some relics and relic caskets from England to Sanchi. In this second impetus, the initial initiative was taken by Buddhist societies. Following a resolution passed at a meeting of the Buddha Society in Mumbai in 1938, various societies made an appeal to the Government of India to request the return of the Sanchi relics that were at the Victoria and Albert Museum in South Kensington, London.[41] These, the resolution stated, should be handed over to the Maha Bodhi Society of Calcutta for being enshrined at Sarnath. Six months later, there was a second request, this time by the Maha Bodhi Society, to enshrine the relics in a vihara at New Delhi. This demand was in line with what had been happening to Buddhist relics that were being discovered in British India, which were usually handed over to that society. For instance, the Bhattiprolu relics, discovered in 1891 and, since then, kept in the Madras Museum, were made over to the Maha Bodhi Vihara at Calcutta in 1922. Again, some of the relics discovered by the Archaeological Survey at Taxila, Nagarjunakonda and Mirpur

Khas were also presented to the Maha Bodhi Society for enshrinement at the Mulagandhakuti Vihara at Sarnath.

By 1939, the Victoria and Albert Museum authorities agreed to return the Sanchi relics to India but due to the outbreak of the Second World War, the transfer was postponed. The decision of the museum, however, was widely reported in the Indian press and this, in turn, brought Bhopal back to the centre of the question of where the relics should be preserved.

A report in *The Statesman* of 3 February 1940 regarding the proposed handing-over was seen by Ali Haider Abbasi, Political Member of the Bhopal government. He immediately wrote to the Political Agent in Bhopal, strongly underlining the *locus standi* of the Bhopal government. Interestingly, he cited Marshall's letter where he had expressed his opinion that Sanchi was the place where such objects should be rightfully kept:

> The Government of Bhopal have always been most anxious to have these relics in the Sanchi Museum. They had some correspondence on the subject with the then Director-General of Archaeology in India, viz.: Sir John Marshall. In the latter's D.O. letter no. 335, dated the 5th February 1920, the opinion expressed is that the most proper place for enshrining the relics, taken away from the Sanchi Stupas, will be the site of Sanchi itself. The question of the restoration of these relics etc. was not pressed in 1920, because the Political Agent did not see much chance of the British Museum agreeing to return them. Now, however, that the Victoria and Albert Museum in London have agreed to hand over these relics to the Mahabodhi Society, to be enshrined at the Buddhist temple in New Delhi, the Government of Bhopal, as owners of the relics, request that these may kindly be made over to them for preservation at the Sanchi Museum which is unquestionably the most suitable place for them. It is hoped that the wishes of the Bhopal government in this matter would receive due consideration, and the relics, instead of being made over to the Mahabodhi Society, will be restored to them on the termination of the war.[42]

A protracted wrangle then ensued over where the relics were to be kept once they were sent back. On the one hand, L.G. Wallis, Political Agent in Bhopal, strongly supported the Bhopal government's request. On the other hand, curiously enough, K.N. Dikshit who, as Director-General of the Archaeological Survey, headed an organization that favoured keeping objects at the sites to which they belonged, maintained that 'the right of the community who holds them sacred should be given precedence over those of Sanchi'.[43] Eventually, the Bhopal government negotiated with the Maha Bodhi Society and its request prevailed. The relics left England in February 1947 and were brought back to Sanchi after travelling to various countries, including Ceylon, Burma and Nepal.[44] It was the Bhopal government which donated land for constructing a vihara to house them and also contributed several thousand rupees for its construction.

The ceremony around the sacred relics was very much an occasion, as similar ceremonies were, for earning diplomatic brownie points (Fig. 2.3). The relics were brought to Sanchi with great ceremony on 29 and 30 November 1952 and handed over for re-enshrining by Prime Minister Nehru amidst the chantings of hymns by yellow-robed bhikkus from many countries of South Asia and deafening cheers from nearly a 100,000 people. The relics were taken in a mile-long procession by devotees chanting sacred verses, offering flowers and

FIGURE 2.3: PRIME MINISTER NEHRU AND OTHER DIGNITARIES AT SANCHI

burning incense. In the presence of U Nu, the premier of Burma (Fig. 2.4); many prominent Asian envoys; international visitors and national figures, Nehru spoke about the atmosphere of fear and hatred in the contemporary world, and how it was 'only by remembering afresh and by endeavouring to act up to the teaching that illumined India two thousand five hundred years ago' that the world was likely to emerge from the surrounding gloom.[45] This was timely as the trauma of and the scars left by the horrific genocides in Europe, and the deaths associated with the Second World War, were still fresh. Closer home, though, in view of the communal frenzy and killings that marked the aftermath of Independence and Partition, it is strange that Nehru made no mention of the role of the Bhopal Durbar in preserving the stupas that formed the backdrop to his speech. Looking back, he could well have scripted the occasion differently. Apart from the restitution of India's Buddhist heritage as an occasion for strengthening her ties with other Asian nations, Nehru could have used it to simultaneously showcase the quality of Indian

FIGURE 2.4: PRIME MINISTER NEHRU, BURMESE PREMIER U NU AND OTHER DIGNITARIES ON THE STEPS OF THE BUILDING SPECIALLY MADE FOR THE RELICS BROUGHT BACK TO SANCHI

secularism by giving due credit to the erstwhile Muslim rulers of Bhopal for the return of the relics to Sanchi and for their contribution to the conservation of Buddhist monuments there.[46]

There is, though, a final point that is worth mentioning. Apparently, the relic caskets of Sariputra and Mahamogallana which were brought back and enshrined on the Sanchi hill, are the ones that Maisey and Cunningham had removed from the neighbouring Buddhist site at Satdhara. This was suspected as early as 1949 and finally confirmed in 1957.[47] The Sanchi relics of those two disciples are still untraceable.[48]

NOTES

1. For Ambedkar's conversion ceremony, Singh (2010): 195. The affinity of the dome of Rashtrapati Bhawan to Sanchi is mentioned in the official website of the President of India. See http://presidentofindia.nic.in/rb.html
2. See http://www.thaindian.com/newsportal/world-news/an-indian-style-buddhist-temple-gifted-to-sister-civilisation-china-lead_100371841.html
3. Mayaram (2004): 19 and *Census of India, 1901, Volume I* (1901): 370ff.
4. Oberoi (1994): 1.
5. Lyall (1884): 7-8.
6. Rai (1915): 44-6.
7. See Sanyal (2009), Metcalf (2009), Mayaram (2004) and *Census of India 1901* (1901): 375.
8. Metcalf (1982): 5-6.
9. Metcalf (1982): 273-4.
10. Oberoi (1994): 24.
11. Ling (1979): 65.
12. Malalagoda (1976): 260.
13. *Imperial Gazetteer of India* (1907-9): 412.
14. *Imperial Gazetteer of India Provincial Series – Punjab* (1908, rpt., 1991): 376.
15. Seagar (1995): 108-10.
16. For an overview of modern forms of Buddhism see McMahan (2008).
17. Ahir (1989): 55-6.
18. Ahir (1989): 46-9.
19. See correspondence of 1902 in File No. 331903, Department of Revenue and Agriculture – Archaeology and Epigraphy (AE, hereafter), Part B. The subject is 'Visit of Count Otani and Mr. Honda, two members of the Japanese archaeological party, to Nepal Terai'.
20. Almond (1988): 12.
21. Cunningham (1854): 368.

22. Letter of Spooner dated 6 April 1910 in Spooner papers.
23. That the British rulers of India were also viewed as saviours by key figures in the Buddhist revival as it unfolded in India is also worth pointing out. Anagarika Dharmapala, in a letter of June 1918 to John Marshall, Director-General of the Archaeological Survey of India, made this crystal clear when he explained to the latter the source of his funds with which land for housing the Taxila relics would be kept in Calcutta, was purchased. As he put it, 'But for Mrs. Foster the Vihara could not be built, but for the promised relics of Taxila, the impulse would never have come to erect a Vihara, but for you the Relics would have never been discovered – So you will see how closely you are associated with the vihara and the Relics.' See letter of Dharmapala in File 459, 1916, Part 4, Archaeological Survey of India (ASI, hereafter). On the presentation of arms at a relic ceremony, a similar guard of honour was presented by the Bhopal army in 1952 when the relics of Sariputta and Mahamoggalana were brought back to Sanchi. See Report of the Sanchi Functions in *Maha Bodhi* (1953): 43.
24. Lahiri (1999): 41.
25. Cunningham (1892).
26. Ray (1964): 169-70.
27. *All India Reporter Manual* (1989): 581-93.
28. I have discussed this at length in Lahiri (2004).
29. Spilsbury (1835).
30. Cunningham (1854): 269.
31. Note of Griffin dated 2 October 1882, Proceedings of the Home Department – A (Archaeology and Conservation of Ancient Monuments), Nos. 13-15 (July 1882).
32. Report of H. Cousens dated 27 February 1905, Proceedings of the Foreign Department (PFD hereafter) – B (Internal), Nos. 421-2 (August 1905).
33. Note of Marshall dated 24 November 1905, PFD – B (Internal), Nos. 378-9 (May 1906).
34. Note of Curzon dated 15 November 1905, PFD – B (Internal), Nos. 378-9 (May 1906).
35. Note of Marshall dated 12 December 1906, PFD – B (Internal), Nos. 378-79 (May 1906).
36. For this and other details in this paragraph Begum (1922): 233ff and 272. Also Begum (1927): 203.
37. Letter of Marshall to Colonel Spence, Political Agent at Bhopal dated 23 May 1912, Central India Agency, No. 221 (1912).
38. Letter of Begum to W.S. Davis, Political Agent in Bhopal, dated 16 July 1912, Central India Agency, No. 221 (1912). Also, letter of Begum to W.S. Davis dated 23 September in the same file.
39. Marshall and Foucher (1940) I: Preface.

40. Letter of Marshall to the political secretary of the ruler of Bhopal dated 5 February 1920, Central India Agency, No. 251 (1913).
41. This has been discussed at length in the centenary volume of the Maha Bodhi Society. See Maha Bodhi (1991): 183.
42. Letter of Abbasi to Gaisford dated 24 February 1940, Central India Agency, No. 251 (1913).
43. Letter of Dikshit to the Political Agent in Bhopal dated 21 March 1940, Central India Agency, No. 251 (1913).
44. The return journey of the relics and their re-enshrinement in India and Burma make for a fascinating story and has been described in *Maha Bodhi* issues of 1952 and 1953, as also in Daulton (1999).
45. Nehru (1952): 203-4.
46. Nehru's presence and involvement as the prime minister in the religious ceremonies involving the restoration of the relics at Sanchi is worth juxtaposing with his aversion in 1951 to the involvement of President Rajendra Prasad with the ceremonies surrounding the rebuilding of Somnath. In his correspondence on Somnath, Nehru constantly mentioned that this was not how a secular state behaved and Prasad seems to have handled all criticism by pointing out that it was not a government function.
47. A letter from N.P. Chakravarti, Director-General of Archaeology in India dated 1949, Archaeological Survey of India, No. 27D/2/49 (1949) to C. Sivaramamurti (Superintendent, Archaeological Section, Indian Museum, Calcutta) asks him to get the caskets photographed: 'You should not only have photographs of the caskets from different angles but also of the lids particularly of the inside where the inscriptions are ... it is imperative that this should be done now for record. Apart from this, I particularly want the photographs for the purpose of identification whether they are Sanchi caskets or those found at Satdhara.' For a confirmation that these were the Satdhara caskets, see Mitra (1957): 44, fn. 1.
48. Willis (2000): 68.

BIBLIOGRAPHY

Archival Sources

Files of the Office of the Director General of Archaeology in India in the Archaeological Survey of India, New Delhi.

Files of Central India Agency in the National Archives of India, New Delhi.

Files of the Department of Revenue and Agriculture (Archaeology and Epigraphy Branch) in the National Archives of India, New Delhi.

Files of the Foreign Department (Internal) in the National Archives of India, New Delhi.

Files of the Department of Home (Archaeology and Conservation of Ancient Monuments) in the National Archives of India, New Delhi.
Spooner papers at the Stanford University Libraries, Stanford.

Published Sources

Ahir, D.C. 1989. *The Pioneers of Buddhist Revival in India*. Delhi: Sri Satguru Publications.

All India Reporter Manual. 1989. *The AIR Manual Unrepealed Central Acts*, vol. 1. Nagpur: All India Reporter Limited.

Almond, P.C. 1988. *The British Discovery of Buddhism*. Cambridge: Cambridge University Press.

Begum, S.J. 1922. *An Account of My Life*, vol. II. Bombay: The Times Press.

———. 1927. *An Account of My Life,* vol. III. Bombay: The Times Press.

1901. *Census of India, 1901,* vol. I. Calcutta: Superintendent of Government Printing.

Cunningham, A. 1854, rpt. 1997. *The Bhilsa Topes*. New Delhi: Munshiram Manoharlal.

———. 1892, rpt. 1998. *Mahabodhi or the Great Buddhist Temples under the Bodhi Tree at Buddha Gaya*. Delhi: Munshiram Manoharlal.

Daulton, J. 1999. 'Sariputta and Moggallana in the Golden Land: The Relics of the Buddha's Chief Disciples at the Kaba Aye Pagoda', *The Journal of Burma Studies* 4: 101-28.

1907-9. *Imperial Gazetteer of India: The Indian Empire,* vol. 1. Oxford: Clarendon Press.

1908. rpt. 1991. *Imperial Gazetteer of India Provincial Series: Punjab*, vol. 1. New Delhi: Atlantic.

Khan, S.M. 2000. *The Begums of Bhopal: A Dynasty of Women Rulers in Raj India*. London: I.B. Tauris.

Lahiri, N. 1999. 'Bodh-Gaya: An Ancient Buddhist Shrine and its Modern History (1891-1904)', in T. Insoll (ed.), *Case Studies in Archaeology and World Religion*. Oxford: Archaeopress, pp. 33-43.

———. 2004. 'From Ruin to Restoration: The Modern History of Sanchi', in T. Insoll (ed.) *Belief in the Past*, Oxford: Archaeopress, pp. 99-114.

Ling, T. 1979. *Buddhism, Imperialism and War: Burma and Thailand in Modern History*. London: George Allen and Unwin.

Lyall, A.C. 1884. *Asiatic Studies Religious and Social*. London: John Murray.

Maha Bodhi. 1991. 'The Sacred Relics of the Sriputta and Mogallana Arhans', *Centenary Volume*, pp. 182-93. Calcutta M. Wipulasara Maha Thera.

Malalagoda, K. 1976. *Buddhism in Sinhalese Society 1750-1900: A Study of Religious Revival and Change*. Berkeley: University of California Press.

Marshall, J.H. and A. Foucher. 1940, rpt. 1983. *Sanchi* (3 vols.). Delhi: Swati Publications.

Mayaram, S. 2004. 'Beyond Ethnicity? Being Hindu and Muslim in South Asia', in I. Ahmad and H. Riefeld (eds.), *Lived Islam in South Asia*. Delhi: Social Science Press, pp. 18-39.

McMahan, D.L. 2008. *The Making of Buddhist Modernism*. New York: Oxford University Press.

Metcalf, B. 1982. *Islamic Revival in British India: Deoband, 1860-1900*. Princeton: Princeton University Press.

_____. 2009. 'A Historical Overview of Islam in South Asia', in B. Metcalf (ed.), *Islam in South Asia in Practice*. Ranikhet: Permanent Black, pp. 1-39.

Mitra, D. 1957, rpt. 2001. *Sanchi*. New Delhi: Archaeological Survey of India.

Nehru, J. 1952, rpt. 1997. 'Opening of the Sanchi Vihara', *Selected Works of Jawaharlal Nehru,* Second Series, vol. 20 (19 October 1952-31 December 1952). New Delhi: Jawaharlal Nehru Memorial Fund.

Oberoi, H. 1994. *The Construction of Religious Boundaries: Culture, Identity and Diversity in the Sikh Tradition*. Delhi: Oxford University Press.

Rai, L. 1915. *The Arya Samaj*. New York: Longmans Green and Co.

Ray, B.G. 1964. *Religious Movements in Modern Bengal*. Santiniketan: Ranajit Ray.

Report of the Sanchi Functions. 1953. *The Maha Bodhi* 61(1-2): 40-7.

Sanyal, U. 2009. 'Sufi Ritual Practice among the Barkatiyya Sayyids of U.P.: Nuri Miyan's Life and 'Urs, Late Nineteenth-Early Twentieth Centuries', in B. Metcalf (ed.), *Islam in South Asia in Practice*. Ranikhet: Permanent Black, pp. 166-72.

Seager, R.H. 1995. *The World's Parliament of Religions: The East/West Encounter, Chicago, 1893*. Bloomington and Indianapolis: Indiana University Press.

Singh, U. 2010. 'Exile and Return: The Reinvention of Buddhism and Buddhist Sites in Modern India', *South Asian Studies* 26(2): 193-217.

Spilsbury, Dr. 1835. 'Note Regarding the Bhilsa Monument', *Journal of the Asiatic Society of Bengal* 4:17.

Willis, M. (ed.) 2000. *Buddhist Reliquaries from Ancient India*. London: The British Museum.

CHAPTER 3

Buddhism, Archaeology and the Nation

Nagarjunakonda, 1926-2006

UPINDER SINGH

ONE OF THE INTRIGUING aspects of Indian Buddhism is that its symbolic importance has always been in much greater proportion to the number of practising Buddhists in the subcontinent. The doctrines, followers and patrons of this religion have consistently enjoyed a privileged position in the historiography of ancient India, both in colonial as well as post-colonial discourse. One of the reasons why Buddhism has consistently attracted more interest than any other Indic religion is the fact that it spread far beyond the subcontinent and had a major cultural impact on many regions of Asia.[1] In the colonial period, Buddhism came to be considered by many European historians and archaeologists as the best of all non-Christian religions, and there was a romanticization of its rationalism and egalitarian social ethos.[2]

After Indian independence, these factors coalesced with another important one – the importance of non-violence in the Indian freedom struggle. As a result, Buddhism retained an importance not only in interpretations of the Indian past but also assumed an iconic position in representations of the Indian nation. Apart from the conversions of members of Scheduled Castes to this religion, associated most closely with the leadership of B.R. Ambedkar, Buddhism's ideas and ideals also found strong support among other nationalist leaders such as Jawaharlal Nehru. This explains the adoption of the Aśokan Sarnath capital as the symbol of the Indian nation and the *cakra* as the central symbol of the national flag. Thus, in independent India, there was not merely a retention but a strengthening of a vision of ancient India that privileged Buddhism (especially at the political level), along with its chief patron, Aśoka, and the ideal of *ahiṁsā*. This highly influential understanding of the ancient Indian past in which Buddhism was assigned an exalted place had an important impact on archaeological and conservation policies, both in colonial as well as independent India, and that is the focus of this paper, albeit in the context of a specific important site, namely Nagarjunakonda.

Situated on the banks of the river Krishna and surrounded on three sides by offshoots of the Nallamalai hills, Nagarjunakonda, in the Guntur district of Andhra Pradesh in India, was a 15 sq km site rich in remains ranging from the prehistoric to the medieval periods. In spite of its long history and variegated religious landscape, the site was especially celebrated for Buddhist remains of the third and fourth centuries, when it was known as Vijayapurī, capital of the Ikṣvāku dynasty. Apart from the vast amount of data generated by excavations here, Nagarjunakonda is also important because it offers excellent material for a study of the presuppositions and agendas of archaeological research in pre-colonial and independent India.

The history of the exploration, excavation, documentation and interpretation of the remains at this site reveals several distinct phases. Discovered in 1926 by A.R. Saraswati (Assistant to the Archaeological Superintendent for Epigraphy), it was excavated in early 1927 by Muhammad Hamid Kuraishi and subsequently by A.H. Longhurst.[3] Longhurst's report represents the first stage in the interpretation of Nagarjunakonda, one in which it was seen essentially as a Buddhist site.[4] The second series of excavations were conducted by T.N. Ramachandran in 1938. The results, published many years later in 1953, drew attention to the many Hindu temples in the early historic

FIGURE 3.1: VIEW OF THE EXCAVATED BUDDHIST REMAINS AT NAGARJUNAKONDA (COURTESY: ARCHAEOLOGICAL SURVEY OF INDIA)

city for the first time.[5] This report situated Nagarjunakonda within a framework dominated by regional history and the sentiment of regional pride.

In the 1950s, during the heyday of Nehruvian socialism with its emphasis on heavy industry and big dams, plans for building a massive irrigation dam across the Krishna were drawn up. A major implication of these plans was that once the dam became functional, the spectacular site of Nagarjunakonda would be permanently drowned in the river waters. This led the Archaeological Survey of India (hereafter, ASI)

FIGURE 3.2: SITE OF THE *MAHĀCAITYA* BEFORE EXCAVATION (COURTESY: ARCHAEOLOGICAL SURVEY OF INDIA)

FIGURE 3.3: THE *MAHĀCAITYA*, RECONSTRUCTED ON NAGARJUNAKONDA HILL

to initiate a massive project of exploration, excavation and documentation. Before the valley was turned into a gigantic lake, about 136 new structures and structural complexes were unearthed; nine of the most important structures were transplanted and rebuilt on top of the Nagarjunakonda hill and on the banks of the reservoir; and smaller-scale replicas of fourteen other structures were made. This project is unique in the history of archaeological research and conservation in India. The first part of the report of the 1954-60 excavations, published in 1975, focused on the site's prehistoric and megalithic remains.[6] The second part, published as recently as 2006, was suffused with the sentiment of national pride, with frequent, rather florid eulogies of the site and of the Ikṣvāku dynasty.[7] The report offers a consolidated view of the early historic remains, artefacts and inscriptions of the ancient 'city of victory'.

This paper uses hitherto unexamined archival sources to discuss two important moments in the modern history of Nagarjunakonda. The first comprises the discovery and early interpretations of the site in colonial times, and how these intersected with the issue of the appropriate repository of the Buddhist relics found here. The second moment is located in post-Independence times, and touches on the place of Buddhism in the nationalist imagination, archaeological policy, and the conflict between the preservation of the ancient historical heritage of India and the developmental concerns of the new Indian nation.

THE ANNOUNCEMENT OF THE DISCOVERIES AT NAGARJUNAKONDA

In early February 1927, John Marshall, Director-General of the ASI, received a short letter from Muhammad Hamid Kuraishi, officiating Superintendent with the Southern Circle of the ASI. It said:

> You will be glad to know that I have discovered at Nagarjunikonda a number of stupas and Monasteries, two Apsidal chaityas and some 20 long Brahmi inscriptions all belonging to the 2nd-3rd century A.D. Minor antiquities such as seals and coins or Relics have not been coming forth. But I have found two bricks which bear clear marks or symbols somewhat similar to those discovered by Mr. Yazdani sometime back.[8]

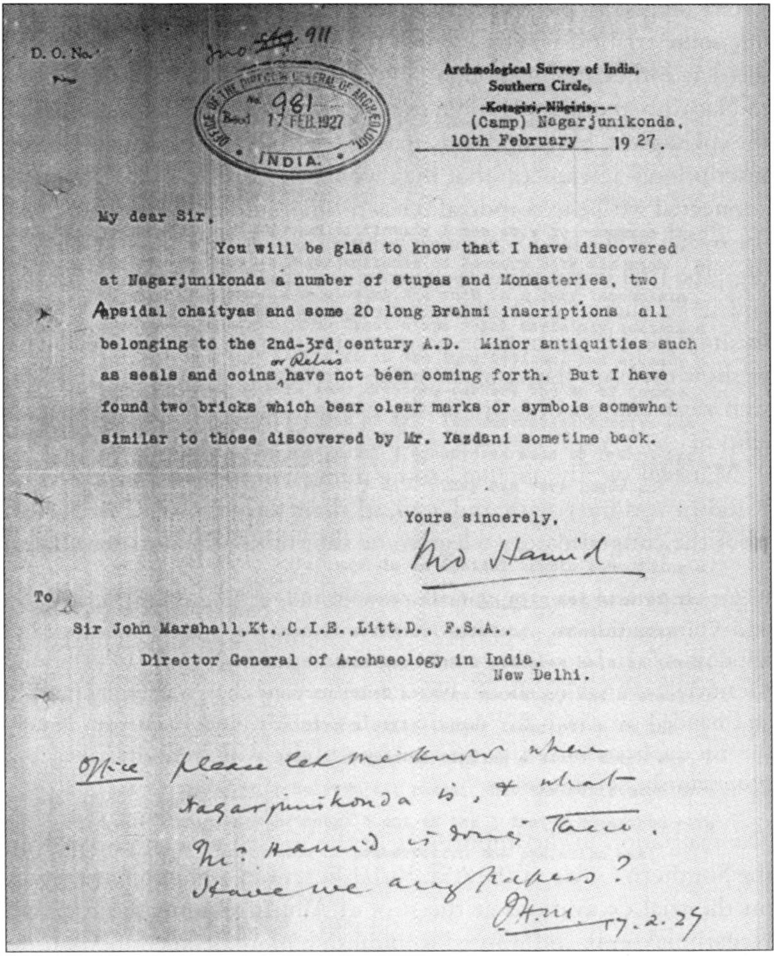

D. O. No. ~~549~~ 911

Archæological Survey of India,
Southern Circle,
~~Kotagiri, Nilgiris,~~
(Camp) Nagarjunikonda,
10th February 1927.

OFFICE OF THE DIRECTOR GENERAL OF ARCHAEOLOGY · INDIA · No. 981 Recd 17 FEB.1927

My dear Sir,

You will be glad to know that I have discovered at Nagarjunikonda a number of stupas and Monasteries, two Apsidal chaityas and some 20 long Brahmi inscriptions all belonging to the 2nd-3rd century A.D. Minor antiquities such as seals and coins or Relics have not been coming forth. But I have found two bricks which bear clear marks or symbols somewhat similar to those discovered by Mr. Yazdani sometime back.

Yours sincerely,
Md Hamid

To

Sir John Marshall, Kt., C.I.E., Litt.D., F.S.A.,
Director General of Archaeology in India,
New Delhi.

Office please let me know where Nagarjunikonda is, & what Mr. Hamid is doing there. Have we any papers?
JHM 17.2.27

FIGURE 3.4: KURAISHI'S LETTER ANNOUNCING HIS DISCOVERIES AND JOHN MARSHALL'S NOTE (COURTESY: ARCHAEOLOGICAL SURVEY OF INDIA)

The name of the site clearly did not ring a bell because a week later, Marshall penned the following note on the letter: 'Please let me know where Nagarjunikonda is and what is Mr. Hamid doing there. Have we any papers?'[9]

Before going on leave in 1926, A.H. Longhurst, Superintending

Archaeologist of the Southern Circle, had directed Kuraishi to carry out some trial excavations at Alluru and Gummadidurru in Kistna district, and Nagarjunakonda in Guntur district. Kuraishi had gone to Nagarjunakonda with high expectations. He was accompanied by the epigraphist, Hiranand Shastri, who was hopeful (because of certain inscriptional references) that they would be able to locate the *caitya* connected with the corporeal relics of the Buddha.[10] Unfortunately, the owner of the land was uncooperative and withheld permission to dig. The trial excavations eventually took place between 24 January and 12 February 1927 and Kuraishi had to sorrowfully leave the work incomplete. However, as he pointed out, there was enough evidence to show the importance of the place – in fact, he hoped that it might well rival Hampi, the site of the capital of the great Vijayanagara empire.

Marshall swiftly obtained some information about the sites that Kuraishi was busy with and realized their importance. This is clear from the congratulatory telegram he shot off to Kuraishi soon after:

> Hearty congratulations on your important finds at Nagarjunikonda Alluru and Gummadidurru. . . .Please take measures to protect all sites and antiquities found stop Orders will issue later regarding disposal of latter stop Meanwhile everything should be retained in your charge carefully marked and handed over with full descriptive lists to Mr. Longhurst stop Kindly furnish duplicate of lists to me and report fully as to measures taken and proprietorship of three sites.[11]

The realization of the importance of the site led to a conflict within the Southern Circle of the ASI. Kuraishi sent in a preliminary report on the trial excavations at the sites of Alluru, Gummadidurru and Nagarjunakonda and wanted to publish a more detailed memoir on the subject. He wrote to Longhurst, requesting the preparation of a site map and photographs that had been taken during the excavations. Longhurst curtly told him that there was no need to include Nagarjunakonda in the memoir as the excavations at that site were incomplete, that Marshall had instructed him (Longhurst) to carry out further excavations there and that he (Longhurst) would write the report himself.[12] The turf war reached Marshall's door and the Director-General supported the idea of the publication of Kuraishi's report, provided it was edited and published in the annual report of the ASI, not as a memoir (since the excavations were incomplete).[13] In this conflict between an Indian subordinate and a British superior, Marshall unambiguously supported the former.[14] He was very sharp and critical of the piece written by Longhurst for the 1926-7 report of the ASI, describing it as below standard and noting that due to this, he was publishing Kuraishi's account instead. Marshall also expressed the hope that in his report for the next year, Longhurst would discuss his own work at the sites where he had subsequently taken up excavations and not poach on Kuraishi's work.[15]

Apart from internal conflicts within the ASI over who should get credit for the Nagarjunakonda finds, two major problems, at this stage, were how to protect the ancient remains on the 13 acres of land on which the discoveries had been made, and where to deposit the antiquities and relics.[16] The land was declared protected under Section 5 of the Ancient Monuments Preservation Act of 1904.[17] The owner had been difficult – he had apparently demanded that the antiquities from the site should be kept in a museum connected with Andhra University, so that he could have the opportunity of seeing them whenever he liked. The problem was that there was no museum attached to the University![18] The Southern circle of the ASI was of the view that the artefacts found at the site should be kept at the site itself till the land was acquired and then perhaps sent off to the Madras Museum. Marshall was keen that the collection be kept together so that the tragedy of dispersal, which had happened at Amaravati, be avoided.[19] The Indian Museum, Calcutta, was keen to acquire some of the sculptures and Marshall was sympathetic to their request.[20] Alarm bells were set off when Longhurst reported an attempt to steal some sculptures and inscribed pillars and whisk them off to France, and arrangements were swiftly made for a watchman at the site.[21] Throughout, Marshall expressed keen interest in the finds, and sought information about the work at the site and its antiquities.

The question of where the material unearthed at these sites should be deposited also excited some public interest and stirred up the sentiment of Andhra pride. An article dated 5 April 1928, published in the *Swarajya* newspaper, observed, with reference to Marshall's announcement of the discoveries of the Buddhist remains at

Gummadidurru, that the ancient treasures of Andhra should be kept in Andhra itself and that it was alarming that the Archaeological Department of Madras was thinking of sending them off to far-off Calcutta. These remains should be kept at Bezwada to form the nucleus of an Andhra museum, or failing that, be sent to the Madras Museum. As the article noted: 'We are sure the Andhra public will make their voice felt and see that the sentiments of the people are respected in this matter.'[22]

One of the most sensitive issues was that of the relics that had been found at Nagarjunakonda in the stūpa known as the *mahācaitya*. These had been discovered by Longhurst and are described in his preliminary report. There was a pea-sized bone fragment in a tiny round gold box. This had been placed in a silver stūpa-shaped receptacle (which was very corroded, when found) with some gold flowers, pearls and garnets. This, in turn, had been placed inside a red earthenware pot, along with a few white and coloured crystal beads.[23] Longhurst was aware that the relics were 'a matter of some political importance'.[24] In 1928, Marshall relinquished charge to write his monographs and Harold Hargreaves officiated as Director-General of the ASI from March 1928-31. When it came to the issue of the

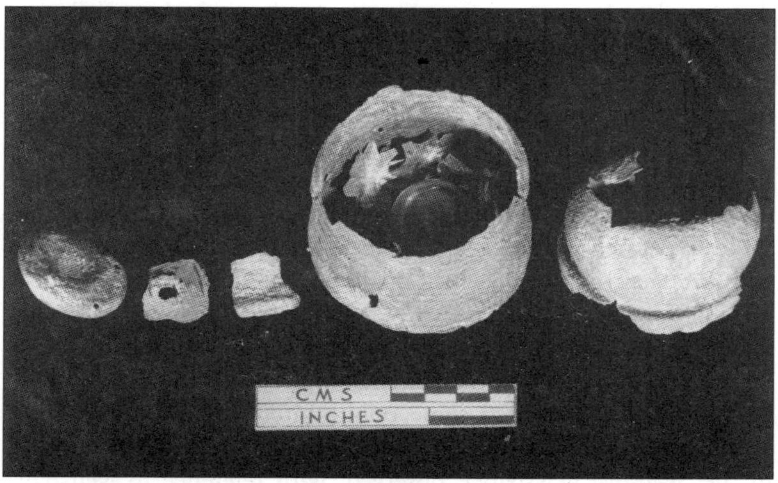

FIGURE 3.5: RELIQUARY AND RELICS FOUND IN THE *MAHĀCAITYA* (COURTESY: ARCHAEOLOGICAL SURVEY OF INDIA)

announcement of the dramatic discovery of the Nagarjunakonda finds, especially the relics, it was Hargreaves who called the shots. In fact, for a long time, the relics issue was carefully kept under wraps.

There was a major difference of opinion between Longhurst and Hargreaves on where the announcement of the discoveries should be made, and this conflict reflects the changing perspectives within the ASI. Longhurst reported to Hargreaves that he had sent a brief account of 'my discovery' to the *Illustrated London News* and to the noted German Sanskritist and epigraphist, J. Ph. Vogel 'so that scholars in Europe may know of the discovery'.[25] The reply was a curt telegram telling him to stop any such publication.[26] In 1924, Marshall had announced the discovery of the Indus civilization in the *Illustrated London News*. But now this route of publicizing a major archaeological discovery in India was vetoed on the grounds that the discovery must first be published in a publication of the ASI or in an Indian newspaper. According to Hargreaves, doing otherwise went against clear government policy and was bound to arouse objections in the Legislative Assembly.[27] Longhurst, on the other hand, was keen on creating a splash in the European press and initially refused to comply with the instructions communicated to him. Finally, confronted by the threat of disciplinary action, he was obliged to fall in line and instructed the *Illustrated London News* not to publish his piece.[28]

Buddha relics were hot news and the *Illustrated London News* was desperate to carry the story but their plea for permission to do so elicited a terse reply in the negative from the Archaeological Department.[29] When the editor pressed the issue, asking for reasons for the denial of permission, Hargreaves replied that according to Government of India orders, officers of the ASI were not allowed to publish the results of their research in any journal other than that of the ASI without government approval.[30] The *Illustrated London News* then sought permission to publish only the story of the Buddha relics, promising to carry an acknowledgement to the Government of India and the Director-General of the ASI, but permission for this, too, was denied.[31]

Ultimately, with Longhurst fretting and fuming at the delay, the story of the discovery of the Nagarjunakonda relics was published in the *Hindustan Times* and the *Anand Bazar Patrika* on 31 January

1930, over a year after they had been discovered.[32] The story was essentially an official communiqué drafted by Hargreaves and moderately edited by Longhurst. In the piece, Nagarjunakjonda was presented as a Buddhist site and the discovery of 'an authentic relic' of the Buddha was highlighted. The relics had completely overshadowed the other remains that had been found at the site. The names of the Indian officers, Saraswati, who had discovered the site, and Kuraishi, who had first excavated there, were not mentioned. Hargreaves and Longhurst got all the credit for the exciting discoveries at Nagarjunakonda.

The bone relic itself was initially kept in Longhurst's office safe and was subsequently transferred to a locker in the Imperial Bank of India in Madras.[33] However, it was recognized that the disposal of the relic was not a matter that could be left to the judgement of archaeologists. Higher-level government agencies and national sentiment were also involved.

THE POLITICS OF RELICS

In the early 1930s, with the relic safe in a bank vault in Madras, the Government of India narrowed down its options to three – to keep the Nagarjunakonda relics at the site itself, to send them to a Ceylonese vihāra (monastery) at Kelaniya near Colombo, or to hand them to the Maha Bodhi Society. The latter two had applied for the relics to the Viceroy. The Madras government and the ASI were of the view that the ancient remains should be kept in a site museum at Nagarjunakonda itself, and that the place should be made more accessible to visitors by road.[34] Yet this did not apply to the relics, which were recognized as antiquities of an entirely different order.

The claims of the Ceylonese vihāra were put forward in early 1930, soon after the announcement, and were supported by the Governor of Ceylon, who addressed the Governor of Madras on the subject thus:

> I have the honour to enclose a copy of a letter . . . addressed to me by the Venerable Mapitigama Dhammarakkhitta, incumbent of the Buddhist Vihara at Kelaniya, near Colombo. I attach, in original, the documents which accompanied his letter. . . .The writer of the letter asks me to approach the

proper authority and to represent the fervent hope of Ceylon Buddhists that it may be possible to obtain from India, for preservation in the Kelaniya Temple, the relic of the Buddha recently discovered at Nagarjunikonda. The letter was handed to me by two very distinguished Buddhist laymen, who may be regarded as exponents of Buddhist opinion among the Low-country Sinhalese and the Kandyans respectively. They assured me that Buddhists throughout the Island would be very grateful for the gift of this relic, and would regard the Kelaniya Temple as eminently suitable for its custody. I understand that there have been precedents of such presentations of relics discovered in India to Buddhist communities outside India, and I venture therefore to submit the request to Your Excellency with an expression of my support.[35]

The Maha Bodhi Society jumped into the fray at a later stage, in mid-1932:

We have learnt with great pleasure that recently a number of Buddha's relics were discovered at Nagarjunikonda. As a Buddhist society which is interested in the preservation of the sacred body relics of Lord Buddha, we are writing to request you to be so good as to obtain the same for our Society. We have already received a number of valuable relics from the Government of India, namely the Bhattiprolu relic at present safely enshrined at the Calcutta Vihara and the Taxila relics enshrined in the Mulagandhakuti Vihara, Benaras. As you are aware relics of Lord Buddha are highly sacred to the Buddhists and are objects of worship, *it therefore wounds the feelings of the Buddhists to see them exhibited in museums for ordinary visitors* (italics mine). As our Society has already made arrangements to preserve them in a proper manner, we hope you will be graciously pleased to obtain these relics and present them to Mulagandhakuti Vihara where they will be placed for worship along with other relics presented by the Government of India.[36]

It is interesting to note that although this formal application for the relic from the Maha Bodhi Society came in 1932, its candidature for custody of the relic had been an issue of discussion within the Government of India from 1930 onwards and seems to have been mooted by Hargreaves, the officiating Director-General of the ASI. Hargreaves had been asked for his opinion on where the Nagararjunakonda relic should be kept. He expressed the view that since the Ceylonese vihāra was a living Buddhist monument and that since Hindus did not worship the Buddha (although they acknowledged him as an avatāra of Viṣṇu), the request of the Ceylonese vihāra was reasonable. Nevertheless, in view of the ideas expressed in the Legislative Assembly, where the issue had apparently been raised on 17 February 1930, it would not be politic to send relics out of the country. Hargreaves suggested that the vihāra being built at Sarnath by 'Indian Buddhists' was the best option. He also drew attention to the fact that the government had already presented some relics from Taxila to that establishment. He pointed out that the completion of the temple was being delayed due to lack of funds and that if pious Buddhists were to find out that a relic of the Buddha was going to be re-enshrined in the temple, the supply of funds would increase enormously.[37]

However, it was not only Buddhist sentiment but also that of Hindu and Indian nationalist sentiment that were perceived to be involved. Hargreaves suggested that Hindu opinion on the matter would probably be satisfied by keeping the relics in the country. G.S. Bajpai, Secretary to the Government of India in the Department of Education, Health and Lands, agreed with Hargreaves' view, pointing out 'that the sending of these relics even to Ceylon would raise a storm in this country'. He added that 'it is not so much a question of religion as a nascent national sentiment that what historically belongs to India should remain in India' and that a Resolution against sending historical remains in India to other countries had been passed in the Assembly in 1928. Bajpai asked the Director-General of the ASI to suggest names of individuals and institutions in India from whom the government could solicit views on the matter of the relic.[38] The earlier track record of the government was also recapitulated; namely, that the relics found at Taxila had been presented by John Marshall to a Buddhist temple in Ceylon in 1916. Much before that, certain other relics had been presented to the king of Siam in 1898, who had distributed them in his own country, and to Burma, Ceylon and Japan. The Government of India consulted the Bengal government and, through them, the Bengal Buddhist Association and Maha Bodhi Society in Calcutta, as well as the Madras government.

That there was an important distinction between regular antiquities and relics was also underlined by an official named J.H. Page, who suggested that while the antiquities of Nagarjunakonda should be kept in a site museum, which should be made accessible by the building of a motorable road, the bone relic should be handed over to a living Buddhist shrine.[39] Also in question was whether the relic was an authentic corporeal relic of the Buddha. Some doubts had been raised on this point by Daya Ram Sahni, who had taken over as Director-General of the ASI in July 1931.[40] In fact, the government was also inclined to test the waters of public opinion (this was the suggestion of Fazl-i-Husain, member of the Viceroy's Executive Council in charge of archaeology) by planting the story of the discovery of the relic in certain newspapers and then taking note of the reactions. Sahni did, in fact, prepare such a note but it was not published.[41] He himself approved of the idea of handing the relic over to the Maha Bodhi Society on the grounds that such a decision would be 'received with acclamation all over the country'. He suggested that a modern silver replica of the original silver casket should also be made and presented. He also pointed out that it was quite customary to make ceremonial presentations of Buddhist relics on behalf of the Viceroy and that the most appropriate occasion to present the Nagarjunakonda relic to the Mulagandhakuti Vihara would be in December 1932, on the occasion of the celebration of its first anniversary. As he put it: 'Buddhists from distant countries are expected to attend this anniversary and will carry news of this valuable gift to their brotherhood'.[42] Two successive Director-Generals of the ASI had strongly endorsed the idea of handing the relic over to the Maha Bodhi Society and their arguments coincided with the views of the government.

The final decision was communicated to the Government of Ceylon:

> . . . after very careful consideration, the Government of India have decided to present the Buddha relic discovered at Nagarjunakonda in the Madras Presidency to the Mulagandhakuti Vihara at Sarnath, Benares. In view of the immemorial sanctity of Sarnath as one of the four principal places of Buddhist pilgrimage, it was thought that this decision would probably be popular with Buddhists throughout the world.[43]

The ASI also transferred to the Society a park that they had laid out around the Mulagandhakuti Vihara.[44]

This is how the antiquities from the site of Nagarjunakonda remained in a site museum that was built for them but the relic was sent off to the Mulagandhakuti Vihara in Sarnath. The ultimate transfer of the Nagarjunakonda relic to this temple has to be seen against the larger background of the history of relic diplomacy in India and decisions made by the colonial state regarding the most appropriate place to house such finds made by archaeologists. It is also connected with the history of Anagarika Dharmapala and the Maha Bodhi Society, and their efforts to establish control over the sacred Buddhist places and to build up a repository of relics in the Mulagandhakuti Vihara at Sarnath. It is to this aspect that we now turn.

THE TRANSFER OF THE NAGARJUNAKONDA RELIC TO THE MULAGANDHAKUTI VIHARA

The Mulagandhakuti Vihara (literally 'the monastery of the principal scented chamber') at Isipatana in Sarnath, the celebrated site of the Buddha's first sermon, was inaugurated on 11 November 1931. *Maha Bodhi*, the journal of the Maha Bodhi Society, described the day as 'preeminent in the History of Buddhism – perhaps of the world.'[45] There were repeated references to the revival of Buddhism at this place, 800 years after Muhammad Ghori's armies had swept across India. The ceremonies had a marked cosmopolitan air with participants, patrons and representatives from various parts of India, Ceylon, Burma, Tibet, China, Japan and Europe. The highlight of the ceremonials was the presentation of a relic from the Dharmarājika Stūpa at Taxila by the Government of India through Daya Ram Sahni, Director-General of the ASI.

An ailing Devamitta Dharmapala (the name assumed by Anagarika Dharmapala after he donned the monk's robes) was present. A message of support from the Hindu Mahasabha was read out on the occasion. Jawaharlal Nehru was there, along with his wife and sisters, and he presented the national flag to the vihāra as a goodwill gesture from the Congress Working Committee. The president of the Maha Bodhi Society received the Taxila relic from Sahni, declaring that the merit arising out of the ceremony establishing the vihāra should be

FIGURE 3.6: MULAGANDHAKUTI VIHARA, SARNATH

transferred to all beings, and expressed a hope for the long life of Dharmapala. Dharmapala had brought three saplings from Anuradhapura to be planted near the temple – one by himself, another by Sahni and the third by two monks from Ceylon. The Taxila relic was enshrined by Dharmapala in the vault of the temple on 13 November. Dharmapala's speech on the occasion explained the importance of this temple. He talked about how it had been his long-cherished dream to see the Holy Isipatana in Buddhist hands and how this dream had now been fulfilled.[46]

The Maha Bodhi Society had a long-term involvement in conserving and developing Buddhist sacred places in India. The Society had an archaeological section, which exhorted the public to supply information about any Buddhist monuments or ruins in their locality. It was in response to the Society's petition that the Maharaja of Nepal had sanctioned Rs. 20,000 for 'improving' Lumbini. Many pages of the Society's journal were often filled with accounts of the discoveries made in the course of explorations and excavations at sacred sites, of the pathetic conditions there and of the need to do something about this. Conservation was linked to control. An article by Bhikkhu Ottama of Burma, published in the *Maha Bodhi* in 1932, thanked

Alexander Cunningham and John Marshall for discovering Buddhist relics at many ancient sites, and urged that the chief Buddhist sacred places should be handed over to Buddhists so that they could be restored and developed for devout pilgrims.[47] The most well-known of the Society's attempts to establish control over such places was its attempt to stake its right to control the Maha Bodhi temple.[48] However, this was part of the Society's larger agenda of extending its control over *all* the major sacred places of Buddhism in India.

The first anniversary of the opening of the Mulagandhakuti Vihara was scheduled to take place in the winter of 1932. The *Maha Bodhi* announced the forthcoming festivities and invited Buddhists from all over the world to come and participate. It was also announced that on the occasion, the Taxila relic, which had been kept enshrined at Taxila for twenty centuries, would be displayed for worship. The festivities were finally held from 27-29 December 1932 and the highlight of the events of the first day was the presentation of a corporeal relic, supposedly of the Buddha, found at Nagarjunakonda. Devamitta Dharmapala was not there because he was ill, but he sent a message.

The stamp of pan-Buddhist internationalism was writ large on the event.[49] The gifts to the temple included a huge brass gilded bell presented by the United Buddhist Society of Japan and a beautiful drum gifted by a Japanese priest. The bell contained inscriptions in Japanese and Sanskrit, symbolizing the meeting of the cultures of India and Japan. A gold-gilded image of the Buddha was presented by an official from Darjeeling. But the most spectacular gift was the one made by the government of India – the Nagarjunakonda bone relic. The relic was ceremonially presented to the temple on behalf of the Viceroy of India, the Earl of Willingdon, by Daya Ram Sahni, the Director-General of the ASI.[50] The Maha Bodhi Society had initially invited Fazl-i-Husain, but he could not attend and had deputed Sahni to take his place. In his address to the gathering on 27 December, Sahni gave a brief account of the Nagarjunakonda excavations and the inscriptions found at the site, and described the *mahācaitya* where the relic had been found. What was especially important in his address was his certification before the devout gathering, on the basis of inscriptions found at the site that the bone relic was an *authentic* corporeal relic of the Buddha.

The relic was handed over by Sahni to a Sinhalese high priest, who carried it on his head in a procession from the Sarnath site museum around the Dhamekh Stūpa to the temple.[51] After three circumambulations of the temple, it was taken inside to a strong room where it was displayed for worship in a glass case for three days, and we are told that thousands of people turned up for *darśana*. Devamitta Dharmapala's message was read out by Pandit Sheo Narain, the Collector of Banaras, who added that:

> . . . the name of Mr Sahni will go down to posterity when the history of the revival of Buddhism is written. Mr. Sahni as an excavator at Sarnath, as a Superintendent of (the) Archaeological circle and now Director-General of Archeology will be remembered by generations to come as a person of learning, scholarship and research, a gentleman who always has been taking keen interest in Buddhistic matters and to whose labours and zeal (the) Maha Bodhi Society is deeply indebted.[52]

Various lectures were delivered on issues ranging from how the Buddha's *dhamma* would save a decadent world and the tenets of Tibetan Buddhism, to 'the burning question of the day' – Buddhism and untouchability.[53]

The first anniversary celebrations at Mulagandhakuti Vihara and the celebration of the receipt of the Nagarjunakonda relic were overshadowed by the death of Devamitta Dharmapala a few months later on 29 April 1933. The importance of the temple in the agenda of the Maha Bodhi Society is evident from the fact that one portion of his corporeal relics were, according to his wishes, enshrined in this very temple.[54] This temple was visualized as becoming a receptacle of relics from major Buddhist sites and more so, as a major international centre of Buddhism.[55] A strong pan-Buddhist internationalism was evident in the various activities there, including the painting of frescoes on the temple walls by the well-known Japanese artist, Kosetsu Nosu.

It may be noted that on the occasion of the second anniversary of the establishment of the Mulagandhakuti Vihara (celebrated from 11-13 November 1933), the Nagarjunakonda relic was once again carried out in an international procession and venerated. Rahula

FIGURE 3.7: STATUE OF ANAGARIKA DHARMAPALA OUTSIDE MULAGANDHAKUTI VIHARA, SARNATH

Sankrityayana presided over the anniversary meeting in the temple hall and Jawaharlal Nehru, who happened to be at Sarnath at the time, also attended. Further, during the Buddhist conference held on 13 November in the vihāra hall, Dharma Aditya Dharmacharyya, General Secretary of the All-India Buddhist Conference, mooted the idea of an international university at Sarnath. This idea was greeted with great enthusiasm by many other speakers, although one M.M. Barua of Chittagong suggested that in spite of the fact that the

Buddhists were poor, if they concerted together, they could easily create a Nalanda University within a few years.[56] In fact, several of those present made donations for the foundation of a Buddhist university. In this airing of the idea of an international university at Sarnath, we see a precursor of the idea of an international university of a different kind recently established at Nalanda.

THE POST-1947 ISSUE: HERITAGE *VS.* DEVELOPMENT

In independent India, Nagarjunakonda became the centre of an entirely different issue with much larger ramifications. The economic agenda of the new India involved an emphasis on heavy industry, and big dams such as Bhakra Nangal, Damodar, Hirakud and Nagarjunasagar. Dams symbolized 'the nation's will to march forward with strength, determination and courage'.[57] The Nagarjunasagar dam was supposed to be built across the Krishna. What made this project different from others was that the dam would completely destroy what had come to be widely recognized by then as an extremely important and valuable archaeological site. During the time that the issue was under consideration, various options were aired and considered – to build the dam somewhere else, to wall in the ruins by building a subsidiary dam and to relocate the historical monuments.[58] The larger context of what was essentially a development *versus* heritage issue included subsidiary issues such as the role of museums in independent India.

Not surprisingly, the Ministry of Irrigation and Power had a perspective that was different from that of the Ministry of Education and the ASI. The irrigation project was estimated as having the potential to provide water for vast tracts of parched land. 'Dead monuments are a great heritage and we should not let them get perpetually buried but of greater importance is the feeding of the hungry millions of this area. Are we going to let the dead starve the living?'[59]

The ASI pointed out that the Ministry of Irrigation and Power was not being helpful and had not understood the international importance of the site. The then Director-General, M.S. Vats, suggested that a committee of which he should be a member should review the whole issue and see whether it was possible to find an alternative location for the dam.[60] The technical committee of engineers set up by the Planning Commission had said no other site was possible. However, the Ministry of Education agreed with the ASI that the engineers had not properly appreciated the historical importance of the site and agreed that an expert committee should be set up. In view of the conflict between the Education and Irrigation/Power ministries, the former asked for a review of the whole matter by a committee set up by the Planning Commission.[61] In the meantime, at a meeting of the Central Advisory Board of Archaeology, Hiren Mukherjee made a strong plea for the saving of the Nagarjunakonda site, arguing that the submergence of the site would be a 'disaster of the first magnitude to the cultural heritage of the country'.[62]

In 1954, it was decided to send a joint inspection team to the site, including representatives of the Department of Archaeology, Government of Hyderabad, the Andhra Planning Commission, and the Ministry of Irrigation and Power. It was also agreed that the views of the governments of Hyderabad and Madras should be ascertained. Ultimately, the engineers won the battle, with the committee concluding that no other site was possible for the dam.[63]

Prime Minister Nehru took a great personal interest in this problem. In his speech, while laying the foundation stone of the Nagarjunasagar dam on 10 December 1955, he had described it as one of the greatest temples of modern India. But he was keenly aware of the heavy price that would have to be paid for building this temple. The idea of a massive excavation project before the dam became operational and of salvaging the structures had been in the air for many years and had met the Prime Minister's approval. He gave instructions to this effect immediately after laying the foundation stone of the irrigation project.[64] In fact, so seized by the matter was Nehru that that very evening, he shot off a lengthy confidential note on the subject to Maulana Azad, the Education Minister, emphasizing the importance of the site and the measures that must be taken to save as much as could be saved:

> This morning I performed the ceremony of laying the foundation-stone of the great dam of Nagarjuna Sagar. . . . Afterwards, I went to the site of the excavations of the ancient cities of Sri Parvat and Vijayapuri. Nearly all this

vast area is going to be submerged when the dam is built and which will be called the Nagarjuna Sagar. This site of excavations is one of the most important and vital in India. The idea that this place, where so much of our ancient history and culture lie hidden under the earth, should be lost forever under the new lake has distressed me greatly. Yet the choice had to be made for the sake of the needs of today and tomorrow.[65]

It should be noted that during the deliberations over the issue of the dam and the site, the latter was usually discussed as one of the most important Buddhist sites in India, associated with Nagarjuna, the founder of the Mādhyamika School of philosophy. (It is interesting to note that the dam was also named after him.) The sentiments of Buddhists were often also alluded to. This is how Nehru saw it, too – he took special note of the fact that a Buddha relic had been found at the site and that the place was an international centre of Buddhism in ancient times.[66]

Once the decision was made to go ahead with the dam and to initiate a massive excavation project before the submergence of the site, there was the problem of convincing the farmers to agree to the excavations, failing which, it would become necessary to acquire the land.[67] Again at Nehru's instance, it was decided to use quick tactful persuasion rather than go in for lengthy legal processes involving land acquisition, and the Prime Minister suggested that emergency provisions should be invoked wherever necessary, given the urgency of the excavation plan.

Three committees were set up to look into various aspects of the ancient site. One was an Expert Committee, set up at the express instructions of Nehru. It was mooted in December 1955 and officially set up on 14 March 1956, to look into the location of the Nagarjunakonda museum and to examine the feasibility of moving some of the monuments to the top of the hill or to another site altogether, where they would be well above the water level.[68] It was to include the Secretary of the Ministry of Education (as chairman); the Chief Architect of the CPWD, an engineer of the Andhra government with a rank not lower than that of Superintending Engineer; the Principal of the J.J. School of Art, Mumbai; and the Director-General of the ASI (A. Ghosh). The Government of Mumbai suggested the inclusion of H.D. Sankalia, Director of the Deccan

College, Poona, in place of the Principal of the J.J. School of Art on the grounds that the need of the hour was a person who had experience of archaeological excavations and a deep interest in history.[69] The government's response was that the Director-General, ASI, would take care of this aspect and that the Principal of the School of Art was required to give advice on the preparation of models. The committee swung into action and swiftly gave its recommendations. These included the preparation of a scale reproduction on the hill of the entire site, showing the location of the various monuments; the transplantation of selected monuments; and the construction of scale models of some of the most important ones.[70] The recommendations of this expert committee were accepted. Jafar Ali, the chief engineer of the Nagarjunasagar dam, was also co-opted into the committee in May on Ghosh's suggestion.

There were two other committees that were supposed to deal with other aspects of the gigantic irrigation-cum-conservation project. A policy committee was enjoined to ascertain whether the hill that was to be converted into an island as a result of the irrigation project would be able to withstand the water pressure. Its answer was in the affirmative.[71] There was also a coordination committee set up in 1957: its function was to coordinate the activities of the Nagarjunasagar project and the Nagarjunakonda excavation project.[72]

The project presented major challenges for the ASI and these had to be dealt with by making special provisions. A special branch of the ASI was established at the site in 1954 and R. Subrahmanyam was placed in charge of operations as Superintendent, Department of Archaeology, Nagarjunakonda Excavation Project. It was known that the area would be submerged by early 1960 at the latest, when the dam became functional. The archaeological investigations, once initiated, went on with extraordinary gusto.[73] It was also clear that there was a need to appoint a senior, experienced archaeologist as a special officer for a period of three years. At the recommendation of Ghosh, T.N. Ramachandran (Joint Director-General, ASI) was brought in in 1958. Ramachandran was familiar with the site as he had excavated it in 1931 and it was expected that he would write the report of the excavations within the next two years.

It should be noted that as Nagarjunakonda was an isolated site and the work was envisaged as lasting several years, all kinds of provisions had to be made for the staff involved in the dam-building and excavation activities.[74] Schools and medical facilities had to be provided. The hill-top that would house some of the transplanted monuments had to be meticulously landscaped and planned. Funds for the project were to be divided according to the following formula – the cost of the excavations was to be borne by the ASI; the funds for housing and other amenities, the removal of the monuments, the building of the site museum, etc., were to be provided by the Nagarjunasagar irrigation project (subject to an upper limit of 6 lakhs).[75] Monthly progress reports of the excavations were submitted by the archaeological team, and there was both energy and urgency in the reports of the discoveries that were being made at a rapid rate. There were enormous technical problems related to the transplantation of the selected monuments and the scale models that were to be built, and these had to be swiftly addressed. And all this went on under constant scrutiny and pressure from several quarters. Several Members of Parliament took an interest and the Prime Minister himself constantly urged that no expense should be spared in the excavation and conservation work. The idea of moving the museum and the monuments to the hill-top seems to have been Nehru's, and he personally monitored the progress down to minute details such as the placing of an exit door in the front wall of the museum.[76]

THE FINAL PLEA

And yet, as late as in 1957, when work at the site and on the dam had been well underway for many years, the issue became the subject of a lengthy debate in the Rajya Sabha, the Upper House of the Indian parliament. V.K. Dhage, an independent member of the Rajya Sabha, moved a private Resolution on the need to take all steps to preserve the site of Nagarjunakonda.[77] The Resolution was sent for comments to the Director-General, ASI, who gave a resume of all that had transpired, pointing out that no other location was possible for the dam, also giving a description of the massive scale of the ASI operations at the site and detailing the steps being taken for the preservation of the antiquities. A day before the notice for this resolution was issued, a deputation of the Rajya Sabha members, including Dhage, met the Minister of Education and suggested that a committee of MPs be set up to ascertain whether the government had made the right decision.[78] The bill was taken up for discussion in the Rajya Sabha and the government opposed it. It explained the whole sequence of events, the discussions and deliberations, and argued that it was trying to protect as much as could be protected. Dhage pointed out that this site was important 'not only from the point of view of Buddhistic history but also from the point of view of Hindu history'. He pointed out that he was not asking for the abandonment of the irrigation project and made an impassioned plea that the site be saved by building a 500 ft long wall around it *within* the dammed-up waters of the Nagarjunasagar. He also pointed out that if it was preserved, the site would attract Buddhist pilgrims not only from India but from all over the world. The income that would accrue to the government would more than compensate for the cost of building this wall. He argued that taking a utilitarian view on this matter would strike at the root of Indian civilization: '. . . if we destroy this town (of Vijayapurī) I feel that we shall have marked a *kalank* (mark of disrepute) on our face that soon after independence we were so short-sighted that we were not able to save this city at all'.

However, Kishen Chand, an MP from Andhra Pradesh, rose to speak soon after and pointed out the great benefits that would be brought to the farmers of Andhra with the building of the dam and noted that all other alternatives, such as shifting the site of the dam or building a wall, were impractical. B.K.P. Sinha, an MP from Bihar, observed that there were a huge number of historical monuments in India and one could not keep trying to save them all on sentimental grounds. Indian culture was not so fragile that it would perish with the destruction of this one monument: 'I therefore feel that, if it is necessary in the interests of the people of Andhra that a dam should be built and Nagarjunakonda submerged, let it be submerged. Let us take care of the living, and the dead shall be taken care of.'

Nehru also spoke during the lengthy debate, reiterating the government's quandry and final decision, and declaring that the matter was non-negotiable, at this stage. Dhage's resolution was rejected but the Prime Minister suggested that two MPs, one from each House, should be added to the coordination committee. The following amended resolution was also moved, but defeated, after the debate:

> This House is of the opinion that Government should appoint a committee consisting of ten Members of Parliament and two others being persons possessing special knowledge of the subject to inquire into and report on measures to protect and preserve the town of Nagarjunakonda in view of its association with early Buddhist history and the development of various schools of Buddhistic thought.[79]

Nagarjunakonda had again been cast in the now familiar but very one-dimensional role of a site whose importance rested entirely on its Buddhist connections.

During the 1950s and 1960s, there were parliamentary questions on the progress of the excavation and conservation work, details of the various phases of the irrigation project, on whether the central government was considering taking over the irrigation project (irrigation was a state, not a central subject), the escalation of costs, the water requirements of neighbouring states, the building of the site museum, the number of times that the committees had met, new discoveries at the site, and on the development of the site as a tourist centre.[80] During subsequent years, occasionally questions were asked about the conservation activities at the site and developing it as a tourism destination. More recently, there was also a parliamentary question on the publication of the excavation report.[81] The first volume had been published in 1975; the second volume was finally published in 2006, almost half a century after the excavations.

CONCLUSION

The modern history of the ancient site of Nagarjunakonda presents us with many unique features. The scale of excavation and conservation work at Nagarjunakonda was unprecedented and has not been equalled since. The amount of political involvement in the events at the site, including the interest of parliamentarians, was also unprecedented and remains unmatched. What is ironical is that the rich archaeological potential of the site only came to light as part of the preparations for its death by drowning in the waters of the Nagarjunasagar dam.

The excavations at Nagarjunakonda brought to light a wide range of remains, ranging from the prehistoric to the medieval, revealing it to be a complex, multi-layered and multi-period site. However, the official correspondence emanating from different statesmen, ministries and agencies, including the ASI, generally emphasized its early historic Buddhist connections, as well as its fabled connections with the famous Buddhist scholar, Nagarjuna. Nehru himself was acutely aware of the importance of the Buddhist heritage of India and of the Asian ramifications of this heritage, and his vision of India's ancient and modern history left an important imprint on the site.[82] This was not his personal vision alone, but there were other, different visions as well. This is revealed by the parliamentary debate on the national flag, which brought out the different understandings of the symbolism of its colours and the *cakra*. It is interesting to note that while there was a long parliamentary debate on the national flag, there was none on the national emblem – the lion capital of Aśoka's Sarnath pillar, with its strong Buddhist resonance.

Relic diplomacy was something that went on in both colonial and independent India. On 14 January 1949, Nehru made an impassioned speech while receiving the Sanchi relics, which had been sent back to India from the Victoria and Albert Museum, London, before handing them over to the Maha Bodhi Society.[83] He spoke of the Buddha as a messenger of peace and asserted that Buddhism had 'more than anything else laid the foundation of Greater India and established cultural unity of an abiding value between India and many parts of Asia'. In 1955, he presented some of these relics to Ceylon, expressing the hope that the gift would 'further cement the bond of friendship between these two neighbouring countries'.[84] The Indian government was not the only one engaging in relic diplomacy. In 1957, at a ceremony in Nalanda, Nehru received relics of the Chinese pilgrim, Xuanzang (apparently a small part of his skull), along with some books about him from the Dalai Lama on behalf of the Chinese government.[85] The full story of relic diplomacy in modern times still remains to be written.

Underlying the Indian relic diplomacy was an acute awareness of the international ramifications of India as the homeland of Buddhism. Buddha Jayanti was apparently made a public holiday 'for certain international reasons'.[86] In 1957, Nehru saw a ten-reel film on the Buddha entitled *Gotama the Buddha*, produced for the Films Division by Bimal Roy Productions, and suggested that its copies be sent to the principal missions abroad, especially to Burma and Ceylon.[87]

The physical landscape of Nagarjunakonda graphically reveals the various processes that have been discussed in this paper. Over the last few years, the Indian government has been aggressively developing ancient Buddhist sites for international spiritual tourism and Nagarjunakonda has also become part of this circuit.[88] The consistent emphasis on the Buddhist element in the history of the site is writ large all over its landscape.[89] The Indian government is not alone in realizing the benefits to be reaped through such activity, and reference may be made here to recent Chinese attempts to develop Lumbini as a pilgrim-tourist destination and the Nepalese resistance to it. All these developments are important parts of the modern histories of ancient sites.

The issues examined here in the context of Nagarjunakonda continue to be of great relevance even today: Where should ancient artefacts be deposited and viewed? What should be done in the case of artefacts which are associated with special religious significance? Should they be museumized, deposited in places of active worship, or be made objects of worship in museums? The most serious problem concerns the conflict between heavy-investment modernization projects, on the one hand, and the conservation of sites and monuments on the other; a conflict in which fierce battles to preserve heritage are sometimes fought and, more often than not, lost.

ACKNOWLEDGEMENTS

I would like to acknowledge a grant I received from the University of Delhi for this research, as well as the valuable help in collecting data rendered by my research assistants, Kanika Kishore, Kanika Kalra and Tarun Kumar.

NOTES

1. Of course, it was not the only religious tradition to do so. Jainism remained confined to certain regions of the subcontinent but Hindu influences travelled along with Buddhist traditions to the lands of mainland and island Southeast Asia.
2. See Almond (1988); Singh (2004): 47-9.

3. Nagarjunakonda' literally means Nagarjuna's hill (*koṇḍa* is Telugu for hill). An inscription (Vogel 1929-30: 22; 'F') refers to a monastery called Cula-Dhammagiri on Siriparvata on the eastern side of Vijayapurī. This suggests that the early historical city was known as Vijayapurī. A Tibetan tradition refers to the famous Buddhist philosopher Nāgārjuna spending the later part of his life in a monastery at Śrīparvata. This is the basis of the supposed connection of this site with Nāgārjuna. It may be noted that several early writings refer to the site as Nagarjunikonda.
4. Longhurst ([1938] 1999).
5. Ramachandran ([1953] 1999).
6. Subrahmanyam et al. (1975).
7. Soundararajan ed. (2006).
8. Letter dated 10 February 1927, file no. 911 of the Archaeological Department, 1926-30, Subject: Excavations at Nagarjunakonda, in the archives of the Archaeological Survey of India (ASI), p. 126. The rest of the material in this section is also based on this file.
9. Marshall's hand-written note dated 17 February 1927, on the letter cited above.
10. File no. 911, p. 122, ASI.
11. Telegram dated 22 February 1927, file no. 911, p. 129, ASI.
12. File no. 911, p. 20, ASI.
13. File no. 911, p. 38, ASI.
14. There is also a personal angle – Longhurst happened to be Marshall's brother-in-law.
15. File no. 911, p. 172, ASI.
16. File no. 911, pp. 49 ff, ASI.
17. File no. 911, pp. 82, 192 ff, ASI.
18. File no. 911, p. 58, ASI.
19. File no. 911, p. 87, ASI.
20. File no. 911, pp. 30, 32, ASI.
21. File no. 911, pp. 150, 160, ASI.
22. File no. 911, p. 165, ASI.
23. File no. 911, pp. 185-6, ASI.
24. File no. 911, p. 181, ASI.
25. File no. 911, p. 204, ASI.
26. File no. 911, p. 209, ASI.
27. File no. 911, p. 210, ASI.
28. File no. 911, p. 213, ASI.
29. File no. 911, pp. 220-1, ASI.
30. File no. 911, pp. 227-9, ASI.
31. File no. 911, pp. 226, ASI.
32. File no. 911, pp. 228, 229, ASI.

33. File no. 911, pp. 246, 249, ASI.
34. Letter from the Deputy Secretary to the Government of Madras, Finance Department, No. 28890-E.T.-2, dated Fort St. George, 18 November 1930, file no. 317-1/32-F, Notes, Forests, No. 3, Dept. of Education, Health and Lands, National Archives of India (hereafter NAI).
35. Letter from the Governor of Ceylon to the Viceroy, dated 27 February 1930, file no. 317-1/32F, No. 1, Department of Education, Health and Lands, NAI.
36. Letter from the Secretary, Maha Bodhi Society, dated the 7 July 1932, Dept. of Education, Health and Lands, Forest Section, 1932, F.317-1/32F, No. 4, p. 9, NAI. It is not clear who in the government this letter was addressed to.
37. Hargreaves' note dated 5.5.30, Dept. of Education, Health and Lands, Forest Section, 1932, F.317-1/32F, No. 1, p. 1, NAI.
38. Note dated 9 August 1930 by G.S. Bajpai, Dept. of Education, Health and Lands, Forest Section, F.317-1/32F, No. 1, p. 2, NAI.
39. Note dated 1 April 1931, Dept. of Education, Health and Lands, Forest Section, F.317-1/32F, No. 1, p. 3, NAI.
40. Note dated 2 August 1932, Dept. of Education, Health and Lands, Forest Section, F.317-1/32F, No. 1, p. 4, NAI.
41. Ibid.
42. D.R. Sahni's Note dated 8 December 1932, Dept. of Education, Health and Lands, Forest Section, F.317-1/32F, No. 2, pp. 5-6, NAI.
43. Letter to the Colonial Secretary, Ceylon, No. F.317-1/32F., dated New Delhi, 20 December 1932, Dept. of Education, Health and Lands, Forest Section, No. 6, p. 10. NAI
44. File no. 115/2/33/F., Notes, Nos. 1-5, Dept. of Education, Health and Lands, Forest Section, NAI.
45. *Maha Bodhi*, 1931: 520.
46. *Maha Bodhi*, 1932: 232-3.
47. *Maha Bodhi*, 1930: 234-5.
48. See Lahiri (1999); Trevithick (1999).
49. See *Maha Bodhi,* 1933: 38-41.
50. *Maha Bodhi,* 1933: 1-4.
51. The Sarnath museum, established in 1910, is the oldest site museum set up by the ASI.
52. *Maha Bodhi,* 1933: 39.
53. *Maha Bodhi*, 1933: 39-41
54. For a description of this ceremony, see *Maha Bodhi*, 1933: 285-7. The other portion (p. 289) were enshrined in the Maligakande temple in Colombo.
55. Note the comment made in *Maha Bodhi*, 1933: 39 in the account of the anniversary celebrations: 'We have every reason to expect that some day we

shall have larger collections of relics in Sarnath, which is growing into an international Buddhist centre.'

56. *Maha Bodhi*, 1933: 513-20.
57. From Nehru's speech while inaugurating the Bhakra-Nangal canal system at Nangal on 8 July 1954, Nehru (*Selected Works*, 2000), 132.
58. Extract from the notes of Ministry of Education, file no. F.3-30/52-A2, NAI.
59. Note of A.N. Khosla dated 6 September 1952, extract from the notes of the Ministry of Education, file no. F.3-30/52-A2, NAI.
60. Extract from the notes of the Ministry of Education, file no. F.3-30/52-A2, note of M.S. Vats, Director-General, dated 13 July 1952, NAI.
61. Extract from the notes of the Ministry of Education, file no. F.3-30/52-A2, note of E. Kolet, dated 23 April 1953, NAI.
62. As reported in *The Hindu* newspaper dated 17 August 1953. Hiren Mukherjee was a member of the Communist Party of India (Marxist), with a strong interest in history and culture.
63. Ministry of Education, C.I., 1957, file no. 4-6/57 C.I., p. 2, NAI.
64. Ministry of Education, C.I., 1955, file no. 3-125/55 C.I., NAI.
65. Note from Nehru to the Minister for Education, dated 10 December 1955, Guntur, Ministry of Education, C.I., 1955, file no. 3-125/55 C.I., pp. 19-20, NAI.
66. Note from Nehru to the Minister for Education, dated 10 December 1955, Guntur, Ministry of Education, C.I., 1955, file no. 3-125/55 C.I., pp. 21-2, NAI.
67. Letter dated 3 January 1956 from T.S. Krishnamurti, Under Secretary to the Government of India to the Secretary, Public Works Department; letter dated 21 December 1955 from V.V. Subramaniam, Secretary to the Govt., Public Works and Transport Dept., Govt. of Andhra Pradesh, to N. Bhagwandas, Collector of Guntur; Ministry of Education, C.I., 1955, file no. 3-125/55 C.I., pp. 25-6, NAI.
68. Letter from D. Chakravarti, Under Secretary to the Govt. of India to the Director General of Archaeology, Ministry of Education, C.I., 1955, file no. 3-125/55 C.I., pp. 38-9, NAI.
69. Letter dated 14 January 1956 from the Under Secretary to the Govt. of Bombay, Education Dept. to the Secretary to the GOI, Ministry of Education, C.I., 1955, file no. 3-125/55 C.I., p. 31.
70. Minutes of the meeting of the Expert Committee held on 18 and 19 April 1956; Ministry of Education, C.I., 1955, file no. 3-125/55 C.I., pp. 42-9.
71. The members of this committee included K.K. Dutta of the Geological Survey of India and R. Subrahmanyam, superintendent of the Nagarjunakonda excavation project, apart from the administrator of the Nagarjunasagar project or his nominee, and a nominee of the Central Water and Power

Commission. Ministry of Education, C.I., 1957, file no. 4-6/57, C.I., p. 27.

72. This committee consisted of the Governor of Andhra Pradesh as the chair, the chief minister of Andhra Pradesh; the Administrator, Nagarjunasagar; the Joint Secretary, Ministry of Education; the Director General, ASI; and the Chief Engineer, Nagarjunasagar Dam. Ministry of Education, C.I., 1957, file no. 4-6/57, C.I., pp. 27-8. Details of the deliberations of the three committees are also available in file no.F3-51/58 C.I. (1958), ASI archives.
73. Letter dated 19 October 1957 from A. Ghosh, DG, ASI to Dr. Lakhani, Ministry of Education, C.I., 1957, file no. F3-147/57, C.I, p. 30, NAI.
74. Details of all these activities and deliberations behind them are contained in File no. F3-51/58, C.I., 1958 (ASI Archives).
75. Self-contained note on Nagarjunakonda excavations; Ministry of Education, C.I., 1957, file no. 4-6/57, C.I., pp. 25-32.
76. File no. F3-51/58, CI, 1958 (ASI Archives), pp. 160, 165. Nehru (*Selected Works*, 2002): 103-6, 108-9; vol. 32: 95-6.
77. The Notice for the Resolution was issued on March 11, 1957. See Ministry of Education, C.I., 1957, file no. 4-6/57, C.I., NAI.
78. Ministry of Education, C.I., 1957, file no. 4-6/57, C.I., p. 6, NAI.
79. Notice of Amendment to be moved in the Rajya Sabha on 22 March, 1957, Ministry of Education, C.I., 1957, file no. 4-6/57, C.I., p. 35. Details of the debate can be read in the Proceedings of the Rajya Sabha on 22 March 1957, pp. 386-412. V.K. Dhage and N.G. Ranga joined the coordination committee. The MPs were invited to visit the site and two members were co-opted into the coordination committee.
80. Dhage himself raised several of these questions on different occasions.
81. Parliamentary Question No. 2343 raised by MP Charan Das Mahant; date of reply: 14 December 1999.
82. What the Buddha and Aśoka meant to him emerges from his many writings, including *The Discovery of India*.
83. Nehru (*Selected Works*, 1990): 101-3. The relics were supposed to be those of the famous monks Sāriputta and Mahāmoggalāna, but, as pointed out by Debala Mitra, actually from the nearby site of Satdhara. The role of the Bhopal Durbar in ensuring that the relics came back to Sanchi and were housed there has been discussed in Nayanjot Lahiri's essay in this book.
84. *Maha Bodhi*, 1955: 331.
85. Nehru (*Selected Works*, 2005): 185-8.
86. Nehru (*Selected Works*, 2005): 224.
87. Nehru (*Selected Works*, 2005): 194-5.
88. See Singh (2010).
89. See Singh (2010) for details of this aspect.

BIBLIOGRAPHY

Archival Sources

Archival files of the Archaeological Department, Archaeological Survey of India.

Archival files of the Department of Education, Health and Lands (Forest Section); and of the Department of Education, in the National Archives of India, New Delhi.

Proceedings and Debates of the Indian Constituent Assembly, Rajya Sabha and Lok Sabha, Parliament of India.

Published Sources

Almond, Philip. 1988. *The British Discovery of Buddhism*. Cambridge: Cambridge University Press.

Lahiri, Nayanjot. 1999. 'Bodh-Gaya: An Ancient Buddhist Shrine and its Modern History (1891-1904)', in Timothy Insoll (ed.), *Case Studies in Archaeology and World Religion*. Oxford: BAR International Series, pp. 755, 33-42.

Longhurst, A.H. [1938] 1999. *The Buddhist Antiquities of Nagarjunakonda, Madras Presidency: Memoirs of the Archaeological Survey of India*. No. 54. rpt. edn. New Delhi: Archaeological Survey of India.

Maha Bodhi. Journal of the Maha Bodhi Society, vols. 39-41 (1931-3); vol. 63 (1955).

Nehru, Jawaharlal. 1990. *Selected Works of Jawaharlal Nehru*, Second Series, vol. 9, ed. S. Gopal. New Delhi: Jawaharlal Nehru Memorial Fund.

———. 2000. Second Series, vol. 26, gen. ed. S. Gopal. New Delhi: Jawaharlal Nehru Memorial Fund.

———. 2002. Second Series, vol. 31, ed. H.Y. Sharada Prasad and A.K. Damodaran. New Delhi: Jawaharlal Nehru Memorial Fund.

———. 2003. Second Series, vol. 32. Second Series, ed. H.Y. Sharada Prasad and A.K. Damodaran. New Delhi: Jawaharlal Nehru Memorial Fund.

———. 2005. Second Series, vol. 36. Second Series, ed. H.Y. Sharada Prasad and A.K. Damodaran, New Delhi: Jawaharlal Nehru Memorial Fund.

Ramachandran, T.N. [1953], 1999. *Nagarjunakonda 1938*. Memoirs of the Archaeological Survey of India; No. 71. rept. edn. New Delhi: Archaeological Survey of India.

Singh, Upinder. 2010. 'Exile and Return: The Reinvention of Buddhism and Buddhist Sites in Modern India', *South Asian Studies* 26, 2: 193-217.

———. 2004. *The Discovery of Ancient India: Early Archaeologists and the Beginnings of Archaeology*. Delhi: Permanent Black.

Soundararajan, K.V., ed. 2006. *Nagarjunakonda (1954-60):* Volume II (*The Historical Period*). Memoirs of the Archaeological Survey of India, No. 75. New Delhi: Archaeological Survey of India.

Subrahmanyam, R. et al. 1975. *Nagarjunakonda (1954-60):* Volume I. Memoirs of the Archaeological Survey of India, No. 75. New Delhi: Archaeological Survey of India.

Trevithick, Alan. 1999. 'British Archaeologists, Hindu Abbots, and Burmese Buddhists: The Mahabodhi Temple at Bodh Gaya, 1811-1877', *Modern Asian Studies* 33, 3: 635-56.

Vogel, J.Ph. 1929-30. 'Prakrit Inscriptions from a Buddhist Site at Nagarjunikonda', *Epigraphia Indica* 20: 1-36.

CHAPTER 4

Archaeology, Pilgrimage and Heritage

Modern Amaravati, 1900-2011

SONALI DHINGRA

THE AFTERLIVES OF archaeological sites with religious significance often tell a tale of abandonment, rediscovery, reuse and reappropriation. In fact, many of these ancient sites with material vestiges of the past are inextricably linked to modern and contemporary developments. Ancient Buddhist sites have been profoundly impacted by the complex modern phenomenon of the revitalization of Buddhism across Asia; their rediscovery and the so-called revival of Buddhism in India are worthy of scholarly scrutiny and analysis. The context of the rediscovery and early scholarly interpretations of ancient Buddhist archaeological sites have been analysed by scholars in recent times.[1] Others have dealt with the ways in which new and potent imagery conveys different messages to different groups of Buddhists and the physical changes in archaeological remains as a result of modern interventions.[2] Although the orientations of these works vary, one underlying theme is the recognition of the fact that Buddhism, with its two main components of Tibetan Buddhists and neo-Buddhists, is 'living' in India. The degree and dynamics of change vary at each ancient Buddhist site and several factors converge to shape their modern-day histories.

The case-study for this paper is the ancient *mahācaitya* site at Amaravati, Guntur district, Andhra Pradesh, India, active from the third century BCE till the fourteenth century CE. Amaravati is today considered an unusual choice for scholarly research due to its ruined state brought about by the activities of both locals and archaeologists in the eighteenth and nineteenth centuries.[3] The monument, denuded of all its gloriously-sculpted architectural components is now reduced to an artificially-created mound of mud, surrounded by a partial railing of the Aśokan period made of stumpy pillars and a recently-reconstructed fraction of the later ornamental railing that would have encircled the stūpa in its complete state (Fig. 4.1). Lush lawns beautify the monument, demarcated by a barbed-wired fence, making Amaravati a designated 'monument of national importance' safeguarded by the Archaeological Survey of India (henceforth, ASI).

Despite its ruined appearance, the Amaravati *mahācaitya* is not just another obscure Buddhist monument but an important archaeological site, a sacred place of worship, as well as an example of ancient Buddhist heritage in India today. The surviving parts of the stūpa point to the scale and grandeur of the monument in its day, something uncommon in the archaeological record. As an Aśokan pillar inscription suggests, the early stages of the monument were connected with the proselytizing activities of the Mauryan emperor, Aśoka. The *mahācaitya* has yielded crystal and ivory relic-caskets – some with bone remains, precious stones and gold flowers. It is no

FIGURE 4.1: THE AMARAVATI *MAHĀCAITYA* IN 2009
(PHOTO BY SONALI DHINGRA © 2009)

wonder that inscriptions always refer to the Dhānyakaṭaka *caitya* (as it was known in ancient times) as a *mahācaitya* or a 'great *caitya*', as it probably enshrined the relics of the Buddha himself.

Over the seventeen centuries of worship at the *mahācaitya*, it received devotees from outside the Andhra region. Some identifiable places where pilgrims came from are Kaliṅga, Rājgīr, and nearby Ghanṭāśālā and Vijayapurī (modern Nagarjunakonda). It needs to be noted that pilgrimages to the Dhānyakaṭaka *mahācaitya* continued even after the third century CE, and this Buddhist establishment received donations from the local ruling elite in the twelfth century and monks from Sri Lanka as late as the fourteenth century CE.[4] Modern scholarship has focused almost exclusively on the circuit of eight sites in north India that are associated with the life of the Buddha, as described in Chinese sources, whereas there were many other Buddhist establishments that were significant for Buddhists.[5] The fixing of the sacred geography of the Buddha in scholarly writings has created a hierarchy among Buddhist pilgrimage sites, with the result that 'core' sites have received a great deal of attention both from patrons and pilgrims alike.[6]

Taking its rediscovery and subsequent despoliation as a starting point, this paper seeks to investigate the unique trajectory that the history of the ancient archaeological site of Amaravati in Andhra Pradesh has taken in the twentieth and twenty-first centuries, and its connections with the Buddhist revitalization in Asia. Four themes will be discussed through this essay. First, the perceptions about the site that were formed in the nineteenth and twentieth centuries; and the archaeological excavations, investigations and conservation activities conducted at Amaravati will be detailed. Second, the construction of modern iconography and architecture at the site that appears to compensate for the lack of ancient archaeological remains; and the imaginary reconstructions of the permanently-damaged Amaravati *mahācaitya* will be discussed. Third, the multi-religious significance of Amaravati from early medieval times till today, and the overlap between the secular and sacred visitations to the *mahācaitya* site at Amaravati in contemporary times will be analysed. And lastly, the role of local agencies in conserving and promoting the ancient Buddhist heritage in Andhra Pradesh, their pan-Asian outlook and linkages will be considered. Fieldwork at the site, archival research, modern literature published on the Amaravati stūpa, as well as personal interviews form the sources for this study.

AMARAVATI *MAHĀCAITYA*: RE-DISCOVERED AND FORGOTTEN?

Amaravati has had a chequered history through the late nineteenth, twentieth and twenty-first centuries, the reasons for which are significant in understanding its place among Buddhist sites in India today. In 1797, the mound at Amaravati, already disturbed by locals, was the first Buddhist 'tope' to be discovered and later excavated by British colonial archaeologists. With little information on Buddhism at the time, Colin Mackenzie, the surveyor of the Madras Presidency, could not pinpoint the Buddhist affiliation of the large mound that he discovered at 'Amravutty'. Over the next hundred years, the beautifully-sculpted architectural parts of the Buddhist monument were recognized to be among the finest specimens of Indian art and these were torn away, in successive stages, finding their way to museums in London and in Madras. The dispersal of its remnants means that the modern history of Amaravati includes both the history of the site and of its parts.

By the 1900s, the structure of the Amaravati *mahācaitya* was totally destroyed. This was noted as early as 1867 by James Fergusson who compared Amaravati to Sanchi, the site which was to become an object of much fascination for British archaeologists – from Alexander Cunningham to John Marshall: 'Unlike that at Sanchi, the Tope at Amaravati has been so completely destroyed that a traveler might ride over the mounds in which it is buried without suspecting what they covered.'[7]

James Burgess, too, lamented the fact that there was no way for archaeologists to understand the original layout of the Amaravati *mahācaitya*:

> The removal, in 1880, of all the debris and other remains of the stupa within the area of the rails – much of it thrown into and quite filling up the tank dug in the centre by Raja Venkatadri Nayudu – destroyed forever the chance

of recovering any precise dimensions of the central pile, which even a few bricks in situ would have fixed.[8]

Yet the absence of an accurate design of the Amaravati stūpa did not mean that fanciful descriptions of it could not be made. The description offered by Burgess exemplifies this:

Surrounded by a double sculptured rail, the outer one about 13 feet high, and the stupa rising to a height of perhaps 100 feet, this great marble dome must have had a very brilliant effect, while round the outside were numerous small chaityas – miniature copies of it – the monumental records of the hierarchy in whose charge it was; and in a wider circle around were the monastic buildings and dwellings of the yellow-robed fraternity of monks, with the wet season retreats of mendicants from all quarters. On the fortnightly festival occasions, and more especially at the dipavali season, the whole surface of the dome was covered with festoons of flowers, and flags fluttered from the square capital on top, while at night it was dotted over with hundreds of lamps, that covered it with a blaze of light which, amid the darkness, made of it a hill of lamps, and gave it the popular name, still handed down, Dipaldinne.[9]

Imaginary reconstructions of the Amaravati *mahācaitya* have been made ever since and a modern rendering of this monument is today a popular image (this is discussed below).[10] One of the greatest paradoxes in the history of the Amaravati *mahācaitya* is that the steady mutilation of the monument was accompanied by the reassembly of its disconnected parts. The newly-invented technology of photography, in vogue by the 1860s, was employed for attempting the photographic restoration of the monument.[11] The 'Amaravati marbles' at the Madras Museum were photographed by Linnaeus Tripe in 1858 and Fergusson got the architectural fragments in London photographed in 1866. The latter were showcased in the Paris Exhibition where they were well-received by a European audience.

The interest in Amaravati, however, waned by the end of the nineteenth century. The site was excavated by Alexander Rea but his concentration was mainly on the nearby site of Bhattīprolū in Andhra Pradesh. Nevertheless, his digs yielded significant findings – a gold relic-casket in which was kept a piece of bone and small gold flowers among other objects, most notably copper images of the Buddha.[12]

Rea's discoveries were reported in the Maha Bodhi Society's journal[13] for they indicated that 'the site was occupied by Buddhists as far back as the Mauryan epoch'. Thus, archaeological reports and findings were duly reported in the *Journal of the Maha Bodhi Society* as they were tangible and 'scientific' proof of India's age-old Buddhist past.

Concomitant with the rediscovery of ancient Indian Buddhist sites was the process of renewal of the interest of Buddhism in Asia, spearheaded by Anagarika Dharmapala of the Maha Bodhi Society. In the first few decades of the twentieth century, the Archaeological Survey and the Maha Bodhi Society were preoccupied with the search for, and the location and appropriation of Buddhist relics. What is curious about Amaravati's modern history is that even though relic-caskets were found in the *mahācaitya*, they received no attention from the Maha Bodhi Society and no claim was ever made on them even in a climate of the feverish search for the Buddha's relics by British archaeologists and their zealous acquisition by the Maha Bodhi Society.

The lack of focus on the Amaravati relics can be explained in two ways. First, there was the absence of inscriptions on them that might have helped archaeologists identify whose relics were contained within. By contrast, a rock crystal relic-casket with a small piece of bone discovered in 1892 at Bhattīprolū was a 'well-authenticated' relic of the Buddha, as this was ratified by a Brahmī inscription on it dated to the second century BCE.[14] This relic was given by the Government of India to the Maha Bodhi Society and was ceremoniously deposited in a stone vault at a vihara in Calcutta in 1919.[15] The second explanation for the absence of interest in Amaravati is that the site was already explored and excavated, and its most significant features – its gloriously sculpted architectural parts were already taken away from it, leaving nothing behind. With a host of new discoveries every year, the site of Amaravati, with no Buddhist vestiges left *in situ*, was not too appealing to archaeologists or Buddhist revivalists.

Archaeological explorations of the time are well known for their affinity for marking the sacred geography of the Buddha by tracing the footsteps of the Chinese pilgrims Xuanzang and Fa-Hien along the eight sites associated with him in north India. Other spectacular archaeological discoveries such as Taxila, Sanchi, Mathura, Ajanta and Nalanda also received the attention and resources of the ASI.[16]

It is these sites, discussed and written about extensively in the early twentieth century, as Toni Huber argues, that became the locus of pilgrim-activity for modern Buddhists.[17] Other places, such as Amaravati, that were not visited by the ancient Chinese monks, were not seen as places of much religious importance, and found no mention in the numerous public discourses and writings on Buddhist shrines in India. Scholarly writings heavily influenced belief and, consequently, the same sites were visited by Buddhist pilgrims. The 'Amaravati stones' however, continued to be significant as fine examples of Buddhist art and architecture, and found mention in Percy Brown's work (1942) and in C. Sivaramamurti's detailed catalogue of Amaravati sculptures in the Madras Government Museum (1942).

After Independence, the ASI was organized into different circles in order to conduct excavations, restoration and preservation of India's ancient archaeological sites, monuments and material remains in different parts of the country. Post-Independence excavations by the ASI have led to the discovery of significant archaeological material; most notably, the surface find of a fragmentary inscribed pillar attributed to the Mauryan king, Aśoka (r. *c.* 268-232 BCE). The date of the establishment of the Amaravati Stūpa was pushed back to the middle of the third century BCE, thereby establishing a link between the *mahācaitya* at Dhānyakaṭaka and Aśoka. Later, some scholars even suggested the stūpa was pre-Aśokan.[18] The early date of the origin of the Dhānyakaṭaka *mahācaitya* and its historical connection with one of the greatest Buddhist missionaries ever known in India – Aśoka – have been highlighted ever since, both in scholarly and popular literature.

The 1960s-70s appear to be a period when the ASI undertook frequent conservation projects at several ancient Buddhist sites. The site of the Amaravati *mahācaitya* was levelled after the conclusion of the 'clearance operation' in 1958-9.[19] In April 1962, the then Director-General of the ASI, A. Ghosh, was concerned with improving the condition of the site[20] and the roads as both were in a shoddy condition. More importantly, the ASI was concerned about giving a correct impression of what the 'original' stūpa looked like. Ghosh indicated that there were problems in the arrangement of the limestone uprights found in the recent excavations. Set up along the *pra-*

dakṣiṇāpatha, they 'gave a false impression of the layout of the railing and of the chronology of the whole stūpa'. In 1970, spotlights were installed at the ASI's site museum as the museum building was often visited by many distinguished tourists and VIPs, and in order to better display the museum's collection.[21] In 1970, some 'special repairs' were also carried out to the stūpa at Amaravati.[22] The general upkeep and maintenance of the monument has been carried out by the ASI since then.

In 2006, a major event commemorating the Kālacakra initiation, a significant Tibetan Buddhist ritual, was planned with Amaravati as its venue. This event will be discussed in more detail in a section below. Before the Kālacakra event, it seems that the ASI went all out to give the stūpa-complex a facelift.[23] The restoration efforts at the site made unusual changes to the architecture of the stūpa itself. A second drum was built to conserve the mud dome that tended to get washed away during heavy rains. However, this intervention of the ASI altered the original architecture of the *mahācaitya*. The lawns surrounding the ancient monument were tidied and pruned, new paths were paved for devotees to circumambulate, and new metal railings installed to make the complex more presentable and pilgrim-friendly. Later, focus lights were installed at the site to light up the ancient monument.

In addition to these changes, the Government of Andhra Pradesh demanded a few sculptures from the Government Museum, Chennai, and nineteen pieces were procured. These were put together to form a partial railing, so as to give the visitors an idea of the original one. Sculptural fragments from the storage collection of the site museum were also brought out and placed against the second drum. Even a mutilated *āyaka* pillar was erected in the middle of the *pradakṣiṇāpatha*.[24] It is significant that the ASI, using the few fragmentary remains in its possession or those obtained from elsewhere, attempted to remind the visitors and pilgrims of the once-splendid state of the now deplorably barren monument. The changes made to the archaeological site concentrated more on making the place a destination for spiritual tourism and, in the process, some alterations to the structure of the stūpa were carried out, something potentially hazardous to an ancient archaeological site.

The Amaravati *mahācaitya* yielded a large number of reliquaries from each of the four *āyaka* platforms that project from it in the cardinal directions. The caskets contained gold flowers and other precious stones, as well as a bone-relic.[25] The relic-caskets are in the safe custody of the Amaravati Site Museum of the ASI and have not been displayed due to the lack of adequate security measures. During the Kālacakra event, the relic-caskets were brought out, and put on show for visitors and pilgrims in a special separate room amid tight security. Making reliquaries a permanent part of the display is a contentious and unsettled issue as doing so would require extensive safety measures. Relic galleries have already been established in the Andhra Pradesh State Museum in Hyderabad and in the National Museum, New Delhi, to showcase the bodily relics of the Buddha excavated from Bavikonda and Piprahwa, respectively. Buddhist devotees and pilgrims visit the galleries to view these relics, to worship them, and to offer prayers and to meditate.

The stones from the Amaravati *mahācaitya* continue to be held principally by the British Museum, London, the Chennai Government Museum, Chennai, and the ASI Site Museum, Amaravati. The British Museum has some of the best pieces of Amaravati art displayed in a climate-controlled gallery funded by the Japanese glass manufacturers, Asahi Shimbun. The Amaravati stones that reached the Madras Museum in 1883 were arranged arbitrarily and many of them were set in concrete. Recently, the Chennai Government Museum renovated the gallery with the Amaravati sculptures and aims to showcase the larger part of its famous collection.[26] There are also plans to upgrade the display at the Site Museum (which receives more than 80,000 visitors in a year), to mark the sesquicentennial anniversary of the ASI.

THE CHANGED PHYSICAL LANDSCAPE OF AMARAVATI – BUILDING ANEW

New Buddhist architecture, with modern architects and technology at its disposal, is quite different from its ancient counterpart in conception, scale and design. This is because the symbolism of the stūpa is heavily influenced by the heterogeneous character of Buddhism, and it can be simultaneously appropriated as a symbol of world peace, social egalitarianism or political assertion in today's time. The mixture of different styles and elements is noticeable in modern examples of Buddhist architecture, with a trend towards large and monumental statues-cum-buildings becoming tourist attractions.

At Kusinagara (Uttar Pradesh, India), a giant statue of a seated Maitreya, the future Buddha, has been conceptualized, which will be the second tallest statue in the world when complete. In the architect's conception, numerous shrines, meditation rooms and exhibition galleries would be created inside the building, making it a novel, ambitious and spectacular architectural project.[27] A similar, though more modest modern structure is a 125 ft high statue of the Dhyāna Buddha made of concrete, along the banks of the Krishna river at Amaravati. The project was conceptualized in 2003, and is owned and funded by the Andhra Pradesh Tourism Development Corporation.[28] Due to its height, this structure is visible from the *mahācaitya* site and completely dominates the entire landscape of the small town.

This concrete statue of the Buddha (Fig. 4.2) is seated on a lotus and in *dhyāna-mudrā* (a meditation pose with both hands placed on the lap, palm upwards, signifying deep meditation). The architects have integrated a hall with the base of the Buddha statue and four pavilions stand on the corners of this complex. The design of the pavilions takes inspiration from the dome of the Amaravati stūpa model that is displayed at the Amaravati Site Museum. Within the complex stand replicas of Aśokan pillars set in concrete, symbolically reminding the visitor of the connection of the great ancient ruler, Aśoka, not only with Buddhism but also with the Andhra region and Amaravati.

The base of the Buddha statue has been minutely carved to depict representations of the narratives of the Buddha's life and other scenes of worship. The narrative reliefs are replicas of the sculptural panels that once adorned the *mahācaitya*. Originally, they would have belonged to different parts of the stūpa and arranged in a logical scheme according to a plan. Here, though, they are arbitrarily placed to fulfil their decorative function. In fact, in the absence of the original, one of the main aims behind the construction of the Dhyāna Buddha

FIGURE 4.2: THE DHYĀNA BUDDHA STATUE AND BUILDING COMPLEX, AMARAVATI (PHOTO BY SONALI DHINGRA © 2009)

building project, is to 'recreate' the sculpture from the *mahācaitya* to help visitors to get a 'feel of the real magnitude and intricacy of the Amaravathi school of sculpture'.[29]

The Dhyāna Buddha complex was visited by the Dalai Lama during the Kālacakra celebrations in January 2006 and the Buddha statue, though unfinished, was consecrated by him. A deity of the Kālacakras is installed here. Further away from the new building complex and some time during the Kālacakra event, the then Chief Minister of Andhra Pradesh late Y.S. Rajashekhar Reddy, also unveiled a statue of B.R. Ambedkar, the iconic leader of Dalit Buddhists, at a road junction opposite the Amaravati Site Museum.[30] The iconographic programme at the nearby Buddhist site of Nagarjunakonda has a similar flavour. Its newly-constructed landscape combines the iconography of the Buddha, the Buddhist philosopher Nāgārjuna and Ambedkar to symbolically represent the disparate elements in modern Indian Buddhism.[31]

While the exact use of the Dhyāna Buddha complex would only be known after its completion and occupation, the Dalai Lama suggested that the building be used as an international Buddhist learning and interpretation centre. The Tibetan spiritual leader also showed support to the project by donating 300 volumes of Buddhist literature and Rs. 30 lakh as a token of his appreciation.[32] The construction of an exhibition hall, a seminar hall and luxury suites for tourists to stay at the complex is underway. This would contribute towards improving the infrastructure for spiritual tourism at Amaravati. A two-storied museum-complex and a 'sound and light show' is intended to showcase the early history of the 'Andhra Desa' and the history of Buddhism in Andhra Pradesh to visitors.[33] Eighteen acres of land in front of the Dhyāna Buddha statue at Amaravati will be developed into a theme-park where pilgrims and tourists alike can take part in recreational activities.[34] The Dhyāna Buddha complex, even in its incomplete state, draws several visitors every day, many of whom are pilgrim-tourists who visit the famous Amareśvara temple dedicated to Śiva at Amaravati.

The Dhyāna Buddha statue is not the first attempt at the 'reconstruction' of the 'original' state of the ancient Dhānyakaṭaka *mahācaitya.* The ASI created a model of the monumental and highly-ornamental *mahācaitya* to Douglas Barrett's drawing of the Amaravati *mahācaitya* in his publication of 1954. The model stūpa, created sometime in the 1970s, made of concrete, is displayed at the Amaravati Site Museum. Ever since, this small-scale version of the Amaravati *mahācaitya* has become representative of its 'original', glorious past for visitors to the Amaravati Site Museum. This imaginative creation, it appears, is based on the stūpa-slabs from the monument that some scholars identify as representations of the *mahācaitya.* While this claim is debated by art historians, the so-called portraits of the *mahācaitya* are believed to be photographic representations of devotion at the *mahācaitya* in ancient times. This image of the *mahācaitya*-model has travelled far and wide and has gained such popularity that almost any literature on the Amaravati stūpa, whether popular or published by the ASI, displays its photograph. To the visitor, the model *mahācaitya* is certainly more visually appealing than the deserted mound of mud and bricks that remains at the site. The 'fantasy' stūpa is one of the key attractions for visitors to the Amaravati Museum and museum authorities give it pride of place, taking utmost care to safeguard it (Fig. 4.3).

This 'fantasy' stūpa is what may be termed a 'distinct object' that tourists to the site museum at Amaravati 'gaze' upon, and it is this

FIGURE 4.3: MODEL OF THE AMARAVATI *MAHĀCAITYA*, AMARAVATI SITE MUSEUM (PHOTO BY SONALI DHINGRA © 2009)

gaze captured through photographs that has been reproduced, reinforced and disseminated endlessly. Today, it stands for the Amaravati stūpa itself.[35] What effect would the two versions of the Amaravati Stūpa – the former, real and dilapidated and the latter, an idealized form have on a visitor? When looked at together, these contrasting visuals of the *mahācaitya* fill the viewer with awe at the former magnificent state of the stūpa, as represented by its 'model', and at its antiquity, as confirmed by its ruined appearance.

THE LIVING MEMORY OF THE AMARAVATI *MAHĀCAITYA:* TIBETAN LEGENDS AND THE KĀLACAKRA INITIATION, 2006

Even as the Śrī-Dhānyakaṭaka *mahācaitya* lay derelict and 'forgotten', the very spot where it stood was alive in the legends of Tibetan Buddhists, who considered it to be a significant centre of Mahāyāna and Vajrayāna teachings by the Buddha himself. According to one tradition, during a terrible famine, a monk is said to have miraculously caused a rain of rice to fall for twelve days, thus relieving the starving people. The leftover rice was collected and the Heap of Rice (Dhānyakaṭaka) stūpa was constructed out of it.[36] In another more enduring and prevalent Tibetan legend, it is believed that the Śākyamunī taught the Paramādibuddha the original textual redaction of the *Kālacakra Tantra* and other important *tantra* systems, inside the huge and multi-leveled Śrī-Dhānyakaṭaka Stūpa.[37] The legend places this event simultaneously with the Buddha's enlightenment on the full-moon night in the month of Caitra. So Tibetan Buddhists believe that while the Buddha taught the Kālacakra at Dhānyakaṭaka, he dwelt on the Gṛdhrakūṭa (identified to be near Rājgīr) and taught the Bodhisattvas present there the Perfection of Wisdom.

Although several earlier versions of the *Kālacakra Tantra* must have existed, the earliest reference to the Kālacakra system in India dates to the beginning of the eleventh century CE.[38] A few centuries later, the tradition was carried to Tibet where it was studied, preserved and enacted through the centuries.[39] The ritual's history came full circle in 2006 when it was preached near the Dhānyakaṭaka Stūpa and this event, according to Tibetan legends, marked the 2550th anniversary of the Buddha's own preaching of the *Kālacakra Tantra* at the same spot (Fig. 4.4). Toni Huber remarks on the special symbolism of the event: 'Tantric Buddhist history was to be repeated – perhaps for the last time – at Amarāvati, when another manifestation of the Buddha would once again teach the *Kālacakra Tantra* at its exact place of origin; the wheel of time would turn full circle.'[40]

Prior to this, Kālacakra initiations were conducted by the Dalai Lama in India after the exodus of the Tibetan population into India and it is now no more an esoteric Tibetan Buddhist practice. The locations for the staging of this ritual have included major Buddhist archaeological sites.[41] Huber argues that the staging of the Kālacakra ritual at holy places in India associated with the Buddha represents a 'vital symbiosis between Indian interests and Tibetan exile ones'.[42]

Kālacakra events witness a congregation of Tibetans and their supporters from far-flung places that brings about a reinforcement of identity and solidarity for the widely-dispersed Tibetans in exile.

FIGURE 4.4: PILGRIMS AND VISITORS AT THE AMARAVATI *MAHĀCAITYA* SITE DURING KĀLACAKRA 2006 (PHOTOGRAPH COURTESY: TENZING SONAM/WHITE CRANE FILMS)

As Huber argues, 'to consider these events merely in terms of their religious meanings and functions is facile, for they also have a profound social importance and indeed uniqueness for Tibetan refugee society'.[43] The Kālacakra event at Amaravati, too, was not just a religious sermon or ritual but an occasion for the Dalai Lama's meeting with his followers, Tibetan and otherwise.

Catherine Becker describes the ten-day long Kālacakra at Amaravati in detail and argues that during this congregation of Buddhists for the ritual, the ancient *mahācaitya* was 'suffused with new life and meaning', leading to a revitalization of an ancient stūpa.[44] The event certainly helped to publicize the efforts and intentions of the Andhra Pradesh government to make the state an important destination for Buddhists from all over the world. As discussed in the earlier section, a Holy Relic gallery at the Andhra Pradesh State Museum (that now permanently displays the Buddha's relic from Bavikonda) and the Buddha statue that stands in the middle of the Hussain Sagar lake were consecrated by the Dalai Lama.[45] It should be emphasized, however, that the Kālacakra event is but one very recent aspect of the modern history of the *mahācaitya* site at Amaravati. It remains to be seen if a single mega-event can have a lasting impact on the rekindling of interest in any ancient Indian Buddhist site.

VISITORS TO THE *MAHĀCAITYA*: PROFILE AND PURPOSE

Pilgrimage is a religious activity undertaken by followers of all major faiths of the world. For Buddhists, the cluster of holy sites are largely those modern places identified as associated with the life of the Buddha (Lumbini, Bodh Gaya, Sarnath, Kusinagara, Sravasti, Sankissa, Vaishali and Rajgir). The notion of a journey is inbuilt in Buddhist philosophy as life itself is understood as a journey towards enlightenment. Religious travel and tourism for Buddhists, Michael Hall asserts, need to be understood keeping in mind the importance of 'personal experience' for understanding or 'testing' Buddhist teachings.[46] On the significance of spiritual travel in Buddhism, a practising Buddhist said that 'the significance of a pilgrimage is to remind myself of the essential teachings of the Buddha. Visiting places connected with the

Buddha's life focuses my mind on the nature of existence and inspires me to try and practice what he taught'.[47]

Religion and tourism are clearly at a crossroads today as an increase in travel motivated by spiritual reasons has contributed to an upward swing in the tourism industry. India, the homeland of Hinduism and Buddhism, is being promoted in tourist literature as the land of spiritual gain for international tourists.[48] Each Indian state is vying for its share of tourists, and those states with a large number of venerated places and ancient sacred sites are promoting them as holy tourist spots, often as part of pilgrimage-circuits. Places of religious and cultural importance are being commodified and attractively packaged, and sold to both pilgrims and tourists who seek to visit sacred sites.[49] In the midst of pressing governmental concerns for revenue, and the activity of pilgrims and visitors from outside or within the region, archaeological sites – often non-descript markers of sacred spots for religious communities – are subject to change and renewal in recent times.

Tourism campaigns for Andhra Pradesh assertively endorse it as a holy land for Buddhists with a wealth of ancient Buddhist sites dating to as early as the third century BCE. Within the hierarchy of Buddhist sites in the state, prominence is given to Nagarjunakonda where a host of attractions await the tourist, including a 'rare museum on an island, shaped like a vihāra', 'reliquaries', comfortable accommodation and a 'pleasure cruise' to the island. Amaravati is described in tourist literature as 'the most magnificent and widely known', and advertised in grandiose terms as 'the most sacred pilgrim centre of Buddhists in India.' After the Kālacakra event, the state government planned to develop the town into a centre of international Buddhist learning in the attempt to attract a larger volume of tourists to this ancient Buddhist site. However, this idea has not been translated into action so far due to the lack of funds, and the initiator and innovator of this project is trying to collect funds through several novel ways.[50]

The Amaravati *mahācaitya* is regularly visited by an assorted group of Buddhist pilgrims from across the globe. International Buddhists, mostly from Asian countries such as Japan, Korea, Sri Lanka and Taiwan, generally prefer the winter months for conducting their pilgrimage to India. Indian and Tibetan Buddhists also visit the sacred

Amaravati *mahācaitya*. In the absence of a visitors' survey, an accurate idea of the share of the different groups of tourists cannot be ascertained. At an average, more than 11,000 Indians visited the monument each year between 2000 and 2005, and an average of 115 international visitors in the five years before the Kālacakra. What is clear from the visitor records maintained by the ASI is that the Amaravati *mahācaitya* was visited by both domestic and foreign Buddhists even before the 2006 Kālacakra initiation.[51] The number of tourists to the Amaravati *mahācaitya* was not enhanced by any significant degree after that event.[52]

The importance of the Kālacakra in the modern history and revival of the ruined archaeological site of the Dhānyakaṭaka *mahācaitya* must not be over-emphasized. The event received international publicity and was attended by a large number of visitors from all over the world. While a large-scale gathering for worship at the ancient site of Amaravati may be the result of a well-planned, funded and executed event, devout Buddhists had been visiting the site from even before. There is a documented reference to a visit by the Dalai Lama to Amaravati in 1986 and it is difficult to imagine why other pilgrims would not have visited as well.[53] At the same time, pilgrimage to Amaravati is not the preserve of only one section of Buddhists, as the *mahācaitya* is also visited by Dalit Buddhists from Andhra Pradesh and Maharashtra.

The religious history of certain sites (such as Amaravati, Ellora, Varanasi and Bodh Gaya, among many others) with a long period of habitation cuts across the modern divisions of Buddhism, Hinduism and Jainism.[54] Scholarly works seldom highlight the complexity of the larger religious landscape of a particular site. In writings on Amaravati, the Buddhist remains at the ancient Amaravati *mahācaitya* have overshadowed the presence of the living Amareśvara Temple, a significant aspect of the religious history of Amaravati from the ninth-tenth century CE. The *mahācaitya* was under worship till the thirteenth or fourteenth CE, and there is evidence that the two religious centres existed and functioned very close to each other during that period. The religiosity of the *mahācaitya* is recognized even by non-Buddhist devotees, many of whom visit the revered spot to offer their prayers. This points to the special religious significance of the spot where the *mahācaitya* stood from the eighteenth century till today.

It needs to be emphasized that there are different kinds of travellers that visit ancient archaeological sites of sacred importance to Buddhists today. While pilgrims form a part of the tourist flow to places like Amaravati, such ancient Buddhist sites are also visited by a host of others religious and secular. The Amaravati *mahācaitya* is visited by Buddhist devotees from near and far, Hindus who visit the sacred Śaiva *tirtha* of Amareśvara, tourists interested in learning about India's ancient Buddhist past, and local schoolchildren on educational visits to explore their region's history and heritage.

Local perceptions on Andhra Buddhism, in general, and the Amaravati *mahācaitya*, in particular, are also found in school textbooks that describe Buddhism as a significant part of the culture of the region. Large groups of schoolchildren from district schools, well-informed about the importance of the ancient Buddhist *mahācaitya* at Amaravati, visit the site as part of school-sponsored excursions. Last but not the least, Buddhism is also often promoted as a way of life by Buddhist organizations as its teachings are not seen as antithetical to those of other religious traditions, thereby drawing newer adherents to its purely philosophical aspects.

REGIONAL PERCEPTIONS, LOCAL REVIVERS: BUDDHISM AND BUDDHIST ORGANIZATIONS IN ANDHRA

Research on Buddhism in modern times has mainly concentrated on the activities and efforts of Anagarika Dharmapala with his roots in Sri Lanka, founder of the Maha Bodhi Society, to revive Buddhism globally in the late nineteenth and early twentieth centuries. It needs to be stressed that by the medieval period, even as Buddhism declined in India or was pushed to the periphery, a small minority of Buddhists in India survived and maintained their separate ethnic and religious identity. They continue to do so to this day as small organized groups that have attempted to revive both an interest in Buddhism, as well as build a network of Buddhist communities across different Asian countries.

One such community is that of the Baruas, a group of Bengali-speaking Buddhists hailing from Chittagong, Bangladesh. The community migrated to India in the last few centuries, and is now widely dispersed across the subcontinent and the world. The Ananda Buddha Vihara, an organization of Indian origin, was founded by the descendants of members of the Barua community who moved to the Hyderabad area in the nineteenth century to work for the Nizam as well as the British. Today, membership of the Ananda Buddha Vihara is open to all and its local followers consist of an eclectic group. In addition to the dwindling Barua community, its members include Chinese Buddhists settled in Hyderabad, neo-Buddhists (or Dalit Buddhists) from Andhra Pradesh and Maharashtra who aspire for a 'life of dignity', as well as 'intellectual Buddhists' who embrace the spiritual essence of the teachings of the Buddha.[55]

The Ananda Buddha Vihara was established in 1974. Its present complex was built in the 1990s, with a Buddha statue installed in its main hall in 2003 and consecrated by the Dalai Lama.[56] It is a large and sprawling 3-acre complex in a tranquil spot in the otherwise bustling metropolitan city of Hyderabad, the capital of Andhra Pradesh, and is even considered a place of tourist interest, open to those interested in knowing more about Buddhism and the aims of this organization.[57] The Ananda Buddha Vihara appears to have multiple aims but its primary one appears to be, in its own words, to make 'a determined effort' to revive 'interest in the Buddhist tradition and culture in a land that once nourished the dhamma, for a thousand years'.[58] It also functions as a centre for resident and visiting Buddhist monks and nuns who seek to study Buddhism, and even assists them in making pilgrimages to Buddhist sites. The organization also appears to promote 'Buddhist values' among people, presenting Buddhism as a way of life rather than a religion. A calendar of Buddhist events like the Buddha Jayanti and other festivals are celebrated at the vihara and are occasions when the Buddhist community gathers here. Discourses on Buddhism and Indian culture are organized from time to time, and meditation and vipassana classes are also held at the centre.

The architecture of the Ananda Buddha Vihara complex, like all modern Buddhist constructions, is a fusion of different architectural elements. The amalgamation of architectural styles in neo-Buddhist architecture goes back to the viharas built in the early 1900s by the Maha Bodhi Society. With the knowledge of ancient Buddhist architecture at the architect's disposal, picking out of the best features of such architecture across the Indian subcontinent is an interesting feature of new Buddhist construction. Two grand Sanchi-*torana* inspired gates greet the visitor to the Ananda Buddha Vihara complex. The building itself, made of granite and cement, draws on several elements of ancient Buddhist architecture. The entrance to the vihara is in the shape of a *caitya* arch, and is reminiscent of the façades of the rock-cut temples of the Western Ghats. The beautifully-carved wooden doors to the vihara, as the head monk proudly points out, were specially procured from Burma.

A Bodhi tree sapling procured by the head monk from Anuradhapura in Sri Lanka is situated in the lawn outside the vihara. This sacred marker of the Buddha's enlightenment adds sanctity to the premises of the vihara and is a spot used for meditation by monks. Thus, even as innovations in architectural design are made, certain aspects of authenticity and legitimacy in new Buddhist sacred spaces remain the same. The architectural design and iconographic programme at the Ananda Buddha Vihara also carefully and subtly highlight its pan-Asian outlook, as it aspires to weave together different strands of Indian and Asian Buddhists to represent itself as a nodal point for them. A plaster cast of the popularly-worshipped Bodhisattva, Kuan Yin, placed in the amphitheatre of the complex, welcomes East Asian Buddhist pilgrims and perhaps makes them feel at home.

For its sustenance, the vihara is dependent on contributions from individual donors and does not receive aid from any national or international organization, except a small annual grant from the Government of India. The Ananda Buddha Vihara is linked to the largest Buddhist monastic and lay organization in Taiwan, Buddha's Light International Association. The organization publishes a monthly journal in English and has brought out several Telugu books on Buddhism, as well as scholarly compilations of the inscriptions and accounts of the archaeological remains from Buddhist sites in Andhra.[59] The latter is done to highlight the rich material remains of Buddhism that are scattered across more than 150 sites in Andhra Pradesh, these being tangible proof of India's ancient Buddhist heritage.

In the literature produced by the Ananda Buddha Vihara Trust, the accent is on the ancient connection of Buddhism with Andhra, its glorious innings in the area and the profound influence that it has had on the culture of the region that is generally referred to as the 'Telugu country'. The antiquity of Buddhism in the Andhra region is established by the claim that 'Buddhism reached the Telugu country, even when the Enlightened One was still alive'.[60] In the publications of the Ananda Buddha Vihara, a connection is drawn with the Mauryan emperor, Aśoka, as he is considered to be the most ardent propagator of Buddhism. Also described is the region's connection with Buddhist philosophers such as Nāgārjuna, another feature that makes it special for Buddhist pilgrims. Lastly, it has been asserted that the geographical spread of Buddhism to the 'far east including China, Japan and Sri Lanka' took place from the Andhra region. Allusion to the distinguished significance of the Andhra region in the history of Buddhism connects the diverse group of Buddhists under its ambit and also imparts a feeling of pride to new adherents.

The disparity between science and belief is evident here. Even though archaeologists do not consider the human relics found in the Amaravati *mahācaitya* to be those of the Buddha, the Buddhists do. K. Sangharakshita Mahathero, the head monk at the vihara – who also spoke for other international pilgrims who visit India to view relics – was displeased by the fact that Buddhist relics are generally kept in the strong-rooms of museums and that getting permission from the ASI to view them is a cumbersome process. The monk also informed me that he had been closely associated with the excavations carried out by the ASI at Bavikonda. The relics found there were housed for a few days in the temple of the Ananda Buddha Vihara but were then taken away to the Holy Relic Gallery in the Andhra Pradesh State Museum.

It is not difficult to notice the significance that the Amaravati stūpa has for the Buddhist community at the Ananda Buddha Vihara. The very logo of the organization derives from the imaginative construction of the Amaravati Stūpa – here modified slightly so that the revered stūpa emerges out of a lotus. The brochure of the organization has a picture of the model-stūpa at Amaravati, and there are plans to build a meditation hall styled on the dome and architecture of the ancient *mahācaitya* itself. Clearly, the symbolic value of the Amaravati *mahācaitya,* one of the largest Buddhist monuments ever to be built, is still very great for Buddhists.

CONCLUSION

This paper aimed to situate the archaeological site of Amaravati in the midst of the developments related to the revitalization of Buddhism in the twentieth and twenty-first centuries. While there has been an expansion in the popularity and patronage of Buddhist sites in the nineteenth and twentieth centuries, this has not occurred in equal measure at all ancient Indian archaeological sites with any vestige of Buddhism, as the hierarchy in Buddhist sites has been influenced, to a large extent, by scholarly discourse.

Despite the varying degrees of revival at different Buddhist sites, it is apparent that in view of the expanding spiritual-tourism industry, governmental authorities recognize the need for enhancing infrastructural facilities at Buddhist archaeological-cum-spiritual tourism sites, as Buddhists form a significant portion of the Asian population. In the last two decades, concerted attempts towards the revitalization of ancient holy Buddhist sites have been made by the central and state governments, especially during special years commemorating events from the life of the Buddha. A vital aspect of this revival is linked to the relics of the Buddha that have been unearthed from several locations across India. In the context of the travel of Asian Buddhists to Indian Buddhist sites, the issue of ownership, display and movement of relics is a crucial one. There has been concern over the proper and regular maintenance and exhibition of Buddhist relics found in India since the 1980s.[61] The sharing of India's rich Buddhist heritage with other Asian countries is now also a significant part of diplomatic dialogue and cultural relations.[62]

However, the process of revitalization of Buddhism is not a 'revival', in the true sense of the word, as the forms of Buddhism that exist today differ from its ancient forms in a considerable way. The development of new Buddhist religious architecture, aided by both state governments and foreign agencies, is clearly noticeable across archaeological sites in the country. As there is greater scope for the exercise of the imagination and no obligation to follow Buddhist architectural or iconographic conventions, modern Buddhist imagery and architecture is almost always a reinvention of ancient forms of building. The modern architecture at Amaravati and other places reflects this characteristic. While tangible remains of the *mahācaitya* at the site itself are scanty, it has been revivified in public memory through the construction of new popular imagery and literature. A general feature of new Buddhist architecture is that it is a blend of several features of Indian and Asian Buddhist art and architecture, so that it appeals to the widely dissimilar and heterogeneous group of Indian and international Buddhists.

Some sites, such as Amaravati, owing to their modern histories of rediscovery and archaeological excavations, are today mere physical markers that commemorate the presence of Buddhism at the spot. Far from being an desolate archaeological site, the *mahācaitya* was recently visited by a large number of pilgrims who had gathered at Amaravati to attend the Kālacakra ritual performed by the Dalai Lama, the spiritual leader of Tibetan Buddhists. While this event is significant in the *mahācaitya's* modern history, it would be erroneous to believe that it somehow magically transformed an extinct archaeological site into a living entity teeming with pilgrim activity in the long-term. Pilgrimage to Amaravati has been a sustained activity for several years and its sanctity is recognized even by Hindus who visit the Amareśvara Temple dedicated to Śiva, located close to the ancient *mahācaitya* site. Possibly, the overlap in visitors to the Amaravati *mahācaitya* and the Amareśvara Temple goes back to ancient and medieval times. It also needs to be stressed that visitor activity at the *mahācaitya* site and, in fact, at several other ancient sites is not confined to those with spiritual interests. With heritage and culture being sold as a commodity, archaeological sites, the repositories of tangible remains of Indian history, are also visited by enthusiastic travellers with non-religious interests.

In view of the flow of ideas beyond India, some Buddhist organizations, such as the Ananda Buddha Vihara, have become points of intersection for interactions between domestic Buddhists and Buddhists from Asian countries. This revivalist organization consciously seeks to provide cohesion to members of the Buddhist community who identify with its aims and objectives. At the end of the day, the revival of Buddhism in India is dependent on modern-day patrons – the central and state governments and foreign investment in Buddhist sites. The funding of projects and the development of infrastructural facilities are dependent upon the will and whims of policy-makers, and these are not constant. The revitalization of ancient Buddhist sites to put them in touch with modern Buddhist devotees is clearly an ongoing process.

ABBREVIATIONS

EI : *Epigraphia Indica*
ARASI : *Annual Report of the Archaeological Survey of India*
NAI : National Archives of India

NOTES

1. See Trevithick (1999), Lahiri (2004), and Singh (2004) for more on this subject.
2. Tartakov (1991), Kim (2009), Becker (2009) and Singh (2010) have worked on this theme in recent times.
3. Singh (2004) discusses the rediscovery of the Amaravati stūpa and the steady dismemberment and dispersal of almost all of its architectural parts by the end of the nineteenth century.
4. Within the database of 210 donative inscriptions from Amaravati, thirty-six donors identify themselves as belonging to a geographical place and of these, four belonged to Amaravati.

   A famous inscription from Gaḍalādeṇiya that has been identified as the last datable record of the history of the Dhānyakaṭaka *mahācaitya* records the meritorious deeds of the great *sthāvira* Dharmakīrtti, one of the seniormost monks of the Buddhist church in Ceylon in the fourteenth century at Amaravati (see Paranavitana, 1933).
5. For a critique of the scholarly focus on a fixed and singular tradition of Buddhist pilgrimage, see Huber (2008).
6. See Hall (2006) for a discussion on a hierarchy within spiritual-tourism sites.
7. Fergusson (1867): 146.
8. Burgess (1887): 20.
9. See Burgess (1887): 21.
10. Percy Brown (1940) was the first to make a conjectural reconstruction of the monument. See plate xxxv, between pp. 48-9 'Conjectural Restoration of the Amaravati Stūpa'.

11. For more on photography of Indian archaeological sites see Tapati Guha-Thakurta (2010).
12. See archaeological reports of Alexander Rea's excavations in the Krishna valley (Rea 1888-9 and 1908-9).
13. *The Maha-bodhi and the United Buddhist World* 6 (1909):126
14. *The Mahabodhi and the Ancient Buddhist World* 7 (1909).
15. 'Relic given by Government of India to Maha-bodhi Society' *Maha-bodhi Society* 28 (1919): 244 and 'The Bhattiprolu Relic at Shri Dharma Rajika Vihara in Calcutta' *Maha-bodhi Society* 28 (1919): 257-8.
16. *The Maha-bodhi and the United Buddhist World* 30 (1922): 206.
17. For more: see Huber (2008): 267.
18. See Dehejia (1969).
19. See *IAR* (1958-59): 4-5.
20. Note by A. Ghosh, Director-General ASI entitled 'Conservation Note on the monuments at Amaravati, District Guntur, by DGA', April 1962. Document no. 3/AP/1/62-M/1962. Monuments Branch, ASI Archives, NAI.
21. Note entitled 'Providing spot lighting facilities in Museum building at Amaravati'. Document no. 4/6/SE/2/70-Monuments, Monuments Branch, ASI Archives. NAI.
22. Note entitled 'Special repairs carried out to the stupa at Amaravati', Document no. 4/2/SE.7/70-Monuments. ASI Archives, Monuments Branch. NAI.
23. http//www.hindu.com/2006/01/18/stories/2006011813110500.htm retrieved on 10.2.2010.The news report further says that the request to make the changes to the stūpa was made by the organizers of the event.
24. This information was given to me in a personal interview with D. Kanna Babu, then Assistant Superintending Archaeologist, Archaeological Survey of India, Hyderabad Circle on 9 August 2011.
25. Since its discovery, a total of ten relic-caskets have been found from the four *āyaka* platforms of the stūpa at Amaravati. For more see Subrahmanyam (1999).
26. http://www.hindu.com/2010/02/11/stories/2010021157690100.htm, retrieved on 10 February 2010.
27. 'The Maitreya Project is being developed by the Foundation for the Preservation of Mahayana Tradition, founded in 1975 by Lama Thubten Yeshe and now led by Lama Zopa Rinpoche – a well funded organization. The budget for this project is $390 million. The plan includes a park dotted with ten thousand *stūpas*, schools, a teaching hospital, and eventually, a university. The "heart shrine" of this building is to house a rare collection of relics, most notably the blood-relic of the Buddha himself, donated by

the Meitktia Relic Museum, Myanmar' (see Singh and Mathur 2007: 151). Also, see www.maitreyaproject.org.

28. This Rs. 1.7 crore project was conceptualized by the then Guntur Deputy Director of Social Welfare, Mallikarjuna Rao.
29. Information taken from, http,//www.hindu.com/2007/05/02/stories/2007050211270400.htm, retrieved on 10 February 2010.
30. This information was reported in http//www.business-standard.com/india/news/amaravati-to-be-made-intl-buddhist-learning-centre/226130/htm
31. For more see Singh (2010): 16-22.
32. From http,//www.tibet.net/en/index.php?id=1293&articletype=flashold&rmenuid=morenews&tab=1.
33. The two-storeyed museum complex, built at a cost of Rs. 4 crore, is part of the Rs. 20-crore Lower Krishna Valley Buddhist Circuit. It will have exhibits on the early history of Andhra Desa, the history of Buddhism in Andhra Pradesh, the changing phases of Buddhism and other relevant topics. It would also house a theatre for a Sound and Light show, which was to be commissioned later. Information published in *The Hindu*, see http://www.hindu.com/2006/01/10/stories/2006011004690500.html, retrieved on 10 February 2010.
34. 'We have decided to finish the pending works on the monolithic statue', confirmed the UDA vice-chairman Vijayakumar. He said a theme park would be developed in front of the statue for which UDA has requested the district administration to allocate an 18-acre land. Information from http://articles.timesofindia.indiatimes.com/2011-03-25/india/29187975_1_tallest-buddha-statue-guntur-uda, retrieved on 10 February 2010.
35. For more on the 'tourist gaze', see Urry (2002).
36. kLong rdol (1765): 47, contained in Lokesh Chandra (1973) cited in Newman (1985): 83 fn.3.
37. See Hopkins (1985): 59.
38. For more see Newman (1985): 65.
39. There is a large corpus of Tibetan sources as well as scholarly material on the Kālacakra rite. This practice, it seems, was confined to the cultural region of Tibet, including parts of Nepal, Bhutan, Mongolia and Siberia. It has not reached China, Korea, Japan or Southeast Asia (Hopkins 1985: 64). This makes the Kālacakra a tantric rite especially associated with Tibetan Buddhists.
40. For more, refer to Huber (2008): 374.
41. In fact, the Kālacakra has been performed very frequently almost every other year in the past two decades or so, at important Buddhist sites (Bodh Gaya, Sarnath) and places with considerable Buddhist population (Kalpa, Spiti and Tabo in Himachal Pradesh and Gangtok in Sikkim, among others) in

India, as well as several places abroad (Toronto, Canada, Graz, Austria, Sydney, Australia, Ulanbator, Mongolia and recently at Chicago) ostensibly, with a view to promote world peace.

42. From Huber (2008): 373-4.
43. See Huber (2008): 372.
44. Refer to Becker (2009).
45. http://www.dalailama.com/news/post/9-hh-the-dalai-lama-to-address-the-inauguration-of-holy-relic-gallery, retrieved on 10 February 2010.
46. See Hall (2006): 173.
47. Tenzing Sonam, personal interview, 23 August 2011.
48. Newspaper reports reveal the efforts of the state government towards developing Amaravati and other places as spiritual tourism destinations. See http://www.business-standard.com/india/news/amaravati-to-be-made-intl-buddhist-learning-centre/226130/ and also http://www.blonnet.com/2006/01/06/stories/2006010601631900.htm, retrieved on 10 February 2010.
49. Reports such as this one clearly point to the aspirations of the Andhra Pradesh state government of developing Amaravati and other places as spiritual tourism destinations. See http://www.business-standard.com/india/news/amaravati-to-be-made-intl-buddhist-learning-centre/226130/ and also http://www.blonnet.com/2006/01/06/stories/2006010601631900.htm, retrieved on 10 February 2010.
50. http://www.thehindu.com/news/cities/Visakhapatnam/article2153570.ece
51. These numbers exclude children below the age of fifteen and the exact composition of the group is not available to us.
52. I am thankful to the Hyderabad Circle of the ASI for providing the visitor statistics for Amaravati and Nagarjunakonda.
53. Information taken from, http://www.dalailama.com/biography/travels/1980 – 1989, retrieved on 11 August 2011.
54. A visitors' survey conducted in 2009 by Yaaminey Mubayi and her team in Ellora (as part of the preparation of the Ellora Site Management plan by CRCI commissioned by ASI) highlights the multi-religious significance of the site. As results of this survey show, visitors to the site belong to a variety of groups, and come here for both religious and non-religious reasons.
55. This information is contained in the brochure published by the Ananda Buddha Vihara that I obtained from the monastery on my visit. This booklet gives the details of the monastery's history and aims.
56. I got this information in a personal interview with Venerable K. Sangharakshita Mahathero, head monk of the Ananda Buddha Vihara in August 2011.
57. On my visit to the complex in August 2011, groups of curious young people could be seen exploring the place and inquiring about its purpose.

Publications on Buddhism and images of the Buddha kept in the main hall are provided free of cost to visitors who want to take back a few publications as a reminder of their visit to the vihara.

58. These claims about the monastery's purported aims are made in the brochures that are produced by the Ananda Buddha Vihara. See especially pp. 3-5 of the brochure on the monastic complex for quotes given in the paragraph.
59. A journal *Suhrullekha*, currently discontinued, was being published by the Ananda Buddha Vihara. It contained a series of articles, both spiritual and scholarly. Other publications that were available free-of-cost at the vihara include those on Buddhism and Buddhist thought. These also included several books for children which were published by the sister concern of the vihara, the International Buddha's Light Association. The Ananda Buddha Vihara has also published two books on the archaeology of Buddhism in Andhra Pradesh. See the bibliography for complete references.
60. See the brochure of the Ananda Buddha Vihara, p. 5.
61. As early as 1984, a Task Force was set up by the Union Ministry of Tourism to identify sites at Piprahwa, Vaishali and Amaravati for constructing stūpas to house the relics of the Buddha. See, 'Parliamentary question on relics', Unstarred question no. 5359, Lok Sabha, 2003. http://164.100.24.208/lsq/quest.asp?qref=60641, accessed on 12 October 2011.
62. For example, the Kapilavastu relics of the Buddha travelled out of India to Sri Lanka in January 2012 to begin a process of symbiotic relationship based on enhanced tourism for India and better infrastructural facilities for Sri Lankan pilgrims travelling to Indian Buddhist sites. See http://www.thehindu.com/arts/history-and-culture/article2441897.ece, retrieved on 9 September 2011.

BIBLIOGRAPHY

Primary Sources

Paranavitana, S. 1934. 'Gaḍalādeṇiya Rock-inscription of Dharmmakīrttī Sthavira', *Epigraphica Zeylanica*, 4: 90-110.

Rea, Alexander. 1905-6. 'Excavations at Amaravati', *ARASI*. Calcutta: Office of the Superintendent Government Printing, India: 116-19.

———. 1908-9. 'Excavations at Amaravati', *ARASI*. Delhi: Swati Publications.

Sircar, Dinesh C. 1963-4. 'Fragmentary Pillar Inscription from Amaravati', *EI*, 35: 40-3.

Sivaramamurti, C. [1942] 1998. *Amaravati Sculptures in the Chennai Government Museum*. Chennai: Bulletin of the Chennai Government Museum.

Secondary Sources

Almond, Philip. 1988. *The British Discovery of Buddhism*. Cambridge: Cambridge University Press.

Arya, Samarendra Narayan. 2004. *History of Pilgrimage in Ancient India AD 300-1200*. New Delhi: Munshiram Manoharlal.

Beal, Samuel. 2001 [1914]. *The Life of Hiuen Tsiang*. New Delhi: Gian Publishing House.

Becker, Catherine. 2009. 'Remembering the Amaravati Stūpa: The Revival of a Ruin', in Jason Hawkes and Akira Shimada (eds.), *Buddhist Stūpas in South Asia*. New Delhi: Oxford University Press.

Bharati, Agehananda. 1963. 'Pilgrimage in the Indian Tradition', *History of Religions*. 3(1): 135-67.

Brown, Percy. 1940. *Indian Architecture: Buddhist and Hindu Periods*. 7th rpt. in 1976. Bombay: Taraporevala and Sons.

Burgess, James. 1882. *Notes on the Amaravati Stupa*, Madras: Archaeological Survey of Southern India; rpt. 1972. Varanasi: Indological Book House.

———. 1887. *The Buddhist Stūpas of Amaravati and Jaggayapeta*. London: Trübner; rpt. 1996. New Delhi: Archaeological Survey of India.

Chattopadhyay, Debiprasad, ed. 1970. *Tāranātha's History of Buddhism in India*. Simla: Indian Institute of Advanced Study.

Fergusson, James. 1873. *Tree and Serpent Worship, or Illustrations of Mythology and Art in India in the First and Fourth Centuries after Christ from the Sculptures of the Buddhist Topes at Sanchi and Amaravati*. London: India Museum.

———. 1867. 'Description of the Amaravati Tope in Guntur', *JRAS*, N.S., (3): 132-66.

Ghosh, A. 1979. 'The Early Phase of the Stūpa at Amaravati, South East India', *Ancient Ceylon*, 3: 97-103.

Guha-Thakurta, Tapati. 2010. 'The Many Lives of the Sanchi Stupa in Colonial India', in Sudeshna Guha (ed.), *The Marshall Albums: Photography and Archaeology*. New Delhi: The Alkazi Foundation and Mapin.

———. 2004. *Monuments, Objects, Histories, Institutions of Art in Colonial and Postcolonial India*. New York: Columbia University Press.

Hall, Michael C. 2006. 'Buddhism, Tourism and the Middle Way', in D.J. Timothy and Daniel Olsen (eds.), *Tourism, Religion and Spiritual Journeys*. New York: Routledge.

Hopkins, Jeffrey. 1999. *The Kālachakra Tantra: Rite of Initiation for the Stage of Generation*. London: Wisdom Publications.

Huber, Toni. 2008. *The Holy Land Reborn: Pilgrimage and the Tibetan Reinvention of Buddhist India*. Chicago and London: University of Chicago Press.

Kim, Jinah. 2009. 'What Makes a Stūpa? Quotations, Fragments and the

Reinvention of Buddhist Stūpas in Contemporary India', in Jason Hawkes and Akira Shimada (eds.), *Buddhist Stūpas in South Asia*. New Delhi: Oxford University Press.

Knox, Robert. 1992. *Amarāvatī: Buddhist Sculpture from the Great Stūpa*. London: British Museum Press.

Kumari, M. Krishna. 1989. *Pañchārāmas in Medieval Andhradesa*. Delhi: Agam Kala Prakashan.

Lahiri, Nayanjot. 2004. 'Sanchi, Destruction, Restoration and Restitution', in H.P. Ray and Carla Sinopoli (eds.), *Archaeology as History in Early South Asia*. New Delhi: ICHR.

Ling, Trevor. 1980. *Buddhist Revival in India: Aspects of the Sociology of Buddhism*. London and Basingstoke: Macmillan.

Newman John, et al. 1985. *The Wheel of Time: The Kalachakra in Context*. Madison: Deer Park Books.

Omvedt, Gail. 2003. *Buddhism in India: Challenging Brahmanism and Caste*. New Delhi: Sage.

Pratt, James Bissett. 1993 [1928]. *The Pilgrimage of Buddhism and a Buddhist Pilgrimage*, vols. 1 & 2. Gurgaon: Vintage Books.

Sarkar, H. and S.P. Naihar. 1972. *Amarāvatī*. New Delhi: Archaeological Survey of India.

Sarkar, H. [1966] 1993. *Studies in Early Buddhist Architecture of India*. New Delhi: Munshiram Manoharlal.

———. 1974. 'Some More Inscriptions from Amaravati Excavations and the Chronology of the *Mahāstūpa*', *Studies in Indian Epigraphy*, vol. 1.

Singh, Upinder. Forthcoming. 'Buddhism in the "City of Victory": Integrating Archaeology, Epigraphy, Art-history and History', to be published in the volume emerging from the conference on 'Buddhism Across Asia: Networks of Material, Intellectual and Cultural Exchange', 16-18 February 2009, Institute of Southeast Asian Studies, Singapore.

———. 2010. 'Exile and Return: The Reinvention of Buddhism and Buddhist Sites in Modern India', *South Asian Studies* 26, 2: 193-217.

———. 2004. *The Discovery of Ancient India: Early Archaeologists and the Beginnings of Archaeology*. New Delhi: Permanent Black.

Singh, Kavita and Saloni Mathur. 2007. 'Reincarnations of the Museum: The Museum in an Age of Religious Revivalism', in Vishakha Desai (ed.), *Asian Art History in the 21st Century*. New Haven: Yale University Press, pp. 149-68.

Subrahmanyam, B. 1999. *Buddhist Relic Caskets in Andhradesa*. Hyderabad: Ananda Buddha Vihara Trust.

Tartakov, Gary Michael. 1990. 'Art and Identity: The Rise of a New Buddhist Imagery', *Art Journal*, 49(4).

Trevithick, Alan. 1999. 'British Archaeologists, Hindu Abbots and Burmese

Buddhists, the Mahābodhi Temple at Bodh Gaya, 1811-1877', *Modern Asian Studies*, 33, 3: 635-56.

Urry, John. 2002. *The Tourist Gaze*. London: Sage.

Vaidehi, A. Srimathi. 1956. 'Temples in Medieval Andhra', *Journal of Andhra Historical Society*, 24.

Verghese, Anila. 1995. *Religious Traditions at Vijayanagara as Revealed through its Monuments*. New Delhi: Manohar.

Willis, Michael. 2009. 'Relics of the Buddha: Body, Essence, Text', in Jason Hawkes and Akira Shimada (eds.), *Buddhist Stūpas in South Asia*. New Delhi: Oxford University Press.

CHAPTER 5

Relics, Ruins and Temple-building

Archaeological Heritage and the Construction of the Dharmarajika Vihara, Calcutta

SRAMAN MUKHERJEE

IN 1892, ALEXANDER REA, during his excavations at the Buddhist site of Bhattiprolu (in the Kistna district of the erstwhile Madras Presidency), discovered a small piece of bone encased in a rock-crystal casket. The Brahmi inscriptions on the casket attested the identity of the corporeal remain as a '. . . well authenticated relic of the Buddha' himself.[1] For purposes of safe-keeping, this relic was soon carted away from the site to be housed in the Government Central Museum in the city of Madras. On 30 June 1916, the Government of India proposed to present the Bhattiprolu relic along with a cache of Buddhist relics unearthed by the Archaeological Survey of India (henceforth, ASI) from sites in and around Taxila (in the Rawalpindi district of Punjab), to two Buddhist associations – the Maha Bodhi Society and the Bengal Buddhist Association. The government offer came with the condition that both these societies had to guarantee that the relics would be enshrined in worthy viharas and adequately safeguarded, and that the shrines had to be constructed before the relics were distributed by the government.[2] Above all, these new Buddhist temples had to meet the approval of the ASI to be certified as worthy repositories of these ancient relics.

In the years that followed, the Maha Bodhi Society constructed the first new Buddhist temple of colonial India, the Dharmarajika Vihara, in the city of Calcutta. During its opening ceremony in 1921, the Government of India, through Lord Ronaldshay, the then Governor of Bengal, presented the Bhattiprolu relic to the Society for enshrinement in the new temple. Taking the opening of the Dharmarajika Vihara as an entry point, this essay will move back in time to explore the politics at work in the construction of the first new Buddhist vihara in colonial India. The key players involved in the building of this new shrine were the ASI and the Maha Bodhi Society. The Calcutta vihara, and other subsequent temples built by the Society at Sarnath and Sanchi during the 1930s and 1950s, embodied the complex co-configurations of the secularization of archaeological heritage and the politics of Buddhist religious revival. The negotiations between these two were mediated through the interplay between two distinct and often overlapping objects and categories – the relic and the ruin.

At the most fundamental level, relic (origin, Latin word *reliquae*) '. . . is a material object that relates to a particular individual and/or to events and places with which that individual was associated'. Usually, it is the body or fragment of the body of a deceased person revered as holy.[3] Alongside corporeal relics are non-corporeal items that were possessed by, or came into direct contact with, the individual in question.[4] Durability, resistance to decay, transportability and mobility are frequently taken to be the defining features of a relic. While uniqueness is often regarded as a crucial attribute of relics, critical scholarship has demonstrated that throughout history, relics have been subjected to practices of 'forgery', 'fabrication' and 'reproduction', which do not necessarily diminish their hallowed status in the eyes of the community of believers. The word 'ruin' (origin, Latin *ruina*), in turn, simply means a dramatic structural collapse or decline, as in the remains of a building or structure that has suffered much visible damage.[5] Thus, while both relic and ruin broadly imply a certain physicality in the sense of remnants and remains, 'relic' carries something of a bodily implication, while 'ruin' carries with it a sense of physicality which has nothing essentially bodily about it. Again, and more importantly for our present purposes, while 'relic' carries a sacral if not religious connotation, the word 'ruin' does not necessarily involve something which can be marked either as sacred or religious.

Material remains per se, thus, have no intrinsic status as relics. As Alexandra Walsham put it, 'The former become the latter as a consequence of the beliefs and practices that accumulate around them. . . . The symbolic and semiotic value of such objects is a reflection of the subjectivity of the society that honours and prizes them.'[6] However, unlike other material objects (images, icons, etc.), a relic requires a frame in space and time that explicitly signals its status as a sacred object. As we shall see in the course of this essay, a relic without its reliquary/casket loses its identity as a hallowed object. But like most other objects and categories, the plethora of meanings ascribed to either relics or ruins were, and never are, static. The lines separating them are extremely nebulous, the distinctions between and blurring of their meanings often produced out of divergent social and political networks, and different historically contingent circumstances under which these objects come to be invoked.

Looking at the networks of communication between the officials of archaeology and museums, and the representatives of the newly-[re]formed associations and communities of the Buddhists, I will explore how Buddhist corporeal relics and structural ruins came to be simultaneously secularized and sacralized in colonial South Asia. In other words, the essay will explore how the interplay between relics and ruins was integral to the tortuous negotiations between, and the fraught passages from the spaces of the archaeologically-conserved sites and the galleries of museums to the sanctums of newly-constructed practising Buddhist temples. Drawing on the methodological insights provided by the 'cultural biographies' and 'social lives' of material objects;[7] recent religious studies, historical and art-historical explorations of particular historical and political processes at work in the production of 'value' in relation to material culture in modern South Asia;[8] and critical Buddhological scholarship on the political implications of the study of Buddhism under colonialism,[9] this essay examines how the political, economic and social dimensions of the identification, discovery, preservation, fabrication and circulation of Buddhist relics were instrumental in the production of memory, history and heritage within Britain's colonial empire in South Asia. To explore the contending claims of secularization and sacralization at work around ancient Buddhist corporeal relics and modern Buddhist viharas, let us begin by trying to unpack some of the historically specific connotations of Buddhist 'relics' in colonial South Asia.

INTERROGATING BUDDHIST RELICS: EVALUATION EXERCISES IN THE COLONY

The earliest traceable Buddhist corporeal relic in colonial India was unearthed at Sarnath in north India at the close of the eighteenth century. In 1793-4, Baboo Jagat Singh, the Dewan of Raja Chait Singh of Benares, started excavating the ruins of Sarnath for obtaining bricks, stones and other building materials for the construction of a marketplace in the neighbouring city of Benares to be named after him as Jagat Gunj. In the course of the excavations, Jagat Singh's workmen dismantled a large brick stupa in the immediate vicinity of the great tower locally known as Dhamekh (Fig. 5.1). In January 1794, the workmen found '. . . two vessels of stone and marble, one inside the other'.[10] The inner vessel contained a few human bones, some decayed pearls, gold leaves and other jewels.[11] The bones in the inner casket were thrown into the Ganges, the outer stone urn retained

FIGURE 5.1: WATER-COLOUR DRAWING BY 'ABDULLAH SHAIKH OF THE STUPA AT SARNATH DATED JANUARY 1814. INSCRIBED ON FRONT IN INK: 'THE SAMAUDH OF RAJAH BOOTH-SAIN AT SARA-NAAT NEAR BENARES, JANUARY 1814. COPIED BY SHEIK ABDULLA. APRIL 1819 (COURTESY: BRITISH LIBRARY, ONLINE IMAGE GALLERY)

and covered up by earth *in situ*, and the inner urn of green marble with the precious stones and jewels was presented to the Commissioner of Benares, Jonathan Duncan. In 1798, Duncan presented this casket to the Asiatic Society of Bengal. Thus, the earliest exposure of Buddhist corporeal relics in colonial India was marked by a narrative of 'native vandalism' of ancient ruins and the untraceable destruction of an ancient relic.

Subsequent excavations at Sarnath failed to yield any Buddhist relics. However, other sites in colonial India did. By the middle of the nineteenth century, hunting for Buddhist corporeal relics had become a most engaging pastime of amateur antiquarians and early archaeologists. In the early 1850s, Alexander Cunningham and F.C. Maisey had ferreted out several Buddhist funerary caskets with charred pieces of bones, etc., from Sanchi and the neighbouring sites of Sonari and Satdhara, in the territory of the Begum of Bhopal, which eventually found their way into the great metropolitan museums of Britain, the British Museum and the India House Museum, later renamed the Victoria and Albert Museum.[12] As late as the 1890s, Buddhist corporeal relics continued to travel from archaeological sites to museums in India and Britain.

Thus, there was nothing in principle in the early colonial archaeological discourse which could prevent a corporeal relic from being treated as an unsuitable object of specialized scholarly analysis, scientific preservation and public display. However, at the turn of the twentieth century, as further Buddhist relics were discovered by the Archaeological Department in the neighbourhood of Taxila, the ASI allowed and encouraged the government to present these relics to Buddhist associations so as to be 'returned' to their sacral meaning and usage. While accounting for this change of attitude, we need to explore whether practising Buddhist communities or specialist scholars maintained any stable distinction between relics as essentially sacred objects and ruins as devoid of any particular sacrality or religious connotations, which would render the latter eminently suitable for archaeological analysis and museumization. The religious sacrality of relics and the historical sanctity of the ruins did not remain fixed and permanently coded over time. The plethora of meanings and associations woven around these objects unfolded across deeply overlapping, constantly shifting and often mutually exchangeable registers. As the following section will try to show, three distinct trajectories unfolding over the closing years of the nineteenth and the opening years of the twentieth century shaped this official stance regarding Buddhist relics.

TRANSNATIONAL BUDDHIST REVIVAL, THE MAHA BODHI SOCIETY AND THE POLITICS OF RECLAMATION

The first course which shaped the colonial archaeological department's disposition towards Buddhist corporeal relics by the turn of the twentieth century was the consolidation of a transnational Buddhist revivalist movement spearheaded by the Maha Bodhi Society and led by the Sinhalese Buddhist monk, Anagarika Dharmapala. Founded in Colombo in 1891 with the noted Sinhalese Buddhist High Priest, Hikkaduwe Sri Sumangala Mahanayaka Thero, as the first President, the renowned Theosophist, Colonel Henry Steele Olcott, as the Director-General, and Dharmapala as its first General Secretary, the Society started off with a programme of reforming Theravada Buddhism as it was practised in Ceylon and in other practising Buddhist territories of the colony, namely Burma. Without going into the detailed institutional history of the Maha Bodhi Society, it may be useful to briefly outline the larger political and cultural context within which transnational neo-Buddhist associations like the Society could emerge and claim the position of sole spokesman for the Theravada Buddhists of Asia, specifically of colonial South Asia.[13]

The formation of the Maha Bodhi Society in the late nineteenth century has been usually situated within the larger politics of the consolidation of a Buddhist religious reformation and revivalist movement in Ceylon and Burma, especially in the major urban cities of Colombo and Rangoon. The reform and revival of Buddhism in colonial Ceylon initially developed as an early response to the aggressive proselytizing by Christian missionaries, the implicit complacency of the colonial state with this Anglican zeal, and the consequent failure of the state to safeguard the institutions and interests of the Buddhists. The consequent emergence of a reformed or 'Protestant Buddhism' in late nineteenth-century Ceylon was intrinsically linked to the imperial network of print capitalism, transport networks of steamships and railways, larger international networks of neo-Buddhist associations, the spread of Western education and the development of English as a common *lingua franca* of the Empire, the rise of a Western-educated class of native elites, and a complex fashioning of nationalist consciousness.[14] The resurrection of a reformed and authentic Buddhist tradition in response to the Christian propaganda offensive in Colombo saw the growth of Buddhist reformist associations, secondary schools and colleges, printing presses and newspapers. These associations used the new media of print, public oratory and public debates to counter the Christian missionary 'offensive' in print and public lectures. It is in this context that the noted Theosophist, Colonel Olcott, in the company of the renowned occult practitioner, Madame Helena Petrovna Blavatsky, arrived on the island. Their propaganda tour during the 1880s marked the beginnings of direct Theosophist involvement in the politics of Buddhist revival, culminating in the formation of the Buddhist Theosophical Society in Colombo in 1880.[15]

The critical editing, translation and publication of pre-colonial Pali manuscripts by noted scholar-administrators like T.W. Rhys Davids and his Pali Text Society also had a great impact on the variant of reformed Buddhism propagated by Colombo's Buddhist associations. The editing and translations of the classical Pali canon *Mahavamsa* or the 'Great Chronicle of Ceylon' assumed a special significance. Initially translated by the civil servant and orientalist scholar George Turnour in 1837, extended revised versions and translations of the manuscript into English and Sinhalese recounted the political and cultural glories of an ancient Sinhala nation, and were designed to foster an emergent national consciousness. As Buddhist reformism in Colombo increasingly came to reflect the concerns of the capital's Buddhist elite lay population, these associations emerged as enclaves of cultural nationalism, which came to be increasingly couched in the language of internationalism. Thus, the Buddhist revival, which had initially taken off as a resistance to certain cultural politics of the colonial state, also emerged as a buttress to it. It is precisely in this context that Anagarika Dharmapala and the Maha Bodhi Society emerged as a prominent neo-Buddhist voice, first in Colombo and then in other cities of the British Empire.[16]

Usually portrayed as the founding and most celebrated figure of Sinhalese nationalism, Dharmapala was born into a family of wealthy Sinhalese merchants with strong connections to the lay branch of the Buddhist Theosophical Society. Receiving a strong Christian education at school, while remaining a practising Buddhist at home, Dharmapala worked as a clerk in the Education Department of the colonial government. Following Colonel Olcott's and Madame Blavatsky's visit to Ceylon in 1880, he became actively involved with the Theosophical Society, an association that would continue for the next twenty years.[17] This Theosophist connection proved to be crucial in fashioning Dharmapala as a public reformer and the consolidation of the Maha Bodhi movement. It was Dharmapala's early exposure to the transnational Theosophist network and financiers which provided the initial organizational and financial support for the Maha Bodhi Society.

Soon after its establishment in Colombo in 1891, and drawing on the network of transnational connections provided by the Theosophists and the emerging community of readership for printed newspapers and Buddhist periodicals, the offices of the Maha Bodhi Society were set up in Calcutta, Madras, Rangoon and other cities of the British Empire. Resembling other Buddhist societies and associations of Colombo, Dharmapala's Maha Bodhi Society sought to promote a brand of reformist Buddhism, which aimed to be more 'scientific' and 'rational' than Christianity could ever aspire to be.[18] Like other Buddhist organizations, it sought to create a new Buddhist order, halfway between the status of a monk and layman.[19] His occasional strident and militant pronouncements on behalf of the Sinhalese Buddhists against the colonial state notwithstanding, Dharmapala's positioning as a public activist and a Buddhist reformer, and the Maha Bodhi Society's promulgation of a distinctive type of Theravada Buddhism thus depended on the survival of the empire and the transnational network that it had opened up in some form or the other.[20]

As years passed, under Dharmapala's guidance, the transnational aspirations of the Maha Bodhi Society, however, began to move in a different direction from Olcott's concerns for a 'United Buddhist World' and attempts at a doctrinal consensus between the Buddhists of different countries. Dharmapala's transition from an emphasis on text and the written word to the physical site and space of Buddhist pilgrimage in Ceylon, India and Burma, while opening up a space for spreading the message of Buddhist transnationalism to a wider audience than the Western-educated Buddhist elite, also marked a moment of sharp departure from his Theosophist mentor and the larger associational politics of Buddhist reformism in Colombo. Above all, this spatial turn brought the world of practising Buddhism into intimate encounters with the historicist vision of the archaeological conservation of ancient monuments.

Soon after its foundation, the Society's initial programme of religious reformation and revivalism in practising Buddhist lands spilled over into a prolonged campaign for the recovery and restitution of ancient Buddhist sites in India, the land of its initial origin. This process drew on the same authenticating tactics of colonial archaeology that sought to discover an essentially Buddhist past for ancient India by reading into objects and structures a priori histories of Buddhism.[21] In fact, the Maha Bodhi Society carried it one step further. Now that archaeology had established, beyond doubt, the original Buddhist character of objects and monuments, they were to be returned to their original sacral meanings and associations, to the communities of the reformed practising Buddhists of whom the Society claimed to be the sole spokesman. This was a demand somewhat unanticipated by the Archaeological Department at the end of the nineteenth century. In fact, the perception that Buddhism had long ceased to be a practising religion in India enabled early colonial archaeologists to label objects associated with Buddhism as antiquities and subject them to scholarly scrutiny within the space of the museum.

The initial struggle of Buddhist repatriations started off at Bodh Gaya in 1892, only a year after the establishment of the Maha Bodhi Society. Recent scholarship on the Maha Bodhi Temple at Bodh Gaya has argued that its archaeological identification as essentially Buddhist and its contentious restoration propelled a long-drawn acrimonious struggle, from 1892 onwards, between the Hindu Shaivite Giri Mahant proprietors of the temple and the newly-configured community of the Buddhists under the aegis of the Mahabodhi Society headed by Dharmapala.[22] The new battle over the monument centred on the crucial rights of religious practice, custodial authority, and legal and ethical propriety over it. By the early years of the twentieth century, though the Maha Bodhi Society failed to gain any real control over the Maha Bodhi Temple itself, what became apparent for the various parties involved were the ways in which 'scientific' authenticating practices of archaeology could open up monuments and antiquities to a new set of re-sacralization claims. For the archaeologists, what the Bodh Gaya case also demonstrated was the fact that there would be no easy way in which objects and antiquities identified as ancient Buddhist could be marked as remains of a non-practising religion, and easily appropriated within the disciplinary and institutional spaces of archaeology and the museum. A whole range of religious revivalist politics had consolidated around such antiquities which reclaimed them as sacred objects of belief and ongoing religious practice. It is within this changed context that corporeal relics unearthed in Buddhist funerary stupas in the course of archaeological excavations emerged as potential objects of neo-Buddhist re-consecrations. However, even this does not fully explain why the archaeological department, by the turn of the twentieth century, apparently started shying away from anything religious or potentially sacred. The answer can, in many ways, be traced back to the provisions of the Ancient Monuments Protection Act of 1904.

THE ANCIENT MONUMENTS PRESERVATION ACT AND THE PROMISE OF 'SECULAR' ARCHAEOLOGY

George Nathaniel Curzon's appointment as Viceroy in 1898 and the subsequent appointment of John Hubert Marshall as the Director-General of Archaeology in 1901 saw far-reaching changes both in the institutional organization of the ASI and in the disciplinary parameters of archaeological practice. Both the Viceroy and the new Director-General were keen on conservation. It was this preoccupation with onsite conservation of ancient structures that would constitute a major break in the way monuments and antiquities came to be configured in the early twentieth century. State control over the colony's ancient monuments now moved beyond the practices of survey, textual and visual documentation, and predominantly offsite collections into a deep physical onsite engagement with the structures. The programme of conservation involved an actual physical refashioning of sites, a practice that hinged on the discourse of secular, scientific recovery and the retention, as far as possible, of the 'authentic' structure unadulterated by later 'unauthorized' accretions and erosions.[23] More intensely than before, the state's control over the ancient monumental remains of the colony came to be articulated in a programmatic manner.

In his speech of February 1900 delivered at the Asiatic Society of Bengal, Curzon signalled the emergence of a new regime of 'secular' archaeological conservation of built heritage in the colony.[24] Through a series of legal enactments, Curzon's government passed the famous Ancient Monuments Preservation Act (henceforth, AMPA) in 1904, which encoded the policy of preservation of ancient structures as the central concern of the newly-reorganized Archaeological Department.[25] For the protection of the monument and its site, the Act entitled the state to take up the land for 'public purpose' under the Land Acquisition Act of 1894.[26] By passing the AMPA, the government also sought to gain control over movable antiquities by trying to restrict and criminalize the traffic in these 'objects of historical interest'.[27] The government's powers of compulsory purchase were again invoked as one of the prime measures designed to control unauthorized circulation of movable antiquities. However, it was strictly guaranteed that the government's powers of compulsory purchase would not be exercised in case of '. . . any building or structure . . . *used for religious worship*' or to '. . . *any image or symbol actually used for the purpose of any religious observance* . . .'.[28]

The AMPA, thus, envisaged greater imperial control over monuments than ever before. At the same time, there was a conscious steering away from granting protected status to the buildings or objects still in 'religious' use. The sacrality of Buddhist corporeal relics, as they emerged in the context of Buddhist reform and revivalist movements in Ceylon, were further asserted by the provisions of this Act which shied away from material remains with religious or even potentially sacred connotations. The increasing symbolic sacrality of the relics was also produced by a completely different brand of politics that marked the diplomatic exchanges of the colonial government in India with the practising Buddhist territories at the frontiers of the empire. Even then, there was no simple trajectory which allowed an easy passage of Buddhist relics from the specialized preserve of archaeology and the museums to the sanctums of the newly-constructed Buddhist viharas.

The Colonial State and Relic Diplomacy

Colonial states' involvement with relics, particularly with Buddhist corporeal relics in South Asia, was not without precedents in the early twentieth century. The earliest association of Western colonial regimes with Buddhist corporeal relics in South Asia has been usually traced back to the Portuguese capture of the Buddha's 'Tooth-Relic' in Ceylon and its subsequent destruction by the then Portuguese Viceroy and by the Archbishop of Goa in 1561. Studying the responses of the different parties involved in the capture, attempted recovery and subsequent ritual destruction, and by the conflicting accounts of the resurrection of the relic, John Strong argues that this event demonstrated an early modern colonial historical juncture when Catholic Christian and Theravada Buddhist notions of relics and their symbolic potential could converse with one another. In their act of the ritual destruction of Buddha's Tooth Relic, the Portuguese participated in the pre- and early modern vocabulary of the potential sacrality of relics, an act that allowed the various contending parties to resurrect the physical presence of the relic and perpetuate its myth of indestructibility.[29]

In contrast to these early modern narratives, the British association with the relic of the Buddha's tooth marked a sharp departure. By the early nineteenth century, when the British had acquired control over Ceylon, the Tooth Relic had come to be housed in the Daladā Māligāva or the temple of the Tooth Relic in Kandy, encompassing the shrine, the palace and the hall of audience of the Kandyan kings (Fig. 5.2). The resurrected Tooth Relic had, by then, assumed an immense symbolic potential in the island, so much so that its control was deemed to be a necessary prerequisite for gaining legitimate sovereign authority. After defeating the Kandyan royal dynasty, the

FIGURE 5.2: THE DALADĀ MĀLIGĀVA OR THE TEMPLE OF THE TOOTH RELIC AT KANDY, 2011

British, in an attempt to legitimize their newfound political and economic control over the island, assumed custodianship of the relic. British scholars and officials were, thus, compelled to refute the narrative of the Portuguese capture and destruction of the relic in the sixteenth century, and fashioned themselves as the new custodians and official sponsors of the cult of Buddha's Tooth. This active British involvement with the cult of the Tooth Relic in Kandy can be situated within the wider context of the early colonial regime's attempts to legitimize its newly-established authority in South Asia by participating in pre-colonial forms and rituals of sovereignty. By the mid-nineteenth century, under the increasing censure of Christian missionaries, such involvement with the rituals of pre-modern sovereignty would be abandoned by the colonial state.

In the face of increasing criticism of the British association with the cult of the Buddha's Tooth by missionaries and the Church of England, the British finally divested themselves of the role of custodians of the Tooth Relic in 1847, handing over the administration of the temple to a committee of elders constituted by representatives of prominent Buddhist monasteries, a committee which had no claims to any kind of temporal sovereignty. In the face of staunch opposition from the Kandyan chiefs and monks, this disassociation by the British proved to be even more destructive than the alleged capture and destruction of the Tooth by the Portuguese authorities. Strong argues that while the early modern Portuguese ritual destruction of the Buddha's Tooth had provided room for its refabrication and resurgence, the British, after initially entering into and endorsing the cult of the relic, and later withdrawing from it, left the Buddha's Tooth in limbo from which no 'recovery' was possible, divesting it of all symbolic associations with political authority.[30] However, contrary to Strong's apprehensions, Daladā Māligāva continued as a major seat of symbolic power in the island. While its symbolic value for the legitimization of political authority might have waned by the mid-nineteenth century, in a very narrow sense, the Tooth Relic survived as a major site of sacrality well into the twentieth century and beyond.

As in colonial India, in Ceylon, too, despite official pronouncements to the contrary, the late nineteenth and early twentieth centuries saw the continued intervention of the colonial state, in various capacities, in the space of the religious practice of the colonized population. The transnational network of Buddhist reform and revival in which Ceylon had emerged as a major centre of reformed Buddhism opened up the cult of the Buddhist Tooth Relic to a wider Theravada Buddhist audience from Burma and Siam. Alongside renewed circuits of transnational Buddhist pilgrimage to Daladā Māligāva, the late nineteenth century saw repeated demands from the Burmese Buddhists and the Buddhist king of Siam for replicas made of the sacred tooth or its use for consecrating oil and other transportable objects, which could then be circulated out of Kandy to these Theravada Buddhist lands. Even after relinquishing its formal role as the custodian of the Temple of the Tooth and the sponsor of relic tours, the British colonial establishment in Ceylon acted as the major broker in these negotiations.

Thus, far from being marginalized in the public life of Sinhalese Buddhism, the late nineteenth and early twentieth centuries saw the increasing replication and circulation of the cult of Buddha's Tooth in the wider Theravada world. These renewed travels of the cult of the Tooth Relic have to be situated squarely within the larger transnational network of Buddhist revival, a network buttressed, in many ways, by the British colonial regime in South and Southeast Asia. It might be worthwhile to note that this growing international prominence of the Tooth Relic probably led to a most curious configuration of reformed Buddhism in South Asia. In the previous section, we have already seen how major Buddhist associations and societies in Colombo, including the Maha Bodhi Society itself, promoted a brand of 'Protestant' Buddhism as a rational, almost non-ritualistic faith. For all their commitment to promote a scientific, rational Buddhism, almost none of these societies entirely rejected the cult of the Tooth Relic, although their negotiations with it remained tortuous. Making space for relic worship within the reformed Theravada Buddhism stemmed from the growing transnational visibility of the relic in the late nineteenth and early twentieth centuries.[31] This possibly accounts, at least to some extent, for the desire of Buddhist societies like the Maha Bodhi to reclaim Buddhist corporeal relics from the jurisdictions of archaeology and museums.

With the passage of time, the colonial state's involvement with Buddhist corporeal relics moved from the cult of the Buddha's Tooth in Ceylon to other Buddhist corporeal relics unearthed by the archaeological department in colonial India. Buddhist relics now emerged as new sites and media for diplomatic exchanges. In 1898, certain Buddhist relics unearthed at Piprahwa Kot (widely assumed to be the site of Kapilavastu), on W.E. Peppe's estate in the United Provinces, were, on the advice of the local government and the noted linguist scholar, G.A. Grierson, presented to Rama V, the King of Siam as '. . . the only reigning Buddhist sovereign . . .', which he, in turn, distributed, on the government's suggestion, to the practising Buddhists of Burma and Ceylon, the Buddhists in India being regarded, at that time, as too few to be considered.[32] In 1910, a few years after the passage of the AMPA, Buddhist relics discovered by the Archaeological Department at Shah-ji-ki Dheri near Peshawar were presented by the Viceroy Gilbert Elliot-Murray Kynynmound, the 4th Earl of Minto to a Burmese delegation, representing the Buddhists of the Indian Empire, to be enshrined at Mandalay. Such presentations of relics to Burmese delegates and the King of Siam represented the acts of frontier and foreign diplomacy of the colonial government. The presentation of the Piprahwa relics to King Rama V of Siam reflected the British anxieties to increase their political influence over Siam, which had emerged as an important geopolitical buffer between the British and French colonial interests in mainland Southeast Asia. The presentation of relics from 'Kanishka's stupa' at Shah-ji-ki Dheri to Burmese delegates from Mandalay was intended as a symbolic gesture to consolidate the newfound British political hold over Burma. The relics were specifically intended as compensation to Burma after its political and economic subjugation in the late nineteenth century after three bloody Anglo-Burmese wars, and in the aftermath of the embargo placed by the colonial government on the Burmese mission to restore the temple of Bodh Gaya.[33] Thus, at these junctures, what mattered to the government, alongside the new-found religious sacrality of the relics in question, were the symbolic potentials of these corporeal remains which made them a favourite object of colonial diplomatic presentations.

The reframed sacrality of Buddhist relics reflected a cautious positing of the colonial state vis-à-vis these corporeal remains. While the relics in all their stark corporeality definitely attested for colonial archaeology, even if not the actual physical presence of a historical Buddha, an important material index to map the spread and extent of an ancient Buddhist civilization in South Asia, they provided the government the means to enter the world of modern Buddhist transnational revival even while remaining ritually unconnected to religious overtones of the cult of relics. In the early twentieth century, as competition for colonial control among European powers (especially the British and the French) and an emergent Japan intensified over South and Southeast Asia, the presentation of these relics to practising Buddhist territories and countries on the frontiers of the British Empire (Burma and Siam) provided the British state in South Asia an opportunity to fashion itself in the image of pre-modern ancient imperial benefactors of the Buddhists like Ashoka. In fact, the role of this ancient Mauryan emperor in the rise, spread and establishment of the Buddhist Dhamma emerged during this time as a historical lineage to the colonial state's act of gifting Buddhist relics, evolving as a discourse producing its own precedent.

It is quite important to note that even at this juncture the colonial government and its archaeological department was quite loath to relinquish its control over all Buddhist corporeal relics unearthed during archaeological excavations beyond what was absolutely necessary for diplomatic exchanges. In 1900, when the Government of Madras proposed to gift the Bhattiprolu relic from the Madras Museum to the King of Siam, the Government of India intervened against the proposal. Citing the resolution of the Home Department, dated 8 June 1883, the government argued that such relics should remain in the country in which they were discovered and ordered that '. . . the relic in question should remain in the Madras Museum'.[34] After publicly declaring this offer, in the face of the strict opposition of the imperial government, an embarrassed Madras government was forced to retract. In 1910, in the immediate aftermath of the presentations of Buddhist corporeal relics unearthed at Shah-ji-ki Dheri to the Buddhists of Burma, the Home Department passed a fresh resolution ordering the various local governments that objects of archaeological interest, beyond which what was absolutely necessary for diplomatic exchanges, should not be lent or given away for purposes of devotional worship.[35] The objects in question remained completely unspecified and it was not guaranteed that Buddhist funerary relics would not be considered as worthy objects of archaeological investigation.

FROM THE MUSEUM TO THE VIHARA: THE BHATTIPROLU RELIC AND THE CONSTRUCTION OF THE DHARMARAJIKA VIHARA IN CALCUTTA

In 1916, when the Government of India, on the advice of the ASI, decided to present certain Buddhist relics to Buddhist organizations, it was again political considerations that reigned supreme. Against the backdrop of the First World War and the intensified militarization of colonies in South and Southeast Asia, the colonial state was pressed to secure the loyalty of its frontier provinces and territories – of Burma,

Ceylon and Siam – for replenishing the rapidly diminishing exchequers of the British government and for acting as bases of large-scale military recruitment. The situation was further complicated by the particular turns that nationalist politics took both in India and Ceylon, at this stage, which tended to move beyond the associational politics of the urban middle-class intelligentsia towards mass movements. These developments in South Asia put the colonial state into disquiet, especially with the war spreading from nations in Europe to European colonies in South and Southeast Asia. The situation was, thus, urgent enough for the colonial state to override the historical sanctity of Buddhist corporeal relics and propose a fresh round of presentations.

John Marshall, the Director-General of the ASI, initially proposed that portions of these relics should be distributed to the King of Siam, the Dalai Lama of Tibet and the Buddhists of Ceylon.[36] However, as soon as news of the discovery of the Taxila relics was made public, Marshall recorded that Indians, particularly Indian Buddhists, began to take a keen interest in their disposal. Numerous petitions followed from the Maha Bodhi Society and the Bengal Buddhist Association for a share of these relics. In 1916, Marshall apprehended that after much press publicity, if the decision to present the relics to foreign countries were made public, it would give rise to widespread disappointment which the government could ill afford in the heart of the colony with the ongoing war. The only way out of this quandary, Marshall envisaged, was to present the relics, including the Bhattiprolu relics, to the Buddhists in India to be retained in this country and enshrined at viharas constructed across sites associated with the Buddha's life. This, he was convinced, would '. . . produce an excellent impression and give the greatest satisfaction throughout India'.[37] Following Marshall's advice, the government decided that the claims of the Buddhists of the colony would reign supreme. Portions of Buddhist corporeal relics were to be presented to the Maha Bodhi Society and the Bengal Buddhist Association, and a third share to Ceylon.[38] The years that followed saw Marshall and the ASI negotiating on two fronts: with Dharmapala and the Maha Bodhi Society regarding the plans and designs of the new Buddhist temple to be built at Calcutta, and with the Madras Museum and the local government of Madras on the terms of acquisition of the Bhattiprolu relic. Such negotiations would now drag the archaeological department outside its cherished forte of 'secular heritage conservation'.

Of Old Bones and New Caskets: Shifting Locations of the Bhattiprolu Relic

As the Government of India's decision to present Buddhist corporeal relics to the Maha Bodhi Society were being formalized, Marshall started negotiating with the Madras Museum regarding the terms of official transfer of the Bhattiprolu relic. At this point, the relic, identified as the skull bone of the Buddha, and its caskets, were deposited in an empty cigarette tin and stored away from public view inside a strong safe of the Madras Museum.[39] With the Madras government displaying keen enthusiasm to gift the Bhattiprolu relic to the King of Siam only a few years earlier, Marshall hoped that neither the Museum officials nor the Madras government would now raise any objections to the relic being transferred to the custody of the Maha Bodhi Society for ritual consecration. Dr. Henderson, the Madras Museum Superintendent, agreed to hand over the relics but argued that the Museum would '. . . retain both the crystal casket and the inscribed stone receptacle in which the relic was preserved' at its moment of discovery.[40] Faced with this custodial demand, Marshall now addressed the Madras government directly.

In his official correspondence with the Madras government, Marshall asserted that such relics are indeed '. . . devoid of interest from the *museum point of view*, and moreover for *sentimental reasons* ought not to be exhibited in a museum'.[41] He contended that the Buddhists would appreciate that the old caskets in which the relics were discovered be handed over to them, along with the corporeal remains of the Buddha. Marshall, however, left the final decision to the Madras government, stating that if it decided to second the claims of the Museum authorities, a copy of the original reliquary had to be prepared by the ASI for repatriating the relics to the Maha Bodhi Society. Negotiations followed and the Madras government, once publicly snubbed by the Government of India for its eagerness to make a gift of the Bhattiprolu relic to the King of Siam, now decided to firmly back the Madras Museum's claims over the relic caskets. In a stern rejoinder, it now ordered that the original caskets remain in the custody of the Madras Museum as material documents of historic and artistic importance, having no special religious significance for the Buddhists. Only the bare corporeal relics, defined by the Museum authorities as the prime object of Buddhist religious veneration, were allowed to travel out of the confines of the Madras Museum for re-sacralization.[42]

As crucial as this demand of the Madras Museum might have been in deciding the ultimate course of the journey of the Bhattiprolu relic, it needs to be emphasized that the situation was not without precedent in South Asia. Except for the Sanchi, Sonari and Satdhara relics which had travelled, with their relic caskets intact, out of India to the confines of museum collections in London, the occasions of the presentation of the Piprahwa and the Shah-ji-ki Dheri relics to Siam and Burma had witnessed the divorce of the relics from the reliquaries. In both cases, officials involved in the transfer, particularly archaeologists and antiquarians, had put forth the argument of the absolute historical sanctity of the relic caskets and the repatriability/dispensability of the corporeal remains for ritual veneration. In both these cases, the relic caskets remained within the disciplinary and institutional confines of museums in the colony and the government presented communities of Buddhists with the bare corporeal remains (Ray 2008). Faced with these precedents, the Government of India refrained from pushing the Madras government on this issue. Marshall now decided to go ahead with the making of a duplicate relic casket. The noted jewellery firm, Messers Hamilton and Company, on a special commission from the ASI, designed a new silver relic casket in which the Bhattiprolu relic, now shorn of its 'ancient' reliquaries and reduced to its bare corporeality, was deposited[43] (Fig. 5.3). This is where matter stood in 1920, at the moment of the final delivery of the Bhattiprolu relic to the Maha Bodhi Society.

At this point, it might be useful to explore the particular politics at play by which archaeologists, antiquarians and other government officials from the late nineteenth century onwards arrived at this rather curious distinction between bones as essentially sacred and ancient caskets enshrining them as objects of art and history, so much so that while the former could be classified as objects unsuited for

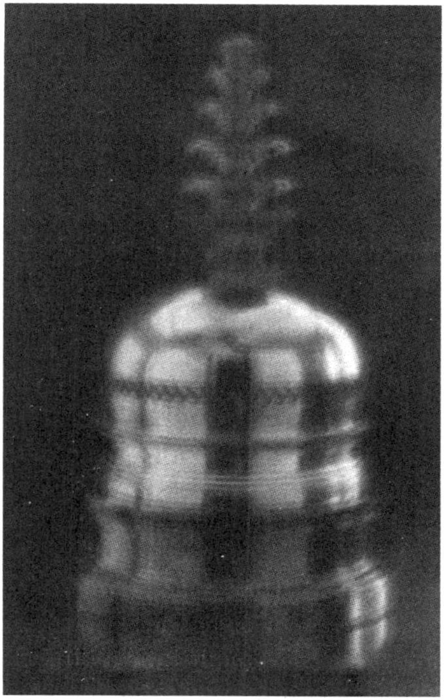

FIGURE 5.3: THE NEW CASKET MANUFACTURED BY MESSERS HAMILTON AND CO. FOR ENSHRINING THE BHATTIPROLU RELIC, 1919 (COURTESY: ANAGARIKA DHARMAPALA TRUST, COLOMBO)

museum displays and, hence, safely repatriated to Buddhist associations, the later remained a prerogative of the custodial hold of the museum and history. More importantly, we need to probe why the ASI, sharing the similar historicist concerns of the museum, took upon itself the duty of delivering the old bones in their 'original' caskets to the Buddhists and when restrained in this, went to the extent of making a duplicate relic casket for the occasion. In the different context of the repatriation of the Sanchi relics from the Victoria and Albert Museum in London to the Maha Bodhi Society in the 1950s, Torkel Brekke has argued that the idea of making copies of reliquaries by the museum authorities reveals that they did not believe in the sacrality of these objects, '. . . not primarily because the objects belonged to an alien religion, but because of their modern secular worldview'.[44]

Keeping in mind Brekke's point about the different epistemologies of knowledge and belief, I argue that the ASI's commitment to the making of duplicate reliquaries in 1916 can only be explained by the material particularity of the relics, especially in their relation to their caskets in general, and in the historical peculiarities of colonial South Asia in the early twentieth century.

Relics, as we have seen earlier in this essay, are marked out from other material objects by their stark corporeality. Robert Sharf has persuasively argued that the allure of relics has to be located in their 'pure corporeality', rather than in their representational or iconic qualities.[45] Unlike other material objects, the symbolic potential of relics are constructed in the ways in which they are physically and ritually framed.[46] Thus, in sharp contrast to icons and images, the relic's absence of representational features and its recognition as a moment of unmitigated corporeality is construed by the denotative work done by its frame, its reliquary. In the context of colonial South Asia, the different contending parties involved with Buddhist corporeal remains displayed a remarkable comprehension of the significance of reliquaries, which now emerged as new sites of power play and negotiations. In the case of the Bhattiprolu relic, for the different concerned parties, the inscribed relic caskets bore the ultimate marker of the identification of the enshrined piece of bone as the corporeal relic of the Buddha himself. The historicist concerns of the Madras Museum authorities were, thus, well-shared by the Archaeological Department with its particular disciplinary focus on ancient Buddhism and its belief in the infallibility of material remains, particularly inscribed ancient remains, as the only reliable source for reconstructing the scientific history of the colony. In the archaeological and museological discourse, relic caskets could well emerge as 'authentic' objects of ancient art and history. The aspirations of neo-Buddhist reformist associations like the Maha Bodhi Society, its programme of reform and revival of Buddhism as a practicing faith and reclamation and re-consecration of ancient Buddhist sites and objects, though not always sharing the same historicist commitment of archaeology and museums, drew, to a large extent, on the same authenticating desires of these colonial disciplines and institutions.

The refusal of the Madras Museum and the Archaeological Department to display corporeal relics within the space of the museum cannot be read in the context of ethical concerns attending the display of human remains, which were yet to emerge in the context of post-colonial repatriations only from the 1950s and 1960s. The Museum's decision to give away the bones to the Maha Bodhi Society was probably predicated on the modern sacrality of Buddhist corporeal relics as it emerged during the late nineteenth and early twentieth centuries. With the Government of India's decision to embark on a new round of relic presentation against the political backdrop of the First World War and critical turns in nationalist politics across colonial South Asia, the Museum authorities could ill-afford to hang on to the bone itself, which now came to be increasingly classified as an object unworthy of exhibition in the museum gallery. However, in holding on to the inscribed relic caskets as objects of art and history outside the jurisdiction of religious sentiments, the authorities asserted their jurisdiction over an important antiquity of the province.

With the Madras Museum, backed by the local government, continuing to hold custody over the reliquaries, the Bhattiprolu relic, divorced from its authenticating frames, was now threatening to turn into a meaningless piece of scrap. The Archaeological Department, who had been entrusted by the Government of India to facilitate this transfer, feared that this critical divorce of the reliquary from the bone of the Buddha would enrage the Maha Bodhi Society.[47] In an ultimate effort to prevent the corporeal relic of the Buddha from being turned into just another bone fragment, the ASI now took it upon itself to get fresh relic caskets made in duplication of the originals in the Madras Museum. The new casket, now inscribed with a brief statement of the discovery of the relic and a translation of the original inscription, sought to attest the enshrined bone's identity as an authentic relic of the Buddha.[48] Above all, this divorcing of reliquaries from corporeal remains in the case of Piprahwa, Shah-ji-ki Dheri and Bhattiprolu now set a precedent for the production of a new order of Buddhist relics centred only on the symbolic sacrality of the bones that would be invoked by archaeology and museums both in India and England with varying degrees of success in the context of the repatriation and re-consecration of Buddhist corporeal remains.[49] However, the question still remains as to why the Maha Bodhi Society, despite its grasp over the symbolic potential of the relic frames, did not object to the particular course of action taken in the case of the Bhattiprolu relic. The answer, in many ways, has to be sought in the preoccupation of the Society and the ASI with an extremely complex set of negotiations over the plans and designs of its new Buddhist temple in Calcutta.

Ancient Designs and Modern Buildings: Planning the Dharmarajika Vihara

With the announcement of the government's decision to gift Buddhist corporeal relics to the Maha Bodhi Society and the Bengal Buddhist Association in 1916, Dharmapala started an active campaign of repeatedly assuring the Archaeological Department and the Government of Bengal that the new vihara of the Society would replicate the principles of ancient Buddhist architecture. At this juncture, it is important to trace the precise reasons that led a neo- Buddhist reformist association to commit to the building of its new vihara as per the designs of ancient Buddhist architecture. More importantly, we have to explore how the Archaeological Department, officially committed to the principles of the scientific conservation of ancient structures as against restoration and rebuilding, came to be embroiled in the planning of the new temple as a re-creation of ancient Buddhist monuments. The process was, in no way, easy. If the transfer of the Bhattiprolu relic had witnessed the ASI championing the claims of the Society against the Madras Museum, even if fleetingly and primarily as a pragmatic stance adopted under larger political contingencies, the building of the Dharmarajika Vihara at Calcutta saw a greater and more acrimonious clash between the principles and practices of colonial archaeology, particularly its commitment to a certain vision of heritage conservation in the colony, and the religious revivalist aspirations of the Maha Bodhi Society. The initial directives for involving the ASI in the plan and design of the new Buddhist temple at Calcutta came from the Government of Bengal.[50] This government order dragged the ASI not only outside its principles of secular commitment to heritage but also towards a much-abhorred practice of building new structures.

From the various communications that followed, it now appears that the suggestion for incorporating the designs of ancient Buddhist architecture in planning the Maha Bodhi Society's new temple at

Calcutta initially came from the Director-General of the ASI himself.[51] Responding to Dharmapala's request for a plan for the Calcutta Vihara of pure Buddhist architectural type, Marshall deputed J.A. Page, the then Superintendent of Mohammedan and British Monuments of the Northern Circle of the ASI, for preparing the designs and plans of the proposed temple.[52] He himself sent detailed suggestions regarding the plans of the Calcutta Vihara which, it was decided, should be modelled on the Karle chaitya hall. However, even while he was substantially involved in designing this new building, Marshall would repeatedly assert that such work did not fall within the usual official purview of his department. He asserted that Page's selection as the architect of this new temple hinged on the fact that besides being an employee of the ASI, he was also a trained architect. His involvement was to be classified as 'private work', without any overt involvement of the ASI or any questions of its flouting its principles of secular heritage conservation.[53] However, such efforts at self-distancing notwithstanding, both Marshall and the ASI would now be increasingly drawn into the muddle of building a new practising temple, and not only in matters of plans and designs.

As Marshall and Page were busy preparing the plans, Dharmapala started an active campaign in Calcutta to raise funds for the proposed vihara. A study of the donors of the Maha Bodhi's cause in Calcutta reveals the crucial links that the Society was able to forge with powerful international bankers, landed magnates, political leaders and civil servants in India. These connections played a critical role in the self-fashioning of the Society as the sole spokesman of the Buddhists of colonial South Asia.[54] In the face of increasing contacts and exchanges with rich and powerful public figures in India, one notices the certain tendency of the Maha Bodhi Society to espouse strong links between the reformist variant of Buddhism promoted by it and 'Sanatan Hinduism'.[55] Such reconciliatory approaches on the eve of the building of the new vihara at Calcutta were not just essential for immediate financial support. They were cautiously designed to amend the public image of Dharmapala and the Society, especially in the aftermath of the staunch public stance taken by them against the Shaivite Giri mahants of Bodh Gaya only a few decades ago. In fact, it might be worthwhile to note that from the 1910s, as the government began to distance itself from the affairs of the legal entanglement at Bodh

Gaya and the Maha Bodhi Society failed to gain any decisive custodianship of the temple, Dharmapala moved away from the strictures of legal appeals and started negotiating with the major political parties in the colony, the Hindu Mahasabha and the Indian National Congress.[56] This would gradually turn the Society into a formidable force, which government departments, especially the Archaeological Survey, had to take account of. These powerful connections notwithstanding, the Maha Bodhi Society's claims of being the sole spokesman of the Buddhists continued to be deeply fractured.[57] In the particular context of the building of the Society's Calcutta Vihara, the challenges came from different communities of Buddhists in the colony, specifically from the Burmese Buddhists and the Bengal Buddhist Association.

Established in 1892 under the leadership of Kripasharan Mahasthavira, only a year after the foundation of the Maha Bodhi Society in Colombo, the Bengal Buddhist Association belonged to the world of neo-Buddhist institutions professing a reformed variant of Buddhism. By the turn of the twentieth century, the Association fashioned itself as the representative of the interests and concerns of the Bengali Buddhists, particularly the Buddhists of Chittagong who constituted its main support base. By the early years of the twentieth century, the Association had built its headquarters in Calcutta, not far from the Maha Bodhi Society's College Square property, in Babu Lalit Mohan Das Lane at Kapalitola. In early 1916, when the exact terms of giving away Buddhist corporeal relics to neo-Buddhist associations of Calcutta were yet to be formalized by the government, the Bengal Buddhist Association started campaigning actively for their share of relic portions. In a passionate memorial to the Director-General of the ASI, Kripasharan Mahasthavira and Gunalankara Mahathera, the president and vice-president of the Association, sought to establish the credentials of their institution as the one and only rightful representative of the Indian Buddhists, especially the Buddhists of Bengal.[58] Referring to the earlier decision of the government to gift certain Buddhist relics unearthed by the ASI at Shah-ji-ki Dheri to the Burmese Buddhists, the petitioners now urged that the '. . . *disappointment* caused to the *Indian Buddhists* by the disposal of the sacred ashes and charred bone of the Lord Buddha . . . to *countries beyond the limits of India* . . .' should now be removed '. . . by graciously allowing that the relics discovered this time will be preserved . . .' in the Association's headquarters in Calcutta.[59]

While the Bengal Buddhist Association had initially cordial relations with Dharmapala and the Maha Bodhi Society, its assertion of certain territorial and national rights over Buddhist relics and its claims of being the flagbearer of the 'Indian Buddhists' now ran counter to the Society's public fashioning of itself as the sole representative of the interests of the Buddhists of colonial South Asia. In April 1916, when Dharmapala tried to coax Lord Thomas Gibson Carmichael, the Governor of Bengal, to act as the official patron of the Society's Calcutta Vihara, the Secretary to the General Department informed the Governor's Office, in a confidential note of the bitter rivalry, if of not positive enmity, between the Society and the Bengal Buddhist Association. While the Maha Bodhi Society under Dharmapala was trying to emerge as a transnational association of the Buddhists of the colony, the Secretary recorded that it had lost most of its Bengali Buddhist members (mainly Buddhists from Chittagong) to the Bengal Buddhist Association. In view of these complicated circumstances, the General Department advised the Governor to refrain from meddling with Buddhist politics.[60] Thus, while the political contingencies of the war and the complications of nationalist politics in India forced the government and the Archaeological Department to take recourse to relic diplomacy, such considerations also demanded that the colonial government take a neutral non-interventionist stance in matters of rivalries between two similarly-placed neo-Buddhist organizations.[61] However, contrary to its hopes of remaining uninvolved in internal disputes between the Buddhist communities and associations, the colonial government and its archaeological department would now find themselves further embroiled in such complications.

In August 1916, Dharmapala wrote to Marshall complaining that the Buddhists of Burma and Ceylon were displaying a remarkable unwillingness to contribute towards the building of the Calcutta Vihara. Dharmapala recorded on a rather bitter note that Taw Sein Ko, the Archaeological Superintendent of the Burma Circle, was against building viharas in India and was inciting the Burmese Buddhists not to contribute money to the fund collections for the Calcutta Vihara.[62] Marshall's official intervention on behalf of the

ASI was necessitated by the fact that with the involvement of an officer of his department, the matter ceased to be a case of intra-Buddhist rivalry and could potentially complicate the situation further.[63] Responding to Marshall's official appeal, Taw Sein Ko now reported that most of Burma's money was already invested in war funds. In such a situation, the Burmese Buddhists could not be persuaded to contribute towards '. . . building of Buddhist religious buildings in India, with which they have nothing in common, in race, language or religion'.[64]

Contrary to Taw Sein Ko's assertions the Burmese Buddhists had a deep involvement with Buddhist affairs in India.[65] In 1916, his refusal to contribute Burma's finances to the building of the Calcutta Vihara of the Maha Bodhi Society probably reflects the response of the Buddhists of Burma who had not been approached by the colonial government for a further share of Buddhist relics. However, rather than reading it as another case of intra-Buddhist rivalry, we probably need to take account of the fact that the incident reflected a deeper chasm between the variant of reformist Buddhism espoused by the Society and the traditions of Buddhist practice prevalent in Burma.[66] It is this deep divide that led the highest archaeological officebearer of Burma to refuse the requests of his departmental superior. In the context of the political and economic contingencies of the war situation, where securing the allegiance of a frontier province like Burma was crucial to the colonial state, Marshall decided not to push the matter further and nor did the Maha Bodhi Society, for it had other scores to settle with the Archaeological Department regarding the plans and designs of its new temple.

As the plans and designs prepared by Marshall and Page for the Calcutta Vihara were forwarded to the Maha Bodhi Society, Dharmapala assured the Director-General that the Society would stick to the design provided by the archaeologists and, following their advice, would approach the Bengal government for acquiring the land adjacent to its plot under the Public Land Acquisition Act for its temple.[67] When contacted, the Government of Bengal flatly refused to exercise its compulsory acquisition powers, arguing that such legal enactments could not be pressed into service for a sectarian affair like the building of a new temple.[68] Citing financial difficulties and space crunch, Dharmapala now started to modify the specialist designs, and plans of the archaeologists. To modify Marshall and Page's designs, Dharmapala approached Percy Brown, the Principal of the Government School of Art in Calcutta, who deputed the modelling teacher of his school, Acharya, to prepare clay models of the proposed Calcutta Vihara[69] (Fig 5.4). These models not only reflected the contingencies of the financial and space crunch faced by the Maha Bodhi Society but also Dharmapala's personal aspirations for his vihara, which now differed substantially from the archaeologists' conceptualization of the temple. As the photographs of the models were forwarded to Marshall for approval, the enraged archaeologist saw in them a gross

FIGURE 5.4: THE CLAY MODEL OF THE PROPOSED DHARMARAJIKA VIHARA PREPARED BY MR. ACHARYA, MODELLING TEACHER, GOVERNMENT SCHOOL OF ART, CALCUTTA AT ANAGARIKA DHARMAPALA'S REQUEST, 1916 (COURTESY: ANAGARIKA DHARMAPALA MUSEUM, SARNATH)

pulverization of their specialist designs and asserted that the models of the vihara sent by the Society would not hold ground 'structurally and artistically'.[70] In the correspondence that followed, while Dharmapala repeatedly cited the Society's lack of funds and space as the main reasons for changing the archaeologists' specialist designs, Marshall continued to assert that the best path for the Society was to follow the plans and designs provided by him and Page. While the physical site of the proposed Buddhist vihara in the heart of the colonial city lay well beyond the jurisdiction of the Archaeological Survey, the plans and designs of the proposed temple would now unfold as the register through which the archaeologists tried to retain some semblance of control over the new vihara enshrining the ancient relics. As these tortuous negotiations over the design and plan of the Calcutta Vihara were in progress, Dharmapala tried to affect a coup d'état over the archaeologists. In a public advertisement issued in 1917, he declared in print that 'Sir John Marshall, Director-General of Archaeology, *has kindly prepared the plan of the proposed vihara. . . .*'[71] Marshall took great exception to this unsolicited name-dropping. In an irate note, he reminded Dharmapala that the revised designs of the Society were anything but satisfactory and neither his name nor that of his department should be attached to a building '. . . which is architecturally faulty and totally different . . .' from that which the archaeologists had suggested. Rounding up on a stern note, Marshall reminded Dharmapala: 'If you propose to put up anything of the kind in Calcutta you must be careful to make it clear that *it is not my handiwork*!'[72] Although Dharmapala assured Marshall that the Society would adhere to the recommended designs, in the June 1917 issue of the Maha Bodhi Society's journal, he published a photograph of the clay model of the Calcutta Vihara, one that had been earlier rejected by Marshall, as the finalized design.[73] Though Dharmapala assured Marshall that this was an editorial mistake, he continued to use the latter's name on various occasions, particularly in his official correspondences with the Bengal government.

By early 1918, the modified plans of the proposed Calcutta Vihara had been sanctioned by the city's Municipal Corporation. These bore little semblance to the original designs prepared by Marshall and Page. In a series of letters to Dharmapala, the irate Director-General of Archaeology now asserted that his name and that of the Department was to be completely disassociated with the Society's Calcutta Vihara.[74] Dharmapala's reconciliatory overtures notwithstanding, Marshall now strongly refused to have any more associations with the Society's Calcutta temple.[75] These tortuous negotiations over the designs and plans of the Maha Bodhi Society's Calcutta Vihara thus held important lessons for the archaeologists. For Marshall and Page, these negotiations revealed that the specialist knowledge of archaeologists concerning the ancient Buddhist monuments of the colony could now be used and modified freely by neo-Buddhist revivalist associations in building new practising temples over which the specialist would have no official control.[76] As for the Calcutta Vihara of the Maha Bodhi Society, the building was ultimately supervised by an eminent civil architect, Mono Mohan Ganguly, and finished in 1920. On the occasion of its opening ceremony in 1921, the new casket with the old bone of the Bhattiprolu relic was handed over to the Society's president, Sir Asutosh Mookerjee, by the Governor of Bengal, Lord Ronaldshay (Fig. 5.5). Along with the statue of the Buddha from Japan, which

FIGURE 5.5: LORD RONALDSHAY, GOVERNOR OF BENGAL, HANDING OVER THE BHATTIPROLU RELICS TO SIR ASUTOSH MOOKHERJEE, PRESIDENT OF THE MAHA BODHI SOCIETY, DURING THE INAUGURAL CEREMONY OF THE DHARMARAJIKA VIHARA AT CALCUTTA IN 1921 (COURTESY: ANAGARIKA DHARMAPALA MUSEUM, SARNATH, 1921)

FIGURE 3.6: THE DHARMARAJIKA VIHARA OF THE MAHA BODHI SOCIETY IN CALCUTTA, 2011

Dharmapala had earlier tried in vain to install in the Maha Bodhi Temple at Bodh Gaya, the relics were enshrined in a new temple in Calcutta, now named Dharmarajika Vihara, in imitation of the ancient vihara complex of the same name unearthed by Marshall and the ASI in Taxila (Fig 5.6). The relics enshrined in the Dharmarajika Vihara soon paved the way for a series of religious and national repatriation claims over the disciplinary and institutional preserves of archaeology and museums.

ACKNOWLEDGEMENTS

This research was assisted by a Social Science Research Council Postdoctoral Fellowship for Transregional Research with funds provided by the Andrew W. Mellon Foundation and a Ford Foundation India Postdoctoral Fellowship. The study was conducted in libraries and archives across India, Sri Lanka, Myanmar, Thailand, the Netherlands and the United States – at the archives of the Office of Director-General of the Archaeological Survey of India, New Delhi; the Library, Archives and Museums of the Maha Bodhi Society in Calcutta, Sarnath, and Colombo; the Siam Society, Bangkok; National Archives of Myanmar, Yangon; at the I. Kern Collections of the Leiden University Library and the AMES South Asia Collections of Library of the University of Minnesota. I sincerely thank the staff of these institutions for providing access to their collections. The research was made possible by a number of institutional supports at various points by the Maulana Abul Kalam Azad Institute of Asian Studies, Kolkata; Centre for Studies in Social Sciences, Calcutta; International Institute of Asian Studies, Leiden; and the Department of Art History and Institute for Advanced Study, University of Minnesota. I would like to record my sincere gratitude to Prof Tapati Guha-Thakurta, Prof. Lakshmi Subramanian, Prof. Hari S. Vasudevan, and Dr. Bodhisattva Kar in Calcutta; Prof. Nayanjot Lahiri, Prof. Upinder Singh; and Prof. H.P. Ray in New Delhi; Dr. Ellen Raven, Dr. Philippe Peycam, Dr. Marieke Bloembergen and Prof. Nira Wickramasinghe in Leiden; Prof. Frederick M. Asher in Minnesota; and Prof. Tansen Sen, Prof. Prasenjit Duara and Dr. Gitanjali Surendran for their support and encouragement in shaping this study through dialogues and debates.

NOTES

1. Letter No. 1766, dated Simla, 30 June 1916, from The Hon'ble Sir E.D. Maclagan, Secretary to the Government of India, Department of Education, to the Secretary to the Government of Bengal, General Department, File No. 459, Part 2, 1916, Office of the Director-General of Archaeology in India (henceforth, DGASI). For an account of the discovery of the Bhattiprolu relics, see *New Imperial Series of the Reports of the Archaeological Survey of India*, vol. XV, pp. 11-12. For a translation of the inscription on the Relic Casket, see 'Luders' List of Brahmi Inscriptions', *Epigraphia Indica*, vol. X.
2. Letter No. 1766, 30 June 1916, from Maclagan, to the Secretary to the Government of Bengal, File No. 459, Part 2, 1916, DGASI.
3. Walsham (2010): 11.
4. According to the *Oxford English Dictionary* 'relic' connotes more generally an outdated object of interest, custom or belief surviving from an earlier time, or more specifically a part of a deceased holy person's body or belongings kept and treated as an object of reverence after his/her death (*OED* 2001: 704).
5. Ibid.: 731.
6. Walsham (2010): 14.
7. Appadurai (1986).
8. Davis (1997); Guha-Thakurta (2004); Mathur (2008).
9. Ibid.
10. Cunningham ([1871] 2000): 113.
11. Duncan (1799): 131-2; Cunningham ([1871] 2000): 113-14.
12. Brekke (2007): 270-303; Mathur (2008); Guha-Thakurta (2010).
13. Guha-Thakurta (2004); Trevithick (2006).
14. Malagoda (1976); Gombrich and Obeyeskere (1988); Gombrich (1988); Bond (1988).
15. The anti-Christian tracts provided by the Theosophists along with translations of major anti-Church tracts by Western philosophers were increasingly used by propagandists of the Buddhist revival movement (Frost 2002: 937-67).
16. Ibid.
17. Trevithick (2006).
18. Moving away from 'traditional' modes of Buddhist practice, like the practice of meditation under the apprenticeship of a *bhikku*, Dharmapala propagated new modes of sexual and ritual conduct. While the popularization of meditation through a study of printed and translated Pali hymns rendered the role of the spiritual master marginal in the practice of Buddhism, Dharmapala's prescriptions of a disciplinary code of conduct for the Buddhist laity, encompassing table manners, toilet habits and a regime of sexual

puritanism, embodied in his book *Gihi Vinaya* (published in 1898), aimed at the making of new responsible citizens out of the Buddhists. By the late 1880s and early 1890s, Olcott and his Theosophist Society published the *Buddhist Catechism* which sought to standardize and establish Buddhism as a rational non-superstitious faith (see Olcott, 1947).

19. Frost (2002): 956-7.
20. In fact, in the aftermath of the Ceylon riots of 1915 and the imprisonment of the major neo-Buddhist leaders of the island, all except Dharmapala, upon their release, attested their loyalty to the colonial state and the imperial order. Frost (2002): 937-67.
21. Guha-Thakurta (2004).
22. Guha-Thakurta (2004); Trevithick (2006); Mukherjee (2010).
23. Roy (1961); Lahiri (2005).
24. Curzon, 'Speech before the Asiatic Society of Bengal, 7 February 1900', in *Lord Curzon in India, being a Selection of his Speeches as Viceroy and Governor-General, 1898-1905*, London, 1906.
25. Marshall (1922): 2006.
26. A Bill to provide for the preservation of monuments and objects of historical or artistic interest, Draft, in Accompaniments to the Letter to the Government of India, No. 689, dated 5 February 1902, File No. 89, April 1902, DGASI.
27. Ibid.
28. Ibid., italics mine.
29. Strong (2010): 184-98.
30. Ibid.
31. In his diary entry of 12 August 1927, Anagarika Dharmapala recounted that Colonel Olcott's public criticism of the cult of Dalada as superstitious and degenerate eventually led to a rift between the Maha Bodhi Society and his Theosophist mentor. See, 'Diary of Anagarika Dharmapala, 1927', unpublished. Colombo: Anagarika Dharmapala Trust.
32. Note No. 58, dated 11 January 1916, File No. 459, Part I, 1916, DGASI.
33. Ray (2008): 417-49.
34. Note No. 58, dated 11 January 1916, File No. 459, Part I, 1916, DGASI.
35. Resolution dated Simla, 21 May 1910, from H.G. Stokes, Deputy Secretary to the Government of India, Home Department, to the various local governments and departments. File No. 117, Serial No. 1, 1910, DGASI.
36. He, in fact, pointed out that rather than the fresh relic casket unearthed at Taxila, which was in a state of advanced ruin as most of its contents had practically crumpled to dust, it was more advisable for the Government of India to offer the King of Siam the Bhattiprolu relic in the Madras Museum which besides being in a state of excellent preservation, was authenticated beyond doubt as the corporeal relics of the Buddha himself. See, Note, dated 17 February 1916, from John Marshall, Director-General, ASI.

File No. 459, Part I, 1916, DGASI and Letter No. 292, dated, Sanchi 17 February 1916, from John Marshall, Director-General, ASI, to Sir James Du Boulay, Private Secretary to His Excellency, the Viceroy, Delhi. File No. 459, Part 2, 1916, DGASI.

37. Note, dated 17 February 1916, from John Marshall, Director-General, ASI. File No. 459, Part I, 1916, DGASI.
38. Note, dated 22 May 1916, from John Marshall, Director-General, ASI. File No. 459, Part I, 1916, DGASI.
39. Letter dated, Camp Sanchi, Bhilsa Post Office, 24 February 1916, from John H. Marshall, Director-General of Archaeology in India, to Dr. J.R. Henderson, Superintendent, Government Museum, Madras. File No. 459, Part 2, 1916, DGASI. Marshall stressed in this letter that in its present state of preservation, the existence of the Bhattiprolu relic had almost been forgotten, with scarcely anyone having the opportunity to view it.
40. Keeping in mind the recent developments and involvements of the colonial state in the cult of Buddhist corporeal relics, Henderson, in fact, argued that it was not fitting that the relic be exposed to 'public view' within the exhibitionary complex of the Museum. See Confidential Note No. 126, dated 28 February 1916, from Dr. J.R. Henderson, Superintendent, Madras Museum, to John H. Marshall, Director-General of Archaeology in India. File No. 459, Part 2, 1916, DGASI.
41. Letter No. 647, dated Camp Saraikala (District: Rawalpindi), 20 March 1916, from John H. Marshall, Director-General of Archaeology in India, to the Hon'ble A.G. Cardew, Member of Council, Somerford – Adyar, Madras. File No. 459, Part 2, 1916, DGASI.
42. D.O. No. 1329-1, dated Ootacamund 1 May 1916, from the Educational Department, Government of Madras, to Sir John H. Marshall, Director-General of Archaeology in India. File No. 459, Part 2, 1916, DGASI.
43. Letter No. 204, dated 19 January 1917, from John H. Marshall, Director-General of Archaeology in India, to Messers Hamilton and Co. File No. 459, Part 4, 1916, DGASI.
44. Brekke (2007): 289.
45. In the case of Buddhist relics in Southeast Asia and Japan, Sharf has shown that the distinction between relics and religious icons and images is often blurred, especially in the case of ash icons and dried lacquered mummies of departed Buddhist teachers, all of which bear an uncanny resemblance to sculptures and icons. Sharf (1999).
46. Drawing on Gregory Bateson's notion of framing, Sharf argues that while an explicit or implicit frame of some kind is necessary to distinguish the signifier from the signified, the 'map' from the 'territory', the status of the frame remains couched in a logical ambiguity, stemming from the compulsion

of the frame to straddle both the signifier and the signified and yet belong to neither, and from the frame's obligation to draw attention to itself and remain almost invisible at the same time. On the notion of framing, see Sharf (1999); Bateson (1972); and Goffman (1986).

47. In 1910, when the Government of India gifted the Buddhists of Burma a share of Buddha's corporeal relics (unearthed by D.B. Spooner at Shah-ji-ki Dheri), for ritual enshrinement in Mandalay, Marshall had initially made an offer to present the relics in a newly-made casket on the grounds that the old casket in which the relics had been discovered was shattered. The Burmese delegation sent to Calcutta to receive the relics and headed by Taw Sein Ko, Superintending Archaeologist, Burma Circle, had urged for a loan of the original dilapidated casket to convince the Burmese public of the antiquity and authenticity of the relics. After some deliberations, Marshall convinced the Government of India to give the original casket to the Burmese Buddhists on a loan for two months. (See Letter No. 165/6 B.R., dated Mandalay 7 March 1910, from Taw Sien Ko, Office of Superintendent Archaeological Survey, Burma, to J.H. Marshall, Director-General of Archaeology in India and Letter dated 18 March 1910, from John Marshall, Director-General of Archaeology in India to Sir Harold Stuart, Government House, Calcutta, and Stuart's undated no-objection note on the same letter. File No. 204, 1909-10, DGASI.) This might have set a precedent and in 1916-17, with the political contingencies of the war-time situation and the growing transnational prominence of the Maha Bodhi Society, the Director-General apprehended strong protests from the latter over the divorce of the reliquaries from the bones in the context of the transfer of the Bhattiprolu relic.
48. Letter No. 204, dated 19 January 1917, from John H. Marshall, Director-General of Archaeology in India, to Messers Hamilton and Co. File No. 459, Part 4, 1916, DGASI.
49. Despite reservations about the particular disassociation of the reliquaries from the corporeal remains by the Madras Museum in 1916, the ASI soon adopted this course of action in subsequent cases of 'repatriation' of Buddhist remains at Ceylon and Sarnath. In 1917, responding to appeals from Ceylon, the Government of India, through the personal attendance of John Marshall, presented two shares of the relics unearthed at Taxila to the Temple of the Tooth in Kandy and to the Buddhist Nunnery of the city. In both cases, relics were taken out of their original caskets and presented in new cases specially commissioned by the ASI for the purpose. (See Letter, dated Kandy 24 February 1916, from Sister Suddhamachari, Superior Buddhist Nunnery, Kandy, Ceylon, to the Governor-General of India and Memorandum, dated Simla 20 January 1917, from the Superintendent, Department of Education,

Government of India, to the Director-General of Archaeology in India. File No. 459, Part 2, 1916, DGASI; and Letter No. 204, dated 19 January 1917, from John H. Marshall, Director-General of Archaeology in India, to Messers Hamilton and Co. File No. 459, Part 4, 1916, DGASI.)

50. See Letter No. 1766, dated Simla, 30 June 1916, from The Hon'ble Sir E.D. Maclagan, Secretary to the Government of India, Department of Education, to the Secretary to the Government of Bengal, General Department and Letter No. 218, dated Simla 28 August 1916, from E.D. Maclagan, Secretary to the Government of India, Department of Education/Branch, Archaeology and Epigraphy, to the Secretary to the Government of Bengal, General Department. File No. 459, Part 2, 1916, DGASI.
51. Letter No. 645, dated Delhi 18 March 1916, from John Marshall, Director-General, ASI, to Anagarika Dharmapala, General Secretary, Maha Bodhi Society. File No. 459, Part 2, 1916, DGASI.
52. Letter No. 1469, dated Calcutta 30 May 1916, from Anagarika Dharmapala to John Marshall; Letter No. 2939, dated Simla 16 October 1916, from John Marshall, Director-General, ASI, to J.A. Page, Superintendent, Muhammadan and British Monuments, Northern Circle, Agra. File No. 459, Part 2, 1916, DGASI.
53. See Letter No. 845, dated Agra 18 October 1916, from J.A. Page, Superintendent, Muhammadan and British Monuments, Northern Circle, Agra, to Sir John H. Marshall, Director-General of Archaeology in India; and D.O. No. 3075, dated 14 November 1916, from John Marshall to Anagarika Dharmapala. File No. 459, Part 2, 1916, DGASI.
54. Mary Elizabeth Foster of Honolulu, wife of the rich American banker, T.R. Foster, emerged over the years as the prime financial benefactor of the Maha Bodhi Society. After an initial meeting with Dharmapala in 1893, when the latter was on his way back to Ceylon via Japan after attending the World Parliament of Religions in Chicago, Foster started contributing regularly to Dharmapala's various projects in India, Ceylon and later, London. Besides regular annual contributions, Mrs. Foster often contributed lump sum amounts for particular projects undertaken by the Society, like the setting-up of schools and hospitals and later, the building of new Buddhist temples. After contributing a substantial sum amounting to Rs. 22,000 for the buying of the College Square plot, in response to Dharmapala's requests, she made another donation of Rs. 18,000 for the expenses of building the new temple. In fact, it was this financial break which allowed Dharmapala and the Society to go on with planning the new temple even in times of strict financial contingencies occasioned by the war. Besides, Dharmapala's own resources and those of his family and acquaintances in Ceylon that mobilized for the building of the new Buddhist temple, the other major contributors to the cause included Maharaja Saheb Gaekwad of Baroda; Ashutosh Mookerjee,

well-known Judge of the Calcutta High Court and a powerful member of the Calcutta University's Senate who had accepted the post of President of the Maha Bodhi Society; Prafullanath Tagore; Kumar Manindra Chandra Cinha of Paikpara Raj; Kumar Arun Chandra Sinha; Sarada Charan Mitra, Judge of the Calcutta High Court; and Hirendranath Dutta, President of the Bengal Theosophical Society. (See Advertisement of the 2461st Anniversary Celebration of the Parinirvana of the Tathagata Buddha at Calcutta organized by the Maha Bodhi Society, enclosure to letter No. 38610, dated Gulmarg 31 July 1917, from John Marshall to Anagarika Dharmapala. File No. 459, Part 2, 1916, DGASI.)

55. The resolution adopted by the Society on the building of the Calcutta Vihara asserted in unequivocal terms: 'Buddhism and Sanatan Dharma are not in opposite poles as erroneously thought by some, but they are sister forms of Hindu faith and their points of resemblance are far greater than points of difference.' See Copy of the Resolution, dated Calcutta 17 May 1916, adopted at a Public Meeting held on Buddha's Birth Anniversary regarding the building of the vihara in Calcutta to enshrine the relics of the Lord Buddha. Attachment to letter No. 1469 dated Calcutta 30 May 1916, from Anagarika Dharmapala to John Marshall. File No. 459, Part 2, 1916, DGASI.
56. Trevithick (2006).
57. In his private diary entries and in the public announcements in the Society's Journal, Dharmapala had often bitterly complained about the lack of financial and infrastructural support of the Buddhists of Burma, Ceylon, Japan and Siam to the cause of the Maha Bodhi Society, particularly in the legal battle over the Bodh Gaya temple. Such pronouncements, while reflecting the limits of the appeal and acceptance of the variant of Buddhism espoused by the Society in the larger Theravada Buddhist world of South and Southeast Asia were also consciously designed by Dharmapala in his self-fashioning as the lone crusader of the Buddhist cause. See, Trevithick (2006). By the 1910s, when the negotiations around the building of the Society's Calcutta Vihara were in full swing, Dharmapala hoped that the Buddhists of Burma, Ceylon, Siam and Japan would contribute generously to this cause of building the first of the new temples. Public appeals for funds were made by the Society in the newspapers and in the pages of its own journal. However, the building of the first Buddhist vihara in Calcutta was never really a joint enterprise where all the Buddhists of the Indian empire jointly rallied. (See Letter dated Sri Saddharma Mandir, 4 A, College Square, Calcutta, 5 February 1916/2459 B.E. (Buddhist Era), from Anagarika Dharmapala, General Secretary, Maha Bodhi Society, to Sir John H. Marshall, Director-General, ASI, Simla. File No. 459, Part 2, 1916, DGASI.)
58. Letter No. 456, dated Calcutta 29 February 1916, from Kripasharan Mahasthavira, President, and Gunalankara Mahathera, Vice-President,

Bengal Buddhist Association, to Sir John Marshall, Director-General, Archaeological Department in India. File No. 459, Part 2, 1916, DGASI.

59. Ibid., italics mine.
60. Confidential Note, dated 5 April 1916, from Mr. K.C. De, Secretary, General Department, Government of Bengal, to W.R. Gourlay, Private Secretary to the Governor of Bengal, enclosed with letter no. 1011, dated Darjeeling 21 April 1916, from W.R. Gourlay, Private Secretary to the Governor of Bengal, to John Marshall, Director-General of Archaeology in India. File No. 459, Part 2, 1916, DGASI.
61. In August 1916, the Government of India thus formalized its decision to divide the Buddhist corporeal relics between the Maha Bodhi Society and the Bengal Buddhist Association.
62. Letter No. 2308, dated Calcutta 10 August 1916, from Anagarika Dharmapala to John Marshall. File No. 459, Part 2, 1916, DGASI.
63. For a critical biographical study on Taw Sein Ko, see Penny Edward (2004): 277-335.
64. Letter no. 740/10 G.C., dated Mandalay 7 September 1916, from Taw Sien Ko, Superintendent, Archaeological Survey, Burma, to Sir John Marshall, Director-General of Archaeology in India. File No. 459, Part 2, 1916, DGASI.
65. Well into the late nineteenth century, there had been a steady flow of Buddhist pilgrims and royal restoration missions from Burma to the Maha Bodhi Temple at Bodh Gaya. In fact, it was the Burmese Restoration Mission from the royal court of Ava (in Burma) in the 1870s which sparked off the controversial archaeological restoration of the temple and the subsequent legal entanglements between the Maha Bodhi Society and the Shaivite Giri mahants in the late nineteenth century (Trevithick, 2008; Guha-Thakurta 2004). By the closing years of the nineteenth and the opening years of the twentieth century, the Burmese Buddhists, as noted before, emerged as one of the prime recipients of the Buddhist corporeal relics unearthed by the ASI in Peshawar and, on that occasion, Taw Sein Ko had himself headed the delegation of the Burmese Buddhists to Calcutta.
66. In his diary entries, Dharmapala repeatedly noted that notwithstanding the presence of the offices of the Maha Bodhi Society and other neo-Buddhist associations in Burma (especially in Rangoon), the Buddhists of Burma hung on to their degenerate and superstitious ritual practices. See Diaries of Anagarika Dharmapala, 1901, 1915, 1919, 1921, 1927, unpublished. Colombo: Anagarika Dharmapala Trust.
67. Letter No. 3474, dated Calcutta 26 November 1916, from Anagarika Dharmapala to John Marshall. File No. 459, Part 2, 1916, DGASI.
68. Letter, dated Calcutta 6 August 1917, from Anagarika Dharmapala to John Marshall. File No. 459, Part 2, 1916, DGASI.

69. While Marshall and Page had planned the building keeping in mind the simple and rather stern design of the ancient Karle Chaitiya Hall, the new clay models were designed on the model of the Ajanta cave temple. Moreover, in order to distance himself from his surrounding crowd of 'secular buildings' at College Square and to stress on its 'purely Buddhistic' character, Dharmapala now ordered that the roof of the model vihara should be fitted with a dome in imitation of the Thupārāma dagoba at Anuradhapura in Ceylon. Letter No. 253/C, dated Calcutta 13 July 1917, from Anagarika Dharmapala to John Marshall. File No. 459, Part 2, 1916, DGASI.
70. Letter No. 381/C, dated Gulmarg 26 July 1917, from John Marshall to Anagarika Dharmapala. File No. 459, Part 2, 1916, DGASI.
71. Advertisement of the 2461st Anniversary Celebration of the Parinirvana of the Tathagata Buddha at Calcutta organized by the Maha Bodhi Society, enclosure to letter no. 38610, dated Gulmarg 31 July 1917, from John Marshall to Anagarika Dharmapala. File No. 459, Part 2, 1916, DGASI, italics mine.
72. Letter No. 386/C, dated Gulmarg 31 July 1917, from John Marshall to Anagarika Dharmapala. File No. 459, Part 2, 1916, DGASI, italics mine.
73. Letter No. 354/C, dated Calcutta 7 September 1917, from Anagarika Dharmapala to John Marshall. File No. 459, Part 2, 1916, DGASI.
74. Letter No. 1351, dated Simla 13 June 1918, from John Marshall to Anagarika Dharmapala. File No. 459, Part 2, 1916, DGASI.
75. When asked for a souvenir for the laying of the foundation stone of the vihara by Dharmapala, Marshall flatly refused and only gave in at the end, in the face of Dharmapala's extremely nagging communications. (Letter no. 2628, dated Saraikala 30 November 1918, from John Marshall to Anagarika Dharmapala; Letter, dated Calcutta 5 December 1918, from Anagarika Dharmapala to Marshall; and letter dated, Saraikala 12 December 1918, from Marshall to Anagarika Dharmapala. File No. 459, Part 2, 1916, DGASI.)
76. By the 1920s, in the face of similar passionate applications from the Bengal Buddhist Association for the supply of plans and designs for their proposed temple to enshrine their share of Buddhist relics, Marshall and Page refused to oblige. The work, Marshall now argued, was for the private architect and not the government's archaeologists. After some negotiation, their plan was approved by Marshall as just about meeting the criterion of a worthy receptacle for the Buddhist ruins. The Director-General was, however, quick to assert that the archaeologists and the ASI were only concerned with conserving ancient remains and not building new temples. See correspondences between the Bengal Buddhist Association and the Archaeological Department filed in File No. 385, 1920-21 and File No. 385, 1922, DGASI.

BIBLIOGRAPHY

Select Primary Materials

UNPUBLISHED GOVERNMENT PAPERS

Files from the Office of the Director-General of the Archaeological Survey of India, New Delhi, 1905-33 (exact correspondences cited in the essay).

UNPUBLISHED PRIVATE PAPERS

Diaries of Anagarika Dharmapala, Sarnath Maha Bodhi Society Collection (exact dates cited in the essay).

Diaries of Anagarika Dharmapala, Colombo Maha Bodhi Society Collection (exact dates cited in the essay).

PUBLISHED REPORTS

Cunningham, Alexander, *Four Reports Made During the Years 1862-63-64-65*, vol. I, ASI, 1871, rpt., New Delhi, 2000.

Select Secondary Published Literature

Almond, Philip C. 1988. *The British Discovery of Buddhism*. Cambridge: Cambridge University Press.

Appadurai, Arjun, ed. 1986. *The Social Life of Things: Commodities in Cultural Perspective*. Cambridge: Cambridge University Press.

Asher, Frederick M. 2012. 'Travels of a Reliquary, its Contents Separated at Birth', *South Asian Studies*, vol. 28, no. 2, pp. 147-56.

Blackburn, Anne M. 2010. *Locations of Buddhism: Colonialism and Modernity in Sri Lanka*. Chicago and London: University of Chicago Press.

Bond, G. 1992. *The Buddhist Revival in Sri Lanka: Religious Tradition, Reinterpretations, and Response*, Delhi: Motilal Banarsidass.

Brown, Peter. 1981. *The Cult of Saints: Its Rise and Function in Latin Christianity*. Chicago and London: University of Chicago Press.

Cohn, Bernard. 1998. *Colonialism and its Forms of Knowledge*. New Delhi: Oxford University Press.

Davis, Richard. 1997. *Lives of Indian Images*. Princeton: Princeton University Press.

Edwards, Penny. 2004. 'Relocating the Interlocutor: Taw Sein Ko (1864-1930) and the Itinerancy of Knowledge in British Burma', *South Asia Research*, vol. 12, no. 3, pp. 277-335.

Fentress, James and Chris Wickham. 1992. *Social Memory*. Oxford: Blackwell.

Frost, Mark. 2002. '"Wider Opportunities": Religious Revival, Nationalist Awakening and Global Dimension in Colombo, 1870-1920', *Modern Asian Studies*, vol. 36, no. 4, pp. 937-67.

Geary, Patrick J. 1978, rpt. 1990. *Furta Sacra: Thefts of Relics in the Central Middle Ages*. Princeton, NJ: Princeton University Press.

———. 1994. *Living with the Dead in the Middle Ages*. Ithaca and London: Cornell University Press.

Germano, David and Kevin Trainor. 2004. *Embodying the Dharma: Buddhist Relic Veneration in Asia*. Albany, NY: State University of New York Press.

Gombrich, R.F. 1988. *Theravada Buddhism: A Social History from Ancient Benares to Modern Colombo*. London: Routledge and Kegan Paul Ltd.

Guha-Thakurta, Tapati. 2004. *Monuments, Objects, Histories: Institutions of Art in Colonial and Postcolonial India*. New Delhi: Permanent Black.

———. 2013. 'The Production and Reproduction of a Monument: The Many Lives of the Sanchi Stupa', *South Asian Studies*. 29(1): 77-109.

Lopez, Donald S., ed. 1995. *Curators of the Buddha: The Study of Buddhism under Colonialism*. Chicago and London: University of Chicago Press.

Lowenthal, David. 1985. *The Past is a Foreign Country*. Cambridge: Cambridge University Press.

Lubar, Steven and W. David Kingery, eds. 1993. *History from Things: Essays on Material Culture*. Washington, DC: Smithsonian Institution Press.

Malagoda, K. 1976. *Buddhism in Sinhalese Society, 1750-1900: A Study of Religious Revival and Change*. Berkeley: University of California Press.

Morgan, David, ed. 2009. *Religion and Material Culture: The Matter of Belief.* London and New York: Routledge.

Mathur, Saloni. 2008. *India by Design: Colonial History and Cultural Display*. Berkeley: University of California Press.

Myint-U, Thant. 2004. *The Making of Modern Burma*. Cambridge: Cambridge University Press.

Nora, Pierre. 1987. 'Between Memory and History: Les Lieux de Mémoire', *Representations*, 26, pp. 7-24.

Obeyeskere, R. 1984. 'The Bilingual Intelligentsia: Their Contribution to the Intellectual Life of Sri Lanka in the Twentieth Century', in P. Colin-Thome and A. Halpe (eds.), *Honouring E.F.C. Ludowyk: Felicitation Essays,* Colombo: Tisara Praksakayo Ltd., Dehiwela, pp. 71-91.

Ruppert, Brian D. 2000. *Jewel in the Ashes: Buddha Relics and Power in Early Medieval Japan*. Cambridge, Mass: Harvard University Asia Centre.

Said, Edward, 1978. *Orientalism*. London: Penguin.

Schopen, Gregory. 1997. 'Archaeology and Protestant Presuppositions in the Study of Indian Buddhism', in *Bones, Stones and Buddhist Monks: Collected Papers on the Archaeology, Epigraphy, and Texts of Monastic Buddhism in India*. Honolulu: University of Hawaii Press.

Sengupta, Indra. 2010. 'Sacred Space and the Making of Monuments in Colonial Orissa in the Early Twentieth Century', in Himanshu Prabha Ray (ed.) *Archaeology and the Text: The Temple in South Asia*. New Delhi: Oxford University Press.

Sharf, Robert H. 1999. 'On the Allure of Buddhist Relics', *Representations*, 66, pp. 75-99.

Strong, John S. 2004. *Relics of the Buddha*, Princeton: Princeton University Press.

Thero, Kahawatte Siri Sumedha. 2006. *History of the Mulagandha Kuty Vihara: The Prime Place of Worship at Isipatana*. Kolkata: Maha Bodhi Society.

Trainor, Kevin. 1997. *Relics, Ritual, and Representation in Buddhism*. Cambridge: Cambridge University Press.

Trevithick, Alan. 2006. *The Revival of Buddhist Pilgrimage at Bodh Gaya (1811-1949): Anagarika Dharmapala and the Mahabodhi Temple*. New Delhi: Motilal Banarsidass.

Walsham, Alexandra, 2010. 'Introduction: Relics and Remains', *Past and Present*, Supplement No. 5, pp. 9-36.

PART II

TEXTS, POLITICS AND THE SANGHA IN SRI LANKA

CHAPTER 6

New Manuals for New Times

A Comparative History of *Buddha Ädahilla* and *A Buddhist Catechism*

KITSIRI MALALGODA

SEEKING TO DESCRIBE 'the present form and influence of Buddhism in Ceylon', R.S. Copleston, who had resided there as the Anglican Bishop of Colombo since 1875, felt that there was more than one kind of Buddhism that he needed to take into account. In his view:

> There are two Buddhisms now in Ceylon: the residuum of the old Buddhism of the past centuries, as it lingers in out-of-the way places, and as it has shaped the habits and ways of thought of those not under European influence; and a new revival, much more self-conscious and artificial, which aims indeed only at reviving what Buddhism always professed to be, but which has been influenced, in its estimate of the profession, very largely by Europeans.[1]

He went on to add, however, that the two Buddhisms were distinguishable only 'in their extremes', and that between the two extremes, there was 'every intermediate shade'. He exercised the same sort of caution when he summarized the contents of two contemporary publications – *Buddha Ädahilla* and *A Buddhist Catechism* – in order to illustrate what 'the leaders of the modern school wish the Buddhists of Ceylon now to practise and believe'. For, here again, he added that 'it is not easy to say whether these books represent a new departure, or continue the tradition of the past. In this respect there is probably a wide interval between the two little books'.[2]

The width of the interval between the two books becomes apparent even at first glance. The more recent of the two, *A Buddhist Catechism* (1881), though published simultaneously in Sinhala, was written in

English. It bore unmistakable signs of Christian influence in its very title. Historically, it was a product of the then newly-formed alliance between Buddhism and Theosophy. It had the imprimatur of a leading Buddhist monk, Hikkaduve Sumangala, who held a high office not merely in the local monastic hierarchy (as 'High Priest of Adam's Peak') but also in theosophical associations (as president of the clerical division of the Buddhist Theosophical Society, and as vice-president of the broader and more international Theosophical Society itself). Its author was the president and co-founder of the Theosophical Society, Henry Steel Olcott, who had embraced Buddhism just recently. The immediate purpose for which the catechism was written was its use as a text for religious instruction in newly-opened Buddhist schools, which, in other and non-religious respects, followed the same kind of academic curricula as in Christian missionary schools.[3]

The origin of the other book, *Buddha Ädahilla*, was more obscure. Its title, which Copleston translated as 'Buddha-Faith', was unusual for a book containing Pali verses (*gāthā*) and formulae, and their explanations and translations in Sinhala.[4] Like *A Buddhist Catechism*, it, too, was originally published in Colombo but Copleston did not know its exact date of publication. He estimated it to be about 1872.[5] Thus, unlike the *Catechism*, which was published during his time in Colombo, it had already been in circulation for a couple of years when Copleston first arrived there in 1875. In contrast to the *Catechism*, furthermore, the *Ädahilla* had no known author or authorizer; it only had a compiler or anthologist, Mohottivatte Gunananda, who was as well known a local monk as Hikkaduve Sumangala. Its intended audience was the Buddhist laity, in general, and not a specific group such as school children, in particular.

Just like Hikkaduve Sumangala, whom he had known at least since the early 1860s, Mohottivatte Gunananda, too, was to join the alliance with Theosophy in the late 1870s. He became a 'fellow' in 1879 and, in the same year, his lay supporter, J.R. de Silva, became the local agent of the *Theosophist*. But the *Buddha Ädahilla* belonged to a time which preceded the emergence of that alliance. In fact, it preceded the formation of the Theosophical Society itself (in New York in 1875) and the transfer of its headquarters to India (in 1879). Mohottivatte's fame around that time was as a preacher at Buddhist gatherings and as a debater with Christian missionaries. In a less itinerant capacity, however, he was also a key figure in the emergence of new Buddhist centres in Colombo – a city which, for some three centuries, had been the main military and administrative stronghold of colonial powers, and where Christian churches had a conspicuous presence.[6] Of Mohottivatte's residence at the Colombo suburb of Kotahena, Copleston wrote:

> In Colombo itself there are scarcely any Buddhist institutions that are not new. European passengers often ask to see a temple, and for want of any more genuine temple in the town they are taken to one at Kotahena. It is only within the last thirty years that this temple has been heard of. There was a pansala [monks' residence] there but no vihara [temple] till one was erected and named (it was completed about 1880) by the energetic controversialist, Mohottivatte.[7] This man never rose, I believe, to be more than a novice (sāmanera); but he made himself a considerable name. . . . He started a printing-press, from which a great many tracts against Christianity have issued, and some periodicals.[8]

The immediate reason for starting the printing press had been to respond to tracts against Buddhism, which had been issued, in larger numbers and over a longer period of time, by Christian missionary presses. Once established, though, Mohottivatte's press brought out other and more classical works as well. Notable among these were an edition and paraphrase of a much admired fifteenth-century Sinhala poem, the *Kāvyaśekhara* of Totagamuve Rahula, prepared by Hikkaduve Sumangala; and the more voluminous eighteenth-century Sinhala translation of the Pali classic, *Milindapañha*. The former was published in 1872 and the latter in 1878. Considering the close cooperation that prevailed between Hikkaduve and Mohottivatte during that decade and earlier, it seems very likely that Hikkaduve – who was later to be the authorizer of Olcott's *Catechism* – played some part in the preparation of the *Ädahilla* as well.[9]

Thus, despite the differences between the two works, the distance in time between them was relatively short (from 1872 to 1881), and there was also clear continuity in the personnel involved in their production and dissemination. It is understandable, therefore, that Copleston preferred to view them both as products of the same 'modern school'. Yet, at the same time, this view created problems for his diagnosis that the modern school was largely of external (European) inspiration and artificial, and, therefore, unlikely to have a deep and lasting impact. External inspiration was far less clear-cut in the case of the earlier manual; and far from being of temporary currency, both manuals have been in print more or less continuously for well over a century now. As will be seen later, a different approach adopted by later students was to separate the two books from each other and assign them to contrasting schools: the *Catechism* to the modern school and the *Ädahilla* to the traditional. However, this approach, too, has its problems since it was in the same locality and same milieu – Buddhist networks in Colombo – that both manuals made their initial appearance. A less problematic starting point to explore the new times that generated new needs for new manuals, therefore, is to focus attention on the locality that they shared.

With that focus, then, the rest of this paper will outline first the emergence of Colombo, a colonial capital and port-city, as a centre of Buddhism (Section II). Next, it will examine the historical circumstances in which the two manuals came into being in the latter half of the nineteenth century (Sections III and IV). Moving on, the paper will then explore the subsequent history of the two manuals (Sections V and VI). What this comparative history reveals is that the two manuals are representative of two types of religious literature, partly opposed yet partly complementary to each other. One type, as represented by *Buddha Ädahilla*, kept the present times in touch with words and actions handed down from the past. The other type, as represented by *A Buddhist Catechism*, sought to provide answers to the – real or hypothetical – frequently asked questions of the present about the essential nature of Buddhism, its differences from other religions, and its position in relation to contemporary interests and concerns like science, social issues and the like. While representatives of the latter type need continuous revision and replacement in order to keep up with changing times, those of the other type manage to remain relatively unchanged over longer periods of time. Both types persist because each is as indispensable to a living religion as the other.

II

Copleston was correct when he stated that in 'Colombo itself there are scarcely any Buddhist institutions that are not new'. The prominent ones – like Mohottivatte Gunananda's temple at Kotahena (Dipaduttamaramaya), Hikkaduve Sumangala's college at Maligakanda (Vidyodaya Pirivena), and the still more recent headquarters of the Buddhist Theosophical Society at Pettah – were all new.[10] Yet behind these new developments there was also an older and longer process at work, one quite unnoticed by Copleston even though his book was intended to provide a long-term view of Buddhist history. This longer process was the return of Buddhists to a region from which they (along with other non-Christians) had been driven out, or where they had been compelled to lie low for quite a while. Some attention to that longer process is necessary, therefore, to move beyond Copleston and to gain a better understanding of how Colombo emerged as a Buddhist centre.

In one sense, the convergence of political and religious centres was just a continuation of an age-old process. This had been the general pattern in the island from the very beginning of its recorded history, from the time of ancient Anuradhapura in the third century BC onwards. But Colombo, in contrast to all previous capitals, was a colonial capital and not the seat of power of an independent Buddhist kingdom. Hence, it was a locality where, in the absence of monarchical patronage, Buddhist institutions had to find their bearings in highly competitive and not always welcoming surroundings. Those surroundings naturally had some impact on the kind of Buddhism that evolved there and – in relation to the subject of this particular essay – on the kinds of manuals and related literature that came to be produced. The production of new manuals for new times was closely linked, in other words, to the emergence of an entirely new kind of locality as a centre of Buddhism.

In seeking to regain something of their lost space and lost visibility in this (western) part of the island, the attention of Buddhists was focused at first not on Colombo itself, where, adjoining an older port, the Portuguese had erected a fort in the sixteenth century, thus providing the nucleus of an expanding colonial city. The initial destinations of Buddhists were two pre-colonial cities whose nearest port was Colombo, and whose decline and fall had coincided with the rise of Portuguese power in Colombo. The first of these was Kelaniya, some seven miles north-east of Colombo and long held to be the most sacred spot in this part of the country.[11] The second city was Kotte, slightly closer to Colombo on the south-east, which had been the capital of local kings in the immediate pre-colonial times. It was under the patronage of the kings of Kotte that scholar-poets like Totagamuve Rahula (mentioned earlier) had flourished and their poetry, still read and admired by the literati, had immortalized the splendours of Kotte and Kelaniya in their heyday.

The temples at Kelaniya – like those at Kotte – had been destroyed by the Portuguese in the late sixteenth century. But pilgrims continued to be attracted to the site, and they also aimed to repossess and rebuild the main temple. Their efforts intensified when the Dutch supplanted the Portuguese in the mid-seventeenth century. Unwilling to allow a major centre of Buddhist pilgrimage so close to their own centre of power in Colombo, the Dutch resisted these efforts as long as they could. Yet in the end, realizing the futility of resistance, they gave in and allowed the rebuilding of the temple to begin in the mid-eighteenth century.[12] Quite apart from these local considerations, this was also the period of the Enlightenment among European nations in general. It was a period when the religious intolerance that had characterized the Reformation and Counter-Reformation of the earlier era had lost much of its overtly repressive character.

The reoccupation and rebuilding of the temple at Kelaniya received active support and encouragement from the kings of Kandy (the legacy of Kotte had come to be divided and fought over between them and the colonial powers in Colombo).[13] No such support was to be had, however, when the reoccupation and rebuilding of a temple at Kotte began in the 1820s. By this date, the new colonial power – the British, who had replaced the Dutch in Colombo – had extended their dominion into the interior as well and had extinguished the independence of the kingdom of Kandy. Restoration work at Kotte, therefore, depended chiefly on the energy and enthusiasm of a newly-arrived monk – Pilane Buddharakkhita – and the support he could muster from the local community.

In contrast to the southern parts of the island where Pilane Buddharakkhita came from, the Christian presence was much deeper seated in these western parts. Monks like him, therefore, had to compete harder for local support because the missionaries, too, made efforts to win over and retain the laity exclusively on their side (exclusively because it was not uncommon for lay people to support more than one religion at the same time). This was a contest, furthermore, in which the missionaries themselves had to compete on an increasingly equal footing. No longer allowed to eliminate opposition by destroying and appropriating temples, and driving away their residents and custodians, they now had to limit themselves to the purely verbal weapons sharpened during the evangelical revival (which was as much a part of eighteenth century Europe as the Enlightenment). These weapons were street-preaching and pamphleteering.

For the practice of street-preaching and for distributing polemical pamphlets, places like Kotte and Kelaniya – just beginning to recover from years of ruin – proved irresistible to the missionaries, for these were sites where large crowds of pilgrims and devotees gathered on festive days. Kelaniya was targeted mainly by the Wesleyans, who made day-trips from their headquarters in Colombo. At Kotte, there was a larger and more settled missionary presence for it was here (rather than at Colombo) that the Church Mission Society missionaries established a mission-house, a network of schools and a printing press.

Given the nature of the message that the missionaries wanted to convey at Buddhist festivals – the sin and folly of idolatrous practices – their presence was bound to cause resentment and ill-will.[14] It was the persistent use of these tactics that eventually led to increasing religious polarization and the emergence of militant figures like Mohottivatte Gunananda, who, with no mention of this background, was described by Copleston (in a passage quoted earlier) as an 'energetic controversialist' who 'made himself a considerable name' by starting 'a printing press, from which a great many tracts against Christianity have issued'. Part of that unmentioned background was the curious prehistory of Mohottivatte's press at Kotahena. Its original home was the Church Mission Society mission station at Kotte.

Thus, in the long run, the polemical activities of British missionaries did have some important unanticipated and unwanted consequences: the adoption by Buddhists of the same tactics that were used against them. However, the missionaries were quite unsuccessful in their immediate and desired aim of arresting the resurgence of Buddhist sites like Kotte and Kelaniya. These temples easily retained and even widened their bases of support. Kotte, in particular, became the leader of a network of recently renewed local temples, which shared a common view of their pasts: a golden age under Buddhist kings, a dark age under the Portuguese, and a difficult but hopeful rebirth in recent times. Their shared outlook and aspirations were formalized in the 1850s in a new *nikāya* (monastic fraternity), which, well aware of the past when Kotte and Kelaniya had been more important centres of Buddhism than Kandy, broke away from the authority of the monastic establishment there.[15]

Among those who joined in the formation of the new fraternity and who added considerably to its scholarly standing was another newcomer to the neighbourhood of Colombo. This was Valane Siddhartha, who had taken up residence in a newly-built temple, Parama Dhamma Cetiya, at Ratmalana, a little over 10 miles south of Colombo, in the 1840s. Here, he continued a teaching career already begun further south in his native village of Valana. It was mainly the students of Valane Siddhartha who went on to establish Colombo's supremacy over the rest of the country in the sphere of Buddhist learning. These students included Batuvantudave Devarakkhita of the Kotte temple; Udugampola Ratanapala of the Bellanvila temple; Dompe Buddharakkhita of the Kelaniya temple; Hikkaduve Sumangala, who was to found Vidyodaya Pirivena in 1873; and, closer to home but from a different and older temple in the locality, Ratmalane Dhammaloka, the founder of Vidyalankara Pirivena in 1875.[16]

By the time Vidyalankara Pirivena was founded on the further side of the Kelani river, the distance between Ratmalana and Kelaniya was being greatly diminished by the newly-opened and steadily expanding railway network, enabling the founder to maintain close ties with both places at the same time. The railways were part and parcel of the rapidly changing outward appearance and inner character of Colombo – a changing environment which inevitably had its impact on patterns of life and work in and around the city. The changes were signalled quite strikingly by the fate of its historic fort. No longer needed for its defensive purpose – as a place where colonial settlers could take refuge from besieging armies of local kingdoms – the three-hundred-year old fort was opened up literally and unceremoniously. In reclaimed space, the Fort railway station, retaining the old name but performing a new function, became the meeting point of traffic moving inwards and outwards – north, south and east.

On the western side, where the nearby port provided access to the busy Indian Ocean, the steam engine was having its impact on oceanic traffic as well. The limited natural capacity of the harbour was increased artificially by the construction of a breakwater. New produce for export came from the plantation economy imposed on the territories acquired in the old Kandyan kingdom. By the latter half of the nineteenth century, the combined forces generated by the plantation economy and the long-range effects of the Industrial Revolution had begun transforming Colombo into a colonial city of the Victorian era with its main streets and parks named or renamed after imperial and colonial dignitaries; and with the typical mixture of offices and shops, workshops and warehouses, hospitals and hotels, museums and libraries, printers and publishers, churches and schools, mansions and slums, and so on.[17]

This transformation robbed the city of much of the austere and slow-moving pre-industrial charm that it had acquired under the Dutch in the eighteenth century. Yet if that made the city less appealing visually, more and more people were attracted to it all the same by the widening avenues of horizontal and vertical mobility that it now offered. New residents and migrants came from within the country as well as from without, the latter mainly from Britain and British India. To accommodate them all, the once walled-in and exclusive city began its outward sprawl, absorbing more and more of the adjacent hamlets and open spaces into its orbit. By the turn of the century, Colombo was very much a multi-ethnic, multi-caste and multi-religious conurbation where every major group could find a niche, though, naturally enough, the most powerful community and religion of the time – the British and Christianity – exercised dominance and occupied the commanding heights.

Given that Colombo had become home to a variety of communities, it is not surprising that there were also varied views and representations of the place. British authors, with only a brief history of their own in the locality but looking forward to pleasing prospects in the future, published illustrated guides and handbooks providing 'useful information for the traveller and resident' (e.g. Skeen 1887). Dutch Burghers lovingly remembered monuments left behind by their not-too-distant ancestors (e.g. the watercolours, 1888-9, by J.L.K. van Dort, reproduced in De Silva and Beumer 1988). Having recently recovered some of their lost ground, Roman Catholics recalled the more glorious days under the Portuguese when 'Catholic shrines arose on every eminence and hill-top, giving rise to various suburbs and giving their names to various quarters and streets', and mourned the dark nights that followed 'when all this was swept away by a rude hand [i.e. by Dutch Protestants]' (Perera 1962 [1938]: 70).[18] The re-entry of Colombo into the imagination of the Sinhala literati after a long gap found expression in favourable references to it in their poetry in the latter half of the nineteenth century. In due course, when long-term histories of Sinhala literature came to be written, it became common to refer to the latest stage of that literature as the Colombo Period (Sannasgala 1961).

From the history of literature it was but a short step to the history of religion and the idea of a Colombo Period is implicit in Richard Gombrich's *Theravada Buddhism: A Social History from Ancient Benares to Modern Colombo* (1988). Comparing the title of this book with Copleston's, *Buddhism: Primitive and Present in Magadha and Ceylon* one is, in fact, tempted to see Gombrich's work as a sort of update of the concise but comprehensive history first attempted by Copleston, whom he had previously referred to as 'my learned (though partial) predecessor'.[19] Writing almost a century later than Copleston, Gombrich was able to benefit from monographs on different periods of Buddhist history written in the intervening decades, and which amply illustrated the economic bases and cultural roles of cities in that history. Copleston, in contrast, did his work at a time when basic monographic work had hardly begun (the pioneer study of *Buddhist India* by T.W. Rhys Davids was published only in 1903) and the modern period of Buddhism that he himself was a witness to was still very much in the making. It is not surprising, therefore, to find him resorting to rather rough-and-ready classifications and periodizations. He periodized Buddhist history in relation to the great men of different eras: the Buddha, Asoka and Mahinda, Buddhaghosa, Parakramabahu and Hikkaduve Sumangala.[20] And as mentioned at the very beginning of this paper, he saw two Buddhisms in his time: a residuum of old Buddhism lingering in out-of-the way places and a new externally-inspired Buddhism in the city around him.

Yet this view, as the foregoing sketch of the emergence of Colombo as a centre of Buddhism has sought to demonstrate, was a distorted one. Not all places outside Colombo were homes of a precariously lingering residual Buddhism. On the contrary, it was these places that had sufficient strength to provide Colombo with key religious personnel (such as Pilane Buddharakkhita, Valane Siddhartha, Mohottivatte Gunananda and Hikkaduve Sumangala) for its revival. Furthermore, such monks did not generally migrate all by themselves. They did so with the active encouragement and material support of the lay people who had preceded them into the capital and had improved their worldly fortunes there.[21] As a newly-arrived Westerner himself, Copleston was much more aware of newly-arriving Western influences (notably Oriental philology and archaeology, Free-thought and Theosophy) than of these quieter and longer-term trends in local society and religion.

III

Those who migrated to the capital from the hinterland brought their religious beliefs and practices with them. Therefore, with some obvious variations resulting from differences in densities of population and the resources of patrons, what Buddhists in and around Colombo initially did was not very different from what their co-religionists did elsewhere in the country. Here, as elsewhere, there were various kinds of merit-making activities (*pinkam*) such as building and restoring temples, observing rituals and ceremonials connected with getting them consecrated, admitting novices to the monastic order and getting them ordained in due course, preaching sermons and listening to them, and so on.[22]

These were occasions and activities directed and presided over mainly by monks but in which the participation of the laity, too, played a vital part. The participation of the latter became all the more vital in colonial times because in the absence of state patronage,

Buddhist institutions and practices had to rely more and more on the voluntary participation of the laity. Their participation required a basic knowledge of what to do and say (in Pali) on specific occasions – a knowledge that was generally imparted and assimilated in the process of growing up as a Buddhist. While such informal means of teaching and learning continued,[23] the newly-available medium of print came to supplement the older ones. Thus, in the 1860s and 1870s, there appeared a number of manuals, in print providing basic information and guidance to the laity, and it was to this class of literature that the *Buddha Ädahilla* belonged.

As regards the contents of its original edition (of which no copies seem to have survived), a brief summary was given by Copleston:

> rules for 'taking Refuge in Buddha', etc.; for 'taking', as it is called, or binding oneself to the Five, the Eight, or the Ten Precepts; for the observance of 'poya' (uposatha) days, and for meditation on decay, etc.; with short explanations of the doctrine of Karma and of merit and demerit; and of duties towards the dead, towards the gods, and towards the Buddha.[24]

Out of these items, Copleston gave some special attention to the Five Precepts. In a brief but separate chapter on the subject (Chapter XI), he traced their probable history in canonical and immediate post-canonical times, and he also commented on their place in contemporary practice:

> The obligation of the Five Precepts, being universal, may be taken at home, every day or more frequently; or it may be taken more formally in the presence of a monk at a temple. In this case, the person first offers flowers at the temple; he then kneels or prostrates himself before the monk with hands joined together, says three times, 'Homage to the Buddha,' etc., three times, 'I take refuge,' etc., and then he repeats after the monk the five precepts (or prohibitions). If he has not time to go to a temple, he can 'take sil' before any image of Buddha, or turning himself in the direction in which there is an image or temple, etc. This is the *minimum* of Buddhist observance.[25]

Moving on to the eight and ten precepts, and their closer connections with temples, the *poya* days and the status of a Buddhist devotee (*upasaka*), Copleston noted that the 'devotee of the Ten Obligations, or "dasasil", is almost a monk. . . . This is the upasaka *par excellence*.'[26] Copleston's book, incidentally, contained a rare late nineteenth-century reference to the beginnings of this profession among women:

There are very few men of this profession, but a considerable number of women, generally old, are to be seen about the temples, especially in Kandy, or on the way to Adam's Peak. They usually carry bowls as if for begging . . . and one who had read the books would naturally suppose them to be nuns. Female mendicants they are; but they have not been admitted to the Community [the order of nuns having become extinct], and therefore are not called 'bhikkhunis', but only 'upasikas'.[27]

Listing other items contained in the *Buddha Ädahilla,* Copleston reported that the

Manual goes on to explain how the merit of a man's acts can be imparted to departed friends or to the gods.[28] It contains stanzas used in the worship of dagabas and in offering flowers; and some of the more popular Suttas, viz. Mangala, Ratana, Karaniyametta; and certain Jayamangala gatha, or stanzas for good luck and prosperity. The latter recite certain actions of the Buddha, and each stanza ends with the refrain, 'By virtue of this may your prosperity grow!'

The use of these items had come to be confined mainly to the domestic and monastic realms under colonial conditions. However, keeping them so confined was not easy even under those conditions. In pre-colonial times, monks, householders and rulers had been inter-linked by the reciprocities of a long-standing ideology of merit,[29] which could not be easily forgotten or discarded. This difficulty became manifest in the uses of what Copleston referred to here as 'Jayamangala gatha, or stanzas for good luck and prosperity'.

These stanzas continued to be chanted by monks in welcoming honoured guests, including British dignitaries, a practice to which Christian missionaries raised an objection because they viewed the expansion of European empires as an act of God for the propagation of the Gospel and did not wish to see colonial officials encouraging or condoning non-Christian practices. It was their point of view that found expression, for example, in Gordon Cumming's observation:

Strange to say, they [Buddhist monks] have . . . frequently been privileged on State occasions to chant a solemn benediction in Pali, invoking the blessing of Buddha on their friendly rulers, who remained standing during a ceremony which most felt to be singularly out of place.[30]

The controversial nature of the subject is also clear from Copleston's comment:

It has been said that these verses are not directly religious; but the use of them implies a belief in the Buddha, and their purpose is to obtain for the person congratulated some sort of benefit from the Buddha. It is said that they were once used in welcoming the Governor of Ceylon; but they are no longer admitted on such occasions.[31]

Copleston was mistaken, however, in assuming that the matter had been settled once and for all. Government officials were much less concerned than missionaries with the literal meaning and implications of the Pali stanzas. They were more inclined to promote and welcome expressions of loyalty to the government from all sections of the population. And the idioms of these expressions became more diverse as it became increasingly clear, in the course of the nineteenth century, that early expectations of a spiritual conquest following on the heels of temporal conquest were not quite realistic. Even though some Christians continued to hold 'that all false faiths should fade away before the One True Light of the world',[32] others came to the realization that Christianity would remain only a minority religion in most parts of Asia.[33] Therefore, direct government support for its maintenance and propagation became harder to justify. Among the important official duties that Copleston had to perform during his time as the Bishop of Colombo was to acquiesce in the 'disestablishment' of the Anglican Church, that is, the termination of financial subsidies given to it until then by the colonial government.[34]

At the same time, the government drew on pre-colonial sources of loyalty among the majority community by imitating, to some degree, the roles of pre-colonial rulers. Governor William Gregory (1872-7), for instance, engaged two learned Buddhists, Batuvantudave Devarakkhita and Hikkaduve Sumangala, to bring out an edition and translation (into Sinhala) of the *Mahāvaṃsa*. The final chapter that the two of them added to their edition showed how Buddhist authors themselves had come to accept their current rulers, for all practical purposes, as the legitimate government of the land.[35] This chapter ended with an account of the deposition of the last king of Kandy, which did not differ very much from standard colonial narratives. The deposition was depicted as a just and popular uprising against a deranged tyrant:

> And because the Ruler committed in this way many evil deeds the Sīhalas [inhabitants of the kingdom of Kandy] and the inhabitants of the town of Colombo [the British] rebelled. They all came hither, captured the criminal king alive . . . and brought him to the opposite [Coromandel] coast. After they had brought the King, the torturer of his people, to the opposite coast the Ingrīsi by name seized the whole kingdom.[36]

This acceptance of the status quo did not mean the disappearance of nostalgia for the time of kings. A.M. Hocart, who was archaeological commissioner in the 1920s and who had a special interest in the comparative study of kingship, reported that 'it is . . . commonly believed that the island would be happier and the people more virtuous if a Buddhist king were on the throne once more'.[37] There were also feelings of affinity and sympathy with Buddhist kingdoms in Southeast Asia that outlasted the one in Sri Lanka. However, these feelings, despite their deep ideological and institutional roots, no longer resulted in active rebellions. There were no organizations, cultic or military or both, aimed at restoring pre-colonial kingship.[38] The new voluntary organizations that did come into being at the time had much more limited and perfectly legal aims, such as printing and publishing books and pamphlets in the interest of Buddhism, and thereby adapting the religion to the new (post-monarchical) times. They were the organizations that arranged for the publication of such manuals as the *Buddha Ädahilla*.

Among various manuals that appeared in print at the time, the *Buddha Ädahilla* was not a particularly novel or original work. There were other works of a similar nature published around the same time. For instance, there was a booklet of thirty-one pages, *Pratipatti Dīpaniya*, described by a cataloguer as a 'manual of Buddhist worship, with quotations from the Pali canon',[39] which had been published four years earlier in 1868. This manual claimed to be no more than a revised version of a still earlier publication. Where *Buddha Ädahilla* did differ from earlier publications was in its title. In contrast to a more conventional one like *Pratipatti Dīpaniya* (Illuminator of Practice),[40] *Buddha Ädahilla* was a title that was quite unconventional for a work of this nature.

As mentioned previously, Copleston translated the title as 'Buddha-

Faith'. But he offered no specific comments on the title itself or its translation. Since then, others have commented on the word *ädahilla*, and its etymological connections with *saddhā* in Pali and *śraddhā* in Sanskrit.[41] It may well have been with these etymological connections in mind that Copleston himself translated *ädahilla* as 'faith'.[42] Less explored than the etymology, however, are the practical meanings and associations that the word *ädahilla* had come to acquire by the nineteenth century.

Particularly noteworthy among these new usages in new times was its application across religions – rather like the word *āgama*, which had come to be used as the equivalent of 'religion'. In this case, by adding such adjectives as *kristiyāni* (Christian) or *bauddha* (Buddhist), one could differentiate between one kind of *āgama* and another. Likewise, in the case of *ädahilla,* it now became possible to differentiate between the devotional words and acts of one religious tradition and those of another. It was probably because of this comparative applicability and usage that in the decades that elapsed between the original edition of *c.*1872 (which Copleston consulted) and the later one of 1955 (which Gombrich consulted), the title of the work had shifted from *Buddha* (noun) to *Bauddha* (adjective).[43] The changed title reflected better what its contents had come to do, which was specifying what a Buddhist as a Buddhist (that is, as an adherent of Buddhism as distinct from other religions) was expected to know. It was in this way that Gombrich himself viewed it. He described the *Bauddha Ädahilla* as 'a religious pocket book' containing 'all the Pali verses which a layman is supposed to know or need, with Sinhalese translations and explanations', and he translated the title as 'Buddhist Devotion'.[44] As a religious pocket book, it was comparable to – and, no doubt, influenced in its format by – Christian publications such as prayer books and hymnals, specifying what Christians were expected to know. This type of Christian literature had been available in Sinhala in growing numbers since the Dutch established a printing press in Colombo in the 1730s. Yet, at the same time, older Buddhist roots were reinforced with pride of place being given to Pali. As S.J. Tambiah observed from a comparative perspective:

> In Islam, Hinduism, Buddhism, and Judaism the view has been strictly held that in religious ceremonies the sacred words recited should be in the language

of the authorized sacred texts. The problem whether their congregations understood the words or not was not a major consideration affecting either the efficacy of the ritual or the change in the moral conditions of the worshippers. The Catholic Church maintained the same view with respect to the Latin liturgy until 1967.[45]

In the case of the Pali words in the *Bauddha Ädahilla*, there was nothing particularly exclusive or esoteric about them. Understanding their meaning was encouraged, as indicated by the explanations of them provided in Sinhala. However, in the actual process of learning, getting to know the words and their accompanying actions and contexts generally preceded understanding their meanings.[46] And getting to know the meanings depended, in turn, on levels of education and degrees of devotion. The renaissance of Buddhist learning in and around Colombo in the late nineteenth century – which was mentioned in the previous section – did contribute to higher levels of understanding, and this was a process that continued well into the next century and into other parts of the country. As Gombrich reported on conditions in rural highlands in the 1960s:

> The Five Precepts are almost universally known by rote, and their meanings also are generally known and understood, though the specific meanings of the Pali words are often not known – but this knowledge is on the increase because of *daham pāsal* (Sunday schools) and religious instruction in state schools.[47]

Barely noticeable behind this passing reference to Sunday schools was the adoption and adjustment of an innovation of one religious tradition – acclaimed as 'that mainstay of Protestant Church practice from the eighteenth century'[48]– into the calendar of another religious tradition. Comparable adjustments also took place in relation to the composition and uses of the second manual with which this essay is concerned: *A Buddhist Catechism*. It is time now to turn to the religious and educational context in which this manual came into being.

IV

Colombo, which became a centre of Buddhist learning only after the mid-nineteenth century, had been the main centre of Christian learning in the island for a much longer period. It had Franciscan and Jesuit colleges in the sixteenth and seventeenth centuries,[49] and a Dutch seminary in the next century.[50] Some students of the latter institution went on to pursue higher studies in Dutch universities such as Leiden and Utrecht.[51] The same sort of Western tradition of learning, opening paths to higher studies in Britain for a select few, was continued under the British rule in the nineteenth century.[52]

This was a system of education that was dominated by the Christian clergy though the exact type of clergy who dominated it depended on the nationality and religious preference of the colonial power at a given time. Yet, over time, and reflecting broader social and ideological changes in Europe, there were also other notable changes in this system of education. One such change was in the school curricula. Influenced by the intellectual currents of Renaissance humanism, Enlightenment philosophy and scientific revolutions, school curricula had become increasingly secularized (just as teachers themselves had become increasingly laicized), reducing religious instruction to the status of one subject among many taught in schools (or separately in Sunday schools). Second, secular authorities, who needed expanding state bureaucracies, had begun assuming greater responsibility and power in the area of education, and had, therefore, begun creating government departments to take charge of public instruction.

It was the creation of such a Department of Public Instruction in the colonial capital of Colombo in 1870 that opened up competition for grants-in-aid among different religious groups on a formally equal footing and on the basis of the quality of secular instruction that they were able to provide. It was in the ensuing inter-denominational competition that the Buddhist Theosophical Society (founded in 1880) aspired to take part. And it was as a text to be used for religious instruction in their schools (an area of instruction that was left to the choosing of the managers themselves) that *A Buddhist Catechism* was originally composed in 1881.[53] The title and language of the text would have been suggested quite naturally by the context for which it was compiled. It was to take the place of various catechisms and newer types of apologetic literature, such as William Paley's *Evidences of Christianity*, that had been – and were being – used in Christian schools.[54]

These developments which took place in the field of lay education had some indirect yet significant impact on monastic education as well. This impact can be seen early enough in the transition from Valane Siddhartha's teaching career at Ratmalana in the 1840s-1860s to that of Hikkaduve Sumangala at Maligakanda from the 1870s onwards. Compared with the former place, teaching at the latter was on a larger scale and was more formally organized. In fact, the place was founded specifically as a teaching institution (with a trust deed and board of trustees to ensure that it adhered to that function)[55] in contrast to earlier institutions where teaching and learning were simply one aspect of the wider activities and functions of temples and monasteries. The pedagogic purpose of the institution was also expressed in its name: Vidyodaya ('Dawn of Knowledge').

Over time, Vidyodaya (and its offshoots) came to acquire more and more of the standard features of educational institutions imported from the West: a principal and his assistants, a regular intake of students graded into different classes, prescribed and printed texts, regular examinations and – with the acceptance of a government grant-in-aid – annual inspections, annual reports, prize-giving ceremonies, and so on. In physical appearance, too, Vidyodaya did not differ very much from a modern European-style school. As an American naval officer, who escorted three Korean diplomats on a visit to Vidyodaya in April 1884, reported:

> Knowing it to be a Buddhist institution I expected to see a temple of the usual native architecture. Instead of this however, the college consisted of several very neat nearly European buildings in a small park. One of the buildings, the Library, was entirely European and was an imposing handsome edifice.[56]

To be sure, Vidyodaya derived inspiration and guidance from the pre-colonial past as well. It was from that past that the designation of *piriveṇa* (*pariveṇa* in Pali) was derived: a term which originally meant a monastic cell but which had gradually come to mean 'an institution comparable to the monastic college of medieval Europe'.[57] The term, which had fallen into disuse since the sixteenth century, was revived in the nineteenth. From the same pre-colonial past were also derived the main subjects and texts studied in the modern *piriveṇas*.

For the same reason, however, the contrast with European colleges was all the more apparent. The kinds of adjustments and modifications which had enabled European colleges to continue their pre-eminence into modern times could not be repeated easily or quickly in Buddhist ones. Hence, there was no prospect of a modern *piriveṇa* regaining the same sort of position as its precursors had held in pre-colonial kingdoms. All it could do was to find a place of its own in the current – and more diversified – system of public instruction. In this system, there were primary and secondary schools; schools run by the government and by religious organizations; and more specialized institutions such as a Normal School (1843), a Medical College (1870), and a Law College (1874). Vidyodaya's position within this system – and in the sort of terminology preferred by that system – was that of an Oriental College.

As an Oriental College, Vidyodaya made contributions to the advancement of learning in that field, as well as – in keeping with changing times – to the evolution of a system of formal qualifications pertaining to it.[58] Their effect, however, was to accentuate rather than reduce the differences between those who had an Oriental education and those who had a Western one. Reflections on the resulting problems of religious education can be seen in the message that Hikkaduve Sumangala, as a respected elder of the Theravada School (or the Southern School, as it was often called at the time), addressed to the Parliament of Religions that assembled in Chicago in 1893.[59]

Explaining why a young layman (the twenty-nine-year-old Dharmapala) rather than a senior monk was being sent to represent Theravada (the doctrine of monastic elders), Sumangala wrote: 'We should have been glad to accede to the wishes of your Council in sending one or more of our ordained monks; but being ignorant of Western languages, their presence as active members of the Parliament would be useless'. On the difficulties of gaining access to Western education, he noted: 'Education in Ceylon on Western principles has been backward because until quite recently our children could not procure it save at the risk of the destruction of their religious belief under the interested tuition of anti-Buddhist instruction.'[60]

Though that risk was real enough, in education as in other areas of their activities, Christian missionaries did not always achieve what they intended to achieve. The career of Dharmapala himself was sufficient proof that children from Buddhist homes who attended Christian schools did not always end up as Christians. On the other hand, Sumangala knew of an opposite instance within his own family. His English-educated eldest brother was a Christian.[61]

The 'recent' changes in the ownership and management of schools that Sumangala alluded to in his 1893 message was 'the opening of secular schools by our people under the leadership of the Theosophical Society'; and in that connection, he expressed his appreciation of Olcott to whom 'we owe the very catechism out of which our children are being taught the first principles of religion, and our present brotherly relations with our co-religionists of Japan and other Buddhist countries'. Such cordiality was fitting for the occasion for it was in the company of Theosophists that the Buddhist delegate, Dharmapala – who had previously accompanied Olcott on a visit to Japan in 1889 – was now making his way to Chicago.[62] It was also Sumangala himself who, back in 1881, had certified Olcott's catechism as 'in agreement with the Canon of the Southern Buddhist Church', and recommended it to 'teachers in Buddhist schools and to all others who may wish to impart information to beginners about the essential features of our religion'. But neither at that time nor on subsequent occasions when the catechism was revised and expanded, was the process of reaching an agreement between its author and authorizer quite as easy as is suggested here. The writing of the catechism, in contrast to the compilation of the *Buddha Ädahilla*, was more of a venture into new and unfamiliar territory. While the *Ädahilla* could follow mainly local precedents, the models for the *Catechism* were mainly external. Following their lead, it had to bring difficult and debatable issues relating to beliefs and practices into the open that the other manual could conveniently – and perhaps advisedly – leave implicit. Under the current system of schooling and religious instruction, however, those issues could no longer be left purely implicit. How and with what consequences they came out into the open will get clearer as we examine the later history of the two manuals.

V

Copleston made no direct comparisons on the relative popularity of the two manuals in his time. But his comments suggest that he saw the *Buddha Ädahilla* as the more popular: 'It is largely used, at any rate in the low country. Most Buddhists who can read, at least in or near Colombo, possess a copy; and some of those who cannot read get it read to them'.[63] On the other hand, Olcott, who made no mention of the *Buddha Ädahilla* or any other Sinhala manual, clearly saw his own work as an instant bestseller:

> The Sinhalese and English versions appeared simultaneously, on 24 July 1881, and thenceforward, for some weeks, the hand-presses of Colombo could not strike off copies fast enough to meet the demand. Sumangala ordered 100 copies for the use of the priest-pupils in his College; it became a textbook in the schools; found its way into every Sinhalese family.[64]

If the claim that the catechism 'found its way into every Sinhalese family' was an evident exaggeration (for one thing, not every Sinhalese family was Buddhist), there was one area where its circulation clearly exceeded that of any work written in Sinhala and that was in its distribution overseas. Copleston said nothing in this respect but, here again, Olcott was not reticent in putting forward his claims. Speaking to Japanese Buddhists in 1889 on authors whose publications had popularized Buddhism in the West, Olcott reported:

> There is one book called *The Light of Asia*, a poem by Sir Edwin Arnold, of which several hundred thousand copies have been sold, and which has done more for Buddhism than any other agency. Then there are and have been great authors and philologists like Professor Max Müller, Messrs. Burnouf, De Rosny, St. Hilaire, Rhys Davids, Beal, Fausböll, Biagandet, and others, who have written about the Lord Buddha in the most sympathetic terms. And among the agencies to be noticed is the Theosophical Society, of which I am President. The *Buddhist Catechism*, which I compiled for the Sinhalese Buddhists eight years ago, has already been published in fifteen different languages.[65]

This international circulation continued unabated into the next century and by the time of the author's death in 1907, the catechism had gone through forty editions or reprints and had been translated into twenty languages.[66] In the course of those editions, the title had changed from the relatively modest *A Buddhist Catechism, According to the Canon of the Southern Church* (1881) to the more assertive *The Buddhist Catechism* (1887); and the contents had expanded from twenty-eight pages to nearly a hundred pages divided into five chapters

(1897). The chapters were: The Life of the Buddha, The Dharma or Doctrine, The Sangha, The Rise and Spread of Buddhism, and Buddhism and Science.

The allocation of an entire chapter to Buddhism and science reflected the demands of the time in which the catechism was compiled. Historically, the topic demanded attention in response to some of the missionary critiques of Buddhism: to works like Robert Spence Hardy's *The Sacred Books of the Buddhists Compared with History and Modern Science* (1863). But given that Christianity itself had been the target of criticism from the points of view of history and modern science, a discussion of science was rapidly becoming unavoidable in the presentation of any religion in a modern context. As Jürgen Habermas was to observe later:

> In modern societies, religious teachings must accustom themselves to the unavoidable competition with other forms of faith and claims to truth. They no longer move in a self-contained universe governed, so to speak, by their own absolute truth. Every religious teaching today encounters the pluralism of different forms of religious truth as well as the scepticism of secular scientific knowledge.[67]

As an initial response to such newer issues, the catechism attracted readers well beyond the audience for whom it was originally intended (the schoolchildren of Ceylon); and its publication and distribution, too, were increasingly done by agencies outside the original place of publication (Colombo). Still, the original context continued to have some importance because it was as a manual authored and authorized by Buddhists themselves (rather than by outsiders like Christian missionaries or Orientalists) that the catechism claimed a special status. Just as at the Parliament of Religions in Chicago in 1893, what was attempted here was self-representation rather than representation by others. Hence, Hikkaduve Sumangala's certificate, first issued in 1881 and renewed in 1897, has continued to be included in the publication ever since. Not surprisingly, therefore, it is in the same context that most of the discussions and debates among Buddhists themselves on the content and composition of the catechism have taken place.

One such topic that inevitably came up for discussion quite early in the preparation of the catechism was the definition of *nirvana*.

The topic was a difficult one at any time.[68] It was hardly less so at this time when there were disagreements and debates about it among local monks as well as Western philologists. Olcott has left the following account of how the answer in the catechism was arrived at:

Knowing perfectly well the strong views entertained by the school of Southern Buddhism of which Sumangala is the type, I had drafted the reply to the question: "What is Nirvana" in such a way as to just note that there was a difference of opinion among Buddhist metaphysicians as to the survival of an abstract human entity, without leaning either towards the views of the Northern or Southern school. But the two erudite critics [Sumangala and his Assistant Principal, Heyiyantuduve Devamitta] caught me up at the first glance at the paragraph, and the High Priest denied that there was *any* such difference of opinion among Buddhist metaphysicians. Upon my citing to him the beliefs of the Tibetans, Chinese, Japanese, Mongolians, and even of a Sinhalese school of which the late Polgahawatte [*sic*] was leader,[69] he closed our discussion by saying that, if I did not alter the text, he should cancel his promise to give me a certificate that the *Catechism* was suited to the teaching of children in Buddhist schools, and should publish his reasons therefor. As this would virtually destroy the usefulness of my educational monograph. . . . I yielded to *force majeure*, and made the paragraph read, as it has ever since stood, in the many editions through which the *Catechism* has since passed.[70]

The details of Olcott's recollection are not easy to verify. No comparable recollection has been recorded by Sumangala. What is clear, though, is that Olcott himself was not entirely happy with the answer that appeared in his catechism.[71] Similarly clear is the difficulty of the task he had taken upon himself, namely, 'to condense the whole body of Buddhist *Dhamma* into a little hand-book that one might read through in a couple of hours'.[72] Considering this, some may well have wondered whether a task of this nature was worth being attempted at all. Olcott himself confessed that he could get no monk to undertake it; and even though Christian catechisms and their translations had been available locally for quite a while, no Buddhist until then had tried to emulate them.[73] Many decades later, comparing doctrinal formulations of Buddhism and Christianity, Edward Conze commented:

An Anthology of Christian thought would have to pay special attention to the numerous creeds in which the doctrine from time to time found dogmatic formulation. So essential indeed is creed-making to Christians that . . . these statements of dogma go back to the Apostles themselves. For various reasons Buddhists never felt the need to define their doctrinal position briefly and precisely. We have had to wait 2,500 years for Mr Christmas Humphreys, an English lawyer, to bestow his 'Twelve Points' upon us.[74]

It so happened that the 'Twelve Points' of Humphreys were actually inspired by an earlier list of 'Fourteen Fundamental Buddhist Beliefs' drafted by Olcott (who, too, by the way, had been a lawyer once). And that list, adopted at an international conference at Adyar in Madras in 1891, was a further stage of the same sequence of events which began a decade earlier with the *Catechism*.[75] While the latter sought to condense the teachings of the Southern School, the former sought to arrive at the basic beliefs held in common by both the Southern and Northern Schools in order to move thereby towards greater unity and cooperation between them.[76] As in the case of those fundamental beliefs, so likewise in the case of the catechism: the response to problems of popularization and mass education in the modern age – the Age of Improvement – was not to give up the effort altogether but rather to try and improve the presentation with revisions and amendments.

Olcott's own efforts at improving his catechism through its successive editions resulted, as mentioned earlier, in an increase of its length. This tended to decrease its usefulness for instruction at the more elementary levels. The solution to this problem followed a precedent already established in the Christian tradition, namely, the production of a simpler and shorter version. This was done in 1889 by the British Theosophist (and former Anglican priest), C.W. Leadbeater, who had opened Buddhist Sunday schools as well as the Buddhist High School (later Ananda College) in Colombo in 1886. This shorter catechism was originally published in Sinhala under the title *Bauddha Śiśubodhaya*. Among those who took part in its preparation was Dharmapala, who has left an account of its origins:

Leadbeater was asked by Olcott to prepare a shorter Catechism, which he did compile from the larger one, and Col. Olcott asked me to translate it into Sinhalese, which I did with the help of the High Priest Sumangala.[77] The second part compiled by Leadbeater was translated by the teachers of the Buddhist English school, James Perera and Wimalasuriya.[78]

The *Bauddha Śiśubodaya* was translated back into English as *The Smaller Buddhist Catechism* in 1902 by one of Leadbeater's former pupils, C. Jinarajadasa, who was just embarking on a long career in the Theosophical Society of which he eventually became President in 1945.

While these publications had proceeded within the framework of the Buddhist-Theosophist alliance, cracks within the latter had already begun to appear by the late 1880s. Considering the very different intellectual roots of Sinhalese Buddhism and Euro-American Theosophy, stresses and strains within the alliance were hardly surprising; and they appeared soon enough after the initial honeymoon. The first to abandon the alliance was one of its key architects, Mohottivatte Gunananda, who found himself and his temple at Kotahena losing their centrality to the lay leadership of the newly-created Buddhist Theosophical Society (BTS) headquarters at Pettah. His resistance appeared, among other avenues, in rival publications.

Among these was a newspaper launched in 1888. Its title, *Riviräsa* (Rays of the Sun), was chosen, no doubt, in response to the (abridged) title of the BTS newspaper, *Sañdaräsa* (Rays of the Moon). It was preceded by the first part of a Buddhist catechism of Mohottivatte's own: *Bauddha Praśnaya* (1887). Its title was reminiscent of *Milinda Praśnaya* (Milinda's Questions), of which he himself had brought out a printed edition in his pre-BTS days in 1878.[79] Dedicated to questions and answers on the Buddha, this first part of the catechism also showed a degree of continuity – though in a different format – of the devotional interests of his *Buddha Ädahilla* of the earlier era. In the preface to his catechism, Mohottivatte Gunananda explained that he compiled it in order to resist the incorporation of false (*mithyā*) ideas into Buddhism by its new-found Western sympathizers.[80]

The BTS was secure enough by this time to withstand Mohottivatte's opposition. Olcott himself did not fear it greatly though he did fear the effect it could have on Sumangala: 'Always a specious and silvery-tongued man, [Mohottivatte] had begun to drag the amiable High Priest into his way of thinking, and to make inevitable a breach between us, which to Sinhalese Buddhism at that time would have been very harmful.'[81] Olcott's fears, however, were unfounded. Sumangala knew early enough that Theosophists held ideas that he disagreed with but he did not see these disagreements as serious enough to abandon the alliance with them.[82] He had helped Mohottivatte in the preparation of his catechism, just as he had helped Olcott and Leadbeater in the preparation of theirs. At Olcott's request, in November 1887, he also issued a certificate recommending the former's latest compilation, *The Golden Rules of Buddhism*, 'as a book of instruction for Buddhist youth'.[83] In thus offering his help to all those who sought it, Sumangala may well have seen all these efforts as complementary rather than conflicting ways of popularizing Buddhism among different audiences in his time.[84] Most lay people, too, may well have seen them in the same way. At any rate the same patron, Cecilia Ilangakoon, who had financed the publication of *A Buddhist Catechism*, extended her financial support to the *Bauddha Praśnaya* as well. It is also noteworthy that an external observer like Copleston made no mention at all of the Buddhist-Theosophist tensions. Either he did not know about them or, being no stranger to sectarian conflicts among Christians (or indeed to infighting within his own diocese), he did not see them as particularly significant from the point of view of outsiders.

Mohottivatte's opposition, in any case, did not last long. He was in declining health when it began and he died in 1890, his funeral providing an opportunity for feuding factions to come together. The projected second and third parts of his catechism, which would have been devoted to the Dhamma and the Sangha, respectively, did not appear in print; and the first part, too, never achieved the same sort of circulation – certainly not the same sort of international circulation – as did Olcott's catechism. This did not mean, however, that Olcott's catechism (and the wider Buddhist-Theosophist alliance within which it came into being) remained unchallenged. The next challenger was Dharmapala, who, too, like Mohottivatte before him, experienced a parting of ways from the Theosophists in the late 1890s.

Younger than Mohottivatte by some four decades, Dharmapala's religious career had begun very much in the shadow of the BTS. His grandfather was its president, and his father and an uncle were prominent members. It was by moving into the headquarters of the BTS in 1885 that he began his homeless life. His international career, too, emerged quite naturally out of BTS concerns; in particular,

Olcott's interest in building a platform for an international Buddhist league. It was in Olcott's company that he first visited Japan in 1889 and it was soon after the international conference at Adyar in 1891 to adopt the 'Fourteen Fundamental Buddhist Beliefs' (drafted by Olcott) that he made his fateful trip further north to Bodh Gaya. When he organized the Maha Bodhi Society later in the year and became its general secretary (a position he held for the rest of his life), the managerial, journalistic and fund-raising skills he had acquired in his five-year apprenticeship at the BTS stood him in good stead. Continuity with the past was also reflected in Hikkaduve Sumangala being elected president of the new Society, and Olcott its director and special adviser. For a while, the journal of the Society, launched in 1892, came to have *Maha Bodhi and the United Buddhist World* as its full title. Taking an active interest in the affairs of the fledgling Society, Olcott made a tour to Calcutta, Darjeeling, Akyab and Rangoon in late 1892, canvassing support and helping Dharmapala to organize new branches.[85]

Olcott, who had no problem supporting Buddhism in Ceylon or Burma or Japan, did not find it quite so easy to do so in India, especially if Buddhist and Hindu interests came into conflict with each other – as they soon did over the custody of the Maha Bodhi temple. In the mid-1890s, Olcott began distancing himself from Dharmapala and the Maha Bodhi Society, and formally resigned his position of Director and Special Adviser in 1896.[86] Dharmapala, in turn, sought to distance Buddhism from Theosophy by proposing to eliminate the word 'Theosophical' from the name of the Buddhist Theosophical Society in Colombo.[87] The move was unsuccessful: the BTS, whose activities were mainly educational, continued to value the services of Theosophists who were willing to come and work as schoolteachers. The increasingly uneasy relations between Olcott and Dharmapala eventually resulted in the latter's resignation from the Theosophical Society in 1905.

Having resigned himself, Dharmapala attempted to persuade Sumangala to do likewise and to withdraw the authorization that had been given to Olcott's *A Buddhist Catechism*. Olcott had not helped matters by the new questions and answers that he had included in the latest (40th) edition of this work without consulting the authorizer adequately. Consequently, relations between Olcott and Sumangala became more strained than they had ever been before.[88] However, in the end, there was no formal breach. The mediation of the current leaders of the BTS (R.A. Mirando, D.B. Jayatilaka, and W.A. de Silva) helped to bring about a reconciliation. More moderate than Dharmapala, they were keen to keep old alliances going by mending fences and facilitating compromises.

There is some evidence that Dharmapala, like Mohottivatte before him, drafted a catechism of his own as a rival to Olcott's.[89] But it is unclear whether he got it printed and published. Instead, in the schools under the management of the Maha Bodhi Society, he opted for an alternative catechism that had been available for a while. Reporting on a visit to Ceylon in 1914 (when neither Olcott nor Sumangala were alive), the American philosopher, James Bissett Pratt, wrote:

> Theosophist schools use Colonel Olcott's 'Buddhist Catechism', and Paul Carus's 'The Gospel of Buddha' [1894]; while the Maha-Bodhi schools use Subhadra Bhikshu's 'Buddhist Catechism' [1888] – an excellent book. . . .[90] There is a marked difference between these books: the two latter passing over in silence most of the magical and supernatural elements of Buddhism, or interpreting them symbolically, while Colonel Olcott's 'Catechism' – in true Theosophist style – makes a special effort to teach such things as the 'Aura' emitted by the Buddha and various holy Bhikkhus, as well as from certain dagobas in Ceylon where relics of the Buddha are said to be enshrined [Questions 334-48 in the chapter on Buddhism and Science].[91]

Pratt's observations provide early testimony to the widening choice that was becoming available in relation to the new type of Buddhist manuals written in Western languages. Olcott, who initiated the trend and who sought to improve his own contribution through repeated revisions, aspired to leave *The Buddhist Catechism* 'at my death a perfect compendium of the contents of Southern Buddhism'.[92] Such an aspiration was plainly unrealistic because manuals of this nature, seeking to answer frequently asked questions of a given time, necessarily become dated as questions begin to change with changing times. Accordingly, answers need to change, too, in keeping with changing frontiers of knowledge.

Reporting on 'Buddhism in Ceylon' some three decades after Pratt's visit, Josiah Crosby (1947) made no mention of Olcott's catechism. Instead, in relation to materials in English, he mentioned a newer Buddhist centre in Colombo, the Vajirarama monastery in Bambalapitiya, which issued 'tracts in English upon the subject of Buddhism, as well as . . . a quarterly religious magazine (also in English) entitled *The Bosat*'.[93] Among the preachers and writers at Vajirarama, Crosby mentioned, in particular, the 'head of the establishment [Palane Vajiranana], who is . . . a venerated teacher, whose sermons not infrequently figure in the programmes issued from the broadcasting station at Colombo,' and also one of his pupils, Narada, who was equally well known. Narada travelled extensively within the country as well as overseas, and he was the author of a number of introductory publications, such as *Buddhism in a Nutshell* (1933) and *The Buddha and His Teachings* (1942), both of which were to appear in several editions and reprints.

By this time, with the spread of literacy in English among some sections of the monkhood, the sort of linguistic gulf that prevailed in the generation of Olcott and Sumangala no longer remained quite so marked. An increasing number of local monks had extended their foreign travels, too, beyond Southeast Asia to the West. There was also a reverse flow of Westerners seeking admission to the monkhood and residence in Asia. Narada's early lead in writing introductory works in English was followed in the 1950s – with greater scholarly refinement and to greater international acclaim – by Walpola Rahula with his *What the Buddha Taught* (1959).[94] With the appearance of such works, the appeal of older works like Olcott's was bound to recede; and at the end of the 1960s, Gananath Obeyesekere reported that Olcott's catechism had 'gone out of vogue'.[95]

In the meantime, the Sinhala version of the catechism had fared no better. The translations had not kept up with changes in the English original.[96] A 2007 reprint of the first Sinhala edition of 1881[97] and a fresh translation of the 42nd English edition of 1908[98] have appeared recently. However, these publications were undertaken more for historical and commemorative value than current usefulness. Buddhist Sunday schools have been using primers of a later date than Olcott's (or Leadbeater's) for quite a while.[99]

The historical and commemorative aspects have been prominent in the way that different branches of the Theosophical movement have kept the English version of the catechism in print. These reprints have been part of wider attempts to keep the writings of the founders available more generally. Yet just as competition from later publications has greatly reduced the relative importance of Olcott's catechism, likewise, at a more general level, competition from later movements has greatly reduced the relative importance of Theosophy itself as a global movement.[100]

VI

Compared with the early history of *A Buddhist Catechism*, which, from the moment of its birth, had been chronicled enthusiastically by its author himself, the history of the *Buddha Ädahilla* was more obscure. Unlike Olcott, Mohottivatte claimed no special credit for having compiled it, nor did he try to keep track of its progress. In the absence of this sort of information from the compiler himself, the near-contemporary comments made by Copleston were particularly valuable. He testified to its popularity in and around Colombo in his time, and he provided an excellent starting point for later students by giving the time and place of its original publication, as well as a summary of its first edition. It is unfortunate, therefore, that the information provided by him has not been put to its best use by those who came later.

R.G. Young and G.P.V. Somaratna reproduced parts of Copleston's summary but ignored the date for the text suggested by him.[101] Instead, and without adducing reasons, they assigned it to the same date as Mohottivatte's *Bauddha Praśnaya* (1887). Having thus put the two works together, Young and Somaratna went on to give a sweeping summary of what they saw as the subsequent history of these works:

> *Bauddha Praśnaya* and *Buddha Ädahilla* were simply traditionalist and reactionary in inspiration. They were therefore swept away as society responded creatively to Ceylon's modernization and employed new strategies for finding meaning in Buddhism to cope with these upheavals.[102]

In common with Young and Somaratna, Anderson saw the *Buddha Ädahilla* as a later work than *A Buddhist Catechism*.[103] However, in contrast to them, she did not see as having been 'swept away' by the currents of modernization. On the contrary and with good reasons, Anderson found it to be a work 'distributed widely in a number of different editions and versions'.[104] This wide distribution of the work had previously been attested to by other observers as well, notably Gombrich.[105] Yet, curiously Gombrich too overlooked the date suggested by Copleston, not in order to bring it forward to the 1880s or 1890s (as Young and Somaratna, and Anderson were to do later) but rather to push it further back in order to justify its use as a source for studying 'Traditional Buddhism in the Rural Highlands of Ceylon'.

In thus linking the *Buddha Ädahilla* to 'traditional Buddhism', in contrast to Copleston who had seen it as a product of the 'modern school', Gombrich connected it to pre-colonial capitals rather than the colonial capital of Colombo. Noting the occurrence of many of the verses in the *Buddha Ädahilla* in the daily ritual at the Temple of the Tooth in Kandy (as recorded by A.M. Hocart in the 1920s), Gombrich wrote:

> It seems a fair guess that the verses are the same age as the rituals they accompany, but unfortunately their origin is unknown. The best we can do at the moment is to surmise that these and other popular devotional verses printed in the *Bauddha Ädahilla* and elsewhere . . . were composed in mediaeval Ceylon between say 1200 and 1500. In my opinion a later date is most unlikely, as the sixteenth century saw a great decline in Pali learning. This does at least suggest that Christian influences can have played no part in their formulation.[106]

This statement raised two separate issues: one, relating to individual verses in the *Buddha Ädahilla*; and the other, relating to the collection as a whole. As regards the individual verses, as Copleston had indicated already, there is no doubt that some of them can be traced back not simply to medieval times but even as far back as canonical times. But as regards the collection as a whole, it is equally clear that – as a printed work with a new and untraditional title and a new (lay) audience – it was very much a late nineteenth-century Colombo product. This, at any rate, is what the discussion (in Section III) on the context of the origin of the *Buddha Ädahilla* has sought to demonstrate. If this demonstration is valid, then the colonial capital of Colombo can be deemed to have played a critical role in retransmitting to the provinces what had been derived from the pre-colonial past.

As a religious pocket book printed and published in Colombo, the *Buddha Ädahilla* adopted the format of other works published there, notably by Christian missionaries. At the same time, as a work compiled by conventionally trained monks of provincial origin, its contents had more conventional materials.[107] Among the probable and more immediate of its sources – with necessary adjustments and abridgements to suit lay needs – were the monastic handbooks (*baṇa daham pot*), revised and updated relatively recently in Kandy in the eighteenth century.[108] Given this mixture of older and newer elements, it is not surprising that Copleston found it difficult to decide whether a compilation like the *Buddha Ädahilla* represented a new departure or continued the tradition of the past.[109] His difficulty was a recurrent one not merely in relation to the textual compilations issued by the new Buddhist centres but, more widely, in relation to other activities and interests pursued in them.

At Maligakanda, for instance, Hikkaduve Sumangala was not simply the principal of a new Oriental college. He also held quite an independent appointment as the chief monk of an ancient religious shrine and pilgrimage centre, 'Adam's Peak'. Accordingly, he had a special interest in Buddhist relics that continued and even expanded in keeping with the progress of archaeological explorations both at home and abroad. Hence the report that,

> When the splinters of the Buddha's bowl had been excavated from the Sopārā Stūpa, the Buddhist high-priest of Ceylon [meaning Hikkaduve Sumangala, even though he held no such title] petitioned Government [of Bombay Presidency] that a small portion of the bowl of the world-honoured Gautama might be given to him to deposit in the monastery of Adam's Peak – a petition which, we hardly need say, was readily granted.[110]

At the BTS, the ideas that received attention and dissemination were not merely those of modern authors like Olcott and Carus, whose works were noticed and commented on by Western visitors like Pratt.[111] Unbeknownst to these observers (or, in his time, to Olcott himself), BTS leaders like D.B. Jayatilaka and W.A. de Silva had a deep and abiding interest in pre-modern vernacular writings, which, rather than Pali texts, had been the more immediate source of religious knowledge for the majority of the population. They were leading participants in the wider enterprise of transferring these writings from manuscript to print.[112] Thus, the great pre-modern popularizers of Buddhism, such as Dharmasena (thirteenth century) and Vidagama Maitreya (fifteenth century), had their popularity renewed through the new medium of print.[113] Their writings found a place within school curricula, too, in the field of literature.

At the Maha Bodhi Society, Dharmapala used such contemporary expressions as 'Buddhist Jerusalem' in his English writings; expressions that have come to be closely associated with him.[114] However, these expressions had no place in his Sinhala usage. In his speeches and writings in Sinhala, he used the vocabulary of vernacular Buddhist literature. India was Daṁbadiva (Jambudvīpa), and other toponyms – from Lumbini to Kusinara and beyond – were familiar to all those who knew their Buddhist stories. His campaign to regain control over historic Buddhist sites had local precedents in the near past and quite close to his home in Colombo, at places like Kelaniya and Kotte (as mentioned in Section II). Coming from this sort of background, Dharmapala had much firmer notions of religious space than the Theosophists, who tended to subscribe to much vaguer attachments to the 'East' (or, at a narrower and more elevated level, to the 'Himalayas').

Despite the widened horizons of Dharmapala, his personal career, too – from Colombo to Benares – turned to an increasingly conventional path. After experimenting with a variety of ideas and activities, his energies and resources were concentrated, in the last couple of decades of his life, on building temples in three strategic locations: Calcutta, Sarnath and London. These projects necessarily entailed an adherence to long-established ritual and devotional practices (in particular, the veneration of relics), and a reassertion of the indispensability of monks. While his erstwhile BTS colleagues turned to national politics and councils of state (both D.B. Jayatilaka and W.A. de Silva achieved ministerial positions in the 1930s), Dharmapala turned steadily towards the monastery. And it was as an ordained monk – a status which he conspicuously lacked when he represented Buddhism at the Parliament of Religions four decades earlier – that he ended his life.

Back in Dharmapala's homeland, too, the building and restoration of temples, and the observance of rituals and ceremonies connected with them – the sort of activities that had provided the background to the origins of the *Buddha Ädahilla* in the 1870s – continued unabated. Their continuity was not impeded by newer activities, notably the building and management of schools for lay students that provided the background to the origins of *A Buddhist Catechism* in the 1880s. Newer activities tended to supplement rather than supplant the older, just as newer manuals supplemented the older. Thus, the kind of popularity once claimed for *A Buddhist Catechism* by its author (namely, that it became a household item) has been made for the *Buddha Ädahilla* by others with greater justice and over a longer period of time. Variant products of the same age of print, both manuals aspired to the same goal of mass circulation: entry into every household.

NOTES

1. Copleston ([1892] 1908): 272.
2. Copleston ([1892] 1908): 278.
3. It was the nature and quality of these academic curricula that qualified schools for grants-in-aid from the government, and for which different religious groups competed with each other.
4. According to Young and Somaratna (1996: 208), the fourteenth edition of the work, published in 1912, had a subtitle in English: 'A Manual of the Doctrine and Practice of Buddhism, Largely Composed of Pali Texts with Sinhalese Translation and Exposition.' More will be said on the title in Section III.
5. He did not specify the year but estimated it to be 'about twenty years' before the publication of his own book (in 1892). In the absence of better evidence closer to the date of original publication, this estimate is still the best one we have. It is unclear from Copleston's account whether the original edition did or did not have a date printed on it and locating a copy of this edition has not proved to be easy. Some four decades ago, I reported that I had not seen a copy then (Malalgoda 1972: 162n), and I have not had better luck since. I am also informed by Professor Masahiro Kitsudo, who, during those decades, has searched widely for Pali texts printed in Sinhala characters, that he has not seen a copy either. Some recent authors – e.g. Young and Somaratna (1996: 208), Anderson (2003: 177, 185) – have brought the date of publication forward to the 1880s, thus dating it later than Olcott's *Catechism*. But they

have not explained why they have rejected Copleston's chronology or on what better evidence, if any, the dates they prefer are based. The date's significance for understanding the work will receive further attention in Sections III and VI.

6. There was a wide representation of different branches of Christianity as well. C.F. Gordon Cumming (1892: I, 41-2), British traveller and enthusiast for missionary activities, who visited the colony as a guest of Bishop H.W. Jermyn (Copleston's immediate predecessor) in the early 1870s, reported as follows on venues of Christian worship in Colombo: 'Certainly no one here can plead lack of opportunity as an excuse for non-attendance at church services. Besides several Episcopal churches, there are Roman Catholic, Wesleyan, Presbyterian, Dutch Presbyterian, Baptist, and sundry other churches and chapels scattered over the town, and these (in addition to the services for the English-speaking community) have others in Tamil, Singhalese, and Portuguese, at such times as may best suit domestic servants and others.'
7. Mohottivatte's lecturing tours and temple-building were not unrelated. A touring lecturer and fund-raiser himself, Olcott ([1910] 1975: 257) recorded: 'He built, out of funds collected by himself in lecturing tours, the Temple. . . . which most steamer passengers are taken to see by the local guides.' Gordon Cumming (1892: I, 98) reported that this temple 'though modern, small, and externally insignificant, has recently been highly decorated internally, and has risen to a position of importance in the Buddhist revival'. On outward appearances, a contrast 'within a few hundred yards' of it was provided by the spacious premises of the Roman Catholic Cathedral 'about ten acres in extent' and comprising 'the residence of the bishop and priests, the schoolhouse, and convent'.
8. Copleston (1908): 277.
9. Because she has relied on Anderson (2003) for the date of the *Ädahilla,* Blackburn (2010: 37, 65, 136) has not examined this possibility specifically; but she has commented more generally on the close cooperation between the two monks in the 1870s.
10. Going well beyond Copleston, Young and Somaratna (1996: 130) have seen even the place-name Kotahena as new, explaining it as a Sinhala version of 'Cotton China'. The actual derivation, however, was in the opposite direction: Cotton China was an Anglicization of Kotahena. But unlike other Europeanized place-names in the area (such as Colombo, Mutwal, Pettah, Cotta, Colpetty), Cotton China did not remain in use very long: probably because it sounded too whimsical even in colonial times. It was already on the way out by the time Copleston published his book in the early 1890s.
11. Aspects of the history and historiography of Kelaniya are dealt with in two monographs that appeared in quick succession: Nanayakkara (1994) and Walters (1996).

12. In relation to the early stages of the rebuilding of Kelaniya, the monographs of Nanayakkara (1994) and Walters (1996) could have benefitted from consulting a valuable late eighteenth century Sinhala source, *Sangha-rājasādhucariyāva*. It helps to place this restoration within a much wider programme of restorations in different parts of the country, including the ancient city of Anuradhapura.
13. Kotte itself ceased to be a capital in 1565. On the fate of the most sacred object held at the kingdom of Kotte – the Tooth Relic of the Buddha – there were, as is perhaps to be expected, conflicting claims. The Portuguese claimed that they captured and destroyed it. Buddhists claimed that they rescued it and housed it in new temples: initially at Sitavaka and then at Kandy, where it still remains.
14. Information on these early nineteenth century episodes at Kelaniya, which have not been referred to by Nanayakkara (1994) and Walters 1996), can be found in Young and Somaratna (1996: 61-2) and Harris (2006: 197). The long-term religious history of Kotte has not received the same kind of monographic treatment as has Kelaniya. However, Strathern (2007) deals with the sixteenth century, while the nineteenth-century encounters are mentioned in De Silva (1973: 197-8), Malalgoda (1976: 223), and Young and Somaratna (1996: 63-5).
15. Malalgoda (1976): 136-8.
16. Out of these students, Batuvantudave reverted to lay status in 1845, but his contributions to learning continued and in some respects widened with the greater freedom that the lay status allowed. He was a pioneer journalist as well as an editor and publisher of classical works. He taught a number of people (both lay and clerical), including several Christians. Among the latter were James Alwis (the leading bilingual scholar of his time and Sinhalese representative in the Legislative Council, 1864-78) and Bishop Copleston (who came from an academic background, having been a tutor in classics at St John's College, Oxford). Some of Batuvantudave's sons as well as a son-in-law (D.B. Jayatilaka) were also prominent in scholarship and public life in the early twentieth century.
17. Different aspects of the social history of Colombo are discussed in Roberts (1989), Perera (2002) and Frost (2002).
18. Taking no notice of Colombo's close links with Kotte and Kelaniya and the considerable trading activities in pre-sixteenth century Indian Ocean, Perera ([1938] 1962: 75) also dismissed pre-Portuguese and pre-fortified Colombo as 'a mere Moorish town'.
19. Gombrich (1971): 19n.
20. Copleston (1908): 4. Considering the long intervals between the appearances of these great men, it is clear that he did not see Buddhism as a religion with very much internal vitality, especially in the early modern period: 'it [Buddhism] had little internal vitality when the British occupation began

in 1796. From that time [in contrast to the time of Portuguese and Dutch occupations] all hostile pressure was removed; but the influence and example of the English, and of the most educated and enlightened of the Sinhalese themselves, necessarily operated in favour of Christianity. Buddhism became more and more the religion of the less civilized and the less prosperous; and by the middle of the nineteenth century even intelligent observers thought that it was all but extinct' (Copleston 1908: 14).

21. This process of migration (of both the laity and the religious) occurred in all the religious groups that, at one time or another, had been excluded: Muslims, Roman Catholics, Buddhists and Hindus. It was also among these resurgent and upwardly mobile religious groups that the earliest urban clashes of a violent nature occurred: between Buddhists and Roman Catholics at Kotahena in 1883, and – in a larger number of localities – between Buddhists and Muslims in 1915 (Rogers 1987: 176ff.).
22. Among those who witnessed these expressions of 'Buddhism as a daily religion' were British administrators like J.F. Dickson (1884). What they witnessed and recorded in the provinces was becoming increasingly common in and around the capital as well.
23. Hence, for instance, the autobiographical comment a century later by a professional linguist who grew up in a rural home (Disanayaka 1993: 3): 'I learnt my Pali stanzas listening to my mother and my eldest brother, *loku ayya,* who used to recite these stanzas as he strolled about in the house'.
24. Copleston (1908): 278.
25. Copleston (1908): 278. Among later writers, Conze (1959: 70-3) gives translations of 'The Five Precepts, with Buddhaghosa's Commentary', while Spiro (1970: 193) has described the formula for taking refuge in the Buddha, Dhamma, and Sangha – which precedes the recitation of the Five Precepts – as a Buddhist 'Confession of Faith . . . which is as ancient as Scripture itself.' Also relevant from a comparative perspective is the observation of Gombrich (1971: 253): 'The Five Precepts, preceded by the Three Refuges, are taken so frequently that they may be called the functional equivalent of the Lord's Prayer'.
26. Copleston (1908): 279.
27. Copleston (1908): 279.
28. Copleston (1908): 280). Elsewhere in the book (p. 270), he gave translations of the verses used in transferring merit to kinsfolk and to gods.
29. Tambiah (1976).
30. Cumming (1892): I, 96.
31. Copleston (1908): 280.
32. Cumming (1892): I, 87.
33. India in particular 'was to prove the biggest failure of European missionary enterprise'; and, at the 'Missionary Conference at Edinburgh in 1910, the

largest and most comprehensive of such gatherings so far held. . . . India . . . remained at the forefront of preoccupations' (MacCulloch 2010: 892, 955). Among the missionaries in India who began rethinking the position of Christianity vis-à-vis other religions was J.N. Farquhar, who was also the earliest to attempt a wide survey of *Modern Religious Movements in India* (1915).

34. De Silva (1973): 193.
35. Their allegiance, of course, was not simply given but unequivocally demanded. For example, British appointments to monastic offices – such as the one held by Hikkaduve Sumangala for Sri Pada – bound the appointees 'to obey and execute all such orders as you may receive from us or the Government Agent, and fully to discover or make known to us or the constituted authorities of Government, all things which may come to your knowledge affecting the public interests and all treasons or traitorous conspiracies which you may hear of against His Majesty's Government' (Prajnananda 1947: 86).
36. Geiger (1953): 302.
37. Hocart (1924): 72.
38. This was in contrast to Burma, where there was a major rebellion with that aim (Saya San rebellion) as late as the 1930s.
39. Wickremasinghe (1901).
40. More conventional because there is 'a conventional tripartite division of Buddhism into learning (*paryāpti*), practice (*pratipatti*) and realization (*prativedanā*). Each part is higher than the preceding but also depends upon them' (Gombrich 1971: 270-1).
41. The derivation was along the lines of *saddhā* > *hadahā* >*adahā* > *ädahili*. Gombrich (1971): 58-9.
42. Granting that it 'has usually been translated as "faith"', Gombrich's preference (1971: 59) was to translate *saddhā* as 'confidence'.
43. Gombrich (1971) gives a translation of the table of contents of the 1955 edition as an appendix to his book. There is no direct English translation of the *Bauddha Ädahilla* as a whole, but much of the same material can be found in Dhammananda (1991).
44. Gombrich (1971): 63.
45. Tambiah (1985): 24-5.
46. Thus Disanayaka (1993: 2), who was quoted above in note 23, continued: 'At the Image House, I simply imitated my mother. After offering flowers to the Buddha image, I knelt down, placing my elbows and hands on the white towel spread before me and recited, along with my mother, many Pali stanzas. I chanted aloud the lines that I knew by heart; pretended to repeat the lines that I did not, softly.'
47. Gombrich (1971): 254.

48. MacCulloch (2010): 987.
49. Don Peter (1978).
50. Van Goor (1978).
51. Diehl (1976).
52. Gooneratne (1968).
53. Worldwide, there had been non-Christian and anti-Christian catechisms previously. A famous example was Auguste Comte's *Catechism of Positive Religion* (1852). *The Communist Manifesto* (1848) was also based on an earlier pamphlet on 'Principles of Communism' drafted in catechetical form by Engels in 1845.
54. Gooneratne (1968): 3, 34.
55. Relevant documents are printed in Prajnananda (1947) and are discussed there as well as more recently in Blackburn (2010).
56. Brynn and Bishop (1976): 8.
57. Gunawardana (1979): 9.
58. These qualifications were granted on the basis of examinations directed by a Committee on Oriental Studies convened by the Director of Public Instruction in 1902. Not surprisingly, there were anxieties about the less desirable consequences of examinations: 'The examinations have not been an unmixed blessing. The encouragement of competition has produced cram-work in place of erudition, and it is a lamentable fact that, even among the monks the winning of a medal or diploma has proved a greater incentive to work than disinterested love of knowledge. Knowledge for its own sake has given way to knowledge for recognition' (Malalasekera 1928: 312).
59. This has been reprinted in Prajnananda (1947): 158-61.
60. Prajnananda (1947): 159.
61. A gifted student himself, the elder brother (Don Luis Goonewardena) had become a teacher at the Colombo Academy (later Royal College), a rare appointment for a Sinhalese at that time. The younger brother may well have aspired to create at Vidyodaya his own Colombo Academy/Royal College in the field of Oriental Studies.
62. Olcott was represented at the Parliament of Religions by the new but already well-known recruit to the Theosophical Society, Annie Besant. It was with her party that Dharmapala travelled from London to New York.
63. Copleston (1908): 278.
64. Olcott ([1900] 1974): 301-2.
65. Olcott ([1910] 1975): 116.
66. Among those languages were Sinhala, Burmese, Japanese, French, German, Swedish, Russian, and Arabic.
67. Habermas (2006): 152.
68. 'Buddhist final salvation, one might say, is open-ended. . . . One can say

that it is not nonexistence, and it is a timeless bliss; to say more would be to rush in where Buddhas fear to tread' (Collins 1998: 206).

69. The reference here was to Polvatte Siddhartha, who had passed away just about the time of Olcott's first visit in 1880, and who had been involved in a debate on nirvana (*Nirvāṇa Vādaya*) with another monk of the southern province (Dodampahala Dipankara) in the early 1860s. Even though Olcott did not get to know the original disputants, he considered two younger monks whom he did get to know – Hikkaduve Sumangala and Potuvila Indajoti – as representing the two opposing points of view (Olcott [1900] 1974: 174). Published material on these local disagreements and debates is rather scanty. In contrast, material on debates on *nirvana* among Western interpreters of Buddhism has been substantial enough to generate a separate monograph on the subject (Welbon 1968).
70. Olcott ([1900]1974): 300-1.
71. The answer, as it appears in the forty-fourth edition (1947: 29) of the catechism, is as follows: 'A condition of total cessation of changes; of perfect rest; of the absence of desire and illusion and sorrow; of total obliteration of everything that goes to make up the physical man. Before reaching NIRVĀNA man is constantly being reborn: when he reaches NIRVĀNA he is reborn no more.' It is worth mentioning here that the present paper makes no attempt to examine closely the wording of different questions and answers in successive editions of the *Buddhist Catechism*; nor likewise the contents of the different editions of the other manual (*Buddha Ädahilla*). While such close examinations would indeed be desirable, they are beyond the scope the present paper. It is hoped that the broad comparative history of the two manuals presented here will assist and encourage more minute analyses later.
72. Olcott ([1900] 1974): 301.
73. Christian catechisms available locally (and in printed form since the mid-eighteenth century) included such well known ones as the Heidelberg Catechism (Van Goor 1978: 73, 84). The question-and-answer format was of course not alien to Buddhist literature; and, as was noted earlier (in Section I), Mohottivatte had brought out an edition of *Milinda's Questions* in 1878. But that publication, a volume of nearly 650 pages, was no Sunday-school primer: the sort of work that Olcott ([1900] 1974: 302) wanted his own composition to be.
74. Conze (1959): 181.
75. Olcott's list, appended to later editions of his catechism, was reprinted, along with his own list, by Humphreys in his introductory book on Buddhism (1951: 71-6).
76. As a symbol of that unity, a Buddhist flag was also designed and popularized since 1885.

77. The Sinhala translation of the *Buddhist Catechism*, in its original form in 1881, has also been attributed to Dharmapala by Alan Trevithick (1988: 66-7). Its accuracy, however, is doubtful. Trevithick has provided no evidence in support of the attribution, and he also seems to have overlooked a problem of chronology. At the time the translation was done (in May 1881), Dharmapala was still only a sixteen-year old schoolboy. The translator is likely to have been someone older. A chronological problem arises likewise in relation to the statement that the catechism was 'largely compiled from English translations, many of them the work of the Pali Text Society'. It is of course true that Olcott relied on translations, but the Pali Text Society was formed only in 1881, the same year in which the catechism was published.
78. Dharmapala ([1933]1965): 703-4.
79. The Sinhala translation of Olcott's catechism used a neologism (*kathopakathanaya*) to express the idea of catechism. It, too, thus avoided the word commonly used by translators of Christian catechisms (*katikismaya*), which bore clear signs of its European origin.
80. Mohottivatte Gunananda ([1887]1966): vi-vii.
81. Olcott ([1904]1972): 419.
82. Sumangala did not go out of his way to broadcast those disagreements. But, if questioned, he made no effort to hide them either. Recalling a meeting with him in December 1883, Moncure Daniel Conway (1906: 130) wrote: 'In the recent attack of Catholics on the Buddhist procession, Colonel Olcott had hastened to Colombo and demanded of the government redress for the Buddhists. These were naturally grateful to him, but Sumangala was troubled by the expositions of Buddhism given by the Theosophists. The pretended Mahatmas such as Kothume, [from whom Theosophists claimed to receive communications] he declared non-existent.'
83. Olcott ([1910]1975): 33.
84. More advanced studies were a different matter, requiring years of dedicated work with original texts and commentaries. As on the question of *nirvana* and a variety of other topics, these studies also entailed discussions and debates among monks themselves.
85. Olcott ([1910]1975): 485-510.
86. Prothero (1996): 161-3.
87. Malalgoda (1976): 253.
88. Blackburn (2010): 137-8.
89. Blackburn (2010): 137.
90. Subhadra Bhikshu was the pen-name of the German Buddhist layman Friedrich Zimmermann. His catechism enjoyed considerable success and popularity around the turn of the century. It appeared in a number of German editions and was translated into ten other languages. Not particularly happy about the competition, Olcott ([1900]1974: 302-3) accused

Zimmermann of plagiarism. The use of Zimmerman's catechism in Ceylon was more limited than that of Olcott's catechism for quite a different reason, however: the number of schools under the management of the Maha Bodhi Society was smaller than the number under the BTS Pratt (1915: 362) gave the figures of 22 and 250 respectively.

91. Pratt (1915): 362-3.
92. Olcott [1910]1975): 245.
93. Crosby (1947): 171.
94. By Rahula's time, furthermore, a greater number of monks were pursuing modern secular education. Rahula himself, after his initial monastic training, continued his studies at universities in Colombo, Calcutta, and Paris.
95. Obeyesekere (1970): 46.
96. In his preface to the 36th edition (1903), Olcott reported that a 'fresh version in Sinhalese is . . . preparing at Colombo'; and again in the preface to the 40th edition (1905): 'The new Sinhalese version (38th edition) which is being prepared by my respected friend, D.B. Jayatilaka, Principal of Ananda (Buddhist) College, Colombo, is partly printed, but cannot be completed until he is relieved of some of the pressure upon his time' (Olcott 1947: xi, xiii). It is unclear whether this translation was ever completed.
97. Cited in Blackburn (2010): 138n.
98. Olcott (2007).
99. Gombrich (1971): 83.
100. These later developments have gone unnoticed in the quick summary of the catechism's history given by Stephen Prothero (1996: 101): 'It [*Buddhist Catechism*] first appeared, in both English and Sinhalese, on July 24, 1881. Hugely influential, it is still used today in Sri Lankan schools.' Relying on that summary, the dubious claim that Olcott's catechism is still in use in schools has been continued into the twenty-first century by others, e.g., Frost (2002: 961), McMahan (2008: 99).
101. Young and Somaratna (1996): 208-9.
102. Young and Somaratna (1996): 209.
103. Anderson (2003). On the exact date of *Buddha Ädahilla*, Anderson (2003) is not consistent. In one place (p. 177), she says that 'one biography [of Mohottivatte] provides 1889 as the date of the first edition'. But in another place (pp.185-6): '*Buddhist Catechism* was . . . published in 1881, twelve years earlier than . . . *Buddha Ädahilla*.' The latter statement implies a posthumous date of 1893.
104. Anderson (2003): 171.
105. Gombrich (1971).
106. Gombrich (1971): 115.
107. It seems unlikely that many completely new compositions were included in the collection. One item that can definitely be dated to the nineteenth

century, though, is a set of verses composed by King Mongkut of Siam (Malalgoda 1972: 162). It is worth mentioning by the way that, in addition to printed copies, *Buddha Ädahilla* is also available in manuscript form in temple libraries. But, as Anderson (2003: 176-7) has noted already, these manuscripts are not necessarily older than printed copies.

108. Sannasgala (1961): 477-80, Blackburn (2001): 205-8. Already in eighteenth-century Kandy there were monastic handbooks written on paper (rather than on palm leaf), but it was only later in Colombo that they too began to appear in print (Sannasgala 1961: 72, 712).
109. Copleston (1908): 278.
110. Jolly 1920: 903-4.The relics were received at Vidyodaya in 1882. Among those who saw the relics at the college were the Korean diplomats who visited the place in April 1884 (Brynn and Bishop 1976: 9). A longer and more second hand account also appears in Gordon Cumming (1892: I, 93-6).
111. Pratt (1915).
112. Wickremasinghe (1901).
113. Among the books edited by Jayatilaka were Vidagama Maitreya's *Buduguṇālaṃkāraya* (1894), Dharmasena's *Saddharma-ratnāvaliya* (1928), and the collective thirteenth-century Sinhala version of the *Jātaka* tales (1932). W.A. de Silva's main interests were on more demotic compositions of later centuries. He also translated into English (in 1910) Vidagama Maitreya's *Lōvāḍa Saṅgarāva*. A concise survey of Sinhala materials can be found in Wijayawardhana (1979). That survey (pp. 75-6) makes reference to *Buddha Ädahilla* as well: a work of 'recent origin' but which 'invariably finds a place in many Buddhist households'.
114. Trevithick 1988.

BIBLIOGRAPHY

Anderson, Carol S. 2003. '"For Those Who Are Ignorant": A Study of the *Bauddha Ädahilla*', in John Clifford Holt et al. (eds.), *Constituting Communities: Theravada Buddhism and the Religious Cultures of South and Southeast Asia*. Albany: State University of New York Press.

Blackburn, Ann M. 2001. *Buddhist Learning and Textual Practice in Eighteenth-Century Lankan Monastic Culture*. Princeton: Princeton University Press.

———. 2010. *Locations of Buddhism: Colonialism and Modernity in Sri Lanka*. Chicago: University of Chicago Press.

Brynn, Edward, and Donald Bishop. 1976. 'An American-Korean Diplomatic Mission in Sri Lanka, 1884', *Ceylon Journal of Historical and Social Studies*, n.s., VI, 2: 1-18.

Collins, Stephen. 1998. *Nirvana and Other Buddhist Felicities: Utopias in the Pali Imaginaire*. Cambridge: Cambridge University Press.

Conway, Moncure Daniel. 1906. *My Pilgrimage to the Wise Men of the East*. London: Archibald Constable.

Conze, Edward, ed. 1959. *Buddhist Scriptures*. Harmondsworth: Penguin Books.

Copleston, R.S. [1892] 1908. *Buddhism: Primitive and Present in Magadha and Ceylon*. London: Longmans Green.

Crosby, Josiah. 1947. 'Buddhism in Ceylon', *Journal of the Royal Asiatic Society of Great Britain and Ireland*, 166-83.

De Silva, K.M. 1973. 'The Government and Religion: Problems and Policies, *c*.1832 to *c*.1910', in K.M. De Silva (ed.), *University of Ceylon History of Ceylon*. Peradeniya: University of Ceylon.

De Silva, R.K. and W.G.M. Beumer. 1988. *Illustrations of and Views of Dutch Ceylon, 1602-1796*. London: Serendib Publications.

Dhammananda, K. Sri. 1991. *Daily Buddhist Devotions*. Kuala Lumpur: Buddhist Missionary Society.

Dharmapala, Anagarika. [1933] 1965. 'Reminiscences of My Early Life', in Ananda Guruge (ed.), *Return to Righteousness: A Collection of Speeches, Essays and Letters of the Anagarika Dharmapala*. Colombo: Ceylon Government Press.

Dickson, J.F. 1884. 'Notes Illustrative of Buddhism as the Daily Religion of the Buddhists of Ceylon, and Some Account of Their Ceremonies before and after Death', *Journal of the Ceylon Branch of the Royal Asiatic Society*, VIII, 29: 203-36.

Diehl, Katherine S. 1976. 'Ceylon Students Abroad in the Eighteenth Century', in Katherine S. Diehl (ed.), *Historical Essays: Primary Printed and Manuscript Sources for Sixteenth to Nineteenth Century Available in Sri Lanka*. Colombo: Hansa Publishers.

Disanayaka, J.B. 1993. *The Monk and the Peasant: A Study of the Traditional Sinhalese Village*. Colombo: State Printing Corporation.

Don Peter, W.L.A. 1978. *Education in Sri Lanka under the Portuguese*. Colombo: Colombo Catholic Press.

Frost, Mark. 2002. '"Wider Opportunities": Religious Revival, Nationalist Awakening and the Global Dimension in Colombo, 1870-1920'. *Modern Asian Studies* 36, 4: 937-67.

Geiger, Wilhelm, tr. 1953. *Cūlavaṃsa, Being the More Recent Part of the Mahāvaṃsa*, Part II. Colombo: Ceylon Government Information Department.

Gombrich, Richard F. 1971. *Precept and Practice: Traditional Buddhism in the Rural Highlands of Ceylon*. Oxford: Clarendon Press.

Gordon Cumming, C.F. 1892. *Two Happy Years in Ceylon*, 2 vols. Edinburgh: William Blackwood and Sons.

Gooneratne, Yasmine. 1968. *English Literature in Ceylon, 1815-1878*. Dehiwala: Tisara Prakasakayo.

Gunananda, Mohottivatte. [1887] 1966. *Bauddha Praśnaya*. Kalutara: Vikarama Press.

Gunawardana, R.A.L.H. 1979. *Robe and Plough: Monasticism and Economic Interest in Early Medieval Sri Lanka*. Tucson: University of Arizona Press.
Habermas, Jürgen. 2006. *Time of Transition*. Cambridge: Polity Press.
Harris, Elizabeth J. 2006. *Theravāda Buddhism and the British Encounter: Religious, Missionary and Colonial Experience in Nineteenth-Century Sri Lanka*. London: Routledge.
Hocart, A.M. 1924. 'The King's Justice', *Man*, XXIV: 71-3.
Humphreys, Christmas. 1951. *Buddhism*. Harmondsworth: Penguin Books.
Jolly, J. 1920. 'Stupa', *Encyclopaedia of Religion and Ethics*, XI, 901-4.
MacCulloch, Diarmaid. 2010. *A History of Christianity*. London: Penguin Books.
Malalasekera, G.P. 1928. *The Pali Literature of Ceylon*. London: Royal Asiatic Society of Great Britain and Ireland.
Malalgoda, Kitsiri. 1972. 'Sinhalese Buddhism: Orthodox and Syncretistic, Traditional and Modern' (Review Article), *Ceylon Journal of Historical and Social Studies*, n.s., II/2: 156-69.
———. 1976. *Buddhism in Sinhalese Society, 1750-1900: A Study of Religious Revival and Change*. Berkeley: University of California Press.
———. 1997. 'Concepts and Confrontations: A Case Study of *Āgama*', in Michael Roberts (ed.), *Collective Identities Revisited*, vol. I. Colombo: Marga Institute.
McMahan, David L. 2008. *The Making of Buddhist Modernism*. New York: Oxford University Press.
Nanavimala, Kirielle, ed. [1955] 2002. *Bauddha Ädahilla*. Colombo: M.D. Gunasena.
Nanayakkara, Vesak. 1994. *The Temple of Kelaniya*. Mattegodagama: Academy of Sri Lankan Culture.
Obeyesekere, Gananath. 1970. 'Religious Symbolism and Political Change in Ceylon', *Modern Ceylon Studies*, I/1: 43-63.
Olcott, Henry S. 1947. *The Buddhist Catechism*, 44th edn. Adyar: Theosophical Publishing House.
———. [1904] 1972. *Old Diary Leaves: The History of the Theosophical Society*, Third Series, 1883-7. Adyar: Theosophical Publishing House.
———. [1900] 1974. *Old Diary Leaves: The History of the Theosophical Society*, Second Series, 1878-3. Adyar: Theosophical Publishing House.
———. [1910] 1975. *Old Diary Leaves: The History of the Theosophical Society*, Fourth Series, 1887-92. Adyar: Theosophical Publishing House.
———. 2007. *Bauddha Kathopakathanaya*. Colombo: Dayawansa Jayakody & Co.
Perera, Nihal. 2002. 'Indigenising the Colonial City: Late 19th-century Colombo and its Landscape', *Urban Studies*, 39, 9: 1703-21.
Perera, S.G. [1932] 1962. *Historical Sketches*. Colombo: Catholic Book Depot.

Prajnananda, Yagirala, 1947. *Sri Sumangala Caritaya.* Colombo: Associated Newspapers.

Pratt, James Bissett. 1915. *India and its Faiths: A Traveller's Record.* Boston: Houghton Mifflin.

Prothero, Stephen, 1996. *The White Buddhist: The Asian Odyssey of Henry Steel Olcott.* Bloomington: Indiana University Press.

Roberts, Michael. 1989. 'The Two Faces of the Port City: Colombo in Modern Times', in Frank Broeze (ed.), *Brides of the Sea: Port Cities of Asia from the 16th-20th Centuries.* Kensington, NSW: New South Wales University Press.

Rogers, John D. 1987. *Crime, Justice and Society in Colonial Sri Lanka.* London: Curzon Press.

Sannasgala, Punchibandara. 1961. *Sinhala Sāhitya Vaṃśaya.* Colombo: Lake House.

Skeen, George J.A. 1887. *The Passenger's Guide to Colombo, With a Map; to Which is Added a Compendium of Useful Information for the Traveller and Resident.* Colombo: A.M. & J. Ferguson.

Spiro, Melford, E. 1970. *Buddhism and Society: A Great Tradition and Its Burmese Vicissitudes.* New York: Harper & Row.

Strathern, Alan. *Kingship and Conversion in Sixteenth-Century Sri Lanka: Portuguese Imperialism in a Buddhist Land.* Cambridge: Cambridge University Press.

Tambiah, Stanley J. 1976. *World Conqueror and World Renouncer: A Study of Buddhism and Polity in Thailand against a Historical Background.* Cambridge: Cambridge University Press.

———. 1985. *Culture, Thought, and Social Action: An Anthropological Perspective.* Cambridge, Mass.: Harvard University Press.

Trevithick, Alan Michael. 1988. 'A Jerusalem of the Buddhists in British India: 1874-1949', Ph.D. dissertation. Harvard University.

Van Goor, J. 1978. *Jan Kompenie as Schoolmaster: Dutch Education in Ceylon, 1690-1795.* Groningen: Wolters-Noordhoff.

Walters, Jonathan S. 1996. *The History of Kelaniya.* Colombo: Social Scientists' Association.

Welbon, Guy Richard. 1968. *The Buddhist Nirvāṇa and its Western Interpreters.* Chicago: University of Chicago Press.

Wickremasinghe, D.M. de Z. 1901. *Catalogue of the Sinhalese Printed Books in the Library of the British Museum.* London: British Museum.

Wijayawardhana, G.D. 1979. 'Literature in Buddhist Religious Life', in John Ross Carter (ed.), *Religiousness in Sri Lanka.* Colombo: Marga Institute.

Young, Richard Fox and G.P.V. Somaratna. 1996. *Vain Debates: The Buddhist-Christian Controversies of Nineteenth-Century Ceylon.* Vienna: Sammlung De Nobili.

CHAPTER 7

The Buddhist Utopia

An Aspect of the Buddhist Revival in Sri Lanka

H.L. SENEVIRATNE

WHILE 'THE BUDDHIST REVIVAL' undoubtedly comprises a dimension of regeneration, it is, by no means, a simple efflorescence but a multi-faceted phenomenon fraught with contradictions, ambiguities and unintended consequences that have had both beneficial and deleterious effects on societies subjected to it. This applies no less to the personalities involved as to the phenomenon itself, and no revivalist personality illustrates this more clearly than the Sri Lankan reformer, Anagarika Dharmapala (1864-1933). While Dharmapala spent most of his working life outside Sri Lanka (then Ceylon) he exerted a decisive influence on the course of the island's history, especially on crafting an identity for the majority Sinhala Buddhists and thereby contributing, in no small measure, to both a cultural regeneration and a malaise rooted in this identity that afflicts Sri Lankan society today. Dharmapala, on the one hand, was universalist, internationalist and cosmopolitan and, travelling extensively in the East and West, was able to experience and admire the orderly, rational and affluent societies of the world. He desired his native Ceylon to reach similar social and economic heights, yet was unable to extricate himself from a narrow ethno-religious world-view that was fatal to this project. He failed to address the diverse communities that constitute the citizenship of the island, limiting himself to exclusively addressing his own ethno-religious group. Besides, he kindled in this group, albeit with the best of intentions, a past-glory-imbued pride that has turned out to be shallow, parochial and pathological, and which has ultimately led to the flames of majoritarianism and ethnic supremacism.

It is, then, no surprise that within Sri Lanka, especially among the more discerning scholars, and in international Sri Lankan scholarship, Dharmapala is remembered as the founder of an ethno-religious nationalism and the resulting ills that afflict the island at present. This, however, does not diminish the reformer's heroic contribution to Buddhism's regeneration in the land of its birth, including the mundane aspect of trying to wrest control of its Buddhist religio-archaeological sites for the Buddhists, and his unrelenting efforts to make Buddhism a global missionary religion. It is also no surprise that Indian scholars have shown a greater appreciation of Dharmapala, while, by no means, approving of his exclusivist sanitization of Buddhist sites and monuments (in which imperial archaeology was complicit), thereby contributing to a more balanced assessment of the reformer than would be possible from merely examining his religio-ethnic-bound activities in his homeland. This paper deals precisely with the latter project and outlines Dharmapala's attempt to build a Buddhist utopia, which, instead, has prevented the crafting of a stable, multi-ethnic nation, a task that India successfully achieved in the aftermath of its independence. The project led, rather, to the disruption of inter-ethnic relations and civil war, and has prevented the utilization of even the highly favourable post-conflict space to build a harmonious, happy and prosperous society.

THE IDYLLIC SOCIETY OF THE PAST

Dharmapala's project in Sri Lanka was a movement for the restoration of a Buddhist utopia believed to have existed in the heyday of the island's ancient civilization. The basis of the presumed happiness and perfection of this utopia was the morality it derived from Buddhism; not the contemporary Buddhism that Dharmapala considered degenerate but an idealized, true and pure form. This idyllic society was also 'Aryan', and since it was a moral society, we can use the latter term as a convenient label for it.

What did Dharmapala mean by true and pure Buddhism? It was none other than the doctrine known as the Middle Path, also called the Noble Eightfold Path. It was a path that led to success and happiness in this life, as well as subsequent lives, until the eventual attainment of *nirvana* or liberation from the cycle of births and deaths. As conventionally stated, this Path consisted of Ethical Conduct (*sila*),

Mental Discipline (*samadhi*) and Wisdom (*panna*). These are conventionally explained as Right Thought, Right Understanding, Right Action, Right Speech, Right Livelihood, Right Effort, Right Attentiveness and Right Concentration. It is a return to these virtues that Dharmapala and his followers advocated over and over again in their project to regain the lost paradise.

THE END OF THE MORAL SOCIETY

In Dharmapala's view, the moral society had come to an end and the reasons for this were twofold. First, four centuries of consecutive Western imperial domination meant not merely a political subjugation but a cultural one as well. The Westerners, especially the British who held the island from 1815 to 1948, established a system of schools with the help of Christian missionaries. These schools, as well as the prevailing broader cultural influences, produced a class of deracinated citizens who blindly embraced the habits and customs of the invader. They adopted foreign food and drink, dresses, names, habits, customs, religion and anything else the foreigner introduced to them. Besides, the foreigner instilled a distaste for indigenous food, dress, language, habits, customs and religion in the mind of this class, so that its members looked down upon the indigenous culture and its practitioners. In time, these ideas trickled down to other classes until they were woven into the social fabric and reached even the remotest villages in the countryside.

The second reason for the extinction of the moral society was the system of ritual and false beliefs that had developed over the centuries and encompassed true Buddhism, undermining its ethical content. The project of reviving the moral society was, thus, a project to reverse these two developments. In this paper, I will briefly mention the anti-Western culture project, and discuss the anti-ritual and folk belief project in more detail.

THE REVIVALIST PROJECT 1: THE ANTI-WESTERN PROJECT

The anti-Western culture project used two approaches. The first consisted of propaganda rallies held over the length and breadth of the country, much like modern campaign rallies with which we are familiar. The main attraction in these was the project's founder and leader, Dharmapala, whose venom against his enemy was undisguised. He candidly practised verbal abuse on even his audience, sometimes calling them by animal names. Rather than disapproval that would be the normal reaction to such abuse, it secured for him a trademark that made him extremely popular – so popular that even being verbally abused by him was considered something of an honour. His self-presentation added to his oratorical skills. To begin with, he abandoned his given Western name, Don David, and took the name Dharmapala, meaning 'one who is disciplined by the dharma'. Anagarika, meaning 'homeless', is a descriptive title that he gave himself. Next, he renounced the world in an innovative way by becoming a semi-monk, a new status he created that was neither layman nor monk. He wore the clothing of a layman but its colour and appearance was that of the Buddhist monk's robe. However, unlike the shaven-headed Buddhist monk, he wore his hair long. This ambiguous image conferred on him a certain charisma that was added to by the widely-publicized favourable impression he was deemed to have made at the Parliament of World's Religions at Chicago in 1893 (which was also attended by Hindu thinker and reformer, Vivekananda, then thirty years old).

The second approach in Dharmapala's anti-Western project was the use of the printed word. Due to the prospering colonial economy, the spread of literacy and the advent of the printing press, the late nineteenth century was a period of great dynamism, especially in the city of Colombo and its suburbs, and in the rapidly urbanizing provincial centres. There was a proliferation of daily and weekly newspapers, other weekly and monthly publications, pamphlets, broadsides and books. These became vehicles for Dharmapala and his supporters to publish writings that propagated their project. Among these was the newspaper titled *The Sinhala Buddhist*, published and edited by Dharmapala himself, in which, among other anti-Western writings, he wrote a popular column titled 'Facts that One Should Know'. Another notable contribution to the project were literary works, especially novels, and less frequently, plays, that were read more than performed. Among the novelists, the most influential was Piyadasa Sirisena whose novels typically depicted the moral decay and misery of the villain who had embraced Western culture in contrast to the virtue, uprightness and happiness of the hero, whose habits and customs were pure Sinhala and Buddhist.

THE REVIVALIST PROJECT 2: AGAINST RITUAL AND FALSE BELIEFS

To understand Dharmapala's anti-ritual project, it is useful to get an overall idea of this ritual that he so disapproved of. In a nutshell, it was the cultural expression of Buddhism so beloved of the anthropologists and so much the livelihood of the anthropologists of Buddhism. The anthropology/sociology of Buddhism contains volume after volume of the faithful documentation of a 'transformation of Buddhism', from the esoteric doctrine of an urban elite to a religion of the rural masses. The founding father of the theory of the transformation of Buddhism and of the sociology of Buddhism in general, was the sociologist Max Weber. Despite the lapse of a century and a new understanding of the workings of Buddhism in different cultural contexts, Weber's sociology of Buddhism remains useful and, I believe, generally valid.

What is relevant for our purposes is Weber's insight that mass religiosity demands the satisfaction of two psychological needs: first, intercession in physical and psychic distress in this world and second, the promise of heaven in the hereafter. Buddhism of the earliest texts, which Weber called 'ancient Buddhism', had neither of these. In his view, ancient Buddhism was not a religion but a starkly goal-oriented cultivation of the mind. He called it 'a religious technology for the intellectually schooled mendicant monks', and 'a religion without a deity and without a cult'.[1]

Its aim was not eternal life but an eternal death of sorts because it aimed at ending the cycle of birth and death. Nevertheless, Buddhism, as we find it on the ground is, by any standards, a mass religion and to explain this, Weber reasoned that Buddhism went through a 'transformation' that let in, through the back door, the two ingredients he listed as indispensable to a mass religion – intercession in distress and an eternal existence.

This meant that Buddhist cultures everywhere, if they were to survive as Buddhist cultures, were paradoxically compelled to borrow from non-Buddhist cultures, or from pre-existing non-Buddhist systems of beliefs and practice, drawing on ingredients that met the demands of popular religiosity. This the Buddhist cultures did so successfully that it has enabled Buddhism not just to survive but to thrive as a popular religion. The syncretistic cultural Buddhism that resulted also adapted to different social and economic conditions, enabling its professionals, the monks, to become an elite, often a landowning aristocracy and a dabbler in politics, and capable of making or unmaking kings and governments. In this cultural Buddhism, the Buddha himself, who was a human being and insisted he was one, was made into what the anthropologist Gananath Obeyesekere has called a super deity, a god of the gods. He was made the head or the 'presiding deity' of a stratified pantheon, whose upper rungs were populated, in the Sri Lankan case, by gods borrowed from the Hindu pantheon.[2] Provincial and local deities occupied the lower rungs with other mystical beings, sometimes described in English as demons and goblins, assigned to the lowest stratum. The benevolent among these beings were propitiated and the malevolent exorcised, which necessitated the invention of a system of myths and rituals, replete with music, drumming and other performative acts.

Other aspects of the 'transformation of Buddhism' included the borrowing or invention of a series of divine worlds which the virtuous would be reborn into and hells to which the sinners were destined. A concept of 'merit' was developed so that good acts could be performed that would accrue merit, enabling those who engaged in them to be reborn into a heavenly existence or to luxury in the human world, both temporary stations on one's way to *nirvana*. The idea of merit was expanded to facilitate the transfer of one's merit to others as well, especially departed kin. *Nirvana*, which in 'ancient Buddhism' was no more than the 'extinction of attachment' (*tanhakkhaya*),[3] and often described as beyond the conceptions of existence and non-existence, was now made into a super heaven and an eternal existence of unimaginable bliss.

CARRYING OUT THE PROJECT

Dharmapala considered the challenge in front of him of combating Western culture and the ritualism and false beliefs of the peasantry no less than a war. A war needs soldiers and using military imagery, he asked for recruits, particularly among the Buddhist monks, the social group that he considered the obvious choice as well as the one ideally suited for the task. Buddhist monasteries and resident monks were found in practically every village, and they were influential among the rural masses, the overwhelming majority of the population. So he exhorted the monks to join him in his patriotic mission. Hardly a mincer of words, he did not hesitate to scream angrily and in fairly harsh language at the monks whose response to him was less than he expected.

Many monks were, in fact, able to respond to Dharmapala's clarion call enthusiastically. Prominent among these were the gifted young monks who were students of the monastic colleges, Vidyodaya and Vidyalankara, established in 1873 and 1875 respectively, with the aim of reviving the lost tradition of monastic education known as the *pirivena* system. These two colleges were located within the bustling colonial commercial and administrative centre, the city of Colombo, and the young monastic students had the capacity to absorb some of the dynamism of this environment that included a nationalist zeal and a world-view more encompassing than that of the cloistered rural monk. (Following Dharmapala's usage I call these monks 'soldier monks' or 'monk soldiers'.)

In their task of the de-ritualization and ethicization of Buddhists, these monks adopted three main strategies. The most widely-used and the best-known, was a programme of social and economic development aimed at the largely illiterate rural population. The second was the invention of a new sermon in place of the existing one, which was a formalized ceremonial enactment. The third strategy was the use of the printed word in the form of books, pamphlets, and popular articles in newspapers and journals. Let us look at each of these in some detail.

Strategy 1: Rural Regeneration (*Gramasamvardhana*)

The first strategy, a movement for rural regeneration, was known as 'rural development' (*gramasamvardhana*). It was based on the idea, rooted in Dharmapala, of a happy, prosperous and moral society of idyllic village communities that constituted the ancient Buddhist

Sinhala kingdom, ruled by a paternalistic and benevolent king. The monks involved in this movement came from the monastic college Vidyodaya, and three names stand out – Kalukondayave Pannasekhara, Hinatiyana Dhammaloka and Hendiyagala Silaratana. Their programme consisted of a broad spectrum ranging from (a) educating the rural masses in literacy, civic duty, health and sanitation, cleanliness and so on; issues of the village and household economy, the methodical cultivation of crops, and the proper use of fertilizers and pest control; (b) the building and maintenance of local public works like roads, bridges and wells; and (c) law and order issues like crime prevention, policing and conflict resolution. In putting this programme into practice, these monks tapped local talent, both ordinary citizens and the elite, and local resources. And they also used the newly-invented sermon we will discuss shortly. The most sociologically striking aspect in the work of these monks is their advocacy of a balance of these mundane activities with spirituality, one derived from the Middle Path and achieved through minimal consumption, that is, while you produce with vigour, you consume in moderation. Minimal consumption also included temperance and the avoidance of luxuries, and was conceptualized as *samajivakata*, 'balanced living'. It was a comfortable, moderate and moral life that assured the achievement of both this and the other world, expressed in another concept, *ubhayalokartha sadhana*, the 'realization of both worlds'.[4] This balance is echoed in the startling statement of one of the three monk leaders of this movement, Hendiyagala Silaratana, that 'economic development is inner development'.[5] To sum up, this was a theory of honest, dedicated hard work and minimal consumption within a framework of spirituality. It was a doctrine that bore remarkable resemblance to what Max Weber called 'this worldly asceticism'. It was a basis for action that had extraordinary potential for the realization of a happy and prosperous society but events in Sri Lanka have proved that this was not to be. The society has ended up going in quite a different direction, as we shall see in the concluding section of this paper.

Strategy 2: A New Sermon

The second strategy of Dharmapala's soldier monks in the task of regenerating the moral society was the invention of a new sermon.

By the beginning of the Buddhist revival, that is the mid-nineteenth century, the traditional sermon, known as *dharmadesana*, had developed into an elaborate ritual. However, Dharmapala's soldier monks saw that it presented extraordinary potential in the task of regaining the moral society if shorn of its ritual accretions. The traditional sermon was an all-night performance and consisted of a standardized sequence of events. According to one account,[6] these were:

1. The arrival of the preacher
2. Giving merit to the preacher's seat, the first time
3. Invitation to preach, in two different types of verses
4. Giving merit to the preacher's seat, the second time
5. Invitation to the gods
6. Verses of obeisance
7. Benefits of hearing the sermon in verse, rendered lullabically
8. Benefits of hearing the sermon, a second time, in a different poetic mode and rendition
9. The discourse (homily), *sutra*
10. The commentary
11. Ode to the next Buddha
12. Giving merit
13. Giving gifts to the preacher

In addition to this, there were other ritual acts like the ceremonials associated with the preacher. In this list, the doctrinal content of the sermon is limited to the Discourse and the Commentary. The Discourse was probably in Pali or, even if in Sinhala, remained unintelligible to the majority. Even the Commentary, which ostensibly would explain the Discourse, could well have been a conventional chant beyond the comprehension of the congregation. In both the Discourse and the Commentary, the emphasis was on the sound rather than the meaning because the intention of the audience was not to understand the latter but to acquire merit, which was only possible through hearing as opposed to listening. Stanley Tambiah describes the same phenomenon in Thailand, when he talks about 'liberation through hearing'.[7] Sound is the message, meaning is dispensable.

The traditional sermon was even more elaborate when, simultaneous with it, dramatic events in the biography of the Buddha or in the history of Buddhism, and fund-raising devices like processions, bazaars, fireworks and dances were enacted elsewhere on the temple grounds. Other elaborations included the auctioning of flowers and enactments like the 'sermon of the double seat' in which a monk chanted a question using a text and another chanted the answer. It is quite obvious that such a chant, which would be in Pali, would not have been understood and its value for the audience lay not in its semantic content but in its potential for merit-making.

However potent this sermon was for merit-making, it was of no use for social and moral amelioration, which required the communication of ideas, not the hearing of sacred syllables. In fact, it could be argued that the ritualist sermon was inhibitive as regards social and moral reform. What Dharmapala wanted in the sermon was not a ritual but an instrument of regeneration, a time-framed and thematically focused address that would get a message across effectively. The traditional sermon was also of no appeal to a social stratum that Dharmapala considered crucial for regenerating the moral society, the educated urbanites, who, in any case, had regular work schedules in clerical, professional or other jobs that prevented them from participating in an all-night affair as part of their routine religious experience. They preferred succinctly presented doctrinal ideas and moral instruction for which their appetites had been whetted by the late nineteenth-century Buddhist-Christian debates and by the activities of the Buddhist Theosophical Society, both of which heralded a new scripturalism. Besides, their general acquaintance with modern knowledge and the exigencies of their modern urban existence made a short, modernized sermon entirely suitable and desirable. The traditional sermon was too long and too rustic to constitute any kind of entertainment for the city audiences unlike its role for the rural population.

Thus, at the beginning of the twentieth century, there was a convergence of interest between the urban laity and the newly-emerging Buddhist missionary monks of the city inspired by Dharmapala towards a time-framed, thematic, non-ritualist sermon that was doctrinal in content, morally and economically didactic, and free of emotion. Given the rising urbanism, a new kind of sermon would have probably emerged anyway but Dharmapala's vision of social and religious regeneration gave it a particular structure and content. Besides, Dharmapala had perfected a sermon of sorts as he traversed the country exhorting the people to awaken and act, which he had made available in a printed form in his column 'Facts One Should Know', mentioned earlier. This would serve as a model for the kind of sermon he and his soldiers needed.

The new sermon that they crafted was a radical departure from its traditional counterpart. It was confined to about an hour, a remarkable shrinkage into about one-tenth of its original duration. Next, it was free of the elaborate ritualism that conferred most of its length on the traditional sermon. The new sermon was not a performance in the sense that the traditional sermon was and it lacked the dramatic elements that we noticed in the latter. Above all, it was focused on a theme that was announced at its beginning in the form of a Pali verse and its Sinhala gloss, which, therefore, were structurally and functionally integrated to it.

The new sermon was the result of Dharmapala's attempt to apply what he considered to be 'true Buddhism' to daily life.[8] It has been claimed by some, especially monks of the Vajirarama, the elite temple in Colombo, that it was their founder, Palane Vajiragnana, who invented the new sermon. According to one of them, Palane revolutionized the traditional sermon by (1) confining it to one hour and (2) making it relevant for modern living. Let me quote Palane himself:

> A sermon should be preached according to times and circumstances. Since in these days men do not have more than one hour for listening to a sermon, it is inappropriate to preach a sermon for longer than an hour. It is better to listen to a sermon for 15 minutes per 2 or 3 days than for two or three hours each day. . . . What is preached must be intelligible to even a child. . . . Auctions, collections, music, dancing and fireworks . . . should not be allowed during a sermon. A sermon is meant to teach ethical conduct and improve virtue and wisdom, and not to collect money by swaying people by the use of music, dancing and gymnastics, invitations to preach, fireworks and so forth. Such brief sermons will help the development of wisdom, and the decline of crime, theft, and bad manners in the villages, and promote harmony.[9]

STRATEGY 3: THE PRINTED WORD

Let us now come to the third strategy for regenerating the moral society: the use of the printed word. I must mention here that the three strategies were not mutually exclusive and that there were areas of overlap. For example, all the three monastic leaders of the rural development movement were prolific writers. The output of two of them, Kalukondayave and Hendiyagala, was prodigious by any standards. Kalukondayave, in addition to a host of other publications, is the author of the longest book in the Sinhala language, *Puvatpat Sangara Itihasaya* (History of Newspapers and Journals), running into over 4,000 pages. Their books are strewn with the ideas about society and its reconstruction that we have been talking about, and, in particular, a critique of rural life, which they saw as deficient in cleanliness of surroundings, personal cleanliness, civility in day-to-day relations, politeness in speech, efficiency, manners and so on. This is in stark contrast to the fantasy of a romanticized rural life held by the contemporary urban middle and upper classes, propagandized by the popular media, and used by the ruling politicians as part of the opiate for gaining and remaining in power.

For Dharmapala and his soldiers, the other favourite subject of criticism was the folk religion mentioned earlier, especially its false beliefs in magic and astrology. The conviction that the Middle Path alone was the true Buddhism constituted the armour that gave strength to Dharmapala and his soldier monks in their crusade against the ritualism and false beliefs adhered to fervently by the vast majority. This explains the recurring emphasis on inner development in their writings, sermons and community action, and their insistence that ritual actions were external and irrelevant. Ritual action, indeed, was worse than irrelevant. It was negative because its ethical vacuum impeded both worldly happiness and liberation in a future existence. Ritual, they unabashedly declared, was self-deception, at best, and the refuge of scoundrels, at worst; the latter a profound insight into the exploitative and opiatic dimension of ritual. As we have seen, they maintained that it was not ritual but ethical conduct that led to the twin goals of worldly happiness and ultimate liberation.

To illustrate their use of the written word as a strategy for reviving the moral society, especially the critique of ritual, I use a series of pamphlets that are remarkable for their trenchant nature and sheer brilliance. They also stand out for their courageous challenge to the monastic establishment itself, which designed and perpetuated a complex of Buddhist ritual through the centuries, thereby seriously compromising its own integrity and inner purity.

The author of the pamphlets was the internationally known scholar monk, Walpola Rahula, the author of several important books on the history and philosophy of Buddhism, including *What the Buddha Taught*, one of the best-known introductory books on Buddhism that was available in a dozen languages and was a classroom favourite in college-level courses. The pamphlets were first published between 1933 and 1934 by the Granthaprakasa Press in Colombo for free distribution, the costs being borne charitably by the press and a group of donors. They were an elaboration of a previous publication, a booklet of thirteen pages in a pocketbook format titled *Uttma Pujava* (The Noble Offering), published in 1932. In 1992, seventy years after their original publication, the pamphlets were reprinted in a slim volume of eighty-one pages under the title *Satyodaya* (Dawn of Truth).[10] Though originally published as separate essays, the pamphlets represent a unity of conception, content and style, and constitute a coherent and credible single volume. Except for one, they are in catechistic form, echoing the influence of the widespread Christian missionary activity of the time. It is important for us to note that Rahula was in his mid-twenties at the time that he wrote these essays, long before his mature works were to be produced. So the essays are full of youthful vigour, enthusiasm and zeal, teeming with a critical and irreverent spirit, and recalling the Buddha's own rebellious discovery, and denunciation of the mighty Brahmanical orthodoxy that was his social and intellectual milieu.

The basic premise on which Rahula levels his critique is the inverse relation between ritual and ethics, quite familiar to us by now. This is an essentially Dharmapalist position. We have seen how Dharmapala bases his moral society on the Middle Path. Ethical Conduct is the very first step in that Path. The rest of the Path logically follows. As we have repeatedly seen, it is by treading the Middle Path that one reaches success in this world and progresses towards *nirvana*. On this Path and the balanced life it entails, there is no place for ritual. To worship the Buddha and to make offerings to him are externalities that people have developed in the hope of receiving benefits in the form of merit. According to the Buddha, an act is the same as its intention, so the intention to receive merit degrades the act of offering into a profit-making exchange, obliterating its ethical basis. Therefore, acts of ritual are of no use and are only dabbled in by those deficient in inner development and wisdom.

I shall try to illustrate Rahula's critique by first conveying an idea of the conventional ritualized method of making offerings to the Buddha. This method, widespread in Sri Lankan Buddhist worship, is modelled on the form of Hindu worship known as *puja*. In essence, *puja* consists of treating the image of a deity as if it were a living god by making a series of offerings. While the Buddhist ritual is less elaborate, it is, nevertheless, based on the same central idea: the treatment of an image of the Buddha as if it were the living Buddha. Food and other offerings are placed before the image and the prescribed verses chanted to ritually make the offering. Rahula's favourite method of criticism is to pour scorn on the practice by reducing it to absurdity. He notes: 'In some places, Buddhists prepare a seat to invite the statue to sit on it. After that they prepare and offer water to rinse the mouth, followed by items of food, chewing betel, and a spittoon. Just think what a laughable and childish act this is.'[11]

On the custom of placing food in front of an image and imagining that it will consume it, Rahula says: 'Imagine what a sight it would be if you placed food in front of the statue of one of our national heroes'. He considers these acts as appealing to men who are 'deficient in wisdom and virtue'.[12] These, to him and other soldiers, are 'external' acts that betray the absence of 'inner development'. He contends that it is impossible for us to honour the Buddha in a manner worthy of him by means of external offerings, and points out that the Buddha exhorted us to honour him not by offering him externalities like food and entertainment but by adherence to a standard of ethical conduct (*patipatti*) in our daily life.

Taking his scorn further, Rahula says,

Supposing we had the opportunity to fetch the Buddha some medicine when he got sick, Oh, what a good fortune would that be. However, if a deeply religious person were to imagine that a statue got sick, and were to duly arrange a bed, make the statue recline on it, cover it with a blanket, and scream, 'Come, ho, the Buddha has got sick', spend money and rush in a doctor, boil a concoction, and offer it to the statue, imagine what a farce that would be.[13]

Rahula then points out that the acts of service that one can do for the living Buddha cannot be done when he is dead. Instead of trying to do the impossible, it is wise to try and find out what services we can do *now*. The Buddha preached that to treat the sick and the infirm with kindness would be to serve him. So instead of imagining that a statue is sick and trying to cure it, a true Buddhist should try to cure a living being. Instead of trying to feed a statue that cannot eat, a true Buddhist should feed the hungry.

Rahula takes on the entire range of ritual and ceremonial acts that constitute popular Buddhism. His main objection to them is their motivation for gaining merit, which, to him, is devoid of any ethical foundation because such acts are simply business transactions contracted to gain benefits in this world or the next. He objects strongly to money-making activities that go on in temples in the guise of merit-making ceremonies. Let me quote him again: 'Look at a vihara (Buddhist shrine). There are traps all over designed to plunder money. In front of the seated Buddha statue is a box wrongly labeled "the merit box. . . ." A stranger can only conclude that the Buddha was a person who sat down and waited to collect money.'[14]

The traditional sermon that we encountered includes an invitation to the gods to listen to it. Rahula reduces this too, to absurdity, and does so with his characteristic skepticism and irreverence. To quote him:

I don't think the gods need a special invitation. People come to know about a sermon through flyers posted in public places. . . . These flyers are in Sinhala and if the gods do not read Sinhala, they will also not understand the sermon, because it is in Sinhala. If their language is Pali as some people believe it is, they will not understand the sermon because it is in Sinhala. On the other hand, if the gods do not attend a sermon just because they are not given a special invitation, we are left with only one conclusion, that they are a bunch of arrogant beings that think no end of themselves. If they fail to attend a sermon for such a trivial reason, it is a regretful matter. It is of course the duty of the sermon's organizers to inform the gods just as they inform humans. They should either print a separate flyer inviting the gods, or insert "gods included" in the general flyer they print for humans. Anyhow, if they can hear the chanted invitation, we must assume that they are nearby somewhere, within hearing distance. If so, they can hear the sermon anyway. Inviting them is superfluous.[15]

CONCLUSION: FATE OF THE MORAL SOCIETY AND THE BUDDHIST REVIVAL

While these enthusiastic young monks and other followers of Dharmapala worked tirelessly to regenerate the moral society, they did not realize that it had a built-in problem, namely, the identification of the entire territory of the island of Sri Lanka with the majority ethnic group and the majority religions: the Sinhalas and Buddhism. This identification was expressed in their stirring slogan 'Country, Nation and Religion' (*rata, jatiya, agama*) that became the rallying point of the project. They little realized that Sri Lanka was a multi-ethnic and multi-religious society, and that it would be both practically impossible and morally indefensible to identify the land with any one ethnic or religious group. Not all these monks were exclusivists but by the mid-1950s, the voice of the inclusivists was near-completely drowned in the cacophony of ethno-religious majoritarianism. Thus, by its very definition, the moral society, was immoral. The tension between the moral society propagated from platforms and the rejection of pluralism on the ground increasingly became the marker of the socio-political scene, and the engine of its direction.

Instead of comprehending this ground reality and overcoming it in the interest of the nation as a whole, the movement lost its social and political morality and its humanism that was its justification. As it progressed, the youthful monastic leaders grew older and a new generation of leaders took over. The definition of the universe of people whose interests they were allegedly defending grew narrower, and became focused exclusively on the majority ethnic and religious group, the Sinhala Buddhists. We can indeed say that the focus became yet narrower in that it got increasingly intertwined with the interests of the indigenous elites – the Buddhist monks, indigenous school teachers and indigenous physicians. Another way to put this is that the project of the dreamers was hijacked by those elites who stood to lose the most from British rule. It was British rule that broke the feudal bonds that kept the masses enslaved by these elites. Thus, in effect though not in actual usage, the term *jatiya* (nation) meant not even the Sinhala people as a whole but its indigenous elites. However, this fact was kept well under wraps since in an electoral-based political system, 'the people' mattered a lot as it was their vote that counted to get the representatives of these elites elected to power and to justify the claim that the government they formed was 'the people's'.

There was a further political dimension. While the pre-colonial system oppressed the people, colonialism was, nevertheless, foreign domination. As it got established and perpetuated its own oppression, it was easy to attribute all the ills of society to colonial rule, and to portray the pre-colonial past as perfect, unique, moral and glorious, thereby appealing to parochial national pride. This, in fact, was the essence of Dharmapala's domestic project – to portray the past society as idyllic and listing its components, such as its irrigation system and religious monuments, as iconic of a culture and civilization unmatched anywhere in the world. So stigmatizing the colonial system and its political and cultural remnants became the obverse of valorizing the indigenous culture and civilization. These two sides of the same coin could be used in building an ethnic and religious identity that would drug the masses into voting for those who championed this allegedly immemorial but, in fact, newly-manufactured 'culture' and 'civilization'.

So in this process, the language, religion and culture of the majority ethnic group were redefined as the foundation of a new identity, and as the general election of 1956 approached, these three issues were made the central ones. With its promise to make the majority language, Sinhala, the only state language in twenty-four hours (known as the 'Sinhala Only Act'), and to give 'due place' to Buddhism and 'national culture', the nationalist coalition of 1956 exploited the emotional content of this ethno-religious identity to the maximum with disastrous consequences, as we now know. As soon as they were elected as the new government, they added a new department to the bureaucracy, the Department of Cultural Affairs, which dealt with religion and culture. Thus, in the 1956 electoral victory of the nationalists, the Dharmapala project, which began in the late nineteenth century, finally came to fruition. The history of Sri Lanka since then has been one of taking that project further, which means a march backwards to allegedly restore the erstwhile moral society. As we have seen, the obverse of this is an increasingly vociferous condemnation of the west and its culture, along with any of its local manifestations. Ever since the nationalist agenda of 1956 began to be gradually implemented, the twin exercise of relentless harking back to a former idyllic society and the hysterical resentment towards the west has meant the assertion of a majority hegemony and the marginalization of minorities, with the parallel development of dismantling the edifice of democracy and good governance that the British had built at the time they relinquished imperial control over the island.

Eventually, to ensure their own political survival, the secularist and democratic opposition to the 1956 regime gradually embraced the hegemonic policies of their opponents as well, and accepted the Sinhala Only Act. When they returned to power in 1977, they established a Ministry of Buddhism and the new constitution they enacted made Buddhism virtually the state religion. By then, the nationalist government of 1956 had already 'improved' on their own record and constitutionally accorded, in 1972, 'a special place' to Buddhism.

This process of harking back to a past glory ostensibly for the empowerment of 'the people', which, in effect, was a nullification of the beneficial effects of colonial rule as well as a departure from the universalist ethic of Buddhism, was carried further in other ways by the Constitutions of 1972 and 1978. At the centre of the ill-effects of these moves is what the Colombo University's political sociologist, Jayadeva Uyangoda, has called the 'illiberalization of the state' brought about by the concentration, at the centre of state power, of two illiberal forces: majoritarian ethnic nationalism and a command economy.[16] The 1972 constitution was brought into being by means of what another Sri Lankan analyst, Asanga Welikala, has described as an 'extra constitutional legal revolution that established a precedent for further acts of constitutional manipulation'.[17] To sum up on what happened to the moral state, I can do no better than quote the same author:

> In giving full expression to the constitutional vision of Sinhala-Buddhist nationalism – in the form of a constitutionally privileged status for Buddhism

and Sinhalese, and the entrenchment of the unitary state – but aggressively rejecting even a moderate accommodation of Tamil aspirations to autonomy, the 1972 Constitution repudiated the loyalty of the Tamils to the new republic, radicalised that community's politics, and contributed to the later descent into separatism and armed conflict. The 1972 Constitution instituted the pervasive politicisation of governance from which we continue to suffer, and may never escape.[18]

NOTES

1. Weber (1958): 204-30.
2. For a discussion of this, see Obeyesekere (1963, 1966).
3. Rahula (1959): 35.
4. Pannasehkara (1970): 332
5. Silaratana (1951). The entire booklet of 76 pages elaborates on the inner dimension of development.
6. Silaratana (1971): 85-90.
7. Tambiah (1970):195-222.
8. The theme of what Buddhism properly is runs through all of Dharmapala's writings on Buddhism. See Guruge (ed.) (1965): 519, 530-1.
9. In 'wisdom' along with 'harmony', we might note here the interest in both worlds, *ubhayalokartha*.
10. Rahula (1992).
11. Rahula (1992): 1.
12. Rahula (1992): 2.
13. Rahula (1992): 3-4.
14. Rahula (1992): 20-1.
15. Rahula (1992): 5.
16. Uyangoda (2010): 40-3.
17. Welikala (2011): http://groundviews.org/2011/03/13/sirimavo-a-review/
18. Welikala (2011): http://groundviews.org/2011/03/13/sirimavo-a-review/

BIBLIOGRAPHY

Obeyesekere, Gananath. 1963. 'The Great Tradition and the Little in the Perspective of Sinhalese Buddhism'. *Journal of Asian Studies* 22: 139-53.

———. 1966. 'The Buddhist Pantheon in Ceylon and its Extensions', in Manning Nash et al. (eds.), *Anthropological Studies in Theravada Buddhism*. Yale University Cultural Reports Series 13. New Haven, 1-26.

Pannasekhara, Kalukondayave. 1970. *Sri Pragnasekhara Caritapadanaya*. Wellampitiya: Sri Press.

Rahula, Walpola. 1959 . *What the Buddha Taught*. Bedford: Gordon Fraser.

———. 1992. *Satyodaya*. Colombo: Godage Brothers.

Silaratana, Hendiyagala. 1951. *Gramasamvardhanaya*, vol. 2. Kuliyapitiya: Sastrodaya Press.

———. 1971. *Mage Jivita Kathava*, vol. 1. Kuliyapitiya: Sastrodaya Press.

Tambiah, Stanley. 1970. *Buddhism and the Spirit Cults in North-East Thailand*. Cambridge: Cambridge University Press.

Uyangoda, Jayadeva. 2010. 'The United Front Regime of 1970 and the Post-Colonial State of Sri Lanka', in Tissa Jayatilaka (ed.), *Sirimavo, Honouring the World's First Woman Prime Minister*. Colombo: The Bandaranaike Museum Committee, pp. 31-45.

Weber, Max. 1958. *The Religion of India* (English tr.). Glencoe: The Free Press.

Welikala, Asanga. 2010. *Review of Tissa Jayatilaka ed. Sirimavo, Honouring the World's First Woman Prime Minister.* Colombo: The Bandaranaike Museum Committee.

CHAPTER 8

The Political Dimension of Buddhism in Sri Lanka

ANURUDDHA PRADEEP

THE LINEAGE OF BUDDHIST POLITICS IN SRI LANKA

THE DEBATE ABOUT THE relationship between monks and politics, which was prevalent in the history of Sri Lankan politics for decades, emerged once again in an intense manner when an all-monk party, the Jathika Hela Urumaya (JHU, hereafter), decided to contest the 2004 parliamentary elections in Sri Lanka. It was not only the frequent critics of Sinhala Buddhist politics but also its ardent supporters who considered the attempt unsuitable and contrary to tradition. However, Buddhist monks in Sri Lanka have been involved in political activities at least from the middle of the nineteenth century and some of them had even contested elections. Baddegama Samitha Thero, a monk-cum-politician, was already a Member of Parliament when the JHU monks launched their party and, therefore, monks entering politics and contesting elections was not a new phenomenon.

However, the JHU's move differed from all previous occasions on which monks had contested elections in both scale (size) and nature and, perhaps, this was the main reason why it attracted such unprecedented attention and criticism. The first difference, in scale, created a theoretical problem which needed immediate resolutions. Although some monks had contested elections previously, these were individual and isolated efforts, and they did not have any chance of acquiring legislative or executive power. However, the situation was different with the JHU since it contested all electorates other than the Northern Province and the Batticaloa district. When a party contests all electorates, it should, at least theoretically, be understood as an attempt to acquire power to govern the country. If people had voted for them in sufficient numbers, the monks of the JHU would have acquired legislative power and, hence, executive power, too. Given the contemporary political reality, there was no possibility for such a success. However, since this was a theoretical possibility for the first time in history, the question of the appropriateness of monks holding the highest political office in the country had to be considered and resolved. Nalin de Silva,[1] a prominent nationalist scholar, summed this up when he noted that the

> Bhikkus had been advisors to the kings without being kings. The Bhikkus were not even members of the 'Rajasabha' of the kings and the advice of the Bhikkus was given to the kings through other 'non formal' channels. The Bhikkus have never played the role of Khomeini-like figures who rule the country nor the role of Brahmins in India who participated in the deliberations in the 'Rajasabha'.[2]

His argument is clear. Sri Lankan monks have never played an executive role (like Khomeini) or a legislative role (like the Brahmins) at any point in history, so it was contrary to their own tradition for the JHU monks to contest elections.

The nature of the JHU politics contributed as much as its scale in evoking serious criticism from some circles of Sri Lankan society. Political activity of JHU was presented not as an attempt of a group of monks who set aside their monkhood and Buddhist nature for a while, but as an extension of it. This will be explained shortly. What is noteworthy is that monks are quite often involved in fields that are considered to fall outside the traditional role of the bhikku, from maintaining orphanages, nursery schools and elders' homes to astrology, indigenous medicine and, on very rare occasions, even witchcraft. As long as they are not in contradiction with the law of the country and morality, these acts are considered by lay people and even other monks to be personal concerns, and such bhikkus usually maintain their traditional religious activities separate from other activities. Baddegama Samitha Thero was seen as a monk-cum-politician, rather than as a monk who was doing something that could be understood as 'Buddhist Politics'. He was a social worker in his electorate in much the same way as almost all politicians in Sri Lanka.[3] Further, since he belonged to a Marxist party, his leftist leanings were more visible in the political sphere than in his status as a Buddhist. Like other ordinary monks, he limited his monkhood to his temple and its lay mass (*dayakas*), and was engaged in leftist politics, which was in no way related to Buddhism.

The politics of the JHU was completely different to the kind of politics practised by Samitha Thero and all other monks who had previously contested elections. The JHU monks entered politics exhibiting their Buddhist identity to the fullest. The words, terms, symbols and behaviour that they used in their electoral campaign were completely Buddhist: their rallies were called 'Bodu Samulu' (Buddhist Assemblies) their goal was described as a 'Dharma Rajya' (Righteous State) and their campaign was called a 'Paramitha Perahera' (Procession of Great Aspirations). The venues of their rallies were decorated with Buddhist flags and people gathered there in plain white attire as if they were participating in a Buddhist 'Pinkama' (traditional Sinhala Buddhist meritorious act or event). The JHU monks proceeded slowly and one-by-one in a very neat line towards the stage with eyes half-closed, and heads inclined towards the ground, (resembling a group of meditating monks in a jungle hermitage) through crowds of lay people chanting 'Saadu Saadu Saadu' (the Sri Lankan Buddhist expression that shows happiness or approval about something or someone). Buddhist identity in the past had never been added to politics by leftist monks or even nationalist monks to such an extent. These were now no longer merely a group of monks who were involved in politics but a group who was involved in a particular kind of politics that could be described as 'bhikku politics' or Buddhist politics. This gave the impression that this kind of politics arose here not when there is a lack of monkhood but as a necessary extension of it. This is what paved the way for all the attention on and criticism of the JHU politics.

As mentioned above, nationalist scholars like Nalin de Silva argue that even though Buddhist monks have been involved in political activities, they have never held executive or legislative power. Some other scholars, who, do not support the idea of monks' involvement in politics, argue that the very idea of bhikku politics is only a recent phenomenon. Mahinda Deegalle states that 'until the dawn of the 20th century, Buddhist monks were passive agents in the political history of Sri Lanka'.[4] Most other critics of bhikku politics largely share this idea; H.L. Seneviratne's criticism is one of the more visible ones. He argues that monks did not have a prominent role in the pre-colonial era and says that such an idea was merely an invention of Anagarika Dharmapala, the Buddhist revivalist and writer. It was Dharmapala who suggested giving the Buddhist monk a key role in the national revival and the laymen a supporting one. According to Seneviratne, one of the two separate groups of monks who followed Dharmapala's paradigm was the monks of Vidyodaya Pirivena,[5] who worked on the economic front and became social workers in impoverished villages. The other group was that of Vidyalankara Pirivena who worked on the cultural front. In a fairly strong critique, Seneviratne argues that bhikku politics started from the latter camp in which the 'Dharmapalite' term of social service was interpreted as simply a political and ideological rhetoric and activism.[6] For this reason, he and most like-minded scholars consider Walpola Rahula Thero's well-known book, *Bhikshuwage Urumaya* (Heritage of the Bhikku 1946), to be the visible starting point of bhikku politics. While some nationalist scholars argue that the JHU monks violated the Sri Lankan tradition of bhikku politics, others claim that bhikku politics never existed in the history of Sri Lanka.

Therefore, the question that this paper will attempt to investigate is how far the variety of politics which was introduced by the JHU could be justified in terms of the Sinhala Buddhist tradition of the country. Available facts contradict the claim that there was no bhikku politics or that monks were just passive agents in the political history of Sri Lanka. Scholars like Deegalle and Seneviratne are mistaken because they failed to understand the changes that took place in the political sphere in Sri Lanka from the middle of the nineteenth century. What we understand as 'politics' today did not exist in its current form before the advent of modern democracy and, more precisely, before its introduction to this country. However, just as there is a particular version of politics that is suited to the needs of the contemporary world, there was a different version of politics that served the needs of the past. Politics can be defined as the 'activity through which people make, preserve and amend the general rules under which they live'[7] and the people in the past were engaged in this 'activity' according to the needs and the means of the time, though these were not similar to those of the current society. Although monks were not engaged in politics in its contemporary form, in the past, that does not mean that they refrained from politics.

The history of Buddhism in Sri Lanka needs to be explored in order to understand both the methods of politics that bhikkus employed in the past and their desired goals. Buddhism in Sri Lanka was established in the time of King Devanampiya Tissa (307-267 BCE) and it soon attained the position of a state religion. It became very prominent and powerful that King Dutugemunu (*c.* second century BCE) was able to use the sentiments of Buddhists in his war effort against the invader king, Elara from the Chola kingdom. According to the *Mahavamsa,* he went to war with a relic on his spear and invited monks to accompany him to the battlefield: 'Bhikkus shall go on with us, since the sight of Bhikkus is a blessing and protection for us'.[8] Further, he gave his war effort a religious goal: 'Not for the joy of sovereignty is this toil of mine, my striving (has been) ever to establish the doctrine of the Sambuddha'.[9] He built huge monuments such as a 300 ft tall Ruwanweliseya to keep his promise of protecting Buddhism and it is clear that he did much more for the development of the religion than for the economy. This means that Buddhism had attained a powerful position by Dutugemunu's time.

Buddhism soon became a way of legitimizing state power. Protecting the Buddha Sasana (Buddha's Dispensation) was declared to be the purpose of political power. This is clear from the fact that taking possession of the Tooth Relic and Alms Bowl was essential for a prince to become the king.[10] This belief became very powerful by the tenth century, so much so that it was apparently stated in an inscription of King Mahinda (982-1017 CE) that only Bodhisattvas and not ordinary Buddhists should become kings of Sri Lanka.[11] Non-Buddhist kings, too, pretended that they supported Buddhism.[12] Tamil kings who reigned in the latter stages of the Kandyan era considered supporting

Buddhism to be their responsibility as well. This sentiment was so powerful that even the British promised to safeguard Buddhism when they signed the Kandyan Convention on 10 March 1815 and the governor, who was criticized by English missionaries for including such a clause into the agreement, later wrote to the Foreign Secretary that 'in truth our secure possession of the country hinged upon this point'.[13] Only in 1847 did the colonial government decide to officially abandon this duty by thrusting it onto a committee of the Chief Priests of Siyam Nikaya.[14] By that time, the British Empire was a strong worldwide phenomenon, while Buddhism in Sri Lanka was too weak to fight against its political authority.

Thus, throughout history, on the one hand, the general public in Sri Lanka considered Buddhism to be the foundation of the collective consciousness and on the other hand, kings supported Buddhism to legitimize their power.

In ordinary situations, bhikkus were involved in their usual activity of protecting Dhamma, but when a threat to the community arose, they came forward to safeguard it since the community was the bearer of the Dhamma. This can be seen in the story of Dutugemunu in the *Mahavamsa*. This war against Elara was important not because of its magnitude but because it formulated this concept of defending the community which was so crucial to the later development of Buddhism in Sri Lanka. The role of bhikkus in Dutugemunu's war must have been the most difficult dilemma ever faced by them because of Buddhism's emphasis on non-violence. It is well known that it was the violence of war that led King Ashoka to convert to Buddhism and he became such an ardent supporter because of the non-violent characteristic of the religion. But ironically, just over a century later, Sri Lanka, which received Buddhism from him, was at war and the question of the role of the monk in that crucial juncture arose. The question was whether monks should secure the principles of the religion without harming any of it, or secure the particular community that bore the Dhamma, disregarding these principles temporarily. The second option was selected and thus began the dual-faceted nature of Sri Lankan Buddhism.

Approaching the question of the relationship of Buddhism and violence from a different angle, it is clear that in any society in the world, invasion is opposed for reasons of survival. Unfortunately, this ordinary and common behaviour is widely criticized when it comes to Buddhists since Buddhism places great emphasis on non-violence. Opting for war against an invader does not make someone a 'bad human being' but it makes him a 'bad Buddhist'. This has led some scholars to come up with explanations about this apparent contradiction within Sri Lankan Buddhism. One of the most commonly referred to is that of S.J. Tambiah who blames the 'mytho-history of the *Mahavamsa*'.[15] The other is the opinion of Seneviratne who blames the Vidyalankara monks for making allowances for bhikkus to take part in war. However, what should be understood is the fact that Buddhists act according to Buddhist principles in ordinary situations and on the occasion of an invasion, as any other society does. In Dutugemunu's time, monks made allowances for this natural and necessary human behaviour within Buddhism itself. It is inappropriate to romanticize non-violence in Buddhism or to attempt to make it an impractical dogma and expect saints rather than human beings from the Buddhist community. Not only Buddhists but all other religious communities in the world breach their religious principles in times of war since survival is more important than safeguarding religious fundamentals. This can be the key to understanding the behaviour of Sinhala bhikkus during the war against Elara in 161 BC and against the Liberation Tigers of Tamil Eelam (LTTE), two thousand years later.

This helped Buddhism survive the many challenges that followed: from Hindu south Indians, the Catholic Portuguese, British colonialists, Evangelical Christians and the LTTE separatists. The objectives of protecting Dhamma and the community have proved contradictory, on some occasions, such as when monks attempted to justify the war against Elara by manipulating Buddhist concepts.[16] On other occasions, they have merged into one, for example, Migettuwatte Gunananda Thero's successful debates against Christian missionaries in the nineteenth century and Gangodawila Soma Thero's Dhamma purification campaign in the 1990s. There have been other occasions where protecting the community resulted in protecting Dhamma.

For example, King Wattagamini Abhaya's (103 BCE) military campaign stabilized the country and, in turn, facilitated the recording of the *Tripitaka* that had been handed down orally through the bhikku order until then.

CHANGES IN BHIKKU POLITICS IN THE NINETEENTH CENTURY

Alhough monks have been involved in politics throughout history, their strategies changed on par with changes in the political and social arena in the middle of the nineteenth century. Bhikkus, who had earlier supported political authority to safeguard the Dhamma and community, started to become actively involved in politics, without the involvement of the government and sometimes even acting against it.

To understand the necessity and nature of this change in bhikku politics, it is necessary to examine the changes that occurred during the colonial period.

The first was that, Buddhism lost its position as the sole architect of Sinhala identity and unity. Earlier, all the Sinhalese were necessarily Buddhists but this changed with the introduction of Christianity by the West in the sixteenth century. In parallel, Tamil and Muslim communities also came into prominence as a result of the space created for them by the colonial government.[17] Christians and Tamils enjoyed privileged positions during the British period in bureaucracy, legislature and professions such as medicine, law and engineering.

The next change was political. As discussed above, Buddhism and the state were interlinked in important ways in the pre-colonial era and this was evident in the decision of the British to include a pledge to protect Buddhism in the Kandyan Convention. However, the British were not ready to work accordingly.[18] Eventually, they decided to terminate even this nominal obligation in 1853, paving the way for Christianity to become the sole religious force behind the colonial government.[19] Buddhists, thus, lost all political authority, after some two millennia. It is worth noting that during all previous periods of invasion, the Buddhists had their own kingdom at least in one place in the country. When Elara and other Cholas ruled Anuradhapura or Polonnaruwa, the Sinhala Buddhists had their own kingdom in

Ruhuna. During colonialism and until 1815, Kandy had actually escaped Western rule. It is, in fact, important to note that titles for the monks in British areas were conferred not by the British but by the kings of Kandy and this was accepted by the British, the rulers of the area.[20] Although the Buddhists had no kingdom of their own till 1815, they had the official guarantee from the British until 1853, and it was only after that that they became completely without a king. Hence, it was not possible to seek government protection for the community or Dhamma anymore and this situation led the monks to find a new strategy to engage in politics.

In their new strategy, defeating the enemy was abandoned along with seeking protection from the government. Instead, the low country Buddhists started to learn from their rivals and attempted to become more competitive, using the same methods used by their rivals. Meanwhile the Buddhists in the Kandyan region still engaged in the old methods. They rose against the colonial government, unsuccessfully, in two great armed rebellions in 1818 and 1848. They also attempted various forms of conspiracies and revolts nine other times between these two rebellions to topple the British rule.[21] On the other hand, the Kandyan high priests pleaded with the British against the termination of the government's pledge to protect Buddhism in 1853 in vain.[22] However, some Buddhists in the low country who had sufficient knowledge and experience of the strength and character of the British did not want to attempt either of these traditional strategies and invented a new one instead.

Let us examine this in more detail. Even though the Buddhists no longer faced an external threat like an invasion from south India, they had an enemy within: Christianity. In the beginning, not knowing about the aggressive nature of Christianity at the time, Buddhist monks not only tolerated but actually supported the activities of Christian missionaries. Karathota Dammarama Thero and Bowala Dhammananda Thero helped to translate the Bible into Sinhala in 1812, while missionaries were given free meals in temples when they went for their work in rural areas. They were even allowed to preach Christianity to the people on temple premises.[23] However, instead of being grateful, the missionaries started a malicious publicity campaign against Buddhism, even attending Buddhist functions as well as temple premises on 'Poya' (fast) days to make speeches and distribute leaflets in derogatory language that condemned Buddhism and its rituals.[24] Parallel with this aggressive campaign, the government also started to implement policies which adversely affected Buddhists, intentionally weakening Buddhist education and the economic strength of temples.[25] In addition, the task of registering births, marriages and deaths was assigned to the Anglican Church. Marriages had to be registered by a pastor to be legal and babies had to be baptized. Meanwhile, the government and missionaries paid a lot of attention to the spread of Christian education.[26] This was immensely successful in that 60 per cent of those who converted did so through such schools.[27]

Low country Buddhist leaders who had realized that there was no room for rebellion and that it was naïve to seek government help, understood, however, that the colonial government provided space for cultural and religious activity.[28] Therefore, the Buddhist monks and lay leaders designed a campaign to counter the missionary 'onslaught',[29] focused mainly on education and publicity since these were the most powerful weapons of Christian aggression.

There can be no doubt that the most colourful and successful reaction against the Christians was the series of verbal debates known as the Five Great Debates from 1865 to 1873. However, the Buddhist reaction started not at that time but in publishing replies to Christian leaflets, pamphlets and books from 1855 onwards. Until then, the Buddhists did not have a printing press and could not do anything to refute the Christians, who used to frequently publish pamphlets and books that violently attacked and condemned Buddhism. The Buddhist reaction, and hence the Buddhist revival, practically started as some prominent monks decided to buy a printing press. It should be noted here that the new strategy was not to plead that the government prohibit the malicious campaign or attempt to demolish the Christian press but to set up their own. The Buddhists began to reply to the Christians and this developed into a debate, in pamphlet form. In 1865, the Christians, who were very confident since they had already defeated local witchcraft performers,[30] challenged the Buddhist monks to a debate. When the Buddhists accepted, the Christians considered it a foregone victory.[31] However, the end result was contrary to their expectations. Migettuwatte Gunananda Thero, 'one of the pioneer imitators of Christian missionary methods to revitalize Buddhism',[32] was victorious in the last debate in Panadura in 1873.[33] Obviously, this provided enormous confidence to the Buddhist leaders about their new strategy.

This was followed by many such reactive activities and successes. What happened in the field of education is especially notable. Until the latter part of the nineteenth century, the education of monks was in an appalling condition. They usually did not know much more than a few Pali stanzas used in routine rituals and were outsmarted by the well-educated missionaries.[34] To turn this situation around, the Vidyodaya and Vidyalankara Pirivenas were established in 1873 and 1876, respectively.[35] The Ananda College and many other Buddhist schools were set up to bring an end to the Christianization process. Many other reactive efforts were seen during that period: Bhakthi Geetha (Buddhist carols) were introduced as a substitute for Christmas carols, as were Vesak cards for Christmas cards and a booklet of 5,000 names as a substitute for Christian names. Daham Pasal (Buddhist Sunday schools), a Buddhist flag and a national dress, too, were introduced. These reactive activities were not always non-violent. Catholics attacked a Buddhist procession in 1883 in Kotahena in Colombo and although they were in the wrong, the government did nothing.[36] The Buddhists reacted to Christians violently over the next two years and, on at least one occasion, initiated violence without provocation.[37]

The new strategy was very successful in the Buddhists regaining their self-esteem. Ponnambalam Arunachalam observed the following: 'Previously it was considered among Sinhalese rather fashionable to be thought Christian, and I have, in my judicial experience, known Buddhists taking [the] oath on the Bible as a matter of course. This is no longer the case. They are rather proud of their religion. And have even become aggressive to Christianity.'[38]

To sum up, the strategy of bhikku politics changed from one that either sought the protection of the government or attempted to topple undesirable regimes to a new strategy which attempted to defeat the rival by being competitive and using the same methods of the latter.

DIFFERENT STAGES OF THE NEW ERA OF BHIKKU POLITICS

The 'new era' of bhikku politics can be divided into three stages: the first, from the mid-nineteenth century to 1915; the second, from 1946 to 1956; and the third, from 1983 till the present.

The First Stage (Mid-nineteenth Century to 1915)

The beginning of the first stage has been described above under the subtitle 'Changes in Bhikku Politics in the Nineteenth Century'. It brought dignity to the Buddhists once again. The initial stage of bhikku politics happened to be a religious and cultural activity as its aim was to compete with Christianity, the religion of the government, but it was not difficult even for the government to understand its political content.[39] The campaign on the cultural front achieved its target successfully and conversions to Christianity came to an end by the end of the nineteenth century.

No leader paid any attention to direct politics in this period. If the Buddhist revival movement had grown into a fully-fledged national freedom movement, monks would have been involved in direct politics during the pre-Independence era. However, because of the very harsh suppression of Sinhala leaders during the 1915 riots,[40] this Sinhala Buddhist camp collapsed. Nevertheless, the targets of the first stage had obviously been met by this time and there was no need for the monks to continue with activities for the cultural and religious revival, which was the original aim. The task of achieving independence from the British Empire was passed over to the anglicized elite and Sri Lanka achieved independence with no notable participation of monks.

The Second Stage (1946-1956)

In the 1940s, neither the Buddhists nor the socialists were satisfied with the emerging political elite in Sri Lanka. From a cultural point of view, the Buddhists thought they were just brown sahibs, while in the eyes of the socialists, they were capitalists because of their economic views. The Vidyalankara group of monks, including Walpola Rahula Thero, was keen to define the role of the monk in this transition, since this category represented Buddhism and socialism at the same time.

Seneviratne and Deegalle attribute the whole responsibility of 'politicising' monks to Walpola Rahula Thero and his well-known book *The Heritage of Bhikshu*. However, the reality was that both monks and lay people had not engaged in 'politics', in terms of its modern meaning and nature. Public participation became the main form of politics only after the advent of modern democracy. Until then, there were no political parties in the modern sense that aim to organize people and expect their regular participation in their actions. In fact, there was no such political organization before the eve of the 1930s in Sri Lanka and there was no political party before 1935. The United National Party (UNP, hereafter) was formed only in 1946; and one of its three main components, the Sinhala Maha Sabha, had been founded only in 1935.[41]

It is a fact that Buddhist monks did not involve themselves in direct politics at the outset when it began in the modern sense in the country. Instead they waited for several decades. Throughout history, monks became involved in politics when necessary and subsequently returned to their usual religious role when the need for their involvement was over. The first stage of bhikku politics in the new era thus came to an end with the 1915 riots and the monks, therefore, entered a quiescent period as before. This was the period in which direct politics (the new form of conducting politics) started. When the monks realized that Buddhist interests were in danger in the hands of the emerging Westernized political elite during the 1940s, they began to seek the means of countering it and they found the method, direct politics, which had been introduced recently. However, this does not imply that the monks started to engage in activities that they had never done, as Seneviratne and Deegalle argue. They continued their work in a different way: politics as usual but now directly since this became the new way of doing politics.

The reasons for the monks' dissatisfaction with the UNP government are obvious and the following observation of Samuel P. Huntington summarizes the situation effectively:

After independence the new government was dominated by a small, upper-middle class, thoroughly Anglicised, urban elite whose political vehicle was the UNP. Its members were, as one observer remarked, like 'the former

> colonial rulers in everything but the colour of their skins'. This group was overwhelmingly urban, although Ceylon was 70 per cent rural. It was largely Christian, although 91 per cent of the Ceylonese were not and 64 per cent were Buddhist. Its language was English, which 92 per cent of the population could neither read nor write. In short, it was drawn from and represented a minority of less than 10 per cent of the population.[42]

The UNP government refused to make any change in the colonial setup and, for the Buddhists, it was nothing but a continuation of British rule. One striking example of the situation is that 60 per cent of the commissioned officers in the navy, which was established after independence in 1949 by the UNP government, were found to be Catholics.[43] Some of the leading monks of the time attempted to persuade the leadership of the UNP to have the Sinhala Buddhist grievances heard and solved, but they were ignored, ridiculed[44] and even threatened.[45]

Buddhist leaders who decided to challenge the undesirable political order opted to follow the example set by monks in the nineteenth century – of competing with the rival using the rival's own strategy. The first Prime Minister of Sri Lanka, D.S. Senanayake's source of power was direct politics in a democratic set up. Therefore, the only possible way of challenging it was direct political action. Understanding this simple fact, the monks became politically active. Walpola Rahula Thero, one of the most prominent, theoretically justified what had already been happening on the ground by that time. Monks began to be involved in politics to defeat the 'anti-Buddhist government' and they were able to bring a 'Buddhist' to power in the 1956 elections. After this, they lapsed into silence for two decades.

During this period, Sinhala Buddhists saw the emergence of a new rival, Tamil nationalism. It is not surprising that the Sinhalese acquired the majority of seats in the legislature when democracy was introduced in the first half of the twentieth century, even though the minority Tamils had earlier enjoyed a somewhat similar level of representation to the majority Sinhalese. Although this was unavoidable, it warned the minority Tamils of possible majority domination. As a result, Ponnambalam Ramanathan, the representative of the Ceylon Tamil Congress, testifying before the Donoughmore Commission which had been appointed to advise on constitutional reforms, requested the British not to grant any type of autonomy to Sri Lanka or make any changes to the governor's powers. Further, Ramanathan opposed universal franchise since it would give majority power to the Sinhalese.[46] His opposition to universal franchise was so strong that he went to England to persuade the colonial government to reverse their decision even after it had been introduced.[47] Similarly, the Tamils demanded fifty-fifty representation for minorities when the Soulbury Commission, came to Sri Lanka in 1945. It should be noted here that the Commission considered this to be an extremist demand. The Tamil leaders even criticized the Anuradhapura Conservation Act of 1942, the aim of which was merely to preserve the archaeological monuments of that well-known ancient Buddhist city. This criticism, too, was condemned by the Commission.[48]

Consequently, the Sinhala Buddhist leaders started to see their Tamil counterparts as obstacles to national independence and revival. Tamil leaders went to the extent of questioning the position of the Sinhalese not only as the more historically rooted community but also as the numerical majority. Their behaviour reminded the Sinhalese of the bitter history of south Indian Tamil invasions throughout history. The end result was that the Sinhalese started to act prejudicially, even rejecting the just demands of the Tamils, such as recognizing Tamil as an official language. It did not matter who was to be blamed since a new rival was emerging in the shape of Tamil nationalism, which later grew into the biggest and most ruthless non-state armed force in the world. If the monks wanted to save the community in which Dhamma was established, they had to act against this new threat.

The Third Stage (Mid-1980s to the Present)

Even though there seems to have been the continuous participation of bhikkus in politics from the 1980s to the present, we can identify two sub-phases. The first stage commenced around 1985 when the LTTE intensified its military campaign for separation and spanned five years or so until 1990. Nationalist Buddhist monks, who had not been happy with the policies of the UNP, sided with the opposition. The best example was the formation of the Mawbima

Surakeeme Vyaparaya (The Movement for the Protection of the Motherland – MSV, hereafter); the leadership of which consisted of the Sri Lanka Freedom Party (SLFP, hereafter), the Mahajana Eksath Peramuna and a front organization of the then-banned Janatha Vimukthi Peramuna (JVP, hereafter).[49] There was extensive participation of monks, including prominent and popular individuals, who wanted to change the government since, according to them, the existing one was not protecting the community from the threat it faced. This was somewhat similar to what happened in the up country during the first half of the nineteenth century. Both the SLFP and the JVP were in the MSV and while the former had the democratic chance of toppling the government, the latter seemed to have the courage and young blood to do it. There was an unprecedented participation of monks in the protest in Colombo against the Indo-Lanka Agreement in 1987. This protest can be seen as a mixture of non-violence and violence. In front of the Pettah Bo tree in Colombo, there were hundreds of monks who courageously remained in an unshaken meditating posture amidst tear gas, smoke and baton charges, and even flying bullets. On the other hand, there were mobs who committed arson and vandalism against government property: Five hundred twenty-nine government buildings, including forty-two local government and assistant government agent offices and forty-seven railway stations, were burnt in addition to five hundred government buses.[50] Similar to this protest, there were a couple of efforts to topple the government during the next two to three years. One was democratic and was led by the SLFP, while the other was an armed uprising led by the JVP. The democratic path was blocked off with Sirimavo Bandaranaike's defeat in the presidential elections of 1988, following which the JVP intensified its campaign, leading to unprecedented terror. This was finally defeated by the government using a well-organized campaign of counter-terrorism, which killed 60,000 people, including around 1,000 Buddhist monks. With these two defeats on both the democratic and military fronts, Sinhala Buddhist aspirations were overshadowed by demands for human rights, democracy and the like. The UNP government lost power in 1994. However, monks did not play a role in this transition of power, although democratic rights groups did.

Throughout the 1980s, monks had been striving to topple the UNP government and finally it happened. However, the change they expected did not come and, in fact, the government became more and more unfavourable towards the Buddhists under the new leader of the SLFP, Chandrika Kumaratunga. Unlike her nationalist mother, Sirimavo, she was a simple mixture of some Marxist and Liberalist ideas. This was not the long-awaited change the monks and other Sinhala Buddhists expected and it was, by and large, similar to what happened in the time of independence when the Buddhists found an undesirable independent government at the long-awaited end of colonial rule. It was this frustration with and eventual anger over Kumaratunga's policies which paved the way for the emergence of the JHU ten years later in 2004.

Among the most prominent of Kumaratunga's ideas was a belief that the Sinhala Buddhist identity and consciousness was the main obstacle to solving the ethnic conflict. Her formula was to demolish it and then to develop a Sri Lankan identity, solving the conflict by integrating all communities to build one nation. Although this formula was simple and attractive, it was inadequate for understanding the complex realities of the conflict. It misjudged the nature and strength of the LTTE, as well as the characteristics of the Sinhala Buddhist community and consciousness. The LTTE had become the most powerful and ruthless non-state military outfit in the world, and had its own existence independent of the Tamil community. It was not possible to tame the LTTE by solving the grievances of the Tamils. The LTTE did not stop the war against the state even though the main grievance, the language issue, had been solved in 1987. Further, the Indo-Lanka agreement had introduced the Provincial Council system, which was already beyond the original demand of the main Tamil nationalist party in 1956. The LTTE had showed several times that it did not have any trust in a political solution and were reluctant to compromise on Eelam. The LTTE restarted the war in 1995, unilaterally breaking the ceasefire.

Kumaratunga then introduced a new formula, 'War for Peace' – a dual strategy, with war against the LTTE and peace or a political solution for the Tamils.[51] Even though it seemed very fair and effective, it proved futile and even destructive when put into practice. Under this strategy, war was made a matter for the armed forces alone while the society was to be prepared psychologically for a political solution to the conflict. Since the government saw the nationalist Sinhala Buddhist ideas as the main obstacle to its programme, a well-planned campaign was launched to attack them through grassroots-level activities like 'Sudu Neluma' and 'Thawalama' by widely using state media, NGOs and leftist intellectuals. However, this government campaign soon became a psychological warfare against its own war effort. For example, on one occasion when the army was in a stalemate in the Vanni with inadequate manpower and striving to recruit people for its ranks, the Thawalama and Sudu Neluma were campaigning against its effort by saying that no child should be given to the *kalakanni yuddaya* (damn war).[52] Finally, the government war effort came to a destructive end.

While the government was rapidly and dangerously losing the 'war' component of its 'War for Peace' strategy, it intensified the other component, the 'peace effort'. This was practically nothing but a constant attack on the Sinhala Buddhist identity and its interests. The government went to the extent of questioning national symbols and ministers sometimes hurt the sentiments of the Sinhala Buddhists. These allegations were mostly baseless and such actions created anger among the Sinhalese since they started to feel that even their mere survival as a community was threatened.

One notable example of such an allegation was the criticism of the national flag, saying that it did not represent minority communities adequately.[53] The lion, the symbol of the Sinhala community, was seen to be in a threatening posture towards the minorities, as it holds a sword facing the stripes that represent minorities (Fig. 8.1). This was baseless. First, this Lion Flag was, in truth, the pre-colonial royal flag of the Kandyan kingdom and what was done after independence was to re-adopt it, adding two stripes into the front for minorities. Second, this was sufficiently inclusive since the two stripes occupied one-third of the flag and represented Tamils and Muslims, who were only one-fourth of the population. Interestingly, even the British Ceylon flag consisted only of a Buddhist stupa and an elephant, clearly representing the Buddhist community alone (Fig. 8.2).

Another criticism was that the national anthem, too, did not

FIGURE 8.1: ROYAL FLAG OF THE KANDYAN KINGDOM

FIGURE 8.2: THE BRITISH CEYLON FLAG

represent minorities and only celebrated Sinhala heritage. However, the truth was that it clearly encouraged unity and harmony, and, furthermore, could be sung in Tamil too, which was rare for a minority language.[54] The English translation of the lyrics are as follows:

Mother Lanka we salute Thee!
Plenteous in prosperity, Thou,
Beauteous in grace and love,
Laden with grain and luscious fruit,
And fragrant flowers of radiant hue,
Giver of life and all good things,
Our land of joy and victory,
Receive our grateful praise sublime,
Lanka! We worship Thee.
Thou gavest us Knowledge and Truth,
Thou art our strength and inward faith,

Our light divine and sentient being,
Breath of life and liberation.
Grant us, bondage free, inspiration.
Inspire us forever.
In wisdom and strength renewed,
Ill-will, hatred, strife all ended,
In love enfolded, a mighty nation
Marching onward, all as one,
Lead us, Mother, to fullest freedom.

The government also forcefully proposed to abolish the nominal article giving Buddhism a foremost place in the Constitution.[55] Even the British had included this in the Kandyan Convention in 1815. At the same time, it was not legally binding and was just a constitutional decoration. The positions and rights of religions were dealt with not by this article but by the third chapter, which included fundamental rights. According to it, Buddhists in Sri Lanka do not enjoy any extra rights or privileges as compared to other religious communities. They do not have anything more than Hindus have in India, while Hindus in Sri Lanka enjoy the same rights that Indian Muslims and Sikhs do. The Buddhists in Sri Lanka felt that a tradition which was accepted even by the British was in danger of being taken away.

At the same time, the Sinhala Buddhists saw the government project of eradicating the Sinhala Buddhist consciousness as an attempt to exclude them from the state. An enormous campaign was launched by the government to induce and persuade the Sinhalese to call themselves Sri Lankans, even at the school level. However, this was not applied to other communities and their Tamilness and Muslimness was glorified. Meanwhile, some prominent government ministers like Mangala Samaraweera humiliated the Buddhists. On one occasion, he razed a Buddhist shrine in Colombo arousing a huge outcry.[56] On another occasion, he held a Buddha statue by the neck in a very degrading manner, while he was participating in a public event. In a press conference later, he called one prominent monk, Uduwe Dhammaloka Thero, Mister Dhammaloka, which is considered very insulting.[57]

It should be noted here that all these things happened while the LTTE was enjoying massive successes. On the one hand, they claimed huge military victories like the attacks on Mullaitivu, the Elephant Pass and the Katunayake Airport. On the other, they intensified their attacks on civilians like the Central Bank bombing, the Dehiwala train bomb and the Gonagala massacre. Under these circumstances, the Sinhala Buddhists became extremely unhappy about the way the government was handling the LTTE issue.

Another main concern for Sinhala Buddhists was the development of Muslim communal politics. Even though the Muslim politics commenced with the intention of protecting the rights of the Muslims in the face of the growth of the LTTE, it soon became powerful to the extent of controlling the government, as 'king-makers'. Due to the proportional representation system, no party could get a simple majority in parliament from 1994 to 2010. For example, the People's Alliance (mainly the SLFP) won only 105 out of 225 seats, while the UNP got 94, in the 1994 elections. In 2001, the UNP won 109 and the PA got 77. Under these circumstances, parties like the Sri Lanka Muslim Congress had king-making powers since they held the balance. At different times, they supported the PA and the UNP, and these parties came to power accordingly. Sinhala voters had divided along party lines so the main parties had to rely on minority parties like the Muslim Congress and the Indian Tamil parties.

Contemporary Sinhala Buddhist politics, of which the emergence of the JHU was the most notable event, began as a response to these developments. The Buddhists wanted to use the same strategy that was formulated by Buddhist leaders during the latter half of the nineteenth century – learning from their rival and competing with it by using those very strategies. The government and its allies were attacking the Sinhala Buddhist identity and interests. At the same time, minority parties were powerful in the government since they had bargaining power. On top of all this, there was an unparalleled enemy, the LTTE, who had pushed the country to the brink of separation while the government was trying to solve the problem through negotiations, which were used by the LTTE to become stronger. On the other hand, the opposition UNP was more untrustworthy than the government. Sinhala Buddhists started to organize themselves. Almost all the Sinhala Buddhist organizations which finally came together to form the JHU were established during

Kumaratunga's time and it was certainly in response to the policies of her government.

Ranil Wickramasinghe came to power in 2001. His term can be considered as a strong version of Kumaratunga's. The background had already been set for a movement like the JHU by the time of his arrival. He only aggravated the situation. Wickramasinghe was wise enough to abandon Kumaratunga's campaign of attacking the Sinhala Buddhist identity through the media. However, he entered into a Cease Fire Agreement (CFA, hereafter) with the LTTE and this eventually became the biggest ever threat to the Sinhala Buddhists. Wickramasinghe had very high expectations of the CFA as the tool for ending the conflict. He elevated it to be the main programme of his government. He believed that the government should compromise more and, therefore, he agreed to give more concessions to the LTTE in the CFA and the subsequent peace process. This would have been successful if the LTTE had believed in a negotiated settlement. However, contrary to Wickramasinghe's expectations, the LTTE started to violate the CFA, causing him much trouble. Statistics demonstrate the seriousness of the situation. According to the international monitoring mission, by December 2005, the LTTE had violated the CFA 3,471 times, while the government had done so only 162 times. Hence, 95 per cent of all violations had been committed by the LTTE.[58] What really upset people was not the behaviour of the LTTE but the government's effort to cover it up. Meanwhile, the LTTE was behaving as though it was on the brink of achieving a separate state. It forwarded its proposal for an Interim Self Governing Authority (ISGA), which was worse than a separate state since it would have to be funded by Sri Lanka, while it would have all the characteristics of a separate state.

On the other hand, there was a notable rise in Christian evangelical activities during this time. Their actions were viewed as unethical by Buddhists as well as Hindus since they used material benefits to convert people. No other religious group, including the Catholics, attempted to convert people using financial inducements. Not only did the evangelicals have large the financial resources, they also used these while concentrating on one place at a particular time. On the one hand, the Buddhists did not have matching resources; on the other, they had to look after their brethren all over the country if they wanted to prevent conversions. It was obvious that Buddhists and Hindus were in a very disadvantageous position. The gravity of the issue can be understood by the support of some prominent Tamils, including T. Maheswaran, the minister of Hindu Affairs of the UNP government, for the anti-conversion bill brought by Sinhala Buddhists in later years, despite a decade-long fight with the Sinhalese.[59] However, the Buddhists began to think that the UNP government was supporting the evangelical activities. Even though there was not enough evidence for such support, some of their actions triggered a suspicion that they were favouring Christians. On one occasion, the government lit up Colombo for Christmas in a way, as the state media claimed, that 'people have never ever witnessed before'.[60] The police department was ordered to carry this out by its Christian minister and Colombo was kept lit up for the whole month of December.[61] As the country was just recovering from a month-long electricity shortage with daily blackouts of many hours, some people questioned this, and were swiftly told that the same would be done for Vesak and that all religions would be treated equally. However, it was not so and the government did nothing for the Buddhist festival the following May.

By the end of 2003, the frustration of Sinhala Buddhists was nearing boiling point. While they resented the present government, they could remember the policies and actions of the previous government, too. Gangodawila Soma Thero, a popular preacher monk, died at the end of the year, transforming this frustration into a peaceful rebellion during which Sinhala Buddhists gathered in thousands all over the country to show their gratitude to him as well as their dissent to 'anti-Buddhist forces', including the main political parties. It should be noted here that the ISGA proposals of the LTTE had also been sent just one month before this, making the Sinhalese fear of the possibility of a separate state real.

Against this background, there was a need as well as space for a Buddhist revival in Sri Lanka. The establishment of the JHU was the most notable aspect of this revival, even though it was only one event of a greater process. The strategies of this revival were the same as those set by the Buddhist leaders of the mid-nineteenth century: to learn from the rival and compete using the same strategies. The starting point was the establishment of the Jathika Sanga Sabhawa (National Bhikku Council) in 1995. Even according to the founders, the aim was to prepare bhikkus to face the challenges that the Sinhala Buddhists encountered after the election of Kumaratunga.[62] The sister organization of the Jathika Sanga Sabhawa, the Jathika Daham Guru Sabhawa, aimed to give a 'social' objective to Sunday school teachers.[63] In reality, both these organizations tried to organize the monks and lay people politically to face the challenge posed by the LTTE and its 'allies'. The National Movement against Terrorism was founded in 1998 to respond to the propaganda of the LTTE, the government, the NGOs and leftist intellectuals.[64] The Sinhala Weera Widahana, a collective of businessmen, had been established in 1995 to raise funds for these activities of the Sinhala Buddhists. At the same time, it attempted to develop mutual cooperation to enhance the abilities of and opportunities for Sinhala traders to compete, especially with the powerful and well-organized Muslim business community. It is obvious that this was similar to what happened during the latter part of the nineteenth century. At that time, such consolidation took place against the cultural challenge presented by colonialism, but now it was happening against the political and ideological challenge of separatism.

Bhikkus came into electoral politics at the culmination of this process. The Sinhala Buddhist movement realized that the most crucial thing was to gain strength within the political establishment, the parliament, since policies were finally formulated by the forces that held power. The Buddhist nationalists finally decided to form their own party and the first attempt, which failed, was made before the presidential election of 1999.[65] However, the events of the end of 1999 and the first three to four months of 2000, especially the fall of the Elephant Pass army camp, paved the way for a Sinhala Buddhist political party, the Sihala Urumaya (Sinhala Heritage). The objective of the Sihala Urumaya was to dislodge the Muslim and Tamil parties from their king-making position by using Sinhala Buddhist power in parliament.[66] It failed in its attempt. However, the need for a force that would represent Sinhala Buddhist interests in parliament during the government of Ranil Wickramasinghe was more urgent than at any time in history. A new and definite strategy had to be found.

Champika Ranawaka[67] says it was the bhikkus who pointed out that the best way to achieve their target was to contest the election by themselves[68] and he also adds that a good messenger was found to bring the message to the public.[69] This was the only difference between the Sihala Urumaya and the Jathika Hela Urumaya. The electoral success of the JHU proved this decision right and the party won nine seats, while the biggest party, the UPFA, got only 105; that is, eight seats short of a simple majority in parliament. In this way, the JHU became the decisive force.

CONCLUSION

The central argument of this paper is that Sri Lankan Buddhism has had a political dimension throughout history and the JHU was not contrary to this tradition. The visibility of monks in the electoral sphere was the same strategy as had been followed by Buddhist leaders in the nineteenth century. They were merely employing new tactics in response to new social and political changes. The Sinhala Buddhist nationalist movement was able to achieve its main objective of securing the territorial integrity of the country by defeating the LTTE in 2009. At the same time, an obvious revival of the religious and cultural sphere also followed. At no time in recent history have such a large number of children gone to Buddhist Sunday schools or such crowds of youth participated in Seela and meditation programmes. Buddhist religious activities are now noticeably high throughout the country. This situation is similar to that of the nineteenth century and it is difficult to understand what is happening without a comprehensive understanding of the way Buddhist revivals occurred in Sri Lanka throughout history.

NOTES

1. Nalin de Silva is the most prominent figure of 'Jathika Chinthanaya', a Sinhala nationalist ideology and philosophical school.
2. See Nalin de Silva's article, 'Bhikkus in Politics' (http://www.kalaya.org/i040218.html).
3. See Baddegama Samitha Thero's website www.samithathero.lk/charity.himl.
4. Deegalle (2004): 84.

5. Vidyodaya and Vidyalankara were the most prominent 'Pirivenas', Buddhist educational institutions in the latter part of the nineteenth century and in the first half of the twentieth century in Sri Lanka. They were established by leading scholarly monks at the time to compete with the Christian missionary activities.
6. See H.L. Seneviratne, *The Work of the Kings* (1999).
7. Heywood (1997): 4.
8. See *Mahavamsa*, The Great Chronicle of Sri Lanka (M.W., XXV, 3).
9. Ibid: 17.
10. Rahula (1956): 74.
11. Rahula (1974): 12.
12. M.W., XXI, 21,22.
13. Rahula (1974): 71.
14. Somaratne (1991): 219.
15. See S.J. Tambiah, *Buddhism Betrayed*. Tambiah (1992).
16. See the description in the *Mahavamsa* (M.W., XXV, 109-11).
17. Dharmadasa (2002): 142.
18. De Silva (2001): 161.
19. Bandara (2007): 217.
20. Somaratne (1991): 219.
21. Jayawardena (2010): 82-98.
22. Bandara, (2007): 15.
23. Ibid.: 227.
24. De Silva (2006): 8.
25. Bandara (2007): 228.
26. Jayawardena (1972), 31; De Silva (2001): 195, 196; Kularatne (1991): 106, 107.
27. Bandara (2007): 224.
28. Jayawardena (1972): 32; de Silva (2001): 199.
29. De Silva (2001): 198.
30. Ivan (2007): 99.
31. Somaratne (1991): 224.
32. Uyangoda (2007): 59.
33. Ivan (2007): 116.
34. Bandara (2007): 228.
35. Although Paramadhamma Chethiya Pirivena, which was founded in 1839, was the first of this kind and the founders of Vidyodaya and Vidyalankara were students of the institution, the latter institutions became more successful and influential for the purpose.
36. Blackburn (2010): 114.
37. Bandara (2007): 249.

38. Seneviratne (1999): 50.
39. Jayawardena (1972): 136.
40. Armand de Souza, *Hundred days in Ceylon under Martial Law in 1915,* is an eyewitness account of the event. De Souza, neither a Sri Lankan-born nor a Sinhala Buddhist, reveals the harsh suppression of Sinhala leaders during the 1915 riots.
41. Thennakoon (2010): 14.
42. Huntington (2009): 449.
43. Dissanayaka (1975): 38.
44. Hulugalle (2000): 86.
45. Weerakoon (2004): 13.
46. Withanawasam (2007): 55.
47. Ibid.: 62.
48. Ibid.: 164.
49. Ibid.: 81.
50. Gunaratna (2001): 237.
51. Kumaratunga (1996): 51-72.
52. Ranawaka (2004): 121.
53. Gunasekara (2004): 76.
54. D.B.S. Jeyaraj, a well-known Tamil journalist, later commended the Sri Lankan national anthem for its inclusiveness and non-communalist nature. See (Jeyaraj) (2011): 77- 93.
55. Gunasekara (2004): 75.
56. Ratnatunga (2001).
57. Handunnetthi (2005).
58. Department of Government Information (2008): 19.
59. Ranawaka (2009): 106.
60. See the Sunday Observer news article on the event (http://www.sundayobserver.lk/2002/12/01/new17.html).
61. Ranawaka (2009): 106.
62. Abeysekara (2010): 95.
63. Ibid.: 100.
64. Ranawaka (2009): 78.
65. Ibid.: 86.
66. Abeysekara, 104, 105.
67. Champika Ranawaka is the most powerful leader in the Jathika Hela Urumaya. Even though he was not in the limelight during the monks' general election campaign in 2004, he was widely believed to be the main architect of the event.
68. Ranawaka (2009): 124.
69. Ibid.: 128.

BIBLIOGRAPHY

Abeysekara, W. 2010. *Ape Rathana Hamuduruwo*. Rajagiriya: Sadaham Sevena Publishers.

Bandara, A.M.N. 2007. *Brithanya Yatath Wijitha Yugaye Sri Lankawe Jathika Wyaparaya*. Colombo: Fast Publishing.

Blackburn, A.M. 2010. *Locations of Buddhism: Colonialism and Modernity in Sri Lanka*. Colombo: Social Scientists Association.

Deegalle, M. 2004. 'Politics of Jathika Hela Urumaya Monks: Buddhism and Ethnicity in Contemporary Sri Lanka', *Contemporary Buddhism*, vol. 5, no. 2. http://www.wlu.ca/documents/6509/ Politics_of_the_Jathika.pdf

Department of Government Information, Sri Lanka. 2008. *It is Customary to Bury the Dead*. Colombo: Special Media Unit. Department of Government Information.

De Silva, C.R. 2001. *Sri Lanka: A History*. New Delhi: Vikas Publishing House.

De Silva, M.U. 2006. 'Handinweema (Introduction)', in Dodandoowe Dharmasena, Ranjith Amarakeerthi Palihapitiya and Narada Karunathilaka (eds.), *Anagarika Dharmapala Aprakashitha Ath Lipi: Dewana Weluma*. Warakapola: Ariya Publishers.

De Silva, N. 2004. 'Bhikkus in Politics'. *Kalaya.org*. http://www.kalaya.org/i040218.html

De Souza, A. 1916. *Sinhala Marakkala Kolahalaya*. tr. Yasapala Wanasinghe. 2009. Colombo: Godage Publishers.

Dharmapala, A. 2004. *Denagatha Yuthu Karunu*. Boralesgamuwa: Wisidunu Publishers.

Dilrukshi, H. 2004. *The Handicap that is Samaraweera*. http://www.thesundayleader.lk/archive/20051106/issues.htm#pot

Dissanayake, T.D.S.A. 1975. *Dudley Senanayake of Sri Lanka*. Colombo: Swastika Press.

Gunaratna, R. 2001. *Sri Lanka: A Lost Revolution? The Inside Story of the JVP*. Kandy: Institute of Fundamental Studies.

Gunasekara, S. 2004. 'Sri Lankawe Janawargika Wiwidathwaya Samodhanaya Kireema Sandaha Wu Aithihasika Asamarthathawa', in George Furks and Bart Klem (eds.), *Wiwidathwayata Amanthranaya: Getuma saha Samaya Pilibanda Sri Lankeeya Kathika*. Hague: Clingendael.

Heywood, A. 1997. *Politics*. London: McMillan Press Ltd.

Hulugalle, H.A.J. 2000. *Don Stephen Senanayake: First Prime Minister of Sri Lanka*. Colombo: Arjuna Hulugalle Dictionaries.

Huntington, S.P. 2009. *Political Order in Changing Societies*. New Delhi: Adarsh Books.

Ivan, V. 2007. *Pansale Viplavaya: Bauddha Punarudaya Gangodawila Soma Himi Dakwa*. Maharagama: Rawaya Publishers.

Jayasinghe, J. 2001. *Colombo City, Suburbs Light Up*. http://www.sundayobserver.lk/2002/12/01/new17.html

Jayasumana, C.S. 2009. *Demala Janathawage Sankshiptha Ithihasaya*. Boralesgamuwa: Wisidunu Publishers.

Jayawardena, K. 1972. *The Rise of the Labor Movement of Ceylon*. Durham: Duke University Press.

———. 2010. *Perpetual Ferment: Popular Revolts in Sri Lanka in the 18th and 19th Centuries*. Colombo: Social Scientists' Association.

Jeyaraj, D.B.S. 2011. 'Sri Lankawe Jathika Geeye Bhasha Patalawilla', in Jayadeva Uyangoda et al. *Pravada*. Issue 332. March-April 2011. Colombo: Social Scientists' Association.

Kularatne, W.G. 1991. 'Brithanya Yugaye Sri Lankawe Adyapanaya', in P.G.V. Somaratne (ed.), *Lanka Ithihasaye Brithanya Yugaya*. Colombo: University of Colombo.

Kumaratunga, C. 1996. 'Keli Kedena Anathurin Rata Bera Geneemata Athi Ekama Maga', in Chandraratna Bandara (ed.), *Balaya Beda Hereema*. Colombo. Government Information Department.

Mahavamsa or The Great Chronicle of Ceylon. Eng. tr. Wilhelm Geiger. 1912. Dehiwala: Buddhist Cultural Centre.

Rahula, W. 1974. *The Heritage Bhikshu*. Colombo: Godage International Publisher.

———. 1956. *History of Buddhism in Ceylon*. Dehiwala: Buddhist Cultural Centre.

Ranawaka, P.C. 2004. *Koti Winiwideema*. Boralesgamuwa: Sithila.

———. 2009. *Patishothagameewa Thiswasak*. Nugegoda. Neo Graphics.

Ratnatunga, S. 2001. *Lankans Stage Protest Over Razing of Shrine in Colombo*. Gulfnews.com. http://gulfnews.com/news/gulf/uae/general/lankans-stage-protest-over-razing-of-shrine-in-colombo-1.412404

Seneviratne, H.L. 1999. *The Work of Kings: The New Buddhism in Sri Lanka*. Chicago, London: The University of Chicago Press.

Somaratne, G.P.V. 1991. 'Agamika Ithihasaya', in G.P.V. Somaratne (ed.), *Lanka Ithihasaye Brithanya Yugaya*. Colombo: Department of History and Political Science, University of Colombo.

Tambiah, S.J. 1992. *Buddhism Betrayed*. Chicago: University of Chicago Press.

Thennakoon, R.K. 2010. *Maha Sampradaye Kathawa*. Kelaniya. Sarasavi Printers.

Uyangoda, J. 2007. *Religion in Context: Buddhism and Socio-Political Change in Sri Lanka*. Colombo: Social Scientists' Association.

Weerakoon, B. 2004. *Rendering Unto Caesar*. Colombo: Vijitha Yapa Publishers.

Withanawasam, A. 2007. *Sri Lankawe Andukramaya Saha Deshapalanaya*. Maharagama: Tharanjee Printers.

PART III

THE REVIVAL OF BUDDHISM IN CHINA

CHAPTER 9

Taixu's Goodwill Mission to India

Reviving the Buddhist Links between China and India

TANSEN SEN

1940 WAS AN IMPORTANT year for Buddhist exchanges between India and China. It was also a critical period for the Chinese and Indians in their respective struggles against imperialism. While the Indians were trying to end almost two centuries of British rule, the Chinese found themselves facing brutal Japanese military expansion. In this period of anti-imperialism, Buddhism offered the possibility of reconnecting the two regions, which had witnessed vigorous cultural and commercial exchanges in the past. Although Buddhism had weakened in India and China several centuries before, the developing sense of Asianism in the early twentieth century resulted in the invoking of the ancient Buddhist connections as a model for new Asia. It was within this context that two leading Buddhists from China visited India in 1940 and tried to resuscitate the ancient links. During the early part of the year, Taixu (太虛; 1890-1947), the famous reformist Chinese monk, led a Goodwill Mission to South Asia; and in November-December of the same year, a high-ranking Guomindang official and a lay Buddhist named Dai Jitao (戴季陶; 1891-1947) toured several sacred sites in India and met the leaders of the Indian National Congress.

These two visits, as this paper argues, triggered Buddhist interactions between India and China that took place at multiple levels and with diverse objectives. It included interactions between the associates of Taixu, including Tan Yunshan (譚雲山; 1898-1983), the director of the Cheena-Bhavana in Santiniketan, and the Maha Bodhi Society in India; pilgrimages by monks and lay people from China to sacred Buddhist sites; and educational visits to the Cheena-Bhavana for study and research work. Political motives and geopolitical concerns were often part of these activities. It should be noted, however, that there are scant records of activities involving Indian Buddhist monks in China during this period. The doctrinal divergence between Indian and Chinese Buddhists, discussed below, and the chaotic situation in China might account for this disparity.

The revival of Buddhist interactions had been part of the wider effort by intellectuals and politicians in India and China to propagate a sense of Asian unity and solidarity during the early twentieth century. These ideas were initially formulated and advanced by people such as Okakura Kakuzō (岡倉覚三; 1862-1913), Rabindranath Tagore (1861-1941) and Liang Qichao (梁啟超; 1873-1929).[1] For these three intellectuals, the spread of Buddhism had led to a 'brotherly affinity' between India and China, and fostered peaceful interactions within Asia before the European colonization. The revival of such exchanges, they believed, would not only help reinvigorate past exchanges but also result in the creation of a harmonious world.[2]

Taixu, Dai Jitao and Tan Yunshan were three leading Chinese Buddhists who tried to implement the above goals of pan-Asianism by promoting cultural and educational interactions between India and China. The three, however, lived in a more complex world than Okakura, Tagore and Liang. The Japanese invasion of China in the 1930s had seriously questioned the ideals of pan-Asianism. Furthermore, Buddhism exerted nominal influence in both India and China. Thus, their goals, on the one hand, included re-establishing the 'brotherly affinity' between India and China; and, on the other, jointly addressing the threat of Japanese imperialism and making Buddhism relevant in the chaotic world in which they lived. In fact, Taixu, in particular, was deeply involved in reviving Buddhism in China. In a period of warfare and chaos, Buddhism, as Taixu and several of his fellow Buddhists in China believed, had to demonstrate its relevance to the society. As outlined below, they tried to reform the Buddhist Sangha, and establish a new form of Buddhism that engaged with society and did not renounce it. Their efforts resulted in the creation of what has now become known as the school of *renjian fojiao* (人間佛教) or humanistic Buddhism.

THE ISSUES OF BUDDHIST REVIVAL AND AWAKENING IN CHINA

Holmes Welch's book entitled *The Buddhist Revival in China* begins with a paragraph questioning whether the term 'revival' is appropriate to describe the changes within Buddhism during the late Qing and Republican periods (*c.* 1850-1949) of Chinese history. 'Indeed,' he writes, 'the very term "revival" may turn out to be inappropriate, and it is used in this book simply because it is the most convenient and customary way of referring to the varied developments that took place in Chinese Buddhism during the second half of the nineteenth century and the first half of the twentieth.' Welch was ambivalent about the term because he felt uncertain whether 'Chinese Buddhism was in a state of decay when the revival began'.[3]

At the end of his book, Welch returns to this issue in a chapter entitled 'The Meaning of the Revival'. He begins by pointing out that the concept of a 'Buddhist revival in China' was broached in Western literature in 1913 and popularized by Western missionaries, such as K.L. Reichelt and Lewis Hodous.[4] He then explains that between 1850 and 1950, there was no restoration of Buddhism to its original (Tang, Song or earlier) state, no 'renewal of Buddhist creativity in the arts'. He also aptly notes that even during the Tang and Song periods, there were Buddhist practices, such as the commercialization of monastic institutions, which might not have qualified as either moral or ethical for the orthodox followers of the religion. By the twelfth century, he points out, Chinese Buddhism was in the 'process of mutual integration rather than innovative change' and 'had long since entered the state of equilibrium that is characteristic of mature religions. This does not mean it was dead or dying. It had simply passed through its initial, exciting, creative phase and now went on performing the functions required of it by Chinese society, which was itself fairly static'.[5]

FIGURE 9.1: TAIXU WITH JAWAHARLAL NEHRU, TAN YUNSHAN, AND OTHERS AT THE MULAGANDHAKUTI VIHARA, SARNATH.

Based on the above observations, Welch concludes that it was 'trebly misleading to speak of "the Buddhist revival in China"'. He outlines the following three reasons for reaching this conclusion:[6]

> First, most of what occurred was not a restoration of the past, but a series of innovations; not a religious revival, but a redirection from the religious to the secular. Second, it never affected the Chinese population as a whole. The 'occasional Buddhists' who made up the great majority of the laity and the 'call monks' who made up the great majority of the sangha did not take part in it. Third, I believe, it concealed certain trends which, if they had continued, would have meant not a growing vitality for Buddhism but its eventual demise as a living religion.

It is clear that despite the title of his book, Welch did not perceive that Buddhism was going through a phase of 'revival' in the late nineteenth and early twentieth century. Instead, the trend seemed to be towards secularization of the doctrine, particularly under monks such as Taixu. In fact, it was Taixu, who, according to Welch, created this misperception of a Buddhist 'revival' in China through his extensive writings and dealings with foreigners.

In a more recent study, Xue Yu points out his reservations about Welch's views[7] but, in many ways, distorts the latter's unequivocal rejection of the term 'revival' to describe the changes that Buddhism in China went through during the period between 1850 and 1950. For Yu, the term 'revival' is too simplistic to describe the complicated history of modern Chinese Buddhism where there was a 'gradual disappearance of the old and the birth of the new within institutional Buddhism'. Instead, he proposes the idea of 'awakening' to describe the 'Buddhist developments in conjunction with the contemporary social, political, and intellectual movement of national awakening (*minzu juexing* 民族覺醒) in an effort for self-strengthening in China that started after the Opium War in 1842'.[8] According to Yu, the history of modern China and the developments in Chinese Buddhism since the Opium War (1839-42) were intertwined. He explains it in the following way:[9]

> If the awakening of the Chinese nation was prompted internally by self-deterioration and externally by foreign invasions, and if Chinese nationalism was closely associated with internationalism in the sense of learning foreign

techniques for self-modernization, Buddhist awakening was also the result of the external challenges of Christianity, of Japanese Buddhist missionaries, in addition to the state appropriation of temple properties and by self-corruption with the sangha, with the sense of learning from Christian charity work and Japanese Buddhist reform. The dangers that Chinese Buddhism faced forced many Buddhists, both lay and clerical, to realize the importance of self-reform for Buddhist survival and revival, and thus they became actively engaged in Buddhist intellectual studies and social service. They believed that Buddhism would not survive in China if monks and nuns continued to remain inactive inside temples and isolated from society.

There are several problems with Yu's argument advocating the use of the term 'awakening' and his portrayal of Buddhism in China after the Opium War. First, he seems to imply that the Buddhists in China were never awakened before the nineteenth century. If he did not actually mean this, then perhaps Yu intended to use the word 're-awakening' after a period during which the Chinese Buddhists had 'fallen asleep' and had lived 'in the world of illusion', as he states when explaining the Buddhist concept of awakening or enlightenment (*jue* 覺/*juewu* 覺悟/*wu* 悟/*xing* 醒, *juexing* 覺醒). However, he never clarifies when exactly the Buddhists in China 'fell asleep' and started living in a world of illusion so as to awake to the reality.

A second problem with Yu's argument relates to his concept of lay Buddhists. His discussion focuses mainly on 'lay Buddhist intellectuals' such as Tan Sitong (譚嗣同; 1865-98), Liang Qichao and Zhang Taiyan (章太炎; 1868-1936), or lay officials like Dai Jitao, people who were closely connected to the reform movement in China in the late nineteenth century, the discourse on nationalism, or to the state itself. Not part of his analysis are the millions of Chinese who lived in villages and countryside, practicing Buddhism as part of their daily life; for whom Buddhist beliefs and ideas were integral components of their traditional way of life, and not a rigid and distinct form of religion. Indeed, for these people, 'internationalism', 'self-modernization', or even the corruption within the Sangha may not have meant much, nor would these concerns have influenced how they conducted their rituals and ceremonies.

As a result of this narrow focus, Yu's 'awakening' might relate only to the elite lay members of Chinese society. The Buddhist monks associated with this 'awakening' were also those who had an intimate relationship with the state and were known as 'revolutionary monks' (*gemingseng* 革命僧). These included Zongyang (宗仰; 1865-1921), who aggressively promoted educational activities in Shanghai, and Taixu. It does not, in any way, inform us about the thinking of monks and nuns who continued to follow the doctrine without participating in the intellectual discourse among the elites.

Yu also fails to point out that the concerns about the degeneration of the Sangha, the weakening of state support, and the relevance of Buddhism to contemporary society and politics were not new complications for the Buddhists in China. Many of these issues were considered repeatedly ever since Buddhism first entered China. During the Song dynasty (960-1279), for example, the Chinese monk, Zanning (贊寧; 919-1001), made a case for the followers of Buddhism in China to chart their own path and not depend on doctrinal input from India.[10] Other monks and lay Buddhists argued about the proper relationship between the state and the Sangha, and whether the Chinese monks should follow all the Vinaya rules formulated in India. In other words, Buddhism in China was continuously in the process of readjusting, reinventing, and reawakening. The period between 1850 and 1950 was just another phase when Buddhism had to come to terms with the changed political and social situation in China.

Despite its shortcomings, however, Yu's work must be credited for highlighting the concerns of several leading Buddhist monks regarding the ways in which changes within China, caused by political upheavals and foreign invasions, would impact the doctrine they practised. On the one hand, they were apprehensive about the government's policies on regulating the Sangha and confiscating monastic property. On the other hand, they were struggling to address the spread of nationalism among the Chinese population, which was accentuated by the formation of the Republic of China in 1911 and, subsequently, the full-scale Japanese invasion of China in 1937. The 'revolutionary monks' realized that they had to make Buddhism relevant to the contemporary needs of the urban Chinese, irrespective of how the religion was practised at the village and folk levels. According to them, Buddhism needed to engage with the Chinese state and participate in the nation's struggle against foreign invaders. Taixu was one of the leading figures in this movement to transform Chinese Buddhism into a socially and politically engaged religion.

TAIXU AND HIS MISSION

Taixu was born as Lü Peilin (呂沛林) to a poor family in the south-eastern Zhejiang Province. His father, a bricklayer, died when he was one-year old. Brought up by his mother, Taixu was educated at home by his uncle and grandmother. Due to poor health, he was unable to work as a teenager and, perhaps realizing that he would be a burden to the family, became a monk at the age of fifteen. As a monk, Taixu not only engaged in meditation and the recitation of Buddhist texts but was also an avid reader of works by Chinese and foreign intellectuals. Some of his early readings, for example, included the works of Kang Youwei (康有為; 1858-1927), Liang Qichao and Karl Marx.[11] Within a few years, Taixu became acquainted with Buddhist monks who sought to reform Chinese monastic institutions and advocated modern education for the clergy. By the time the Qing empire collapsed in 1911, Taixu had found his way into Nanjing, the capital of the newly-established Republic of China, where he started making his mark as one of the leading 'revolutionary' monks in the country while still in his early twenties.

China had witnessed several decades of turmoil and upheaval prior to the 1911 revolution. Overpowered by the Western colonial powers during the Opium War, the imperial Qing government was in disarray from the mid-nineteenth century. The Empress Dowager Cixi (慈禧太后; 1835-1908), who controlled the court of Emperor Guangxu (光緒; 1875-1908), as well as the Emperors Xianfeng (咸豐; 1850-61) and Tongzhi (同治; 1856-75) before him, decided to retire to the Summer Palace in Beijing. When the loss to Japanese forces in 1894-5 made it apparent that China was significantly behind other polities in terms of technological and educational developments, Emperor Guangxu instituted the so-called Hundred Days Reform in 1898. The aim of these reforms was to rapidly institute educational, political and industrial changes in order to modernize China. The chief architect of these reforms was Kang Youwei whose writings Taixu was familiar with. Opposed to these changes proposed by Kang and his associates, the Empress Dowager Cixi returned from her retirement and terminated the reform movement after only 104 days. Kang Youwei and the other reformers either escaped from China or were placed under house arrest. Kang himself ended up in Darjeeling in British-occupied India.

Shortly after the failure of the reform movement, the Boxer uprising (1899-1901) against the foreign imperial powers broke out in China. This anti-foreign rebellion supported by the Qing court ended in disaster when the colonial powers jointly launched a counterattack and massacred the Boxers. Cixi and Guangxu were forced to flee from Beijing and eventually sign a peace agreement with the foreign powers.

These conflicts, both within the court and throughout the Chinese empire, severely weakened Qing rule. The deaths of Cixi and Guangxu in 1908 ensured that the Qing empire would not last very long. When Sun Yat-sen (1866-1925) overthrew the Qing dynasty and became the head of the provisional government, China was still politically fragmented with local warlords exercising tremendous power in the provinces. Civil wars between the Guomindang and the Communists, and the Japanese invasion of China in the 1930s added more misery to the Chinese people. In fact, even in 1947, when Taixu died, the prospect of a stable and peaceful China still looked bleak.

Throughout these phases of turmoil and misery, Buddhist institutions and monks had to confront their own tribulations. Similar to previous periods in Chinese history, some court officials during the late Qing dynasty questioned the wealth and assets of Buddhist monasteries.[12] Additionally, the Qing government tried to limit the number of Buddhist monks by imposing strict rules on ordinations. The Taiping Rebellion (1850-64) led by a person named Hong Xiuquan (洪秀全; 1814-64), who claimed to be the younger brother of Jesus, also resulted in the destruction of several Buddhist temples and monasteries. Things did not improve during the Republican period even though Taixu often gave credit to the Guomindang government for protecting Buddhism. While several Guomindang officials questioned the validity of Buddhism in the modern world, others simply occupied Buddhist monasteries and turned them into government offices.

Members of the monastic community and lay intellectuals were also concerned about the moral standards of Buddhist monks and what they perceived as various superstitious practices among the common people. In fact, in 1925, Taixu wrote a severe critique of the Buddhist clergy and some of the lay practices. In China, he noted:[13]

> . . . the Buddhist have the following shortcomings: First, they are seldom interested in social service or the work of educating the society. The priests or rather monks are generally ignorant, and their services to the society are confined to the singing of masses or prayers in the funeral services. Secondly, although the monks divide themselves into sects or schools, each pursuing a special object, yet they fail to accomplish that object. Thirdly, the monks are always religious recluses, taking no interest in the affairs of the community or the country and they are in turn slighted by the Government or the ruling classes. Fourthly, most of the Chinese Buddhist monks lack the necessary modern scientific knowledge and are also ignorant of the current thoughts and ideas in the world. In view of such disabilities, they are unable to preach the doctrines of the Buddha in such a way as to appeal to the minds of the modern people.

For the remaining twenty-two years of his life, Taixu devoted most of his energy trying to rectify these shortcomings, recommending steps that had to be taken by the Buddhist community in China. The two most important issues that he highlighted were the need for proper education for the Chinese Buddhist monks and the relevance of Buddhism to the contemporary society. With regard to the former, Taixu proposed a rigorous curriculum for monks and the restructuring of the Sangha. The relevance of Buddhism to the contemporary society emerged as a significant issue when the Japanese invaded China. Taixu's criticism of the Chinese Buddhist monks for their ignorance about the affairs of the country now became more relevant than at any time before. Xue Yu has cited several examples to demonstrate how Taixu and other revolutionary monks argued that the Buddhist clergy in China needed to participate in the anti-Japanese war by joining the army and protecting the state.[14]

Taixu also believed that the Buddhist community should contribute to China's diplomatic relations with foreign polities. This view of Taixu, in addition to his advocacy for the participation of monks in the war against the Japanese, his efforts to make Buddhism relevant to the concerns of the state, and the fact that he had previously interacted with foreign monks and intellectuals, may have been the reasons why he was drafted by the Guomindang government to undertake the 'Goodwill Mission' to Burma, India and Ceylon.

The delegation was to visit these three 'Buddhist' countries to inform the local political leaders about China's struggle against the Japanese colonizers. The aim may have also been to isolate the Japanese Buddhist community, which had failed to take a strong stand against the Japanese occupation of China. In fact, the Japanese Buddhists were perceived as collaborators with the military in the war against China. The mission to Burma, India and Ceylon was Taixu's opportunity to assert his patriotism and put into practice some of the ideas that he had been expounding with regard to creating a socially and politically engaged Buddhism.

REESTABLISHING BUDDHIST LINKS AND CREATING A BUDDHIST WORLD

By the ninth or tenth century, the Buddhist clergy in China had dissociated themselves from the doctrines formulated in South Asia. Instead, they started charting their own path and began establishing their unique doctrinal traditions. They even created pilgrimage sites within China, which were not only frequented by the local clergy but also by foreign monks and officials. Monks from South Asia are known to have travelled to these sites expressly to pay homage to Buddhist divinities such as Mañjuśrī and Kṣitigarbha.[15]

Around the same time, the perception of a decline of Buddhism in India had started to take root in China. This view developed from the reports of Chinese pilgrims who described the decay and desertion of monastic institutions in several important Buddhist towns and cities. Moreover, the Chinese clergy found Tantric Buddhism, which started impacting China in the seventh century, inappropriate for adaption into the local pantheon even though it was popular with the Tang rulers in the eighth and ninth centuries. In fact, the Chinese associated Tantrism with the doctrinal decay of Buddhism and emphasized the need for the Chinese clergy to pursue their own Buddhist philosophical traditions and practices. Thus, by the tenth century, a divergence between the Indian and Chinese Buddhist communities was apparent.

These developments did not mean that Buddhism declined in India and China after the tenth century; rather, they became part of a segmented Buddhist world which had multiple centres, each with its own distinctive doctrinal emphasis, networks of connections and spheres of influence.[16] While the Buddhist centres in India maintained close ties to the monasteries in Tibet with regard to the transmission of Tantric teachings, the Chan/Zen and other Mahayana-focused Chinese Buddhist institutions drew monks from Japan and Korea. Sri Lanka, on the other hand, created a Theravada network across the Bay of Bengal with close links to Burma, Thailand and Cambodia.

With the destruction of Buddhist monastic institutions in northern India in the fourteenth century by plundering armies from Afghanistan and Central Asia, contacts between Buddhists in China and South Asia became negligible. Almost four centuries later, from the late eighteenth century onwards, three new trends with regard to Buddhist interactions between India and China started emerging. First, the spread of the Chinese diasporic community to South Asia resulted in the introduction of Chinese Buddhist beliefs, images and temples into India. Most of this activity took place in Calcutta (now Kolkata), where thousands of Chinese migrants settled between the 1780s and the early twentieth century. These immigrants built several shrines dedicated to Guanyin and other sinicized Buddhist figures, such as Ruan Ziyu (阮子鬱; 1079-1102) and Liang Cineng (梁慈能; 1098-1116). The two are venerated as buddhas by the immigrant Cantonese community from the Sihui County in Guangdong Province.[17]

By the 1950s, this Chinese community in India had established Buddhist temples at almost every major pilgrimage site in India. During the Chinese New Year, members of the community made pilgrimages to these 'Chinese' Buddhist temples to perform rituals and ceremonies. A key person involved in their establishment in India was Tan Yunshan, the inaugural director of the Cheena-Bhavana at the Visva-Bharati University founded by Rabindranath Tagore in Santiniketan in 1937. Tan was 'baptized' by Taixu and had close contacts with leading Buddhist monks and high-ranking lay followers in China.[18] A year before Taixu's visit to India, Tan Yunshan, with funding from a Singapore philanthropist named Lee Choon-seng (李俊承), had renovated the Chinese Buddhist Temple in Sarnath.[19]

Before Taixu's visit in 1940, however, there seems to have been limited contact between the Indian and Chinese Buddhist communities. The Buddhist shrines and temples established by members of the Chinese diasporic community in India were rarely frequented by ethnic Indians. Additionally, because of the doctrinal divergence that took place by the end of the first millennium, there was hardly any common philosophical discourse that took place between the Indian and Chinese monks. Thus, whatever Buddhist ideas or images entered India through the Chinese immigrants remained exclusive to that community.

The second development concerns the discourse on the collapse of India to the British colonizers that took place among leading Chinese intellectuals during the nineteenth and early twentieth centuries. When, in the late eighteenth century, the Chinese suddenly became aware of the military threat posed by European colonial powers, the British invasion of India and the perceived collapse of the Indian civilization emerged as important topics of discussion among the urban Chinese. India was described as a 'failed' or 'enslaved' country (*wangguo* 亡國/ *nuliguo* 奴隶國). For many Chinese, the decline of Indian civilization and its capitulation to the British resulted from its caste divisions and fragmented political geography. The practice of Buddhism, most probably due to its emphasis on non-violence, was also singled out as one of the main causes. A Chinese newspaper called *Beijing nübao* (北京女報) carried the following passage in the early twentieth century:[20]

> You thought that India was just fine, huh? Then why did it invite destruction [*heyi youwang ne*]? It is because they knew superstition. . . . When the British arrived in the cities, they [the Indians] just sat around praying to Buddha . . . praying that their city would not be destroyed. What do you think: are these Indians foolish, or what? Do they deserve to die, or what? After not too long, they became slaves of the British and they're still resting in their dreams. . . .
>
> Ah! Compatriots [*tongbao*]! I would like to ask you if you want to be citizens [*guomin*] of a great and independent nation, or if you want to become slaves [*nuli*] of a lost state? If you want the latter, then I've nothing left to say; if the former, then you should throw away those Bodhisattva statues modeled of clay . . . and you should give that money used for burning incense to your children for their education. . . .
>
> If you don't believe me, then just watch: those red turbans will be wrapped around your heads, too!

This view about Buddhist pacifism as a cause for India's decline may have been widespread in China. Pointing to India several Chinese intellectuals, in fact, argued that Buddhism was 'not only useless but harmful to the nation'.[21] These critics advocated the confiscation of monastic property, and the placing of severe restrictions on the number of monks and nuns. To counter this, some Chinese monks started insisting that India's collapse was not caused by the passivism of Buddhist teachings but because of the 'abandonment of Buddhism, which had made India lose its national identity and spirit'.[22] These monks pointed to Japan, which had emerged as a strong nation because of the emphasis placed on Buddhism. They also strongly felt that China could play an important role in re-introducing Buddhism to India and saving it from colonial rule.

The third trend was associated with the attempt by Indian, Chinese and Japanese intellectuals to create, as noted above, a sense of Asianism in a world that was dominated by European colonial powers.[23] The advocates of Asianism, starting from the first decade of the twentieth century, used the links that Buddhism had forged between various regions of Asia during the earlier times as a model. Liang Qichao and Zhang Taiyan, for example, wrote several essays on the historical development of Chinese Buddhism and its role in transforming Chinese society. They also underscored the contributions of Buddhism in fostering cultural interactions between the two. In fact, Liang strongly advocated a return to the earlier phase of cultural contacts between the two. It was he who hosted Rabindranath Tagore when the Nobel laureate visited China in 1924. Tagore shared Liang's views on both the historical vibrancy of India-China interactions through Buddhism, and the need to revive such exchanges as a way to (re)-establish a harmonious and peaceful Asia.

Closely connected to the ideals of Asianism were the efforts of Buddhist monks in East and South Asia to create a united Buddhist world. Already in the later half of the nineteenth century, the Theosophists, led by Henry Steel Olcott (1832-1907), were trying to establish connections between Buddhist communities in Sri Lanka, India, Japan and China. Olcott's work was supported and continued by the Ceylonese Anagarika Dharmapala (1864-1933), who travelled to Japan and China, and eventually established Bodh Gaya in Bihar as the centre of the Buddhist world. The Maha Bodhi Society, which Dharmapala founded in Colombo in 1891, became the leading international organization engaged in the Buddhist revival movements.[24]

Monks from Japan, and later Taixu himself, also became intimately involved in trying to build what Richard Jaffe calls 'a tightly linked global Buddhist culture'.[25] In fact, in July 1924, at the inaugural conference of the World Buddhist Federation, an organization that he had founded in China, Taixu noted that the purpose of the Federation was: 'First, to unite Buddhists from each province in China; second, to unite Buddhists from each country of East Asia; and, third, to transmit the truths and spirit of East Asian Buddhism to each country of Europe and to the United States'.[26] In the following year, Taixu attended the East Asian Buddhist Conference in Tokyo and presented a paper entitled 'A Statement to Asiatic Buddhists: Only Buddhism can Save the Present World'.[27] The conference, which was attended by Buddhist monks from East Asia, ended with the hope that it would 'become the fore-runner of a great conference in which Buddhists in India, Ceylon, Siam, Burma, Europe, and America will be fully represented and that the day when such an international Buddhist conference is held will arrive in no distant future. Such a conference is a desideratum for world peace, for humanity'.[28]

By the time Taixu visited India, the Chinese clergy, as noted above, had started questioning the role of the Japanese Buddhist community in Japan in promoting world peace. In fact, one of the main reasons for Taixu's visit, as also mentioned above, may have been to gain support for China's anti-Japanese war. Thus, Taixu's mission was not simply a religious pilgrimage or one that intended to unify the Buddhist communities of India and China but it was also intimately related to contemporary political concerns and an attempt by the Chinese Buddhists to demonstrate their relevance to the modern world.

TAIXU'S POLITICAL PILGRIMAGE

When Anagarika Dharmapala visited China in 1893, he asked the Chinese Buddhists present at a meeting near Shanghai to show their 'support and sympathy for the rehabilitation' of Buddhism in India. 'India gave you her religion,' he remarked, 'now I appeal to you to help her in her hour of need.'[29] Yang Wenhui (楊文會; 1837-1911), Dharmapala's host and the future teacher of Taixu, suggested the possibility of recruiting Indian monks for studies in China as an option, 'in order to prepare them for subsequent mission work among their own people'.[30] Although such a collaboration does not seem to have been worked out, Dharmapala's visit to China eventually resulted in a close association between the Maha Bodhi Society and members of the Chinese Buddhist community. Taixu, for example, became a member of the Society in 1928 and, subsequently, a life member and patron.

As a result of these past connections between the Maha Bodhi Society and the Chinese Buddhist community, Taixu's Goodwill Mission to India featured prominently in *The Maha-Bodhi: The Journal of the Maha Bodhi Society*. In its November 1939 issue, the journal announced the forthcoming visit of Taixu to Burma, India, Ceylon and Siam. It included the following message of Taixu to the Chinese overseas communities in these countries: [31]

> The visit has been planned at the request of the devotees of Buddhist shrines in China and the Chinese scattered overseas. We propose to visit Buddhist sites in Burma, Siam, India and Ceylon, to make contact with leaders of Buddhist thought in these various places and hold conferences for the study and discussion of Buddhism. We also hope to have opportunities to explain according to views of Buddhism how China is defending her independence and very existence; and how the Buddhists in China have achieved complete unanimity in regard to this struggle. I wish to add that through our co-operation in the national struggle Buddhism has won national esteem. This esteem is bound to result in positive gains on the day of victory.

Although Taixu writes that the mission was 'planned' by Buddhist institutions in China, it was, in fact, sponsored and instigated by the Guomindang government in order to garner support for the anti-Japanese war. The overseas Chinese were important contributors to the 1911 revolution led by Sun Yat-sen. The Chiang Kai-shek-led Guomindang government also hoped to receive financial and other logistical support from the diasporic communities in their war against the Japanese. Furthermore, the Guomindang government and Chiang

Kai-shek, in particular, desperately wanted the leaders of the Indian freedom movement to support the Allied forces in the Second World War. Thus, in addition to visiting various Buddhist pilgrimage sites in India, Taixu made it a point to not only meet the members of the Chinese overseas communities but also the leaders of the Indian National Congress. He frequently updated the Guomindang government on these meetings and the progress of his Goodwill Mission.

On 17 October 1939, Taixu sent a letter to his disciple, Tan Yunshan, informing him about his forthcoming visits to Burma and India. Tan, as noted above, had been a key figure in the cultural and political interactions between India and China from the time he joined the Visva-Bharati University in 1928. Similar to Taixu, Tan was well-connected with leading Guomindang officials, including Chiang Kai-shek. In India, Tan had developed a close relationship with Jawaharlal Nehru, one of the prominent leaders of the Indian National Congress and the future prime minister of independent India. In fact, Tan had become a key link between the Guomindang and the Indian National Congress.[32] Tan accompanied Taixu throughout his trip in India and also went with him to Ceylon. It is likely that Taixu's itinerary in India and his meetings with Indian political leaders, visits to Buddhist sites and lectures may have all been arranged by Tan, who had recently returned from China where he was involved in organizing anti-Japanese propaganda activities. It is also possible that Tan was the one who instigated the Goodwill Mission in the first place. In early 1939, Rabindranath Tagore, Tan's main Indian patron, sent a letter to him in China, saying, 'The battle-field is hardly a place for a scholar.' He urged Tan to return to India, where, according to Tagore, he would be able to do 'a greater service' for the country by 'disseminating true news about the Sino-Japanese conflict'.[33] Tan perhaps planned Taixu's visit and itinerary with this as one of the main objectives.

On 6 December 1939, Taixu and his entourage reached Rangoon in Burma through the Yunnan-Burma land road. In Burma, Taixu delivered lectures at various gatherings of the overseas Chinese, met members of the local Buddhist communities, visited sacred Buddhist sites and also held discussions with Indian immigrants. Taixu stayed in Burma for little over a month during which time he held several consultative meetings with the Guomindang representatives in Rangoon. At one of them, a Guomindang representative expressed his hope that Taixu's trip would unify the Buddhist communities of India and Burma against the Japanese monks who had collaborated with the army and were 'accessories to murder and killing of innocent people'. Without mentioning the role of Japanese monks, Taixu responded by noting that the Buddhist community would do its utmost to bring 'world peace'.[34]

On the morning of 9 January 1940, Taixu's delegation, consisting of five people, boarded a ship at Rangoon to travel to Calcutta. On the ship, Taixu met P.C. Bagchi, the renowned Indian scholar of China and Buddhism, who was returning from Rangoon. The two discussed the visit of Jawaharlal Nehru to Chongqing in 1939, the activities of the Indian Medical Mission led by Dr. D. Mukherjee and various aspects of Buddhist teachings. Taixu noted that he had met Nehru and Mukherjee in China and hoped that Bagchi could go there some day to teach.[35]

After three days of sailing, Taixu arrived in Calcutta on 11 January. Several hundred people went to the harbour to receive the Chinese delegation, including the leaders of all the major Buddhist organizations based in Calcutta, the Chinese Consul-General and other officials from the Chinese consulate, the heads of Chinese schools and associations, reporters, Tan Yunshan and his wife, and over two hundred members of the Chinese overseas community. Taixu was told that Mahatma Gandhi, Nehru, and Subhas Chandra Bose had sent welcome messages to the Chinese Buddhist delegation through Tan Yunshan.

During his forty-three-day stay in India (11 January to 22 February), Taixu travelled to several cities and Buddhist pilgrimage sites, delivered lectures at key secular and religious institutions, and had in-depth discussions with the political and Buddhist leaders of India. He spent the first week in Calcutta, followed by several days in Santiniketan. At a talk that outlined the important doctrinal issues related to Mahayana Buddhism, Taixu began by mentioning that:[36] 'The present century is the century of spiritual re-awakening of India when the whole nation is reviving its ancient glory. Modern Indian culture is India's original culture infused with the culture of the West and in my opinion Gurudeva is the best representative of the culture and civilization of India to-day.'

Between 24 January and 6 February, the delegation toured Buddhist pilgrimage sites at Bodh Gaya, Nalanda, Lumbini, Sarnath and Benaras. On 7 February, it arrived in Lucknow from where it proceeded to Agra, Mathura, Bhopal and Sanchi, reaching Wardha on 12 February. After an audience with Mahatma Gandhi, the delegation went to Ajanta and finally to Bombay (Mumbai). After a week-long stay there, the delegation departed for Ceylon on 23 February to continue its Goodwill Mission.

One of the first things that the Chinese Buddhist delegation noticed upon its arrival in Calcutta was the dearth of Buddhist monks and monuments. Compared to Burma, the members noted, 'there were very few Buddhist monks; it was also not easy to spot pagodas and monasteries'.[37] Taixu and other members of the delegation considered this as clear evidence of the demise of Buddhism in India. In almost every speech that he delivered in India, Taixu made it a point to mention the state of Buddhism in India and express his hope that the doctrine would revive in its birthplace. In fact, on several occasions, he stressed that the Chinese Buddhists would have an important role in this 'revival' of Buddhism in India.

The themes associated with Buddhism in China, its revival in India, the reestablishment of cultural interactions between India and China, and the anti-Japanese war were the main elements of Taixu's first speech in India.[38] Delivered at a banquet organized by the Chinese overseas community at the Chinese Club in Calcutta on 12 January, the title of his talk was 'The Present Situation of Buddhism in China'. Buddhism in China, he explained, had declined under the Qing empire. As Buddhist monasteries and monks could not contribute to the modern society, the doctrine was considered obsolete and irrelevant. People perceived monks as profit-oriented and Buddhist teachings as mere superstitions. However, Buddhism in China, he argued, was 'back on the track of revival' because of appropriate propaganda work, the stress on the education of monks, the establishment of various Buddhist organizations and the participation of the Sangha in social welfare. Taixu also credited the nationalist government in China with protecting and supporting

Buddhism, a point he made several times during his Guomindang-sponsored mission.

The idea of establishing a branch of the Chinese Buddhist Association in India, which was mentioned by the Chinese Consulate-General in his welcome address, was fully supported by Taixu in his speech. He noted that the establishment of such an organization would help the Chinese migrant community to improve their knowledge about Buddhism. He also pointed out that the Ceylonese and Burmese had their own Buddhist organizations in India. A similar Chinese Buddhist organization, he suggested, could jointly work with these and other Indian Buddhist associations to improve the standing and image of Buddhism in the world.[39]

In his lecture at the Maha Bodhi Society in Calcutta on the following day, Taixu noted that Buddhism in India was no longer flourishing as before, 'but the spirit of Buddhism fills the hearts of every person. The Bengal Buddhist Association, the Maha Bodhi Society and others are making efforts to revive Buddhism'. He added, 'I think, India will soon become the center of world Buddhism'. He explained that while the Chinese clergy fully supported the efforts of the Maha Bodhi Society, they could not be of much help because China was going through a 'difficult phase'. The revival of Buddhism in China itself, he said, would have to wait until this 'difficult phase' was over.[40] The reference here was, no doubt, to the Japanese invasion of China.

The reception at the Maha Bodhi Society was presided over by the mayor of Calcutta, N.C. Sen, who welcomed Taixu by pointing to the intimate cultural and spiritual contacts between India and China during the pre-colonial period. He also noted that a medical mission had been sent by the Indian National Congress to help China in its war against Japan. The welcome address on behalf of the members of the Maha Bodhi Society was read by its General Secretary, Devapriya Valisinha. The address embraced Taixu 'as one of us' and thanked him for his earlier donations toward the construction of the Mulagandhakuti Vihara in Sarnath. It also sympathized with the Chinese people in their period of crisis, expressing the hope that it 'will soon be over and China will again be in a position to play her glorious part for the welfare of the entire human race'. At the conclusion of the reception, Taixu presented a silver pagoda replica gifted by Chiang Kai-shek to the Maha Bodhi Society as 'a token of China's Goodwill'.[41]

Taixu attended several other receptions in Calcutta hosted by local organizations and held meetings with leading members of the society, such as Maharaja Pradyot Kumar Tagore, Subhas Chandra Bose and Jugal Kishore Birla. After these meetings, Taixu travelled to Santiniketan to meet Rabindranath Tagore. His next grand reception was in Benares, where he attended the Asoka Day celebrations with Jawaharlal Nehru on 31 January.

Taixu reached Benares on 29 January and was welcomed at the railway station by members of the Maha Bodhi Society, the Benares Congress Committee and the Hindu Maha Sabha, in addition to other organizations and 'hundreds of citizens'.[42] The following day, he and other members of the Goodwill Mission visited Sarnath where he suggested the establishment of a committee to work towards the restoration of sacred Buddhist sites in India. On the same day, Taixu decided to become a life member of the Maha Bodhi Society and promised to 'continue to co-operate with the Society in its work for the resuscitation of Buddhism in India'.[43]

On the morning of 31 January, Jawaharlal Nehru went from his residence in Allahabad to Sarnath to welcome the Chinese Mission. Nehru and Taixu had a two-hour-long meeting during which the Buddhist monk stressed the fact that the Chinese did not have adequate knowledge of contemporary India. Taixu told Nehru that he hoped some cultural aspects of modern India could be transmitted to China and, at the same time, that Chinese Mahayana teachings could be translated and reintroduced to India. He added that the Chinese could also introduce to India the 'spirit of anti-colonial war and nation building'. Additionally, Taixu sought Nehru's support for the revival of Buddhist pilgrimage sites in India and the establishment of an international Buddhist university. These two ventures, Taixu pointed out, were closely linked to future collaboration among the Buddhist countries of Asia. Nehru responded by noting that the Indian National Congress had, in fact, taken up the issue of reviving Buddhist pilgrimage sites before the resignation of their members from the government (in protest against the unilateral British decision to announce India's participation in Second World War). The Indian National Congress, he explained, had many other tasks at the moment. There were also legal issues related to the ownership of property that had to be sorted out at some of the pilgrimage sites. With regard to the idea of an international Buddhist university, Nehru said that funds had to be raised before establishing such an institution.[44]

Following the meeting, Nehru and Taixu travelled together to Benares to attend the Ashoka Day celebrations. *The Maha-Bodhi* reports the grand reception that the two received on entering the city:[45]

> It was truly a royal welcome that the citizens of Benares accorded to the Mission under the inspiration of Pandit Jawaharlal Nehru. From Dasasumedh Ghat the members of the Mission were taken to the Town Hall in a grand procession organised for their welcome and for the observance of the Asoka Day. His Holiness Tai Hsu and Pandit Jawaharlal Nehru sat in the same carriage while the rest of the party as well as several prominent citizens and Buddhist monks were also accommodated in other carriages. Buddhist emblems, Congress flags, sayings of Asoka written on placards and the yellow robes of the monks lent vivid colour to the procession. His Holiness and Pandit Nehru were profusely garlanded. The procession, after passing through various thoroughfares, entered the Town Hall grounds where arrangements had been made for a mass meeting. The roads through which the procession passed and the shops on both sides were decorated with triumphal arches and garlands. The crowds were so dense that it was with difficulty that the procession reached its destination where nearly 40,000 people were waiting to take part.

Acharya Narendra Dev, the President of the Town Congress Committee, Nehru and Taixu delivered speeches at the event. All three emphasized the friendly relations between India and China in the past and the need to strengthen them in the present. 'The day is not far distant,' remarked Taixu as he thanked his hosts, 'when the cultural relations existing between India and China in the days of Huen Tsang will be re-established between these two countries'.[46]

Taixu repeated these words at a lecture that he gave at the Benares Hindu University on the next day. He noted that ancient India and China had intimate cultural interactions through which the Chinese obtained an in-depth knowledge of India. 'But since there has been a separation of around a thousand years,' he said, 'the Chinese need to understand contemporary Indian culture'. The Chinese should also, he proposed, transmit back to India the teachings of Nāgārjuna and other Buddhist philosophers that were preserved in the translated texts.[47]

Nostalgia for the ancient Buddhist links between India and China and the prospect of reviving them through the visit of Taixu were apparent as the delegation toured various Buddhist sites. Comparisons between Taixu's mission and the pilgrimage of Xuanzang in the seventh century were frequently drawn in welcome speeches and newspaper reports. Taixu's journey through India was remarkably similar to that of Xuanzang in one aspect. Like Xuanzang, Taixu not only visited sacred Buddhist sites but also had audiences with important Indian political leaders – Bose in Calcutta, Nehru in Benares and Gandhi in Wardha. Xuanzang, on his part, was known for his intimate interactions with Harṣa, the king of Kanauj, and Bhāskaravarman, the ruler of Kamarupa. In addition, both Xuanzang and Taixu seem to have successfully accomplished their political pilgrimages and returned to China to promote Buddhist interactions between India and China.

CONCLUSION: THE LEGACY OF TAIXU'S GOODWILL MISSION

On his way back to China, Taixu delivered a lecture in Singapore where he summed up the aims and accomplishments of the Goodwill Mission that he had led in the following way:[48]

> In Burma, we gave a detailed report on the situation in China with regard to the anti-Japanese war. This place (i.e., Burma) is intimately linked to the anti-Japanese war [effort]. International propaganda is either not easy or lacking. After our explanations, the Burmese have decided to form a delegation that will visit China. Later, after arriving in India, we undertook detailed discussion of cultural issues. I have now understood Indian culture and believe that Buddhism is the splendor of its ancient culture. But, in the midst of the past one thousand years, Indian culture witnessed a decline and we (i.e., China) also drifted afar, creating a deep divide between [the two countries]. . . . The aim to visit India was to study contemporary Indian culture and at the same time promote research of Chinese culture there. In Ceylon, the most important work of our Mission was to establish Buddhist

links. . . . Ceylon is the thoroughfare to Europe and America and also a Buddhist country. In fact, since it is the best place to carry out international propaganda, there was a proposal to establish an International Buddhist Federation that would network with the Buddhists in China. Preparations to start this [Federation] have already began.

Taixu ended his report by noting that during 'this time of anti-Japanese war, I hope Buddhist followers will greatly reform themselves, and, according to the needs of the times, support the government. After our victory against the Japanese, we can create a new and invigorated nation and, at the same time, establish a new and invigorated Buddhism. This will be of enormous benefit to our people'.[49]

Indeed, the Goodwill Mission had significantly advanced many of the objectives that Taixu was personally advocating in China: making Buddhism relevant to contemporary domestic and international politics, creating an opportunity for Chinese Buddhist monks to receive in-depth education on various societies and cultures, and uniting the Buddhist communities in Asia. Each of these aspects continued to make progress after Taixu's return to China.

Less than nine months after the departure of the Taixu-led Chinese Goodwill Mission, Dai Jitao arrived in India. Dai had been a key supporter of cultural interactions between India and China since at least the early 1930s. He was instrumental, for example, in raising funds for the establishment of the Cheena-Bhavana that Rabindranath Tagore and Tan Yunshan had envisioned. In fact, throughout the 1930s and 1940s, Dai helped find financial support for educational and Buddhist exchanges between India and China.[50] He also made personal donations to various Buddhist institutions and organizations in India, including the Maha Bodhi Society. Moreover, he played an important role in promoting political relations between the Guomindang and the Indian National Congress. Like Taixu's visit, Dai's trip to India had dual purposes. First, he wanted to publicize the Chinese struggle against the Japanese military expansion. Second, he hoped to encourage Buddhist exchanges between India and China.

Dai Jitao was enthusiastically received by Indian Buddhist organizations, the intellectual community and the members of the Indian National Congress, including Mahatma Gandhi. Dai participated in a grand possession in Sarnath to mark the ninth anniversary of the establishment of the Mulagandhakuti Vihara.[51] He could not, however, meet Jawaharlal Nehru who had been imprisoned by the British government. Even then, Nehru issued a statement from prison for the Indian National Congress and other organizations to cordially receive the Chinese guest.[52] He also entrusted Dai with a letter for Madame Chiang Kai-shek.[53]

Dai Jitao's mission cemented China's relations with the Maha Bodhi Society and also paved the way for Chiang Kai-shek's visit to India in 1942. In fact, after Taixu and Dai Jitao's goodwill missions, Chinese monks, visitors, diplomatic representatives and, in particular, Tan Yunshan became intimately involved with the activities of the Maha Bodhi Society. They frequently donated money to the Society, presided over various ceremonies and contributed articles to the Society's journal, *The Maha-Bodhi*. In 1947, for instance, a few months before his death, Taixu wrote a letter to Ven. N. Jinaratana, the Secretary of the Maha Bodhi Society, in response to the donations that the latter sought to build an International Cultural Religious Centre on the premises of the Maha Bodhi headquarters in Calcutta. The purpose of the Centre, Jinaratna explained, 'was to accommodate those who engage in international cultural and religious activities and especially the professors, students etc. exchanged between India and China'.[54]

Taixu informed Jinaratana that on his request, Chiang Kai-shek had agreed to donate the equivalent of Rs. 10,000 towards the cause. Recognizing his contribution, the Maha Bodhi Society decided to place a memorial tablet in honour of Taixu in its new annex building called the 'China Block'. The 'foundation-laying ceremony' for the annex was performed by the Chinese Consul-General, who noted that the 'China Block will serve as a meeting place of Chinese and Indian scholars whereby the bond of friendship and cordiality existing between China and India will be further strengthened'.[55] The ceremony took place six months after the death of Taixu. The Chinese monk was memorialized by the Maha Bodhi Society with several essays, including an obituary, dedicated to his life and contribution in its May-June 1947 issue of *The Maha-Bodhi*.

For his part, Tan Yunshan continued to support Taixu's international mission by bringing several of his disciples to India. These included Fafang (法舫; 1905-51), Wu Baihui (巫白慧; 1919-) and Zhou

Xiangguang (周祥光; 1919-63), all of whom studied and taught at the Cheena-Bhavana. All three seem to have been initially influenced by a speech that Taixu delivered at the celebrations marking the 'India Day' in China on 17 March 1942. Taixu outlined the ancient Buddhist links between the two regions, pointed to the exchanges between their contemporary political leaders, argued for the need to promote a deeper understanding between the two peoples, and expressed his hope that after attaining independence, the two countries would contribute to the betterment of the world together.[56] Fafang, Wu Baihui and Zhou Xiangguang seem to have taken up this challenge of their master and travelled to India to fulfil his vision.

Similar to Tagore's visit to China in 1924, Taixu's Goodwill Mission to India in 1940 was an important event in the modern history of India-China interactions. Taixu correctly noted that there was a hiatus in the exchanges between the two regions, especially between the sixteenth and eighteenth centuries. Mutual knowledge and understanding declined significantly during these two centuries. While the opium trade and British military interests in Tibet reconnected India and China in some ways, cultural exchanges were limited until the early twentieth century. Tagore's visit contributed to the revival of cultural relations by triggering an interest in Indian literature in China and in scholarship on the historical exchanges between India and China.

Taixu's trip to India also helped revive the Buddhist links between the two countries. Many of his disciples were directly or indirectly responsible for fostering these links. They were, following Taixu's larger mission, trying to make Buddhism a socially and politically engaged religion. Indeed, in a vastly changed world where both India and China were occupied by imperial powers, Taixu had successfully presented Buddhism as a key factor in fostering India-China relations and collaboration. These exchanges, that not only involved the Buddhist communities but also the lay scholars and political leaders of the two countries, continued even after 1949, when the People's Republic of China was established.

The fact that Taixu had left a deep impression on the political leaders he met in India is clear from a letter that Jawaharlal Nehru wrote to his daughter, Indira, a few days after his meeting with Taixu in Sarnath. 'Two hours were spent', Nehru wrote, 'in a laborious conversation with the mission and its leader, the Rev. Abbot Tai Hsu. Laborious, because all conversations through an interpreter are heavy and tiring. The old Abbot – but was far from old looking – was delightful and had the face of a cherub. The more I see of the Chinese the more I like them'.[57]

NOTES

1. Okakura ([1903] 1920), Tagore ([1925] 2002), and Liang ([1925] 2002).
2. For a good overview and writings on pan-Asianism, see Saaler and Szpilman (2011). The India-China exchanges within this context are discussed in Tsui (2010) and Stolte and Fischer-Tiné (2012).
3. Welch (1968): 1.
4. Welch (1968): 254.
5. Welch (1968): 262-3.
6. Welch (1968): 264.
7. Yu (2005): 15. For other criticisms of Welch's study, especially his views on Taixu, see Ritzinger (1999) and Pittman (2001).
8. Yu (2005): 16.
9. Yu (2005): 17.
10. Sen (2003): 137.
11. Ritzinger (1999): 4.
12. Pittman (2001): 29.
13. Pratt (1928): 338-9.
14. Yu (2005).
15. Sen (2003): chapter 2.
16. Sen (2015).
17. Zhang (2014).
18. Tan (1999).
19. Lee (1964).
20. Translated in Karl (2002): 162-3.
21. Yu (2005): 57.
22. Yu (2005): 57.
23. Stolte and Fischer-Tiné (2012).
24. The headquarters of the Society was subsequently moved to Calcutta.
25. Jaffe (2004): 67.
26. Pittman (2001): 107.
27. See Snodgrass (2009): 143 and Pittman (2001): 109-12.
28. 'Japan Far Eastern Buddhist Conference', *The Maha-Bodhi*, vol. 34, p. 81.

29. Pittman (2001): 43.
30. Pittman (2001): 44.
31. 'Rev. Tai Hsu's Goodwill Mission', *The Maha-Bodhi*, vol. 47, pp. 517-18.
32. Tsui (2010).
33. Tan (1998): 135-6.
34. *Taixu dashi quanshu*, vol. 19, p. 31.
35. On Nehru's visit to Chongqing, see Samarani (2005): 8-12. The work of the Medial Mission in China is detailed by B.K. Basu (1984), a member of the medical team. Bagchi eventually went to China as a professor of Indology in 1947.
36. Sarkar (1940): 315-16.
37. *Taixu dashi quanshu*, vol. 19, p. 39.
38. 'Chinese Buddhist Mission in India', *The Maha-Bodhi*, vol. 48, pp. 85-91.
39. 'Chinese Buddhist Mission in India', *The Maha-Bodhi*, vol. 48, p. 85.
40. 'Chinese Buddhist Mission in India', *The Maha-Bodhi*, vol. 48, p. 86.
41. 'Address Presented to His Holiness Tai Hsu', *The Maha-Bodhi*, vol. 48, p. 92.
42. 'Chinese Buddhist Mission in India', *The Maha-Bodhi*, vol. 48, p. 87.
43. 'Chinese Buddhist Mission in India', *The Maha-Bodhi*, vol. 48, p. 88.
44. *Taixu dashi quanshu* vol. 17, pp. 11-12.
45. 'Chinese Buddhist Mission in India', *The Maha-Bodhi*, vol. 48, p. 88.
46. 'Chinese Buddhist Mission in India', *The Maha-Bodhi*, vol. 48, pp. 88-91.
47. *Taixu dashi quanshu*, vol. 18.
48. *Taixu dashi quanshu,* vol. 18, p. 600.
49. *Taixu dashi quanshu,* vol. 18, p. 601.
50. Tsui (2010).
51. 'Ninth Anniversary of the Mulagandhakuti Vihara at Sarnath', *The Maha-Bodhi*, vol. 48, pp. 460-3.
52. Bright (1947): 369-70.
53. Nehru (1960): 454-5.
54. 'Correspondence', *The Maha-Bodhi*, vol. 55, p. 210.
55. 'Notes and News', *The Maha-Bodhi*, vol. 55, p. 219.
56. *Taixu dashi quanshu.*
57. Nehru (1972), 651.

BIBLIOGRAPHY

'Address Presented to His Holiness Tai Hsu', *The Maha-Bodhi: Journal of the Maha Bodhi Society* 48.2-3 (February & March 1940): 92-3.

Basu, B.K. 1986. *Call of Yanan: Story of the Indian Medical Mission to China, 1938-43*. Bombay: All India Kotnis Memorial Committee.

Bright, J.S., ed. 1947. *Important Speeches of Jawaharlal Nehru: Being a Collection of Most Significant Speeches Delivered by Jawaharlal Nehru from 1922 to 1946*. Lahore: The Indian Printing Works.

'Chinese Buddhist Mission in India'. *The Maha-Bodhi: Journal of the Maha Bodhi Society* 48.2-3 (February & March): 85-91.

'Correspondence'. *The Maha-Bodhi: Journal of the Maha Bodhi Society* 55.9-10 (September-October 1947): 208-13.

Jaffe, R.M. 2004. 'Seeking Śākyamuni: Travel and the Reconstruction of Japanese Buddhism', *Journal of Japanese Studies* 30.1 (Winter): 65-96.

'Japan Far Eastern Buddhist Conference', *The Maha-Bodhi: Journal of the Maha Bodhi Society* 34.2 (February 1926): 76-81.

Karl, R. 2002. *Staging the World: Chinese Nationalism at the Turn of the Twentieth Century*. Durham: Duke University Press.

Lee Choon-seng (Li Juncheng) 李俊承. 1964. *Yindu gu Foguo youji* 印度古佛國遊記 [Records of Travels in India, the Ancient Buddhist Kingdom]. Taipei: Fojiao wenhua fuwuchu.

Liang Q. [1925] 2002. 'Introduction', in *Talks in China*, ed. Rabindranath Tagore. New Delhi: Rupa & Co., pp. vii-xxx.

Nehru, J. 1960. *A Bunch of Old Letters, Written Mostly to Jawaharlal Nehru and Some Written by Him*. London: Asia Publishing House.

———. 1972. *Selected Works of Jawaharlal Nehru*, vol. 10. New Delhi: Orient Longman.

'Ninth Anniversary of the Mulagandhakuti Vihara at Sarnath'. *The Maha-Bodhi: Journal of the Maha Bodhi Society* 48.12 (December): 460-3.

'Notes and News'. *The Maha-Bodhi: Journal of the Maha Bodhi Society* 55.9-10 (September-October 1947): 219-20.

Okakura K. [1903] 1920. *The Ideals of the East, with Special Reference to the Art of Japan*. New York: Dutton.

Pittman, D.A. 2001. *Toward a Modern Chinese Buddhism: Taixu's Reforms*. Honolulu: University of Hawai'i Press.

Pratt, J.B. 1928. *The Pilgrimage of Buddhism and A Buddhist Pilgrimage*. New York: Macmillan.

'Rev. Tai Hsu's Goodwill Mission'. *The Maha-Bodhi: Journal of the Maha Bodhi Society* 47.11 (November 1939): 517-18.

Ritzinger, J.R. 1999. 'Taixu: To Renew Buddhism and Save the Modern World'. MA thesis, Lawrence University.

Saaler, S. and C.W.A. Szpilman, eds. 2011. *Pan-Asianism: A Documentary History*, 2 vols. Lanham: Rowman & Littlefield.

Samarani, G. 2005. 'Shaping the Future of Asia: Chiang Kai-shek, Nehru and China-Indian Relations During the Second World War Period', *Working Paper No. 11*. Centre for East and South-East Asian Studies, Lund University, Sweden.

Sarkar, B.K. 1940. 'Tai Hsu on India and Buddhism'. *The Calcutta Review* (March): 315-16.

Sen, T. 2003. *Buddhism, Diplomacy, and Trade: The Realignment of Sino-Indian Relations, 600-1400*. Honolulu: University of Hawai'i Press.

———. 2015. 'The Spread of Buddhism', in *The Cambridge History of the World*, Volume V: *Expanding Webs of Exchange and Conquest, 500 CE-1500 CE*, ed. B.Z. Kedar and M.E. Wiesner-Hanks. Cambridge: Cambridge University Press, pp. 447-79.

Snodgrass, J. 2009. 'Performing Buddhist Modernity: The Lumbini Festival, Tokyo 1925', *Journal of Religious History* 33.2: 133-48.

Stolte, C. and H. Ficher-Tiné. 2012. 'Imagining Asia in India: Nationalism and Internationalism (*c.* 1905-1940)', *Comparative Studies in Society and History* 44.1 (January): 62-92.

Tagore, R. [1925] 2002. *Talks in China*. New Delhi: Rupa & Co.

Taixu dashi quanshu 太虛大師全書 [The Complete Works of the Venerable Master Taixu]. 20 vols. Taipei, 1956.

Tan, C., ed. 1999. *In the Footsteps of Xuanzang: Tan Yun-shan and India*. New Delhi: Gyan Publishing House and Indira Gandhi National Centre for the Arts.

Tan, Y. 1998. *Sino-Indian Culture*. Calcutta: Visva-Bharati.

Tsui, B. 2010. 'The Plea for Asia: Tan Yunshan, Pan-Asianism and Sino-Indian Relations', *China Report: A Journal of East Asian Studies* 46. 4 (November): 353-70.

Welch, H. 1968. *The Buddhist Revival in China*. Cambridge: Harvard University Press.

Yu, X. 2005. *Buddhism, War, and Nationalism: Chinese Monks in the Struggle against Japanese Aggressions, 1931-1945*. New York: Routledge.

Zhang, X. 2014. 'Buddhist Practices and Institutions of the Chinese Community in Kolkata', in Tansen Sen (ed.), *Buddhism Across Asia: Networks of Material, Intellectual and Cultural Exchange*. Singapore: Institute of Southeast Asian Studies and New Delhi: Manohar, pp. 429-57.

CHAPTER 10

Ensouling the Nation through Fiction

Liang Qichao's Applied Buddhism

DAN SMYER YU

LIANG QICHAO was best known for his scholarship on the history of China and his numerous essays on the advent of European modernity into late Qing and early Republican China. His encyclopaedic knowledge of Chinese culture and European philosophical traditions has impressed many generations of Chinese scholars and popular readers in China. Liang Qichao's scholarly works have been well-researched and discussed, especially among historians in both China and North America. However, the influence of his Buddhist background on his prolific thoughts has not been given enough scholarly attention, particularly from the angle of religious studies, in general, and Buddhist studies, in particular. This paper intends to highlight Liang Qichao as a prominent lay Buddhist practitioner and, thus, treat him as a socially engaged Buddhist of his time. Marking its distinction from monastic traditions that are shrouded from the social realm of common people, 'engaged Buddhism' manifests itself as a form of social activism with an orientation towards Buddhist ethics, particularly in Western nations or countries with Western influences. Engaged Buddhists are those who actively apply their Buddhist practice in their social discourses and through activism on the issues of war, social injustice and other collective defilements of a society. As a lay practitioner, Liang Qichao promoted what he called 'applied Buddhism' at the turn of the twentieth century, which, in essence, was a predecessor of engaged Buddhism in the West.

In this paper, I intend to examine how Liang Qichao utilized Buddhist ideals in his promotion of what he called 'political fiction' as an instrument for building a modern China. Buddhism, to him, brought both moral and spiritual perfection to China while, in his opinion, Buddhist soteriological values did not run against modern practices. In Liang's writings that connect religion with nation, it is noticeable that his personifying the Chinese nation with a soul obviously bears the imprint of the romanticism found hand-in-hand with eighteenth and nineteenth-century European nationalism, especially of France and Germany. Like many of his contemporaries, he also felt that the soul of China was comatose and in need of being awakened. In this context, this paper provides an analysis of how Liang evoked Buddhist concepts as the driving force for the awakening of the Chinese people and of how political fiction with his intended Buddhist contents was expected to function as an effective instrument for building national unity toward a modern nation state.

RENEWAL OF THE NATION WITH FICTION

> If one aspires to undertake the renewal of the people of a nation, the renewal of its fiction has to be a priority. Thus, for the renewal of morality, fiction must be renewed; for the renewal of religions, fiction must be renewed; for the renewal of governance, fiction must be renewed; for the renewal of custom, fiction must be renewed; for the renewal of the art of learning, fiction must be renewed; Even for renewal of the mind and personality of people, fiction must be renewed. Why? Fiction has an inconceivable power in shaping humanity.[1]

The voice of Liang Qichao in this statement reveals his passion and expresses not only the urgency of human concerns but also the exigency of immediate understanding of the historical crises during his time. He did not create political fiction; rather, he appropriated it from Europe. In his preface to a collection of translated political fiction, he says,

> Political fiction originated from Europeans. . . . In the past when European countries started their political reformations, their intellectual and noble-minded people infused their personal experiences and their political ideals into fiction. . . . Whenever a work of fiction was published, the opinions of the nation changed drastically. A certain English celebrity said, 'Fiction is the soul of a nation'.[2]

His exuberant spirit for renewing the minds of people came from his assessment of spiritual corruption in China. He attributed this corruption to the type of popular fiction that was self-indulgent and lacked moral concerns for the collective sufferings that the Chinese people were undergoing. According to Liang, this type of fiction had turned Chinese people into 'a senseless crowd of superstitious personalities, arrogant scholars, blood-thirsty murderers, narcissistic young people, and hedonists'.[3] Here, Liang did not blame fiction as the cause of the social degeneration of his time; rather, he blamed its profane content. Liang himself began to use fiction for the purpose of political reformation. He passionately said, 'Today if the reformation for the governance of people is desired, it must begin with the revolution in the realm of fiction; if the renewal of people is aspired, it must begin with fiction.'[4]

Liang's appropriation of the model of European political fiction was meant to resolve his self-posed question – 'Is the soul of China still in existence?' This question was the title of his article published in 1899 in which he asserted that the soul of Japan was its samurai spirit but he was unable to find the soul of China. At the end of the article, Liang proposed to remake the soul of China by integrating the people with the nation and the nation with the people.[5] Obviously, Liang was building an 'imagined nation', i.e. a kind of new China by articulating a common destiny for his compatriots.[6] In his historical reality, Liang witnessed the Chinese people being encroached upon and suffocated by internal corruption and external colonialism. He said, '. . . what I love most is China; the one who suffers most now among sentient beings is China; the one who fills one third of the globe is China.'[7]

In his own work of political fiction titled *An Account of the Future of New China*, Liang, through the protagonist Mr. Kong, voiced both his passion for saving China and his lamentation over his poverty-ridden and spiritually desiccated compatriots: 'China is surely perishing. It isn't dying of foreign invasion; nor is it dying of inhibition of the government, but is dying of these four hundred million people without conscience, without mind, and without courage.'[8] Liang did not blame the destruction of China directly on external elements; instead, he used Mencius's explanation of the cause of the destruction:

'A country must be self-destroyed before outsiders destroy it,' and 'A person must be self-humiliated before others humiliate him'.[9]

Based on this causal explanation, Liang asserted that the Chinese people had been enslaved by the two-hundred-year reign of the Manchus before becoming the slaves of colonial powers. Thus, the slave mentality was deeply embedded in the people's consciousness. In 1901, Liang published his article 'On the Origin of the Weaknesses of China' in which he describes what a slave personality is:[10]

> A slave does not have the ability of self-governance, neither does he have the consciousness of independence. . . . He clothes himself with the clothes given by his master, feeds himself with the food from his master, speaks the words of his master, and carries out the business of his master. Except dependence he does not have other thoughts; except obedience he does not have other qualities; except being a groveller he has no smile; except running errands he has nothing to do; and except for his servility he has no vitality. When being called upon he does not dare to refuse; when being waved away he does not dare to linger around; when being ordered to live he does not dare not to live; when being commanded to die he does not dare not to die. He receives a glance or a smile from his master as if he seized an extraordinary treasure, as if he was awarded with nine royal gifts, as if he ascended to the heaven. . . . He takes whatever others look upon as unbearable humiliation and insult as part of his life. This is slave mentality.

Liang's political fiction aimed at the emancipation of the Chinese people from slavery and the slave mentality, and at a remaking of a new people who 'jump out of old modes of being and create new modes of being'.[11] Although the model of Liang's political fiction came from Europe, the content of it was filled with his vision – the birth of a new modern China. With this potent hope in mind, Liang chose fiction to bring about the renewal of China. His explanation of renewal comprised a twofold meaning: one, to temper and elevate what one has; the other, to add what one does not have.[12] Thus, it was a synthetic renewal in which tradition had to be re-examined and new elements from other parts of the world were to be added. Liang's attempt to renew the Chinese nation was, in essence, a combination of reform and revolution. His intent was not to abolish Chinese cultural traditions but to smash the self-inflicted prison in which one can only act according to the dictate of the ancients. Liang thought this was a result of slave mentality when one dares not say what the ancients did not but takes the body and mind of the ancients as one's own.

Liang was promoting a cultural renaissance in which Chinese traditions needed to be re-evaluated in a new light because China, to him, had a shared responsibility in forming a world civilization. After touring North America and Western Europe, Liang felt that the responsibility of China to this envisioned world civilization was to broaden the horizon of Chinese culture with Western culture and to supplement the latter with it. By synthesizing these world cultures, he believed that a new civilization might emerge.[13]

BUILDING A NEW CHINA WITH BUDDHIST IDEALS

Liang's impassioned advocacy for a Chinese national renaissance was undoubtedly a consequence of a modernity that arose out of an interaction of Chinese intellectuals with Western Enlightenment ideas.[14] It was characteristically a project of secularism but was not intended to separate the religious from the secular or the non-religious; instead, it was ambitiously intended to disseminate and diffuse religious teachings with vernacular expressions into the political sphere of emerging modern China in the late nineteenth and early twentieth centuries. Liang's choice of political fiction, selection of particular types of Buddhist philosophy and ethics, and perception of the position of China in the modern world all point to the fact that Chinese intellectual-led secularism was a forceful ideological movement in which 'the secular and the religious are produced simultaneously'.[15]

The scheme of Liang's revolutionary vision in political fiction was formed with his teacher, Kang Youwei's religious vision of *Datong* or the great commonwealth of humankind. Kang's ideal of the great commonwealth was intended to be a common thread to sew together the collective mind of the entire nation and was meant to be enshrined in the individual souls of the population through the words of ideals uttered by realistically portrayed fictional characters. Liang's exposition of Kang's idea of the great commonwealth was infused heavily with Buddhist and Confucian teachings.

Liang notes: 'The foundational theory of the great commonwealth is that all sentient beings have the same nature as the ocean and all human beings come from the same womb.'[16] This theory is based on Sakyamuni Buddha's teaching recorded in *The Hua-yen Sutra* (or *The Avatamsaka Sutra*) in which the Dharma-realm is a pure land depicted by rich prophetic visions. In this pure land, all the highest ideals existing in the human mind are omnipresent. In addition, it is full of the luminosity of the myriad Buddhas, celestial wonders and the immortality that human beings have been striving for. In the chapter, 'The Inconceivable Dharma of Buddhas' in the *Hua-yen Sutra*, Sakyamuni Buddha says: [17]

> All the Buddhas have infinite pure lands, with inconceivable glories and beauty, revealing the Buddha's domain in conformity with sentient beings' wishes, without attachment. All the Buddhas have infinite Bodhisattva's Paramitas and perfect insight; they sport in all fields with complete freedom. . . .
>
> Oh son of Buddhas, all the World-Honored Buddhas have ten inscrutable peerless capacities: sitting cross-legged, they can manifest themselves everywhere in the universe; with one sentence with one meaning, they can elucidate the infinite Buddha's doctrines; emanating one beam of light, they illuminate the entire cosmos; within one body, they reveal all bodies; at one place, they disclose all world systems; in one insight, they perceive all dharmas without obstruction.

To the Buddhists, the teaching of Sakyamuni Buddha is the communion between two worlds: the world of enlightenment and the world of everyday living. Those who can transform the words of the Buddha into actual visions are set to enter the world of enlightenment. Kang Youwei's great commonwealth, in Liang's political fiction, is a representation of the communion between this world and the world of the pure land. As Liang said,

> Master's [Kang Youwei's] knowledge of Buddhism is purely from Mahayana Buddhism and has its root in Hua-yen. The profound meaning of the Hua-yen teaching lies in the ultimate perfection and the bliss of the Dharma realm. Master inquired into what perfection is and what bliss is. He thought that perfection is unattainable if one abandons this world to seek the Dharma world, and that bliss is unreachable when one thinks living in this world is pain and leaving this world is joy. Thus, he engaged himself in this world to create the world of Dharma.[18]

When Kang moved the world of Dharma to the world of sentient beings, he took Confucius' teaching as the medium to facilitate this movement. In Liang's interpretation, Kang thinks that Confucius' teaching is an incarnation of the Hua-yen school of Buddhism because Confucius 'only speaks of this world but not of the world of Dharma. Thus, this magnificent world is also the world of the magnificent Dharma.'[19] Historically, Confucius and Sakyamuni Buddha did not have an apparent connection. Here, both Kang and Liang creatively used the principles of the Buddha's teaching to assign a soteriological orientation for Confucianism. The role of Confucianism as a set of socially moral principles is either returned to its original state or is restructured with a liberative emphasis, particularly when Kang incorporated what Confucius says to his disciple, Zi You, in *The Book of Rituals* into his great commonwealth:[20]

> The implementation of the great Tao is that everything under the heaven is publicly shared. The virtuous and able ones are encouraged and chosen for the public; integrity and amity are valued by all. Thus, people cherish not only their own parents and children, but cherish the children and parents of others as well. The elderly live their last years in happiness, able-bodied adults are usefully employed; and children are properly reared. Widowers, widows, orphans, and the childless aged, the crippled and the ailing are well cared for. All men share their responsibilities and all women have their respective roles. People pick up belongings of others on streets but do not take them home; People love to use their ability but not only for themselves. In such way, dishonesty and self-closure do not thrive. When robbery, sedition and other crimes do not occur, doors are not locked. Thus, this is the great commonwealth of peace.

The content of Kang's commonwealth was no longer the same as that of Confucius' but broader. According to Liang's explanation, Kang's philosophical system was influenced by the neo-Confucianism of the Song and Ming Dynasties, a system which Liang calls 'Buddha clothed in Confucius'.[21] Culturally, Kang's commonwealth was a mixture of European philosophies and Asian religious thoughts. In Liang's political fiction, these mingled traditions were meant to exercise compassion and wisdom, two major elements in the doctrine of Mahayana Buddhism. Both of them are employed to metamorphose confusion into illumination and superstition into true faith.

What is missing in Liang's praise of Kang Youwei is his secular side, which overtly promoted the physical destruction of traditional religious institutions, literally encouraging the Chinese populace to 'smash temples and burn books'.[22] Kang's secularism was indeed anti-clerical in nature. However, to be historically fair, his anti-clerical act was embedded with his own religious vision of a new Chinese republic: the national moral sources had to come from the wisdom of the ancient religious traditions but needed to be re-dressed in secular garments. To be specific, such secular garments are what Peter van der Veer calls 'scientism and rationalism'.[23] The idea of modern progress had to be instilled in the collective consciousness of the Chinese and, meanwhile, the secularized religious teachings were meant to buttress this progress so that the past of the nation would be reassigned with the mission of building a new modern nation.

Thus, in Liang's nation-building effort, it is obvious that his religious fervour surpassed that of his mentor in rational and comparative terms. Between philosophy and religion, Liang chose the latter. Between Christianity and Buddhism, he chose the latter. In his essay, 'On the Weaknesses and Strengths of a Philosopher and a Religious Teacher', Liang says, in the context of politics, 'If there are no religious thoughts, there is no unification of a nation; if there are no religious thoughts, there is no hope; if there are no religious thoughts, there is no liberation'.[24] In the case of Christianity and Buddhism, Liang thought that although Christianity had been in China for some time, its doctrine went against Chinese tradition and the disciples of Christ were not merely his followers but inferior to him.[25] As for the Buddhists, their innate wisdom was equal to that of the Buddha. Liang's assertion came from *The Nirvana Sutra* in which the Buddha says, 'All sentient beings have Buddha nature'.[26]

This philosophical and doctrinal comparison of Buddhism and Christianity was also an exercise of Liang's 'national defence' against religious and moral traditions coming from the West. The Christianity he refers to was Western Christianity, especially Protestantism, that was known for disseminating canonical and doctrinal contents to the popular realm by the use of the vernacular language. Liang skilfully empowered his compatriots by stating that everyone can be a Buddha but nobody can be a Christ. Once again, his secularization of Buddhism was not meant to separate Buddhist teachings from the secular sphere of the Chinese society but to revive and integrate it into the daily routines of its members.

In this regard, when religious principles are used in Liang's political fiction, they are secularized for the greater community of readers and are directed towards creating a new environment filled with Buddhist liberative ideals. To Liang, environment was an invention of the mind. This invention was accomplished through political fiction which has a spatial quality for the temporal revelations of ideals. These ideals were centred on the renewal of the nation. Due to the influence of Buddhist doctrines, Liang was confident that the entire population of China would comprehend the ideal of renewal. According to him, fiction had four capacities in raising the political consciousness of readers: permeation, immersion, stimulation and elevation.[27] Again, the theory of these four elements was configured with Liang's knowledge of Buddhism. The sum total of the four may enable a reader to reach a certain degree of enlightenment in terms of how an ideal can be transformed into a reality of this worldly life. Permeation, for instance, is based on 'mistaking wisdom as knowledge, and transforming knowledge into wisdom', a passage from the *Lankāvatāra Sūtra*.[28]

The so-called knowledge or *shi* in Chinese is translated from the Sanskrit word *parijñāna*, which, in Sakyamuni Buddha's teaching, means the mind's apprehension of its environment.[29] This apprehension is one's initial contact with the world through sensory activities, such as drinking a cup of hot tea, reading a poem and feeling the vapour in a heavy fog. From these empirical experiences, one may build up a reservoir of knowledge in the mind. According to the Mahayana Buddhist doctrine, this type of knowledge is not the highest state of knowing but it can be metamorphosed into one's ultimate wisdom (*prajñā* in Sanskrit). *Prajñā* is not external to one's capacity; rather, it is an integral part of one's existence. As Hui Neng, the sixth Dharma Master in the Chinese Ch'an tradition, says, 'If one does not recognize *prajñā* in one's own nature, it is like talking about food without sating one's hunger', and 'when a fool learns from a wise one, the wise one tells him of the principles universe. When the mind of this fool is widely opened with the words of the wise one, he is no longer different from the wise one.'[30]

Thus, Liang's strategic usage of permeation was intended to create spatial[31] opportunities for his readers to taste wisdom and to provide the soil for the germination of their 'original seed' of enlightenment.[32] Liang believed that one's own seed would wake the seeds of others and this original seed would eventually spread all over the world. To complement the spatial quality of permeation, Liang introduced immersion as a temporal effect of fiction. This temporal effect was transplanted from Sakyamuni Buddha who 'spoke the immense *Hua Yen Sutra* under a Bodhi tree'.[33] Historically, when Sakyamuni sat under the Bodhi tree, he recognized his past lives and, with his awakening light, re-experienced past events between his countless births and deaths in countless worlds. Finally, he whispered to himself, 'O, jailer, I see you now. How many life times have you confined me in the prisons of birth and death? But now I see your face clearly, and from now on you can build no more prisons around me.'[34]

According to Liang, both permeation and immersion worked together to assist readers to reach a gradual awakening, a Ch'an phrase which originated from Shen Xiu, a contemporary of Hui Neng. After a long meditation, Shen Xiu wrote a verse: [35]

The body is a bodhi tree,
The mind is a mirror.
If one continually dusts the mirror,
No dust can land on it.

In this verse, Shen Xiu advocates one's diligence for daily practice. In other words, one may attain certain enlightening results by temporally enduring days and months and years of practice. This gradual pace would eventually lead one to a moment of sudden awakening, reflected in Hui Neng's verse in response to Shen Xiu's:[36]

The body is not a bodhi tree,
Neither does the mirror reflect.
Originally there exists nothing,
Where can the dust land?

The third capacity of Liang's political fiction, stimulation, was modelled on Hui Neng's experience on reading Shen Xiu's verse. Liang says, 'The power of stimulation is its suddenness: a person may not consciously feel the powers of permeation and immersion, but may be aware of the sudden power of stimulation. Stimulation enables one to experience emerging fresh feelings in a split second without self-control.'[37] Liang further gives an example of 'one whack and one yell', the sudden method used in the Lin-ji Ch'an tradition, to cross a novice over to the other shore, or to liberate the novice from his dull-mindedness to his omniscient Buddha nature.[38]

The culmination of permeation, immersion and stimulation resides at the meeting point of their spatial and temporal qualities and of their gradual and sudden effects. Liang names this meeting point elevation, which is 'a power arising from within, which is the best of the Buddha's teachings'. He continues,

> A fiction reader enters his book and transforms himself into the protagonist. . . . When he enters the book through reading, his body is no longer a possession of the 'I' but, by leaving this world, it goes into the other world. This is how words move people into the world of Hua Yen, into Indra's net, into billions of lotus flowers in one pore, and into thousands of eons in a snap of fingers.[39]

Here, the purpose of Liang's elevation is clear. He is seeking empathy from readers who enter the diachronically arranged events in the world of fiction and begin their empathetic participation in the synchronically structured relationships of fictional characters. Empathy here can be explicated as 'feeling in' or 'getting at the feel of what is inside another person or group of persons'.[40] The aim of empathy may not be to seek an agreement but to discern possible understandings from differences and disagreements. Obviously, Liang puts the reader of fiction in a dialogical mode, in which he starts his inquiry into the meaning of life through his dialogue with various personalities appearing in fiction. The reader as an 'I' encounters numerous characters in fiction and is given an invitation to the space of the discourse of these characters. Thus, the mind of the reader is expanded from the world of his or her own life to the world of others' lives, as well as to the world of others' ideals. In this sense, reading fiction generates a type of spiritual life, which, in Liang's words, 'is independent from the physical environment . . . but which may suddenly transcend reality and break a path into the realm of ideals. That is the paradise of freedom for people.'[41]

BUILDING A NATION OF THE OTHER SHORE WITH APPLIED BUDDHISM

Utopian visions are manifest in Liang's advocacy for political fiction. These utopian ideals are intimately connected with his understanding of the Buddhist Pureland. Liang's utopian ideas exist between two claims: 'ideas constitute a realm of their own autonomous reality and . . . ideas provide guides or models or paradigms for construing experience'.[42] Liang himself said, 'Ideas are the greatest power under heaven, which gives birth to various ethos and endeavors'.[43] The content of his utopian ideas have a visible Buddhist orientation, particularly when Liang uses Kang Youwei's concept of the great commonwealth, which was envisioned to bring about a transformation of human existence from self-centredness to ideal-centredness. In this sense, Liang advocated what he called 'applied Buddhism'. It was derived from his readings on modern European applied sciences, such as applied physics and chemistry. To him, religious practices, like modern scientific practices, had applied aspects that might directly benefit the collective wellbeing of a given society. In his confident promotion of Buddhism, Liang felt that, as a world religion, it had much to offer to the common Chinese people.

Liang's Buddhist social activism did not rely on any organizational resources as many contemporary North American Buddhist organizations do, such as the Buddhist Peace Fellowship and the International Network of Engaged Buddhists. This applied Buddhism was practised through his prolific writings with provocative ideas. Liang's applied Buddhism is synonymous with what contemporary scholars refer to as 'socially engaged Buddhism' that is a blend of Western modern practices and Eastern Buddhist spiritual and moral sources. Socially engaged Buddhism often occurs among Western activists in the contemporary world; however, its inception could be traced to the late nineteenth century when Western modernity and Asian Buddhist traditions began their interaction and mutual appropriation.

Christopher Queen points out that '... the shape and style of contemporary engaged Buddhism does not appear in Buddhist history until about the year 1880'.[44] The late nineteenth and early twentieth centuries were the time when Liang was actively travelling to Europe, North America and Japan, where he absorbed fresh ideas from his hosts. As mentioned, his coinage of 'applied Buddhism' signifies the blending of Western science, rationalism, and the ideas of secularism and progress with traditional Chinese religious practices. Thus, his applied Buddhism, or socially engaged Buddhism, was one of the many results of what James Deitrick calls the 'cultural interpenetration'[45] of the East and West but in the Chinese context.

China, at the turn of the twentieth century, underwent much suffering. With external colonial oppression and internal chaos of all sorts, those who suffered the most were the common citizens. Liang was able to capture the national feelings of China and articulate them in his literary works. In the meantime, he sought solutions to alleviate the collective miseries that the Chinese populace was bearing at the time. This is clearly evident in his applied Buddhism as shown in his writings on Chinese nationalism and the Buddhist faith. The Buddhist ideals that Liang enshrined in political fiction are a series of religious feelings, which signify a string of affective acts arising from human soteriological concerns and a longing to enter the numinous world. In Rudolf Otto's *The Idea of the Holy*, the entrance of the numinous world is not visible for everyone except for those who have had 'a moment of deeply-felt religious experience', or are able to 'recall their intrinsically religious feelings'.[46] Liang once said:[47]

> The nature of human feelings is instinctive, but its power lures people into the realm which transcends human instincts; the nature of human feelings is present, but its power attracts people into the realm which transcends the present. If we want to enter the mystery of life, merge our thoughts with our life as one, and conjoin our life with all sentient beings in the universe as one, there is no other way except to cross the threshold of human feelings. Thus, human feelings are a big secret in the universe.

Liang's religious tone as conveyed in his writings mostly came from his envisioning of a new China as a paradise on earth or a nation of the Other Shore, which signified an enlightened state of being among the social members of the intended new society. This was the entry point of his project for secularizing-diffusing Buddhist teachings to the popular realm of China. From a conventional point of view, Liang's Buddhist ideals appear utopian in nature but are disguised in a set of social and literary terms palatable to the members of the Chinese society of his time.

Although it is a historical fact that Liang envisioned modern Buddhism as the national religion of China (something that never materialized), nevertheless, as a lay Buddhist practitioner and an advocate for the secularization of Buddhist teachings, he gave birth to political fiction as an 'infant' literary genre in modern China. This genre would turn out to be intimately connected with the political history of modern China. The multiple incarnations of this 'infant' have already appeared in such modern writers as Ba Jing, Lu Xun, Ding Ling, Xu Zhi-mo and numerous others. The growth of this 'infant' followed Liang's synthetic world-view – the inclusion of both social reality and spiritual ideality, both intrinsic and extrinsic traditions, such as those of Europe and Asia. He envisioned that 'the twentieth-century is the age for the marriage of two (European and Asian) civilizations. . . . The beauty of the West will bear children for us.'[48] In this historical backdrop, Liang's political fiction was an act of his Buddhist belief on behalf of the greater community of the Chinese populace. The passion and poetic nature existing in the body of his writings on modern Chinese nationalism qualifies him as one who uttered a 'living speech' which was meant to preserve ideality and living presence in all its forms' regardless of the fact that later generations of Chinese intellectuals and creative writers utilized the political fiction genre to abolish religious institutions and practices in their intent to build a new modern China absent of religion – a truly secular nation state in a literal sense.[49]

NOTES

1. Liang (1992), vol. 2.
2. Liang (1936), vol. 2: 34-5.
3. Liang (1992): 6-7.
4. Liang (1992): 8.
5. Liang (1992): 220-2.
6. Anderson (1991).

7. Liang (1992): 319.
8. Liang (1916): 23-4.
9. Liang (1936) vol. 2: 40.
10. Liang (1992), vol. I: 73.
11. Liang (1936): 63.
12. Liang(1992), vol. 1: 107.
13. Liang (1992), vol. 1: 426.
14. Van der Veer (2011): 272.
15. Van der Veer (2011): 271.
16. Liang (1992), vol. 2: 306.
17. Chang (1991): 49.
18. Liang (1992), vol. 2: 317.
19. Liang (1992), vol. 2: 317.
20. Liang (1992), vol. 2: 307.
21. Liang (1992), vol. 2: 236.
22. Van der Veer (2011): 270.
23. Van der Veer (2011): 273.
24. Liang (1984): 139.
25. Liang (1984): 148.
26. Liang (1984): 148.
27. Liang (1992), vol. 2: 4-5.
28. Liang (1992), vol. 2: 4.
29. Ding (1991): 285-7.
30. Price and Wong Mou-Lam (1969): 29.
31. Liang (1992), vol. 2: 4.
32. Liang (1992), vol. 2: 4.
33. Liang (1992), vol. 2: 5.
34. Nhat (1991): 121.
35. Price and Wong Mou-lam (1969): 15.
36. Price and Wong Mou-lam (1969): 16.
37. Liang (1992), vol. 2: 5.
38. Liang (1992), vol. 2: 5.
39. Liang (1992), vol. 2: 5-6.
40. Smart (1983): 16.
41. Liang (1992), vol. 2: 155.
42. Ricoeur (1986): 5.
43. Liang (1992), vol. 1: 66.
44. Queen (1996): 20.
45. Deitrick (2003): 253.
46. Otto (1958): 8.
47. Liang (1992), vol. 2: 22.
48. Liang (1992), vol. 2: 219.
49. Derrida (1973): 9.

BIBLIOGRAPHY

Anderson, B.R. 1991. *Imagined Communities: Reflections on the Origin and Spread of Nationalism*. London: Verso.

Van der Veer, P. 2011. 'Smash Temples, Burn books: Comparing Secularist Projects in India and China', in C. Calhoun, M. Juregensmeyer and J. van Antwerpen (eds.), *Rethinking Secularism*. Oxford: Oxford University Press, pp. 270-81.

Chang, Garma C.C. 1991. *The Buddhist Teaching of Totality: The Philosophy of Hwa Yen Buddhism*. University Park, PA: The Pennsylvania State University Press.

Deitrick, J.E. 1996. 'Engaged Buddhist Ethics', in C. Queen, C. Prebish and D. Keown (eds.), *Action Dharma: New Studies in Engaged Buddhism*. New York: Columbia University Press, pp. 270-85.

Derrida, J. 1973. *Speech and Phenomena*, tr. David B. Allison and Newton Garver. Evanston: Northwestern University Press.

Ding, F. 1991. *Foxue da cidian (Dictionary of Buddhist Studies)*. Shanghai: Shanghai Books.

Liang, Q. 1916. *Xiaoshuo lingjian*. Shanghai: China Commerce Press.

———. 1936. *Yinbingshi heji*, vols. 1 and 2. Shanghai: Commerce Press.

———. 1984. *Qichao Zhexue sixiang lunwen xuan*, ed. Ge Maochun and Jiang Jun. Beijing: Peking University Press.

———. 1992. *Liang Qichao wenxuan*, vols. 1 and 2, ed. Xiaohong Xia. Beijing: China Broadcasting and Television Press.

Nhat Hanh, T. 1991. *Old Path White Clouds*. Berkeley: Parallax Press.

Otto, R. 1958. *The Idea of the Holy: An Inquiry into the Non-rational Factor in the Idea of the Divine and its Relation to the Rational*, tr. John W. Harvey. New York: Oxford University Press.

Price, A.F. and Wong Mou-lam tr. 1969. *The Diamond Sutra and the Sutra of Hui Neng*. Berkeley: Shambhala Publications.

Queen, C. 1996. *Engaged Buddhism: Buddhist Liberation Movements in Asia*. Albany, NY: State University of New York.

Ricoeur, P. 1986. *Lectures on Ideology and Utopia*, ed. George H. Taylor. New York: Columbia University Press.

Smart, N. 1983. *Worldview*. New York: Charles Scribner's Sons.

CHAPTER 11

Theravāda Buddhism as Part of the Buddhist Revival in Mainland China and Hong Kong: Two Paradigms

BILL M. MAK

BACKGROUND

IN CONTEMPORARY BUDDHIST literature, the term 'Buddhist revival' carries different levels of meaning. Very broadly (and somewhat vaguely), it refers to the modern interest in Buddhism as a world religion after the ancient, original teachings of the Buddha were forgotten by many for centuries including in its native India. This definition, however, does not immediately apply in the case of China where Buddhism has had an almost uninterrupted presence for nearly two thousand years and was indigenized, most notably in the forms of Pure Land and Chan, to the extent that Buddhism is no longer recognized as a foreign religion in China.[1] When we talk about the Buddhist revival in the Chinese context, we mostly refer to two distinct concepts: first, the Buddhist modernization movement since the late nineteenth century, which aimed to revitalize Chinese Buddhism after centuries of stagnation and decline;[2] second, the resumption or normalization of Buddhist activities after the disastrous Cultural Revolution (1966-76) during which Buddhism was nearly decimated. In this paper, as we shall see, these three different definitions of 'Buddhist revival' represent different layers of factors which interact with each other to drive the contemporary development of Buddhism in China.

The twentieth century was one of the most tumultuous times in Chinese history. The religious landscape was not spared from all the social and political upheavals, many of which were unprecedented in terms of scope and magnitude. When the Republic of China was founded in 1912 after the collapse of the Qing Dynasty, Buddhism was in dire need of a major reform to face modernization as well as a new world order. In the eyes of the non-Buddhist Chinese, Buddhism retarded the progress of New China.[3] Attempts to revitalize the religion were made, serving as the foundation for subsequent development.[4] During the Republican period (1912-49), foreign travel became possible for the ordinary Chinese for the first time. In the 1930s, contacts with foreign Buddhists, especially those of Theravāda countries, beside the ones of Japan and Tibet with whom there were historical ties, flourished.[5] Meanwhile, Buddhist dialogue at the diplomatic level grew as the Republic of China gradually developed as a modern nation. In particular, Chinese Buddhist leaders demonstrated their patriotism during the national resistance against the Japanese invasion.[6] In sum, though Buddhism itself might not have grown in China during the early half of the twentieth century, it saw some important innovations as a result of the revitalization movement. Furthermore, its influences expanded in the areas of education and diplomacy.

The development of Chinese Buddhism took a sharp turn when the People's Republic of China (PRC) was founded in 1949. Buddhism needed to justify its existence within the socialist ideology and was obliged to collaborate with a government that mistrusted religions in general.[7] None the less, despite the inherent antagonism between Communism and religions, and the mayhem that all religious communities experienced during the Cultural Revolution, Buddhism was, in fact, supported and favoured in China under the Communist regime for the most part.[8] More accurately, the state of Chinese Buddhism since 1949 may be described in three stages, namely, integration, destruction and revival.[9] During the early years of the PRC, Buddhism was recognized as a means for peaceful cooperation amongst neighbouring Asian countries,[10] and the Buddhist Association of China (BAC; 中國佛教協會) was established in 1953 under the auspices of Mao to mainly further various diplomatic initiatives started since the Republican Era.[11] The BAC, a patriotic religious organization supervised by the State Administration for Religious Affairs (SARA), served as a liaison between the Buddhist communities and the government, representing the interests of both parties. During the 1960s and early 1970s, a series of ultra-leftist campaigns, including the infamous Cultural Revolution, which were later denounced, left Buddhism severely desecrated across the country with the number of monastics and functioning temples reaching a historical low.[12] In the 1980s, Buddhism began to show signs of revival as the country was gradually liberalized on various fronts with Jiang Zemin urging a 'more tolerant management of religious organizations' in 1990.[13] However, judging from the number of Buddhist monastics, temples and educational institutes, Chinese Buddhism has yet to recover to its pre-1949 state (Table 11.1).

TABLE 11.1: NUMBER OF BUDDHIST MONASTICS AND TEMPLES IN CHINA[14]

Year	Number of monastics	Number of temples
1930	740,000	–
1940	500,000	–
1949	–	40,000
1976	–	–
1980	–	100
1994	40,000	5,000
1997	70,000	8,000
2006	100,000	15,000

Some scholars have estimated that the current number of practising Chinese Buddhists has reached 300 million, making up around 20 per cent of the Mainland Chinese population, with around 100,000 monastics in the Chinese Buddhist tradition alone.[15] In recent decades, the Chinese government's enthusiastic support of Buddhism was marked by a number of high-profile events, such as the World Buddhist Forum starting in 2005, organized by the United Front Work Department with a multi-million dollar budget. These extravagant events indicate the double role that the Chinese government has envisioned Buddhism as playing in its foreign policy of 'Peaceful Rise' (和平崛起) and internal policy of 'Harmonious Society' (和諧社會) – a role that cannot be played by the other four religions legally recognized in China, namely, Daoism, Islam, Catholicism and Protestantism.

Meanwhile, in places such as Taiwan and Hong Kong, as well as other overseas Chinese communities where Chinese culture was less severely affected, Buddhism did not experience such a dramatic decline and growth and has remained a visible part of the Chinese societies there all along. Although Mainland China and Hong Kong share the same historical and cultural roots, the evolution of Buddhism in these places took separate courses due to the different political and social environments. In the case of Hong Kong, during the British colonial rule for over 150 years (1842-1997), Buddhism was largely unaffected due to the government's laissez-faire policy toward local culture and religions. Moreover, due to the relatively stable environment of Hong Kong, it served as a refuge to those who tried to escape from the turmoil in the Mainland. Among the refugees were the monastics who eventually stayed behind and built some of the earliest Buddhist monasteries in Hong Kong.[16] After the brief flourishing of Japanese Buddhism during the Japanese occupation (1941-5), Chinese Buddhism quickly resumed its role in education and charity in the local society. Prior to the founding of the PRC in 1949, Hong Kong saw a major influx of monastics who escaped communism and brought with them the hope to preserve and spread Buddhism in the British colony. New monasteries and Buddhist institutes were built to cater to the thousands of monastics arriving from the north. Although the influx ended by the 1960s and some of the refuge seekers eventually left Hong Kong, they laid an important foundation for the local development of Buddhism which grew rapidly in the following decades. Due to the generally liberal policy of the government, the Hong Kong Buddhists were able to try new ways to develop Buddhism. Starting from the late 1950s, a number of highly active Buddhist youth organizations were founded.[17] In 1960, Shi Xiaoyun [釋曉雲 (遊雲山)] organized the first Buddhist summer camp for the youth.[18] As an attempt to promote Buddhist knowledge in the modern world, the first 'Chinese Buddhist Bible' was published by Luo Shixian (羅時憲) and other lay Buddhists in Hong Kong in 1961.[19] In the same year, the Hong Kong Chinese Buddhist Association proposed that the government make Vesak (the Buddha's Birthday) a public holiday.[20]

In 1969, the Hong Kong Buddhist College (能仁書院) was founded, which was arguably the first modern Chinese Buddhist college.[21] In 1971, inspired by the novitiate programme in Thailand, Ven. Shi Xichen (釋洗塵) organized the first Chinese Mahāyāna novitiate programme.[22] These examples are all heralded as major innovations in Chinese Buddhism – all made possible due to the unique position of Hong Kong, unlike the Mainland or even Taiwan during its early years before martial law was officially lifted in 1987.

In the present study, Hong Kong, thus, serves as a benchmark when compared to Mainland China where traditional culture and religion, including Buddhism, have been subject to various types of reform and restriction.[23] The comparison would further reveal some salient and common characteristics of Buddhist development in contemporary Chinese societies, as well as details on how Buddhism evolves under different circumstances.

As China gradually rises as a world power, the development of various aspects of contemporary Chinese society becomes a topic of global interest. With the number of Chinese Buddhists estimated from anything between 286 to 690 million (Table 11.2), any future development of Chinese Buddhism will have a significant impact on both the Chinese societies as well as the world at large. The growth of Theravāda Buddhism in China in the past decades may be seen as part of this bigger development as a whole.

TABLE 11.2: ESTIMATED NUMBER OF CHINESE BUDDHIST POPULATION IN 2010

Region	Population (millions)[24]	Percentage of Buddhists[25]	Number of Buddhists (millions)
China (PRC)	1,338.1	20.0[26]-50.0	267.6-669.1
Hong Kong (SAR)	7.0	35.0[27]-66.0	2.5-4.2
Taiwan	23.2	23.9[28]-70.4	5.5-16.3
Total	1,368.3	20.0-50.0	276.6-689.6

THERAVĀDA BUDDHISM IN CHINA[29]

Theravāda Buddhism has an indigenous presence in south-western China dating back as early as the seventh century, and its present form is closely connected with Theravāda Buddhism as practised in neighbouring Thailand and Myanmar.[30] Currently, it is an integral part of the ethnic Dai community (傣族) as well as other ethnic minorities,[31] with the number of ordained monks and novices reaching over 10,000,[32] and the indigenous Buddhist population nearly a million.[33] Theravāda Buddhism in contemporary China, despite the social and political turmoil throughout the twentieth century, has retained much of its traditional character, notably the hierarchical structure of the Sangha, as well as the dynamic interaction between the monastics and the laities.[34] In terms of practice, it shares its orthodox character with that of other Theravāda communities in Sri Lanka and Southeast Asia, such as the adherence to Vinaya concerning ordination, fortnightly *poṣadha*-recitation and daily alms-taking, customs which are no longer practised in Chinese Buddhism.[35] Presently, this indigenous form of Theravāda Buddhism in China shows little growth,[36] although its presence is evaluated by some as representing the traditional values of the indigenous culture.[37]

Contemporary Chinese Buddhists came into contact with Theravāda Buddhists from other parts of the world as equals from the end of the nineteenth century when Theravāda Buddhism began to reach a global audience, starting with Anagarika Dharmapala, founder of the Maha Bodhi Society in 1891, who represented 'Southern Buddhism' at the Parliament of Religions in Chicago in 1893, followed, most notably, by G.P. Malalasekera who was the founding president of the World Fellowship of Buddhists in the 1950s. Among the earliest, though little mentioned anecdotes between the Theravāda and Chinese Buddhists during this early period was Dharmapala's visit to the Longhua Temple and his subsequent meeting with Yang Wenhui, the father of the revival of modern Chinese Buddhism in Shanghai in 1893. Dharmapala, pioneer of the Buddhist revival in India, appealed to the Chinese Buddhists to support the cause of the Maha Bodhi Society in protecting Buddhist holy places in India.[38] His effort did not result in any fruitful collaboration as far as the records go, although Yang's, as well as Taixu's later interests in the World Buddhist Movement were possibly influenced by this Theravāda Buddhist.[39] Reciprocal visits between Theravāda and Chinese Buddhists began in the 1920s and lasted throughout the Republican Period.[40] As the prestige of Theravāda Buddhism continued to rise globally, eminent

Chinese Buddhists such as Taixu gradually realized the values and importance of the Pāli Canon and the Theravāda teachings.[41] A batch of five monks, among whom were Ba Zhou (巴宙) and Ye Jun (葉均) were sent to Sri Lanka in 1935 to master the Pāli language and Theravāda teachings.[42] After the founding of the PRC, a small number of Chinese monks continued to further their studies in Theravāda countries, mostly Sri Lanka, and, in most cases, with government support through the BAC.

Although Theravāda Buddhism belongs to the minority within Buddhism in China, it has had a number of noticeable effects on contemporary Chinese Buddhism starting from the 1920s. First, the close and dynamic monastic-laity interaction (僧信互動) in many Theravāda countries inspired the Chinese Buddhists on how 'Humanistic Buddhism' (人間佛教) may be realized. Some Chinese Buddhists came to realize that Theravāda Buddhism, in fact, demonstrated how the Bodhisattva path is realized, while being unjustly labelled as 'Hīnayāna' in the Mahāyāna polemics.[43] Second, the Western concept of 'Original Buddhism' (原始佛教) based on the unadulterated teachings of the historical Buddha as represented in the Pāli Canon continued to be picked up by the more liberal Mahāyāna Buddhists.[44] Lastly, the practice of the short-term novitiate programme and meditation training for the laity was introduced into Mahāyāna Buddhism.[45]

THERAVĀDA BUDDHISM IN CHINA SINCE 1949

Since the founding of the BAC in 1953, Theravāda Buddhism was recognized as a part of Chinese Buddhist heritage and diplomatic contact with Theravāda leaders, notably with the Burmese Sangha, soon began. Up to 1965, the BAC continued to try but failed to play a leading role amongst other fellow national Buddhist associations, mostly the Theravāda.[46] During the civil disruption in the 1960s and the 1970s, Theravāda temples in south-western China and elsewhere were defaced, Buddhist texts and images were burnt, and indigenous Theravāda monks in Sipsongpannā were forced to flee to Southeast Asia or disrobe.[47] Nevertheless, Theravāda Buddhism remains an important and noticeable part of the everyday life in Sipsongpannā and other indigenous communities in China. As Buddhism quickly revived itself across China in the post-Mao era, local BAC offices, too, resumed their local functions in supporting Theravāda Buddhism through education and temple maintenance, as well as liaising between the government and monastic leaders. At the diplomatic level, the BAC also resumed contacts with Theravāda countries with the notable plan of sending Chinese monks to Sri Lanka for studies.

From the 1970s, with the growing interest in Buddhist meditation practices around the world, eminent teachers such as Mahasi Sayadaw of Myanmar, S.N. Goenka also of Myanmar and Ajahn Chah of Thailand, esteemed for their knowledge of meditation, were first introduced to the West. Subsequently, meditation centres of the Theravāda vipassana tradition were established all over the world.

By the 1980s, a much more globalized form of Theravāda Buddhism, often with emphasis on meditation practise in a variety of forms, entered Taiwan and Hong Kong, and subsequently Mainland China. Besides a growing number of Theravāda temples across China, lay as well as non-denominational Theravāda study and meditation centres were established in almost all the major cities there at a rapid rate.

In the following sections, I shall take a closer look at the development of Theravāda Buddhism and its affiliated organizations in Hong Kong and China respectively, in terms of its operation.

HONG KONG[48]

Four Theravāda temples and one Theravāda centre of Thai tradition were founded between the 1980s and 1990s in Hong Kong.[49] These temples are all affiliated with a home temple in Thailand, managed by Thai monks together with support from the locals, located mostly in the rural area (with the exception of the Theravāda centre), and mostly serving the local Thai communities as a place for worship. Currently, some of these temples also run meditation classes for both Buddhist devotees as well as the non-Buddhist public.

From the 1990s, a continuously growing number of vipassana meditation centres were established across the city (Table 11.3). As stipulated by the local laws, these centres operate either as a company

TABLE 11.3: CURRENT THERAVĀDA MEDITATION CENTRES IN HONG KONG

Organization Name	Location	Lineage [original founder]	Date (official)
Dharma Garden (HK) 香港聞思修佛法中心[50]	Dharma Garden (You Tam Mei Village 攸潭尾村)	Sudhamma 淨法比丘 (Burmese) [Pa Auk]	1994
Association of Spiritual Friends of Godwin 葛榮禪修同學會[51]	Lotus Centre 迴瀾 (Tei Tong Tsai 地塘仔)	Godwin (Sri Lankan)	1995 (2001)
Cultural Department of Chilin Nunnery志蓮淨苑[52]	Diamond Hill 鑽石山	Siu Sik Kau 蕭式球 (Chinese) [Godwin (Sri Lankan)]	1996
Theravāda Meditation Society 香港南傳禪修學會[53]	Tsim Sha Tsui 尖沙嘴	Ajahn Samahito 文比丘 (Thai) [Ajahn Chah]	1997 (2001)
Vipassana Meditation Center, Hong Kong 香港內觀靜坐中心[54]	HK Dhamma House (Hang Tau, Sheung Shui 上水坑頭) and other locations	Goenka (Burmese) [U Ba Kin]	1998 (2000)
Hong Kong Insight Meditation Society香港慧觀禪修會[55]	Fa Hong Monastery法航精舍 (Tei Tong Tsai 地塘仔)	Mahasi (Burmese)	2005

or registered society under the Companies Ordinance and Societies Ordinance, respectively. Besides regular meetings such as Sunday meditation or reading groups, these centres run longer meditation programmes as well, which last from a day to a few weeks.

Among the six vipassana centres, two are affiliated to a meditation master belonging to a certain lineage (Thai or Burmese), three with lay Buddhist founders (Goenka from Myanmar, Godwin Samararatne from Sri Lanka and a former local follower of Godwin) and one is non-denominational. In addition, some of the more progressive Chinese Mahāyāna temples have adopted a non-denominational outlook by introducing Theravāda meditation as part of their educational programme.

Classes on vipassana meditation are offered outside the Theravāda or Theravāda meditation centres mentioned above, most notably under the aegis of Mahāyāna temples or organizations. Since 1996, Theravāda meditation classes have been regularly offered by the

Cultural Department of, Chilin Nunnery (志蓮淨苑).[56] At present, Theravāda meditation classes are also held periodically at the Wang Fat Ching She (弘法精舍), originally a Chinese Buddhist institute of Mahāyāna affiliation, now under the direction of a Theravāda monk. Meditation classes with various degrees of Theravāda elements are also offered by most of the major Mahāyāna Buddhist organizations, as well as non-religious organizations interested in the health benefits or therapeutic values of vipassana.[57]

Beside regular religious events, three types of activities characteristic of these newly-founded Theravāda meditation organizations may be identified: (i) general Theravāda Buddhist education, (ii) meditation programme, and (iii) novitiate programme. General education includes both regular Dhamma talks given by the residing monks or delegates of the organization, as well as special lectures by visiting monks. While these talks or lectures are open to the public without a specific target audience, they mostly serve the needs of their members, introducing to them the doctrine of Theravāda Buddhism (often identified as Original Buddhism; 原始佛教), the Pāli language and chanting. As the majority of the members of these organizations have some exposure to Mahāyāna practices, such educational activities are crucial in developing a Theravāda identity in them. As for the meditation programmes and the novitiate programmes, while the format may vary depending on the organizers, they serve the double purpose of nurturing the members as well as recruiting new ones. These programmes may range from regular weekend camps to intensive ten-day programmes with a rigorous schedule under the supervision of either monks or representatives of the organization. As, traditionally, there is no systematic training in meditation open to lay Mahāyāna Buddhists, the teachings of these new vipassana schools, often offered free of charge, appeal to a large proportion of the Chinese population who are already favourable towards Buddhist teachings.

Since 2005, Theravāda Buddhism has been gaining greater exposure in Hong Kong through the novitiate programme, organized for the first time by the Hong Kong Theravāda Meditation Society.[58] The programme was supported by Theravāda monks and nuns from Thailand, Myanmar and Malaysia, who were experienced in organizing such events in their countries. Besides members of the society, members of the public were also welcome. Such novitiate programmes were organized again in 2008 and 2009, with around thirty recruits each time.[59] These programmes offer the participants an opportunity to experience the 'exotic life' of a Theravāda monk with no specific target participants despite the age limit for practical reasons due to the rigorous nature of the programme. This includes waking up early in the morning, long hours of meditation and soliciting alms in the public. As the mode of interaction between the monastics and the laity in Theravāda Buddhism is very different from that of Chinese Theravāda Buddhism, these novitiate programmes also serve to educate the public on how Theravāda Buddhism may operate within the Chinese society, where the former is largely perceived as a foreign religion.

To sum up, almost all of these activities, characteristic of new Theravāda organizations in Hong Kong, have no specific target recruits. While their teachings are distinctly Theravāda, these organizations have mostly adopted a non-denominational outlook and, in some instances, even a non-Buddhist outlook, as in the case of Goenka's Vipassana Centre, attracting a significant number of non-Buddhists and offering them an opportunity to explore the teachings and practices of Theravāda Buddhism, as well as become potential converts.

MAINLAND CHINA

While the Marxist ideology that the Chinese Communist government subscribes to is antithetical to most religious beliefs and practices, religious freedom is recognized by the Chinese constitution (Article 36) on the condition that religious activities take place within authorized places of worship. New Theravāda organizations, such as those that emerged in Hong Kong, are not legally allowed in China unless special permissions are obtained,[60] and Theravāda teachings and practices may thrive only in indigenous Theravāda temples or mainstream Mahāyāna Buddhist ones if some form of cooperation is established.

The majority of Theravāda monasteries and temples are concentrated in the south-western part of China, centring on the Yunnan province. According to a 1997 Chinese government report, there are around 10,000 Theravāda monks and 1,600 temples.[61] The Theravāda temples in Yunnan belong to local monks of Dai ethnicity and have played an important role in the education of local communities. Some of these temples, besides serving the needs of the local community, also have regular contacts with the neighbouring Thai and Myanmar monastic communities despite monitoring by local authorities for fear of infiltration and foreign influences.[62] Outside Yunnan, two Theravāda temples may be found in Guangdong, one in Chaozhou (潮洲) and the other in Jiaoling (蕉嶺), founded with donations of the overseas Chinese in Thailand and Indonesia, respectively.[63]

The most important present development of Theravāda Buddhism in China was, however, connected to neither the indigenous nor overseas orthodox Theravāda monastics. Mainland China experienced a surge of interest in all forms of spiritual and occult practices from the 1980s, subsequent to the policy of liberalization at the time. Despite various setbacks such as the Tian'anmen crackdown in 1989 and the ban of Falungong in 1999, public interest in traditional Chinese and other forms of Buddhist meditation continued to grow. As Theravāda meditation camps started to emerge in Taiwan, Hong Kong and other overseas Chinese communities in Southeast Asia through the 1990s, the Mainland Chinese Buddhists were also inspired to organize such events.

In 1993, the annual 'Lifestyle Chan Summer Camp' (生活禪夏令營) with elements of Theravāda meditation fused with traditional Chan practices, was organized in the Bailin Chan Monastery (柏林禪寺) in Hebei, specifically targetting university students and young professionals.[64] Since then, a dozen similar events have been held across the country.[65] In 2001, the first ten-day Goenka vipassana course was organized, again in the Bailin Chan Monastery, and was possibly the first Theravāda meditation programme open to the Mainland Chinese public.[66] Subsequently, Goenka vipassana courses have been organized regularly in different monasteries across China on a monthly or even weekly basis.[67] The Mainland Chinese response to Theravāda Buddhism, presented largely through vipassana meditation as a form of spirit-purifying practice or individual cultivation, has been overwhelmingly positive.[68] Due to the restrictions imposed upon religious activities in public, however, Theravāda Buddhism cannot gain an independent existence outside the authorized premise provided by the Mahāyāna Buddhists. As a result, some concerns of the Chinese Mahāyāna hardliners have been noted and the public understanding of Theravāda Buddhism remains largely superficial.

Despite restrictions on religious practices imposed by the government, Theravāda Buddhism has thrived in other unique ways, as in the case of Guangdong Pak Au Real Estate Development Limited (廣東柏奧置業有限公司). This company, supported by a local property tycoon, was a publishing house for Theravāda works, mostly promoting the Myanmar meditation master's teachings.

PARADIGMS FOR THE RISE OF THERAVĀDA BUDDHISM IN CHINA

Broadly speaking, the development of Theravāda Buddhism in China follows the trend of growth of Theravāda Buddhism worldwide, as well as in Asia. During the first half of the twentieth century, the natural course of development of Buddhism was very similar for both Mainland China as well as for Hong Kong due to the liberal attitude towards religious affairs of both the Republican and British colonial governments. As international travel became common, mutual exchanges grew naturally. Chinese Buddhists recognized their religion to be in a state of decline and in need of reform, and were eager to learn from their Theravāda co-religionists. However, due to the political unrests of the time, the doctrinal differences between Mahāyāna and Theravāda Buddhism, and possibly the rivalry amongst the two schools in the international arena, the exchanges between Chinese and Theravāda Buddhists bore little fruit then, and the development of Theravāda Buddhism in China did not take place.

Due to the various policies that the Communist regime imposed upon religious affairs, Buddhism in Mainland China took a very different course than it did in a more tolerant and liberal society such as Hong Kong. In contrast to the vibrant post-war development of Chinese Buddhism, the overall poor reception of Theravāda Buddhism points to the fundamental ideological and cultural differences between Theravāda Buddhism and Chinese culture. The former is still considered alien to this day. The development of Theravāda Buddhism in Hong Kong during the past two decades was, however, dynamic, innovative and organic, demonstrating its great willingness to adapt itself to the needs of the people. As a result, Theravāda Buddhism is no longer confined to the traditional temples originally serving the needs of the local immigrant communities. The great variety of Theravāda organizations in Hong Kong and their activities reflect the freedom and openness that Hong Kong offers to its people. These organizations grow independently with often little interaction with the local Buddhists. Their activities are open to the public in general, without a specific agenda targetting a particular segment of society. Theravāda Buddhism appeals to the Hong Kong public mostly due to the vipassana meditation practice which caters to individual spiritual aspirations, rather than its doctrinal views which are not often compatible with the Mahāyāna values that are largely accepted within Chinese culture. For the Chinese public at large that is less informed about doctrinal details, the international reputation of Theravāda Buddhism, as well as the generally favourable view towards Buddhist teachings, has helped to promote the slow but steady growth of Theravāda Buddhism in Hong Kong.

As compared to Hong Kong where Theravāda Buddhism grew in a reasonably natural and organic way, Theravāda Buddhism in Mainland China encountered much greater difficulties since 1949. Sympathizers of Theravāda Buddhism, government officials or Chinese Buddhists, are often motivated by clearly pronounced goals before they promote or become engaged with anything associated with Theravāda Buddhism. First and foremost, the political leaders in China have recognized the diplomatic value of Buddhism and encourage friendly exchanges between the Chinese and the Theravāda Buddhists, resulting in a variety of collaborations trickling down from a higher level, something not conceivable in Hong Kong or most other secular countries. Second, due to the severe limitations imposed upon religious practices in Mainland China, the development of Theravāda Buddhism has been hampered, relying on the sole support of the Mahāyāna Buddhists. Such collaborations reveal how Chinese Buddhists see the promotion of Theravāda meditation as an expedient to further their cause symbiotically in the Chinese Buddhist revival, as demonstrated by the great success of Theravāda-inspired meditation camps held across the country. However, how these efforts will translate into the actual development of Theravāda Buddhism in China is yet to be seen.

At present, Theravāda Buddhism has no opportunity to gain an independent existence in the major cities across China. As a result, it will continue to depend on the favourable support of its Mahāyāna hosts. While indigenous Theravāda Buddhism in south-western China as well as a small but growing number of Theravāda monks of Han ethnicity may change the picture eventually, the predominance of the Chinese Mahāyāna Buddhists is unlikely to be challenged. It is, thus, fair to contend that the overall positioning of Theravāda Buddhism in China has changed very little from a century ago. However, new opportunities such as the global interest in vipassana meditation, the growing awareness of the values of the Pāli Canon and Theravāda teachings, as well as the rapid revival of Buddhism on the Mainland, create a new space for Theravāda Buddhism to grow as a niche and possibly elitist form of Buddhism in China.

BUDDHISM IN CHINA IN THE TWENTY-FIRST CENTURY

As seen above, the development of Theravāda Buddhism in Hong Kong and Mainland China was the result of Buddhist revival both globally and locally. The rise of worldwide interests in Theravāda vipassana meditation was the main factor driving the new development of Theravāda Buddhism in Hong Kong in the form of meditation centres. In the case of Mainland China, interest in Theravāda Buddhism appears to have been expedient against the backdrop of a major religious revival, as Chinese Buddhism recovered its lost ground since the 1980s. Given such rapid growth, Chinese Buddhism remained a major social force in Chinese societies, in particular, Mainland China. The strategic works of the United Front Work Departments reveal how the Chinese government anticipated this demographic trend in the religious landscape of China in the future.

The awkward development of Theravāda Buddhism in Mainland China also suggests certain traits of the reality of the Chinese Buddhist world which are worth taking note of. First of all, the innate Chinese resistance towards Theravāda Buddhism has been strengthened by the restrictive government policy towards religious practices. The lack of a proper platform for religious expression prevents Theravāda and Mahāyāna Buddhists from engaging in meaningful and otherwise mutually beneficial dialogues, which could have been an opportunity for Chinese Buddhists to embrace a wider global Buddhist world-view. This exchange could also have been an opportunity to make the voice of the Chinese Buddhists heard by a global audience, something envisioned and yet to be achieved since the time of Taixu. Furthermore, the overwhelming success of the Theravāda meditation practice within a Mahāyāna setting also indicates a certain deficiency of traditional Chinese Buddhism, which it has failed to address for a long time. The encounter between the two could, thus, be seen as both a threat as well as an opportunity for Chinese Buddhists. As Chinese Buddhism continues to grow, in order to meet the demands of its growing followers, new generations of charismatic Buddhist leaders of high calibre, who are established in their own traditions as well as capable of carrying on meaningful dialogues with others, are expected. Hopefully, such demands will also be met with more sensible and favourable government policies in which the welfare of Buddhists and non-Buddhists alike would be taken into consideration.

NOTES

1. For general studies in English on modern Chinese Buddhism in China up to the 1950s, see Hackmann (1910), Smith (1912), Chan (1953), Chen (1964), Welch (1967, 1968).
2. The majority of authors on contemporary Chinese Buddhism prior to Welch (quoted above) was unequivocally disparaging toward the state of the Chinese Buddhism in the early twentieth century, describing it as 'in a state of hopeless collapse' . See Smith (1912, 108), as 'moral and spiritual decadence' (Chen 1964: 452), and Chinese clergy as 'notoriously ignorant and corrupt' (Chan 1953: 54). Welch, however, challenged the view and argued that Chinese Buddhism was in a variegated state prior to the so-called 'revival'. Welch (1967) 408. Also, Welch (1968): 1-2.
3. After the collapse of the Qing Dynasty, in a movement known as *Miaochan xingxue* (廟產興學), the large amount of land properties owned by temples

and monasteries were under the constant pressure of both the authority and the public to be turned into schools. For a comprehensive treatment, see Huang 2006. For example of the situation in Yunnan, see Wang (2001): 326, 334, 339.

4. Pioneers such as the eminent lay Buddhist Yang Wenhui (楊文會)(1837-1911) made major attempts to revitalize and modernize Chinese Buddhism through the establishment of Buddhist publishing house, Buddhist institutes and Buddhist organizations. The laity movement, as we shall see, though no longer as prominent as it used to be, continues to be one of the major forces shaping the contemporary development of Buddhism in China.
5. Welch (1968): 160-93.
6. Xue Yu (2005).
7. Though the monastics are by definition those who are devoted to a religious life, both historically as well as contemporarily across different parts of Asia, Buddhist monastics have been much involved in local politics, see Harris (1999). In that sense, the collaboration as well as tension between state and religion is not so unique in the case of Chinese Buddhism.
8. Zhao (1993).
9. Mingshan (2003), cited in Ji (2009); Chen and Deng (2000): 56-8.
10. In 1949, Master Juzan (巨贊) in a memorandum pointed out to Mao that Buddhism was atheistic and could be useful in promoting friendship with Asian countries. In 1952, Master Yuanying (圓瑛) participated the First Peace Conference of Asia and Pacific Region held in Beijing, discussing with fellow Buddhist participants the role of Buddhism in peace development. *Xiandai fojiao* 《现代佛教》(1957).
11. Zhao (1953): 4.
12. Public animosity against Buddhism has been noted during the early years of the Republic Era as Buddhism was viewed by some as a backward and corrupted religion, usurping social resources, in particular, land properties (fn. 3). In that sense, the hysteria against Buddhism as part of the 'Four Olds' can be seen as a continuation of this negative tendency. For topics on how Buddhism was affected during and after Cultural Revolution, see Welch (1969), Welch (1972); Strong (1973); Zhao (1993); Wang (2001): 359-63. A large body of memoires in Chinese is beginning to emerge in recent years and scholarly evaluation of these materials is urgently needed.
13. Overmyer (2003): 1-2.
14. Welch (1968); Ji (2009): 8-15.
15. The figures are based on the field and statistical studies of Ji (2009). A 2005 survey by the East China Normal University gave a lower figure of 200 million Buddhists/Taoist/Folk Religion believers, among the 300 million Chinese (31.4 per cent of Chinese population aged over 16) who considered themselves to be 'religious' Wu (2007). For discussion on the general rise

of religiosity in post-Mao China, see Luo (1991): 184-91. The official statistics appear to be much more conservative. According to the official report 'Zhongguo de zongjiao xingyangziyou zhuangkuang'《中国的宗教信仰自由状况》of 1997, Buddhist/Taoists numbered over 70 millions and there are 13,000 monasteries and 200,000 monastics (120,000 Tibetan, 10,000 Theravāda, *c.* 70,000 Chinese). http://www.china.com.cn/ch-book/zongjiao/zongjiao.htm (accessed 2011.11.11). Some scholars have suggested even greater figures (1999) such as 30-50 per cent and population of 372.75-621.25 million. See Smith (2005): 9-10.

16. For a comprehensive discussion of the history of Buddhism in Hong Kong, see Yongming (1993), Deng (2008.) One of the important differences between Buddhism in Hong Kong and that of the Mainland is that Buddhist monasteries in Hong Kong prior to the 1920s followed mostly the Chan tradition and were practically isolated from the society, with little interaction with the world at large, unlike in some of the Mainland cities where major temples are found within the city. The first lay Buddhist organization found in 1916 and subsequent development of various Buddhist societies, followed the trend in Mainland China, Deng (2008): 41-4, 55.
17. Deng (2008): 121-2.
18. *Yuanquan* (原泉) 46, *Buddhist in Hong Kong* (香港佛教) 1963(40) – both quoted in Deng (2008): 122-3.
19. Deng (2008): 129. Unfortunately, the work *The Selected Buddhist Scriptures* (佛經選要) remained poorly circulated.
20. This was realized eventually in 1999, two years after the handover of Hong Kong to PRC. Deng (2008): 109.
21. Deng (2008): 155.
22. The one-week programme was organized in Wang Fat Ching She (弘法精舍) with 13 participants in total (*Neiming* (内明) 1972(8): 53, quoted in Deng (2008): 116).
23. While the 1997 Government Report on religious freedom (see fn. 1) was correct in pointing out the progress of of the implementation of the policies on religious freedom since the 'reform and opening-up policy' (改革開放政策) of 1978, legally speaking religious practices are categorically confined within authorized places of worship. Religions have no access to the public including the media. On the other hand, as Zhi 2009 pointed out, the development of internet in China since the 1990s has largely changed the picture.
24. '2010 World Population Data Sheet'. Population Reference Bureau, Washington D.C.
25. Estimated figures from Patrick Johnston's *Operation World 1993* with exceptions highlighted individually. Quoted in Smith (2005): 8-10, with an insightful discussion on the definition of 'Buddhist' as compared to 'Christian'.

26. Ji (2009): 8.
27. 'International Religious Freedom Report 2003'. Figure for overall number of people with some form of religious practice excluding Christians and Muslims. http://www.state.gov/g/drl/rls/irf/2003/23826.htm
28. 'International Religious Freedom Report 2003'. http://www.state.gov/g/drl/rls/irf/2003/23825.htm.
29. Major academic studies and survey on Theravāda Buddhism in China, in particular in Sipsongpannā have been made by scholars in China. See Yang 1984[1958], Li (1983), Yang (1994), Wang (2001), Han and Dong (2004). For Thailand and Japan, see Tanabe (1983), Hayashi (2002), and the West, see Davis (1999), Borchert (2006). As pointed out by Borchert (2006: 4 fn.5), the Chinese studies have the tendency of seeing Theravāda Buddhism as a distinguishing feature of the Dai ethnicity; the Thai studies tend to see the form of Buddhism practised in Sipsonpgpannā as a degraded from of Theravāda Buddhism practised in Thailand.
30. Wang (2001): 388. It has been suggested that Theravāda Buddhism was introduced by Siamese monks to the then Nanzhao Kingdom (now south-western China including Yunnan and neighbouring areas) during the seventh century. Theravāda Buddhism was established there probably during the time of Dali Kingdom in the early part of the second millennium, Duan (1994): 202. According to some scholars, however, it was stated in a record dated in 1396 that there was no Buddhist practices in Yunnan and the present form of Theravāda Buddhism in Sipsongpannā (西雙版納) was introduced some time between twelfth and fourteenth century, Liu (1993): 89ff; Wang (2001): 389ff. The history of Mahāyāna Buddhism in Sichuan, however, is much earlier, dating possibly to early second century, although the exact form of Buddhism and the route of transmission cannot not ascertained, Ren (1981): 187. For an overview, see Li (1983); Dao (1985); Li and Wu (1994). For the connection between Sipsongpannā and Dehong (德宏) with Thai and Burmese Buddhism respectively, see Wang (2001): 391ff.
31. Li (1983), Yang (1994), Tan (2005).
32. The figure is taken from the government report of 1997 (see fn. 8 above). In Sipsongpannā alone, according to Borchert's field study in 2002, there were over 600 monks and perhaps 6500 novices in over 550 temples (Borchert 2006: 76). As it is customary in Southeast Asia, most boys disrobe before or soon after becoming monks.
33. Li and Wu (1994): 4; Wang (2001): 368. Some scholars, however, argue that the official figure made for example, the assumption that all Dai people believe in Buddhism, a statement that is no longer true after the Cultural Revolution as reflected by the decreasing number of monastics as a percentage of population, Borchert (2006): 15.

34. While the traditional hierarchical organization of Theravāda monasteries was nominally demolished after 1949, the original system was not replaced as in the case of Chinese and Tibetan monasteries, Li and Wu (1994): 6-7. For a recent assessment of the Theravāda Buddhism in Yunnan, see Dao (1985); Liu (1993): 256-70; Li and Wu (1994): 4-9; Zheng (2011).
35. For differences of contemporary Theravāda and Chinese Mahāyāna practices and how the former had affected the latter, see Welch (1967): 30, 110, 112-14, 207-8, 247, 300-1, 328, 385. Currently, some of the Chinese Theravāda practices such as alms-taking are under pressure of the authority to give up and incoming-generating activities for 'self-sustenance' such as tourism are encouraged, see Li and Wu (1994): 9. According to some, the Theravāda practices in Sipsongpannā are much laxer than those in countries such as Thailand, Borchert (2006): 72 fn.33).
36. The number of monastics in Sipsongpannā stays roughly between 5000-7000 from 1950 up to 1990 with the exception of the 1960s-70s of which statistics are not available (691 in 1981), see Tan (2005): 84. For the problem of increasing number of unmanaged Theravāda temples, see Huang et al. (2006): 117.
37. A number of Western studies such as Evans (2000) and Borchert (2006): 220 have the tendency to attribute the erosion or corruption of traditional indigenous culture solely to the materialistic, atheist Chinese 'colonizers' without taking into full account of the effects of globalization, urbanization, and the economic reality – all the malaise of modernity. To be fair, the problems the indigenous Theravāda culture faces in China are not unlike those other indigenous cultures encounter around the world.
38. Welch (1968): 6.
39. Welch (1968): 180. According to a certain account, however, Yang gave Dharmapāla his 'enthusiastic support', Chen and Deng (2000): 374.
40. The earliest Chinese monk to study in Sri Lanka in modern times was possibly the monk Wanhui who visited Sri Lanka to study Theravāda Buddhism in 1924 (*Eastern Buddhist* 3.3: 274). Later the lay Buddhist Wong Mow-lam (黃茂林) was sent to Sri Lanka by Pure Karma Society of Shanghai to promote dialogue with Theravāda Buddhists. Wong was the editor of an English magazine titled *The Chinese Buddhist* which lasted only a few years before Wong's untimely death during his stay in Sri Lanka. For other contacts during this period between overseas Theravāda and Chinese Buddhists, see Welch (1968): 180-3.
41. However, unlike in Japan where the translation of Pāli Canon systematically began in the 1930s (Beginning with the publication of *Vinaya-piṭaka* and the *Nikāyas* by Takakusu Junichirō and others in 1935/6, continuing up to volume 65 with texts such as the Asoka Edicts published in 1941), the first major Theravāda text was translated into Chinese only in the 1950s, reflecting

the initial lukewarm reception of Theravāda Buddhism amongst Chinese intellectuals, whose attitude toward Theravāda Buddhism was at best 'ambivalent', Welch (1968): 182.

42. Chen and Deng (2000): 374-6.
43. This is the remarkable position taken by Taixu and subsequently, Theravāda Buddhism has been described by most Chinese Buddhists and Buddhist scholars as 'Buddhism of Southern Transmission' (南傳佛教), despite it is still occasionally labelled as the 'Small Vehicle' (小乘).
44. The representation of the Pāli Canon of the Theravāda tradition as the pristine teaching of the historical Buddha was largely the work of Rhys Davids and other textual scholars who, as pointed out by some post-colonial critics, had the tendency of representing 'the complex as the simple' and 'the commingled as the pure' and thus the vernacular and contemporary aspects of Theravāda Buddhism were devalued and dismissed, Lopez (1995): 13 and Hallisey (1995): 31ff. This trend has been most notable in Taiwan, Chen and Deng (2000): 376.
45. Thus, this Theravāda custom was the inspiration for the novitiate programme organized for the first time by Hong Kong Mahāyāna Buddhists in 1971 as we have seen. See also Chen and Deng (2000): 70, 376.
46. Chinese Buddhist leaders were eager to show the diplomatic value of Buddhism but failed repeatedly, and demonstrated their failure by the boycott of 7th Conference of World Fellowship of Buddhist, Welch (1969): 128. Theravāda Buddhism was in a way an indomitable rival to the Chinese Buddhists who tried to make their voice heard amongst fellow Buddhists as well as in the world.
47. Davis (1999): 10.
48. For detailed discussion, see Mak (2012).
49. (i) Wat Buddhadhamaram in Hung Shui Kiu, Yuen Long; (ii) Wat Buddhadhamaram affiliate in Pak Nai, Yuen Long; (iii) Wat Dhammaram (大棠寺) in Tai Long, Yuen Long; (iv) Wat Mekadhamwanaram (aka Wat Tai Wo (太和寺) in Tai Po. The Dharmakaya Centre, located in an apartment of a building in Wanchai may be seen as an hybrid form of a temple in a place where the construction of a temple is impossible.
50. http://www.dhammagarden.org
51. http://www.godwin.org.hk/
52. http://www.chilin.edu.hk/edu/work_professor_detail.asp?id=17
53. http://www.hktheravada.org
54. http://www.hk.dhamma.org
55. http://hkims.org
56. http://www.chilin.edu.hk/edu/work_professor_detail.asp?id=17
57. Theravāda or Theravāda-inspired types of meditation classes are offered in Hong Kong most notably at the Hong Kong branch of the Dharma Drum

Hill founded by the Taiwanese monk Shengyan (聖嚴) and the Plum Village Foundation founded by the Vietnamese monk Thich Nhat Hanh (釋一行). Currently, vipassanā as part of the MBSR (Mindfulness-based Stress Reduction) is promoted by various organizations in Hong Kong such as Wang Fat Ching She.

58. As early as the 1970s, similar programmes for Mahāyāna laities of a somewhat smaller scale were organized in Wang Fat Ching She, organized by local Buddhists, although no such programs are heard of in the recent decades.
59. http://www.hktheravada.org/down/2005%201st%20NC%20Magazine%203pg.pdf. Accessed 2011.11.11.
60. This is technically possible once permissions from BAC and local officials are obtained. However, to my knowledge, no such new, foreign Theravāda organizations have yet established themselves legally in China in this way.
61. See note 2. According to Foyuan.com, as of 1996, there 1702 Theravāda temples in Yunnan (http://www.foyuan.net/article-101162-1.html).
62. Lin (1997). According to Huang et al. (2006), so far Theravāda Buddhism in Yunnan has not been considered by the government as a potential threat to national security as Tibetan Buddhism does.
63. See Bhikkhu Metta's (2007) *Guide*. The first one is currently under the care of Kaiyuansi while the other is under the jurisdiction of the local government.
64. According to Wang et al. (2010), participants of the 'Lifestyle Chan Summer Camp' from 1993-2010 have numbered over 6000. Wang et al. further remarked that beside the age requirement of 18-30, the camp also had gradually increased its demand on the participants' education background, from high school to now university undergraduate, Wang et al. (2010): 23.
65. The summer camp organized by Bailin Monastery has been considered by many as the pioneer of such like events held across the Mainland since then, numbering over twenty annually in both 2005 and 2010 (Wang et al. 2010: 25). Bao 2008 named five of the most well known ones: 1. 'Huangmei Chan Culture Summer Camp' (黄梅禪文化夏令營) in Hubei (湖北); 2. 'Journey of Merit and Wisdom' (福慧之旅) at Guanghua Monastery (廣化寺) in Fujian (福建); 3. 'Lushan Chan Tea Gathering' (廬山禪茶會) at Nuonatayuan (諾那塔院) in Jiangxi (江西); 4. 'Buddhist Summer Camp' (佛子夏令營) at Mount Zhongnan (終南山) in Shaanxi (陝西); 5. 'Buddhist Studies Camp' (佛學營) of Qixia Monastery (棲霞寺) in Nanjing (南京).
66. According to Dr. Bao Shengyong, there have been earlier exchange between Theravāda and Chinese Buddhists including informal organization of Theravāda meditation courses, details of which are yet to be documented (personal communication).
67. Officially according to *zhongguo neiguan wang* (中国内观网) (http://www.vipassana.org.cn/vipassana-schedule.htm), only three temples were listed, namely 1. Nanchan Monastery in Changding, Fujian, 2. Qianfota Monastery in Meizhou, Guangdong, and 3. Huasheng Monastery in Shenyang, Liaoling.

68. Though no statistic is currently available, vipassana meditation and the study of Pāli is largely welcome in Chinese temples though it appears that the majority of Chinese Buddhist monks are opposed to the idea of having Theravāda monks preaching in their temples. A rather exceptional case would be Venerable Yanzhen (衍真) who organized regularly Theravāda meditation training with a Theravāda monk at Baofeng Chan Monastery (宝峰禅寺) in Jiangxi. Such situation is in contrast to Tibetan Buddhism, where Tibetan Buddhist 'programs' targeting students and young professionals are held in private homes or offices rather than temple grounds. For the situation of these Tibetan Buddhist 'programs' and their responses, see Mak (2007).

BIBLIOGRAPHY

Metta, Bhikkhu. *A Guide to Buddhist Monasteries and Meditation Centers in Asia.* Last modified June 2007. Accessed on 26 October 2011. http://www.tt034.org.tw/newrain/books/asia/asia.htm#Hongkong 香港.

Bao Shengyong 包胜勇. 2008. '世俗化抑或大众化：宗教如何应对现代性——. 关于河北柏林禅寺的个案分析.'《中国民族宗教网》*Zhongguo Minzu zongjiao wang.* http://www.mzb.com.cn/html/folder/53.htm=. Assessed on 1 October 2011.

Borchert, Thomas Adams. 2006. 'Educating Monks: Buddhism, Politics and Freedom of Religion on China's Southwest Border'. PhD thesis, University of Chicago.

Chan, Wing-tsit. 1953. *Religious Trends in Modern China.* New York: Columbia University Press.

Chen Bing 陈兵 and Deng Zimei 邓子美. 2000. *Ershi shiji zhongguo fojiao* 二十世纪中国佛教. 北京:民族出版社.

Ch'en, Kenneth. 1964. *Buddhism in China: A Historical Survey.* Princeton, NJ: Princeton University Press.

Dao Shuren 刀述人. 1985. '南传上座部佛教在云南',《法音》*Dharmaghosa* 1985(1): 16-25.

Davis, Sara L.M. 1999. 'Singers of Sipsongpanna: Folklore and Authenticity in Contemporary China'. Ph.D. dissertation, University of Pennsylvania.

Deng Jiazhou 鄧家宙. 2008.《二十世紀之香港佛教》*Ershi shiji zhi xiaogang fojiao.* 香港: 香港史學會.

Duan Yuming 段玉明. 1994. '南传佛教人滇考'.《佛学研究》*Foxue yanjiu* 201-5.

Evans, Grant. 2000. 'Transformation of Jing Hong, Xishuangbanna, PRC', in Grant Evans, Christopher Hutton and Kuah Khun Eng (eds.), *Where China Meets Southeast Asia.* Singapore: Institute of Southeast Asian Studies.

Hackmann, Heinrich Friedrich. 1910. *Buddhism as a Religion: Its Historical Development and its Present Conditions.* London: W.C. Probsthain & Co.

Hallisey, Charles. 1995. 'Roads Taken and Not Taken in the Study of Theravāda Buddhism', in Donald Lopez (ed.), *Curators of the Buddha: The Study of Buddhism Under Colonialism*. Chicago: University of Chicago Press.

Han Lixia 韩丽霞 and Dong Yun 董允. 2004.《云南佛教》*Yunnan fojiao*. 北京市: 宗教文化出版社.

Harris, Ian. (ed.). 1999. *Buddhism and Politics in Twentieth-Century Asia*. London: New York: Pinter.

Huang Yunxi, 黃運喜. 2006.《中國佛教近代法難研究》*Zhongguo fojiao jindai fanan yanjiu*. 台北: 法界出版社.

Huang, Zeshan 黄泽珊 et al. 2006. '云南宗教问题发展动向及对策研究'.《云南警官学院学报》*Journal of Yunnan Police Officer Academy* 68: 114-19.

Ji Zhe 汲喆. 2009. '复兴三十年：当代中国佛教的基本数据'.《佛教观察》*Fojiao guancha*, vol. 5: 8-15.

Li Hongxue 李弘学 & Wu Zhengxing 吴正兴. 1994. '云南上座部佛教考察报告'.《法音》*Dharmaghosa* (7): 4-9.

Li Zhaolun 李昭伦 (ed.). 1983. 傣族社會歷史調查. 西雙版納 *Daizu shehui lishi diaocha - Xishuangbanna*, vols. 1-3. 昆明市: 雲南民族出版社.

Lin Xin 林欣. 1997.《西雙版納佛教考察報告》*Xishuangbanna fojiao kaocha baogao*. http://ttbc.no-ip.org. Accessed on 27 October 2011.

Lopez, Donald, ed. 1995. *Curators of the Buddha: The Study of Buddhism under Colonialism*. Chicago: University of Chicago Press.

Luo Zhufeng (ed.). 1911. *Religion under Socialism in China*, tr. Donald E. MacInnis and Zheng Xi'an. Armonk, NY: M.E. Sharpe.

Mak, Bill M. 2006. 'Ehi Passiko in the Pluralistic World: Challenges and Opportunities of Buddhism as a World Religion in the 21st Century', in《和谐世界从心开始：首届世界佛教论坛文集·征文获奖卷》. 北京: 宗教文化出版社, 333-43.

———. 2007. 'Synergy or Collision: University Students Encountering Buddhism in China', *Bodhi Journal* (3). http://www.buddhistdoor.com/journal/issue003-03.html. Accessed on 27 October 2011.

———. 2012. 'Theravāda Teachings and Meditation in Hong Kong', *International Journal for the Study of Humanistic Buddhism*. Issue 3. 19-38.

McCarthy, Susan. 2004. 'Gods of Wealth, Temples of Prosperity: Party-State Participation in the Minority Cultural Revival', *China: An International Journal* 2 (1-Mar): 28-52.

Mingshan 茗山. 2003. '变革·厄难·复兴：中国佛教三十年', in *Mingshan wenxuan*《茗山文选》. 南京：金陵刻经处.

Overmyer, Daniel L., ed. 2003. *Religion in China Today*. Cambridge: Cambridge University Press.

Ren Jiyu (ed.) 任继愈主编. 1981.《中国佛教史》*Zhongguo fojiao shi*. 北京：中国社会科学出版社.

Smith, Alex. 2005. 'Counting the Buddhist World Fairly', in David Lim and Steven Spaulding (eds.), *Sharing Jesus holistically with the Buddhist World*. Pasadena, Calif.: William Carey Library, pp. 1-10.

Smith, Arthur Henderson. 1912. *The Uplift of China*. New York: Young People's Missionary Movement.

Strong, Sarah and John Strong. 1973. 'A Post-Cultural Revolution Look at Buddhism', *The China Quarterly* 54: 321-30.

Tan Leshan 谭乐山. 1915 南传上座部佛教与傣族村社经济: 对中国西南西双版纳的比较研究 Nan chuan shang zuo bu fo jiao yu Dai zu cun she jing ji: dui Zhongguo xi nan Xishuangbanna de bi jiao yan jiu. Translated by Zhao Xiaoniu 赵效牛 from 'Theravāda Buddhism and Village Economy: A Comparative Study in Sipsongpanna of Southwest China'. Ph.D. dissertation, Cornell University. 昆明: 云南大学出版社

Tanabe, Shigeru. 1988. 'Spirits and Ideological Discourse: The Tai Lü guardian cults in Yunnan', *Sojourn: Journal of Social Issues in Southeast Asia* 3(1): 1-25.

Wang Haitao 王海涛. 2001.《云南佛教史》*Yunnan fo jiao shi*. 昆明: 云南美术出版社.

Wang Minghao 汪明浩 et al. 2001. '宗教在当代社会传播中的内在机理探析 – 柏林禅寺生活禅夏令营与时尚传播个案考察'.《北京青年政治学院学报》*Journal of Beijing Youth Politics College*, vol. 19, no. 4: 17-15.

Welch, Holmes. 1967. *The Practice of Chinese Buddhism*. Cambridge: Harvard University Press, 1967.

———. 1968. *The Buddhist Revival in China*. Cambridge: Harvard University Press.

———. 1969. 'Buddhism since the Cultural Revolution', *The China Quarterly* 40: 127-36.

———. 1972. *Buddhism Under Mao*. Cambridge, Mass.: Harvard University Press.

Wijesekera, Oliver Hector Alwis. 1994. 'Theravāda Buddhism Under Modern Cultures', in M.H.F. Jayasuriya (ed.), *Buddhist and Vedic Studies: A Miscellany*. Delhi: Motilal Banarsidass.

Wu Jiao. 2007. 'Religious Believers Thrice the Estimate', *China Daily*. Updated 7 February 2007. http://www.chinadaily.com.cn/china/2007-02/07/content_802994.htm. Accessed on 27 February 2012.

Yang Xuezheng 杨学政 (ed.). 1994. 云南宗教知识百问 *Yunnan zongjiao zhishi baiwen*. 昆明: 云南人民出版社.

Yang Zhimin 杨志敏. 1984 [1958].《西双版纳佛教调查》'Xishuangbanna Fojiao Diaocha', in《西双版纳傣族社会综合调查》*Xishuangbanna daizu shehui zonghe diaocha*, vol. 1. 148-51. 昆明:云南民族出版社.

Yongming 永明. 1993.《香港佛教與佛寺》*Xianggang fojiao yu fosi*. 香港: 大嶼山寶蓮禪寺.

Zhao Puchu 赵朴初. 1953. '关于中国佛教协会发起经过和筹备工作的报告'. 《现代佛教》*Xiandai fojiao* 6: 1-4.
———. 1993. 《中国佛教协会四十年》*Zhongguo fojiao xiehui sishi-nian*. http://www.foxue.org/article/200212/article_17452.html. Accessed on 27 February 2012.
Zhang Xueying. 2009. 'Buddhism in China', *China Today*. 9 November 2009. http://www.chinatoday.com.cn/ctenglish/se/txt/2009-06/19/content_203310.htm. Accessed on 11 November 2011.
Zheng Xiaoyun 郑筱筠. 2011. '试论中国南传佛教的宗教管理模式'. 《中国宗教》*China Religion* 2011(1): 36-9.
Zhou Bokan [Chou Po-kan] 周伯戡. 1990. '早期中國佛教的大乘小乘觀'. 《文史哲學報》38: 235-71.

CHAPTER 12

Sustainable Development and Karma Logistics

The Moral Discourse of Reformed Buddhism and Capital-linked Business Professionals in Shanghai

WEISHAN HUANG

WHEN SISTER YUFEN CHIOU first showed me the Bodhisattva statue hidden behind the bookshelves, I was surprised by the sophisticated design of this secret closet. 'The first layer of bookshelves only opens when Tzu Chi members gather in the room. It remains closed on a daily basis in case policemen inspect our office spaces unexpectedly,' she said.

In the early 1990s, Shanghai in China was a dark city after 6 p.m. 'They locked the shampoo in shelves as if they were treasures in the shops. You could not find anything to eat after 6:00 p.m. All of the shops belonged to the State,' said Sister Chiou. The State of China not only had overwhelming control of the economic sectors in the 1990s but also penetrated people's private lives. As a pioneer in bringing the Buddhist Tzu Chi to Foundation Shanghai, Sister Chiou has faced harassment, interrogation and short periods of detention by the government.

Like many Taiwanese merchants, Chiou's decision to transplant her manufacturing company from Taiwan to China was not an easy one. They felt forced to relocate their investment because the cost of labour was rising every year. Chiou was losing the capacity to be competitive in the Information and Technology (IT) market. Her son and daughter were old enough, so she left her family and came to Shanghai. In the hope that China was a promised new land for business, she was also determined to bring her faith with her. 'I wanted to be the first seed in Shanghai. They said it was harder for a woman to set up the business in Shanghai. I proved they were wrong.' Tzu Chi had sent missions to China since 1991 when the Huadong (East China) flood took place. The movement also started charity missions to rural areas during this period.

Taiwan has served as an important migrant-sending country contributing to the religious revival in China since its economic liberalization. While many religious practices went underground or disappeared due to the political repression in China during the Cultural Revolution in the decade beginning 1966, Buddhism, Christianity and Daoism have been developing vigorously in Taiwan during the last sixty years, eventually being exported back to China after the opening of its markets. A significant amount of literature has focused on the economic aspects of Taiwanese immigrants/merchants in China, yet the reproduction of Taiwanese culture in China remains an understudied subject. My research examines relations between the Buddhist religious discourse and economic activities in companies, including one of the top exchange listed firms in China. I seek to challenge the old stereotype that Buddhism is anti-commercial and find how it can co-exist with 'development' and the spirit of capitalism in modern China by using the case study of Tzu Chi.

Shanghai has been experiencing large scale social changes since the late 1980s. This chapter will offer an ethnography of transnational Buddhist business people in a highly censorial and increasingly pluralistic city.[1] It is critical to understand how socio-structural challenges, such as immigration and entrepreneurialism, affect faith-based groups within the frame of urban aspirations. Due to governmental restrictions in province-level municipalities, religious practices are invisible in public spaces but they are reviving in private spaces in major Chinese cities.

CAPITAL-LINKED MIGRANTS OR TRAITORS

Two scholars' works are important in defining the sociological meanings of 'capital-linked migrants'. In Sassen's *The Mobility of Labor and Capital*,[2] she links the transnational flow of people and capital. Sassen argues that capital mobility created new conditions for the mobility of labour in which foreign investments provided both cultural and economic contacts between investors and local workers. In Yen-Fen's article, 'The Mobility of Entrepreneurs and Capital', she focuses on the relation between the mobility of capital and that of entrepreneurs.[3]

The world economy has been increasingly characterized by the large-scale transnational mobility of commodities, capital and people. Tseng studies two types of capital-linked Taiwanese immigrant entrepreneurships. One is of capital owners who have been directly recruited by business migration programmes in countries such as Canada, Australia and the United States of America. The other kind involves migrants of the entrepreneurial/managerial class who are attracted to increasing foreign direct investment. [4] While most studies concerning international investment focus on the movement of capital or trade flows, Tseng looks at the Taiwanese migration to Western countries, helping us understand categories who migrate with capital. Taiwanese migration increased by more than four times between 1990 and 1996, predominately by the middle and upper-middle classes, 'pushed . . . by political uncertainty and social dislocations caused by rapid industrialization and urbanization, and pulled by the global economy'.[5] Since the mid-1980s, Taiwan has become a significant capital-exporting country. But what Taiwanese migrants bring with them when they migrate is more than just capital.

Most of the Taiwanese in Shanghai are economic migrants who are seeking better economic opportunities. According to Portes, transnational entrepreneurs are different from immigrant entrepreneurs since the latter are those who 'settled abroad and became progressively integrated into local ways', while the farmer cultivate their networks across space and travel 'back and forth in pursuit of their commercial ventures'.[6]

In China, after the post-4 June 1989 period, the state began to encourage foreign direct investment, which served as a driving force that occasioned the eventual demise of China's state-owned enterprises.[7] Foreign capital, technology, and management knowledge and techniques from the four East Asian newly-industrialized countries

(Taiwan, Hong Kong, Singapore and South Korea) flowed into Shenzhen in China, transforming it into a free-trade zone for multinational factories during the early years of economic reform. A few years later, the government expanded four 'special economic zones', and then fourteen cities, all located along the eastern coast, for joint ventures between foreign companies and the Chinese government. In 1999, the prohibition on foreign-private economic cooperation in China was lifted. By 2000, the government stipulated required quotas of foreign investment. Foreign companies gained permission to establish in China wholly foreign-owned enterprises without joint Chinese state ownership.[8]

There are numerous studies that contribute to the understanding of Taiwanese migrants in China by positioning them in the economic chain of the global division of labour. Scholars often characterize those entrepreneurs who moved their businesses from Taiwan to China as adopting cost-reduction, innovation and quality enhancement strategies. In Lin Man-Houng's study, he found that overseas Chinese merchants tended to maintain their multiple nationalities before 1935 as a means of seeking economic opportunity and reducing commercial risk. The issue of multiple nationalities is an interesting question that should be explored in the case of the overseas Chinese in Shanghai as well.[9] Overall, we have learned that migrant networks and organizations emerged as development agents. In the institutional dimension, agents such as hometown associations, networks of merchant associations, and epistemic networks have emerged as collective actors.[10] Yet in the current round of the migration–development nexus, the manner in which migrant networks interact with local adherents as regards the flow of knowledge and religious ideas has still not been studied.

TRANSNATIONAL NETWORKS

The Buddhist Tzu Chi Foundation (Tzu Chi) is an international Buddhist relief organization founded in 1966 and based in Hualien, Taiwan, with millions of members in Taiwan and overseas. Tzu Chi is indeed the largest social group in Taiwan today, controlling $120 billion Taiwanese dollars in funds, with more than 300 offices in forty countries, four supporting missions and 300,000 certified volunteers worldwide.[11] The founder, Cheng Yen, was initiated as a Buddhist nun in 1963 and was influenced by her master, Yin Shun, who taught his followers to 'be committed to Buddhism and to all living beings'.[12] Unusual among Buddhist organizations, Tzu Chi defines social service rather than religion as its primary goal, a change focusing on social services that dates back to the late 1960s. This reform is truly Cheng Yen's innovation.

Hualien is a sacred land for Tzu Chi members. Every May, the majority of Tzu Chi commissioners in Shanghai, like other Tzu Chi commissioners worldwide, fly back to Hualien to attend the Global Tzu Chi Day on Mother's Day and to participate in a variety of activities during the following week.[13] The Hualien-based mother temple serves as the high commander of its global operation. The flow of religious ideas, practices, publications, and personal and financial resources has established linkages between communities in different countries. Branch directors are required to send reports to the headquarters and to attend board meetings held annually at it. The mother temple exerts direct control over the Shanghai branch and the director and the commissioners operate the branch as they see fit.

Transnational Taiwanese migration is the main factor contributing to the movement's global development.[14] By examining the history of the establishment of Tzu Chi centres in other cities, I have found that the local founders, including its major supporters in Shanghai, drawn from the local immigrants, are largely responsible for the success of the outreach programmes and for the establishment of new missions. I constantly heard Tzu Chi commissioners mention the names of members and leaders in different cities. They knew each other from attending the same events and meetings in Taiwan, as well as from their interaction in cyberspace.

Tzu Chi has 33,389 trained and certified commissioners, and 20,388 Faith Corps members globally.[15] Among them, 29,766 commissioners and 19,064 Faith Corps members are in Taiwan. 3,623 commissioners and 1,324 Faith Corps members are overseas members. Commissioners and Faith Corps members are lay leaders, who are the backbone of the global missions. They require at least two years of training and are certified by the Religious Bureau at the headquarters. Among all the overseas branches, the United States has the most commissioners.[16] Therefore, the study of Tzu Chi USA[17] has significant value. In China, a single branch has 308 commissioners and 79 Faith Corps members on average, making the development of Tzu Chi in the country worth a further careful study. According to my field observations in Hualien in 2010, the process of membership indigenization in China, Thailand, Malaysia, Indonesia, the Philippines and South Africa is significantly different from the practice in the United States.

LAY LEADERSHIP IN CHINA

There are no 'executive directors' in China or Shanghai, which is very different from Tzu Chi's operation in other countries. Tzu Chi Shanghai[18] is directly under the supervision of Master Cheng Yen. During interviews with commissioners in China, I found that they often refer to the significance of the headquarters in Hualien City, Taiwan, and their own experiences of Hualien, which represented a turning point in devoting their life to volunteerism. This is very similar to the stories of commissioners in the United States. Still Thought Abode in Hualien City, the parent and central temple of Tzu Chi's global kingdom, is the Tzuchian sacred place for commissioners and volunteers. Hualien City not only represents the religious sacred pure land for the Tzu Chi people but also functions as a command centre for global missionary activity. Master Cheng Yen is the senior most person in charge of the Taiwan Buddhist Tzu Chi Foundation. The master's charismatic leadership and her representation of a spiritual mother have drawn commissioners to follow her cultivation steps.

Among all the commissioners in Shanghai, Sister Yufen Chiou is the senior lay leader since she is the first person who brought Tzu Chi into Shanghai. Tzu Chi China's headquarters is based in Suzhou. Sister Chiou has travelled between Shanghai and Suzhou every two days for years. Commissioners in Shanghai collectively take responsibility in organizing nationwide activities in China.

All over the world, Tzu Chi's members are mostly women. In addition, we must not forget the fact that Tzu Chi is led by Master

Cheng Yen, who is a nun, and that her teachings are central to the Tzu Chi community – something quite different from other well-known Buddhist organizations of Taiwan, such as Fo-Guan-Shan (Buddha Light International) and Fa-Gu-Shan (Chan Meditation in New York), which are led by male monks. Since most commissioners are female, therefore, we find that it is more common that women form the majority of organizational leaders at both administrative and decision-making levels. According to my observations at the Annual Tzu Chi USA Executive Directors' meeting in Taiwan in June 2008, more than 50 per cent of the regional and branch executive directors were female. What is different in Shanghai is that the heads of companies of Taiwan entrepreneurs provide a space for Tzu Chi's missions and they will usually be named the persons in charge of the operations of a certain district. They are usually the husbands while their wives, who are usually the vice-presidents of companies, are mostly full-time volunteers for Tzu Chi activities. With husbands devoting more time to running companies and wives focusing on charitable works, the division of economic activities and non-profit activities seems to fall along traditional gender lines. Yet the unconventional part of the story is that the husbands are the people who have to implement Tzu Chi teaching into their daily business operations. As for the wives, who might seem to spend more time on non-economic events, they gain actual leadership by planning and leading events, and most of the time, decide Tzu Chi's development in this growing 'alternate civilities'[19] in China.

THE STRUCTURAL RESTRAINT ON TZU CHI'S OPERATION

The post-Mao government in China has permitted limited freedom of religious belief and behaviour, which is subject to legal and regulatory restrictions. From 1979, a limited number of Protestant and Catholic churches, Buddhist and Daoist temples, and Islamic mosques have reopened for religious services.[20]

In 1982, religious toleration was formally reinstated. The basic viewpoint on toleration and the policy on religious affairs during the socialist period were documented in 'Document No. 19th'. It grants legal existence to Buddhism, Daoism, Islam, Protestantism and Catholicism under the government-sanctioned 'Patriotic' associations, but not to any group outside these five religious associations nor to other religions.[21] The post-Mao regime adopted a more tolerant perspective on religion. 'As a component of a new approach to build regime legitimacy, the government accepted a trade-off of broader social and economic autonomy in exchange for continued political loyalty.'[22]

Yet we must note that many religious practices had been preserved through cultural resolutions and revitalized in the Putian area in Fujiang, as Kenneth Dean demonstrated in his study. While religion is still a sensitive issue in China, many scholars contributed to the study of its revival and development, particularly that of Buddhism in urban areas,[23] and that of Christianity in both rural[24] and urban.[25] Yet very little literature touches on the issue of the development of religion in China through transnational networks.

One of the important unspoken regulations among house churches in Shanghai is the separation of 'foreign' and 'non-foreign' congregations or fellowships. It reflects the government's fear of foreign influence on domestic congregations. The government still treats Christianity as a foreign religion. Yet this regulation is not imposed on Buddhists in Shanghai.

How are Tzuchian's practices changed under this structure of restraint? For example, based on my previous research in the US, Tzu Chi conducts a wide array of social service work in New York City. The Mission of Charity commissioners visit the poor, nursing homes and jails, and provide long-term and short-term assistance. Every Saturday, the team of commissioners offers free lunch to elderly people at a Buddhist temple, which is owned and attended by Fuzhouese immigrants in Chinatown. Tzu Chi also distributes winter coats at another Buddhist temple, the Chinese Consolidated Benevolent Association, and other locations in Brooklyn, with assistance from the Guan Ming and Guan Yin temples. In 2001, Tzu Chi New York extended its coat-distribution practice to a Latino neighbourhood, the Charas/El Bohio Cultural and Community Centre on Manhattan's Lower East Side. These kinds of outdoor, interfaith and interracial endeavours may not be easily conducted in current Shanghai, although Tzu Chi received its legal status in 2008.

Another example is the Tzu Chi Mission of Medicine, which provides volunteer services in hospitals and has established a medical clinic on wheels for Chinatown's elderly, conducting blood pressure tests and organizing global bone-marrow donation campaigns in New York. It also supports free clinics for immigrants in Flushing with the help of the Flushing Chinese Business Association, as well as clinics and relief distribution in rural areas. In the last two years, Tzu Chi has been actively negotiating the possibilities of a medical mission in Suzhou city in China and has finally received permits in 2014.

The Tzu Chi Mission of Education in USA has established Tzu Chi Humanities Schools to promote moral teaching, meditation and Mandarin language instruction for the second generation of ethnic-Chinese immigrants. The establishment of Tzu Chi educational institutions was more difficult than it was for the hospitals in China. Some designated Tzuchians in Shanghai would visit elementary schools teachers or principals with the intention to integrate Tzu Chi Still Thoughts into their curriculums.

The Mission of Culture in New York carries out small programmes such as a weekly street clean-up and occasional park beautification projects. Tzu Chi New York also organizes occasional lectures, tea parties and charity bazaars to raise funds for the poor or for disaster relief. In Shanghai, voluntary street cleaning is not possible. Yet private tea parties and charity bazaars are organized at homes or at the Tzu Chi Centre in Changfeng.

BUDDHIST BENEVOLENT PRACTICES IN SHANGHAI IN THE 1920s

The unique aspect of Tzu Chi Buddhism is its emphasis on social service. The concept of benevolent Buddhist practices in China or Shanghai is not new and has been part of Buddhist tradition. According to Zongmao Tang, 'new' benevolent practices in 1920s Shanghai revealed how Chinese Buddhism was socialized in modern China. It also illustrates the significant transition that Buddhism underwent due to modernization in urban areas. Donations for medical treatment, tea and congee were the ways of being a generous Buddhist in the traditional society. Yet these benevolent practices were random and territorially-based. Tang argues that the benevolent practices among the Buddhist laity[26] in the 1920s were significantly different from those of the traditional laity in terms of breaking out of the conventional boundaries of territoriality, kinship and professions in practice.[27]

The Shanghai laity in the 1920s was deeply influenced by Master Yin Guang's[28] teachings on the Pure Land. 'Belief, Vision, and Practice' were taught as the three major essences to achieve the Western Heaven. The Shanghai laity then, unlike those holding to conventional practices, did not affiliate itself with temples or government officials. Therefore, financial resources came from the general public and some major merchants. The people who received aid also included war refugees and children who needed education. Buddhist benevolent works also extended beyond their local adherents. Unlike traditional Buddhists who based their benevolent works around local temples, the laity in the 1920s systematically developed various programmes in the city, which were expanded outside the Jiangshu province. Tang also uncovered how the leadership of benevolent works had shifted from federal landlords and traditional patrons to urban merchants. These merchants, as Tang argued, usually utilized those benevolent works as, first, the presentation of prestige and social status, and second, as the means to advance their businesses.[29]

A SNAPSHOT OF CASE STUDIES

'The More You Give, the More You Receive'

'When I first climbed to the top floor of this manufacturing company for a building inspection, I looked out the windows and there were more than 10 construction sites in the far distance. I felt it in my gut that Shanghai will be the future. It is exactly this spot that I was standing that day. Therefore, I made up my mind to move my business to Shanghai,' said Brother MS[30] during an interview.

Before Brother MS moved his business to Shanghai, he actually started a joint company with friends there. 'Why did I move to Shanghai instead of Shengchen? Most of the labor-intensive factories moved to Shengchen. I went to Guangdong once. I did not like it.' MS was recruited by the Shanghai City government. They sent someone to Taiwan and held a recruitment event in the Danshui

University in the early 1990s. 'Professor CH Lu organized a 32 people tour to come to the development of Pudong in 1990. I joined the tour to visit Shanghai. We were received by the major of A town. . . . They told us the land would be free if we came over and invested our business in Pudong.'

Brother MS converted to being a Tzu Chi follower by a Sister whose company had a union contract with them. When I asked how he incorporates the Tzu Chi spirit into his business management, he said,

> In the beginning when I first joined Tzu Chi, I took some responsibilities to plan activities. I learned business management and time management from my Tzu Chi team. I had to learn to evaluate. I learned how to coordinate different events. I learned how to implement the plan. Business management and Tzu Chi's work really can be integrated. For example, time management. I really respect Tzu Chi's operation. Whenever we plan out an event, we always follow the schedule. From what hour to what hour, we always finish on time. The experience and planning are very important. After all, I have become better in time management and planning in my manufacturing management. In addition, what I learned is loving management (kindness management). For example, Tzu Chi encourages us to promote loving management and caring as incentive for staffs. We used to hold the management tight. We did not dare to relax on our management. We did not know what would happen if we relaxed on our management. In time, I learned how to let go. What I learned at Tzu Chi, I will share with them. It, to certain extent, will change them.

The company office and restaurant were decorated with the Tzu Chi 'Still Thought' phrase. During the lunch hour, there are eight television sets playing Tzu Chi Dai TV programmes. The company provide free vegetarian food, and vegetarian food alone every Friday. Brother MS built a spacious centre inside the company for Tzu Chi to conduct its routine operations and events. Regular classes, such as the Still Thought teachings, are offered and are open not only to all staff members but also to neighbourhood residents.

When I ask Brother MS if he lost time to earn more money when he spent more time on the Tzu Chi mission, he replied:

> Making profit is only for my personal interest. The Shangren said,[31] 'you must give up something in order to get something.' Are you the richest

among richest? Are you the poorest among the poorest? Or are you the richest among the poorest? The Master said that we have to be the richest among the richest. The richest should have to donate more to the needy. . . .

Last time when I was in Sichuan for the earthquake relief, I felt the logic of money going out in a visible way but coming back in an invisible way. Although I was not in the company during that few months, what I earned was more than ever. After I agreed to donate one million (NT dollar), I paid off my villa loan earlier than I expected. This was a fact.

This was how I felt. There was a testimony on myself. Money goes out in a visible way, but comes back in an invisible way.

'. . . A Magnetic Field Generated from People's Benevolence and People's Hearts'

Sister M[32] owns a construction company. She has converted her storefront space into a gathering space for all Tzu Chi activities in Baoshan District. After I was told that there was no public religious display besides tourism sites in Shanghai, I walked into M's office and was greeted by Tzu Chi posters as her storefront decoration. The office is completely converted into a Tzu Chi local centre with clear Tzu Chi interior design elements. At 9 p.m., the office staff gathers in front of a Guanyi Bodhisattva statue and recites the Great Compassion Mantra.[33] When I asked why the Maha Karuna Dharani was recited, M replied that it was relatively short. They recited it three times 8 a.m., 12 p.m., and 4 p.m. during the day. This practice of the three daily prayers has been going on for more than five years in her company.

Tzu Chi's Still Thoughts slogans will be posted at all the construction sites. Sister M believes that these teachings will calm the workers. Bodhisattva statues will be placed at some construction sites. At some sites, workers will listen to Master Cheng Yen's sermon in the morning before they start their daily routine. A vegetarian diet is a must in the office. All the above efforts are done to prevent accidents at the construction sites. 'Those efforts are to create a magnetic field generated from people's benevolence and people's hearts. Imperceptibly, there are more guiren.'[34] The superpower of the magnetic field can be generated by faithful worship and dedicated actions. The appearance of 'guiren' can be understood as the reward of the universe for our benevolent actions.

Community residents can easily spot gatherings on Tuesday and Thursday nights in M's store front office. During the weekends, residents can also hear Tzu Chi music, and witness about seventy-five people singing and dancing outside M's company. Later seventy-five people disperse into four residential communities for an environmental protection campaign, mainly for promoting recycling. A team of sixteen-twenty members set up a booth in the plaza or another open space in the housing community (Xiaoqu) for maximizing the visual impact.

Volunteers start with singing songs and dancing to warm up and catch the attention of passersby. Inevitably, some residents will report this activity to the housing community committee (Juwei), which also includes a party representative. Overall, I observed several very high-profile outdoor campaigns with only one complaint received during the day. Yet the complaint was quickly resolved after Sister M made a few phone calls. How did she manage to get approval in the first place and end the complaint?

Sister M explained to me that she would explain to her community committee the purpose of Tzu Chi missions a few weeks in advance. She would give a DVD presentation and shows selected publications to residential community and party leaders on the nature of Tzu Chi and its NGO missions. For years, the Xiaoqu local party leader only imposed one restriction on Sister M – that Tzu Chi events could conduct any Buddhist rituals.

In this way, Sister M incorporated the concept of sustainable development into her business practice. Ceaseless efforts at communication and the skilful cultivation of personal relationships are the keys for Tzu Chi to develop successfully in some residential neighbourhoods. Sister M also has another religious explanation. She and her company staff have three sutra chanting rituals as a daily routine. After the rituals, she said that she consistently redirects the blessings resulting from chanting to the community party leaders, which might be one of the reasons that they maintain good relationships with Tzu Chi.

'Overcome the Self-Desire is the Path to be a Responsible Entrepreneur'

The Ting Hsin International Group is based in Tianjin, Hengzhou, Xiang and Shanghai with fifty-two units of companies and manufacturers all over China. It is China's biggest instant noodle maker, owning the Kang Shi Fu brand, also known as Master Kang or Ting Yi through its associate, the Ting Yi Holding Corporation. Its business has recently extended to convenience stores,[35] chain restaurants (such as a beef noodle soup business in Shanghai) and other food outlets in China. The TingHsin International Group is also the biggest private shareholder in the Taiwan Financial Center Corporation, which owns the tallest landmark building in Taipei.

One of the company presidents, Wei,[36] is a devoted Tzuchian and follows the teachings on how to be a responsible Buddhist entrepreneur. Master Cheng Yen's overcoming self-desire is seen as a path for cultivating responsible entrepreneurship. For example, Wei believes that everyone should make a concerted effort to reduce their carbon footprint, as Cheng Yen teaches her disciples. As she puts it:

> . . . Environmental awareness should be implemented daily. We hope that we always keep the affection of the heart of the earth, and to promote the concept of 'Keji Fuli' (Overcoming desire, and moral returns for honesty and sincerity). The 'Keji Fuli' New Life Movement is to enhance human morality.
>
> The so-called 'Keji' (self-restraint) is to overcome self-desire. If human beings cannot restrain their desire for pleasure, they will always waste resources, which is not only damaging to human health, but also damaging to the Earth. 'Fuli' (return to ritual or ceremonies) is to discover beauty among human beings. It is the li where we can translate our accomplishments into manners.
>
> We look forward to moving toward a polite and progressive society, to overcome the self-desire, to enhance the humanitarian temperament, to rehabilitate our respect for teachers, filial piety and other traditional rituals.[37]
>
> If so, I believe that it will change the future ecology. Love of everyone which will relieve global warming effect and climatic changes. Society will become harmonious.

Wei is not only a devotee of Tzu Chi; but also the first Taiwanese entrepreneur to establish a Tzu Chi humanitarian department within the human resource office of the TingHsin International Group. Feng,[38] the manager of the department, explains to me how TingHsin integrates Cheng Yeng teaching into corporate culture. 'To be a green corporation we are serious at promoting vegetarianism, recycling, and monetary and energy saving', he says.

Wei expressed how he changed his daily habits since he started to practice 'keji fuli'.

> It is so hard to overcome the inclinations or desires. I have to change my old habits before I can change other company members. . . . I always eat something simple, and I try to be a vegetarian. I do not turn the air conditioner on during the summer. If it is getting really hot, I will still only turn the fan on. We have also changed our faucet to a water-saving one at home. I no longer have a hot bath anymore. Like the rest of Tzuchians, I always bring my own dining set and handkerchief whenever I travel.[39]

Wei also promotes a carbon reduction campaign with his 4,000 employees, fifty-two units of companies and manufacturers. Within six months, the companies have saved about 323 million kilowatt hours of electricity, 20 tons of water, 20 million litres of oil, and 1,900 kg of paper the equivalent of 2.5 million kg of carbon. Yet I could not verify this information when I discussed it with Feng.

SOMETHING NEW FROM AN OLD TRADITION: RELIGIOUS DISCOURSE AND KARMA LOGISTICS

What is Tzu Chi's religious discourse on environmentalism? Cheng Yen uses modern language in her discourse, such as 'Love the Earth'. As a Buddhist, it means to love the pure Hui Ming (the life of wisdom) in our lives. What is the relationship between the earth and Hui Ming? In the world of ten directions (the whole universe), the only place that people can cultivate themselves and become the Buddha is the earth. However, human beings cannot cultivate themselves and become the Buddha in heaven or in hell. Heaven is too comfortable with no opportunity for Buddhist cultivation. Whoever is in hell is too busy suffering. The only place for Buddhist cultivation is the earth. Therefore, if human beings destroy the earth, we destroy our lives of wisdom.

Why do Tzuchians promote environmentalism? They have to

promote the value of the life of wisdom. Environmentalism provides the field for cultivation. Thus, Cheng Yen calls Tzuchians 'Environmental Buddhas', 'Purified Buddhas', or 'Buddhas of Embracing Earth'. She often emphasizes the relationship between 'reviving decency, decorum, ethics and virtue' and environmental protection.

Until 2007, over sixty countries had accepted disaster relief from the Tzu Chi Foundation. Tzu Chi has more than 300 offices in forty countries with over 5 million supporters and over 30,000 certified commissioners around the globe. Tzuchians in China also have worked with the local governments on relief efforts from time to time. This Reformed Buddhist Tzu Chi teaching created a link between traditional Buddhist teaching and modern moral action. Followers of Tzu Chi could not isolate their good deeds to certain contexts; they had to reorganize their lives methodically and cultivate themselves through work in their daily life. To live a simple life is to run one's business wisely in an economical and pragmatic way. To practice diligence is to be prudent and sensible in business. Cherishing resources leads to recycling and reusing material in one's business. Saving resources and energy are moral actions to save the earth. To control desire is a discipline of mind and body requiring methodical cultivation, such as being a vegetarian and practicing thrift. You are not supposed to spend the wealth you earn. The greater wealth is to be able to share your wealth.

If we compare the Tzu Chi merchants with the Buddhist laity in the 1920s, there are three major differences. First of all, Tzu Chi is affiliated with a foreign mother temple in Hualian Taiwan. It is registered as a non-governmental organization in China. The financial resources come from the general public and Taiwanese merchants in Shanghai. Tzu Chi Shanghai is not allowed to publically solicit donations. The benevolence programmes also extend beyond the urban areas for two reasons. The extreme poverty in rural areas has provided a niche for many faith-based organizations, including Tzu Chi, to expand their missions. Tzu Chi's transnational nature suggests that it will not limit its vision for growth to one city. As for the leadership, Tzu Chi merchants have to blend in with other general followers as regular members. As one company's president told me, 'We must shrink ourselves. There is no boss ego in Tzu Chi family'.

Therefore, utilizing charitable works to build a business reputation or social status is prohibited. Tzu Chi merchants cannot use charitable works to advance their business, such as building connections with local or remote governments. On the other hand, they will have to risk their business when they promote their faith.

The discourse that I heard from many Tzu Chi merchants is very similar. They apply the concept of 'keji fuli' to their enterprises. Besides routine donations to the poor, they are strongly encouraged to utilize their profession for public interest. Enterprises should not limit their goal to the pursuit of economic profit but focus on carbon emissions reduction to pursue sustainable development and establish good models of enterprises based on shared responsibility. One quotation that Tzu Chi immigrant merchants repetitively employ is: 'Shagnren[40] told us that we must have gratitude for what we have received from the locals. Our heads are under their sky. Our feet are stepping on their land. We should have gratitude. What we take from the locals, we should return to benefit the locals. We have to love others first before we can be loved by others.' Immigrant merchants take this teaching as a rationale to devote their energies and souls into the work of rural relief and local community building. Of course, the mentality of accumulating karma is a part of these benevolent actions. As Brother MS and sister mentioned, the interpretations of karma exchange are common understanding, yet are expressed differently by individual business people. The businesses are different, the discourse and implementations are different. Sustainable development and environmental protection have translated economically into the practice of thrift in the use of electricity and all other resources, and raw material conservation in manufacturing. Tzu Chi cultivation teaching has translated into the concept of self-management to control or redirect the questionable excessiveness, if not greed, of the employers, as well as to instruct or even discipline the employees.

Furthermore there is evidence of tension between spiritual teachings, censorship and commercial logic. This paper discovered how the tension between the Buddhist Tzu Chi and the Chinese state is different from that between house churches and the local state. Regulations have forced Tzu Chi missions into the private sectors – the companies and manufacturers are dominated by foreign investors, yet the practices are not categorized as illegal activities. This issue will be elaborated in a future paper.

NOTES

1. The fieldwork was conducted in March 2011 for four weeks in Shanghai.
2. Sassen (1988).
3. Tseng (2000): 2.
4. Ibid.
5. Tseng (1997): 143.
6. Portes (1999): 225.
7. Gallagher (2005).
8. Ibid.
9. Lin (2001).
10. Faist (2007).
11. Himalaya Foundation, http://www.npo.org.tw/NPOInfo/list.asp?OrgID=11. Four missions: charity, medicine, education and, culture. Accessed 20 October 2007.
12. Zheng Yen is the Chinese spelling, and Cheng Yen is the Taiwanese Chinese spelling.
13. Since 2008, commissioners have been encouraged to hold the Global Tzu Chi Day locally in their respective host societies.
14. Huang (2003).
15. Commissioners are female lay leaders and Faith Corps members are male lay leaders.
16. 1,407 commissioners and 591 Faith Corps members among 99 US branches.
17. Tzu Chi Foundation United States Branch.
18. Tzu Chi Foundation Shanghai Branch.
19. Robert Weller in his book, *Alternate Civilities: Democracy and Culture in Taiwan*, uses the term 'civil association' to avoid the theoretical assumptions and historical connections of the term 'civil society.' See Weller (2001).
20. Potter (2003): 317-37; Van der Veer (2011): 270-81.
21. Yang (2006): 100-1; Lou (2001).
22. Potter (2003).
23. Fisher (2011).
24. Hunter and Chan (1993).
25. Cao (2007); F. Yang (2005).
26. Buddhist laity, called 'householder Buddhism' by Jushi.
27. Tang (2011).
28. Master Yin Guang, the thirteenth Patriarch of Pure Land School.
29. Tang (2011).

30. The pseudonym for a Taiwanese informant.
31. Master Cheng Yen.
32. Sister M is a pseudonym for a Taiwanese informant.
33. Great Compassion Mantra, Mahā Karuna Dhāranī (大悲咒).
34. Guiren, somebody who helps in time of need.
35. Convenience stores, Quanjia, Family Convenient.
36. A pseudonym for the informant.
37. In original text, it is '期待大家努力朝向有禮的社會邁進，克服自我欲念，提升人文氣質，復興尊師重道、孝道等傳統禮儀。' http://translate.google.com/translate?hl=en&sl=auto&tl=en&u=http%3A%2F%2Fwww2.tzuchi.org.tw%2Fcase%2F2007virtue%2Findex.htm&anno=2 Master speaking in March 2007. Data retrieved at 19 November 2011.
38. A pseudonym for the informant.
39. Public interview (data source)
40. Master Cheng Yen.

BIBLIOGRAPHY

Cao, Nanlai. 2010. *Constructing China's Jerusalem: Christians, Power, and Place in Contemporary Wenzhou*. Standard University Press.

Fais, Thomas. 2008. 'Migrants as Transnational Development Agents: An Inquiry into the Newest Round of the Migration-Development Nexus', *Populations, Space, and Place* 14, pp. 21-42.

Fisher, Gareth. 2011. 'Religion as Repertoire: Resourcing the Past in a Beijing Buddhist Temple', *Modern China*, 15 September 2011.

Gallagher, Elisabeth. 2005. *Contagious Capitalism*. Cambridge University Press.

Lin, Man-Houng, 2001. 'Overseas Chinese Merchants and Multiple Nationality: A Means for Reducing Commercial Risk (1895-1935)', *Modern Asian Studies* 35, 4, pp. 985-1009.

Huang, Julia. 2003. 'Sacred or Profane? The Compassion Relief Movement's Transnationalism in Taiwan, Japan, and Malaysia, and the United States', *European Journal of East Asian Studies*, vol. 2, no. 2, pp. 217-41(25).

Hunter, Alan and Kim-kwong Chan. 1993. *Protestantism in Contemporary China*. Cambridge University Press.

Sassen, Saskia. 1988. *The Mobility of Labor and Capital*. New York: Oxford University Press.

Tang, Zhongmao. 'Minguo shanghai jushi fojiao cishan de jiben yunzhuo moshi, tedian yu yiyi' (The operation model, characters, and meaning of household Buddhists benevolent behaviours in modern Shanghai) Conference paper. Conference on Religious benevolent behaviors, Shanghai University, October 2011.

Tseng, Yen-Fen. 2000. 'The Mobility of Entrepreneurs and Capital: Taiwanese Capital-Linked Migration', *International Migration*, vol. 38(2).

Portes, A., L.E. Guarnizo, and P. Landolt. 1999. 'The Study of Transnationalism: Pitfalls and Promise of an Emergent Research Field', *Ethnic and Racial Studies*, 22(2): 219-37.

Potter, Pitman B. 2003. 'Belief in Control: Regulation of Religion in China', *The China Quarterly*, no. 174, *Religion in China Today* (June 2003), pp. 317-37.

Van der Veer, Peter. 2011. 'Smash Temples, Burn Books: Comparing Secularist Projects in India and China', in Craig Calhoun, Mark Juergensmeyer and Jonathan Van Antwerpen (eds.), *Rethinking Secularism*. New York, NY: Oxford University Press, 270-81.

Weller, Robert. 2001. *Alternate Civilities: Democracy and Culture in Taiwan*, Westview Press, 2001.

Yang, Fenggang. 2005. 'Lost in the Market, Saved at McDonald's: Conversion to Christianity in Urban China', *Journal for the Scientific Study of Religion*, vol. 44, issue 4, pp. 423-41. December 2005.

PART IV

AFTERWORD

CHAPTER 13

The Construction of World Buddhism

PETER VAN DER VEER

HOWEVER LONG AND important the pre-modern history of religious formations in Asia has been, the modern period of imperialism and nationalism provides a specific rupture with the past because of the externality of imperial power and the ideological emphasis in the metropolis on the difference of modern society from both its own past and from other, so-called backward societies. Comparison and an evolutionary perspective on difference became crucial in the high days of the empire. Simultaneously, as Edward Said has argued, the new scientific knowledge of Orientalism provided the colonized with a new understanding of their traditions.[1] Hinduism, Buddhism, Confucianism and Daoism were discovered and evaluated by philologists, archaeologists and other historians, while traders, missionaries and colonial officers tried to deal with the contemporary forms of these traditions.[2] This apparatus of imperial knowledge has created an archive that is still crucial for any understanding of Asian traditions. It is this archive that needs to be understood if one wants to understand the nature of the modern transformation of religion both in Asia and in the West.[3]

One element of the modern transformation of religion is 'the invention of world religions', as Tomoko Masuzawa calls it in her recent book.[4] 'World Religions' as a category is a product of comparative theology and the science of religion. Comparative theology begins and ends with the singularity of Christianity in comparison to other religions, while the science of religion attempts to be a science that deals with all religions evenhandedly. In addition, the science of religion derives part of its scientific status from being closely connected to historical linguistics and philology.

THE 'DISCOVERY' OF BUDDHISM

Of special importance is the 'discovery' of Buddhism as another world religion besides Christianity, which came to be recognized in the nineteenth century as existing in various parts of Asia and, thus, as transnational. In contrast to the old enemy, Islam, it was also regarded as an ethically high religion with universal significance like Christianity. Scholars like Monier Monier-Willams (1819-99), the Sanskritist at Oxford, declared that Buddhism was a philosophy or system of morality but not a religion. This is certainly an important issue that is debated over and over again till the present day but besides such discussions on the nature of Buddhist thought, mainly debated on the basis of textual research, there were also crucial material findings in Asia. Above all, there were archaeological attempts to find ancient Buddhism under the layers of Hinduism in India in the same period. Alexander Cunningham (1814-93), the founder of the Archaeological Survey of India, found and explored long-forgotten Buddhist sites in India, such as the famous Sarnath. The archaeological surveys undertaken by him aimed at 'attributing visual materiality to the "textual object" so that a physically absent religion could be fashioned into a visible living "thing", which was possible to locate artifactually and which could be grasped through its own unique archaeological landscape.'[5] The unearthing of Buddhism in India was coupled with a deliberate marginalization of later and contemporary worship at sites like Sarnath. Even the Jain presence that was accepted to be as old as the Buddhist one was happily ignored. Sarnath came to stand for a timeless Buddhist spirituality that, according to the famous art historian, Ananda Coomaraswamy, was represented by the Sarnath Wheel of Dharma, later adopted in the Indian flag as India's national contribution to universal spirituality. Even today, the Buddhist king, Asoka, is a symbol of ancient Indian secularism and tolerance, a notion that Indian secularists have happily (and unwittingly) adopted from colonial anti-Brahmanism.

These findings were an important element in establishing an ancient Indian history in which Buddhism was portrayed as the enemy of Brahmanism, and came to be destroyed by Islam and ultimately supplanted by Hinduism.[6] This was essential to the grand narrative of Indian history in which Buddhism was also seen as an alternative to caste-ridden Hinduism and taken up as such by egalitarian reformists like the leader of untouchables and a leading politician of modern India, B.R. Ambedkar (1891-1956). It is this simultaneous production of Buddhism as native to India and as a world religion that could be universally respected for its modern, egalitarian message that becomes so important in the Indian location.

In Sri Lanka, something else happened. Here, Buddhism was reframed first by the publication of 26,000 pages of Buddhist texts (in Roman transliteration!) by the Pali Text Society, founded in1881 by T.W. Rhys Davids (1843-1922) who had been a British civil servant in Sri Lanka and, as such, was involved in the excavation of a famous archaeological site, the ancient city of Anuradhapura. Subsequently, it was the Theosophist, Colonel H.S. Olcott (1832-1907) who designed the Sri Lankan flag and created a Buddhist catechism which aimed to transform Sri Lankan Buddhist traditions into a recognizable religion. And finally, and most importantly, it is the efforts of the reformist monk, Anagarika Dharmapala (1864-1933), who had been deeply influenced by Theosophy, that created Sinhala Buddhist nationalism which is of central importance in contemporary conflicts between the Tamils and the Sinhala in Sri Lanka. It is precisely because of the reconfiguration of Buddhism in Western scholarship as a world religion within the imperial framework that enabled it to become such an important element of religious nationalism among the Sinhalese in Sri Lanka. The dialectics of orientalism and nationalism is of great importance to both sides of the imperial imagination. On the side of the metropolis, it is the development of a universal spirituality of which Buddhism is seen as a prime example that fits uneasily with the institutional religion that many intellectuals were familiar with at the end of the nineteenth century.

Simultaneous to and congruous with the scholarly production of cosmopolitan knowledge on Buddhist traditions in different parts of Asia, one finds the development of an audience for universal spirituality. A major step in this was the World Parliament of Religions held on the occasion of the Columbian Exposition of 1893 in Chicago. This event was meant to celebrate the rise of Chicago after the devastating fire of 1871, the 400th anniversary of Columbus' 'discovery' of the Western hemisphere and the superiority of a Judeo-Christian tradition (already a new amalgamation of Protestantism,

Catholicism and Judaism) in relation to other religious traditions of the world.[7] Representatives of ten great traditions – Confucianism, Taoism, Shintoism, Hinduism, Buddhism, Jainism, Zoroastrianism, Judaism, Christianity and Islam – came together for seventeen days to discuss their religions before an audience among which was a considerable press attendance. Despite the unitarian and liberal Christian agenda of the Parliament, media attention was captured by a relatively small (around twenty representatives of seven traditions) Asian delegation. South Asian delegates like Swami Vivekananda and Anagarika Dharmapala became famous overnight. Due to their oratorical skills, they were able to use the Parliament as a platform for their anti-imperialist, spiritual message that extolled the spiritual merits of Asian traditions while condemning Christian missionary aggression. The impact of their success in the American press was such that it was communicated to their home audiences, and paved the way for their reformist and nationalist agendas there.

Anagarika Dharmapala, a Buddhist layman from Sri Lanka, used the World Parliament to launch his campaign. Dharmapala was born in a Buddhist family as Don David Hewavitharana. When Colonel Olcott and Helena Blavatsky came to Sri Lanka, he acted as their assistant. Due to Theosophy, he became interested in the Buddhist traditions of his native land and was shocked by what he considered to be the degenerate state of Buddhism of his time. Under the influence of Theosophy, he set out to reform Buddhism with an emphasis on its spirituality and worldwide message. The irony of the history of both Vivekananda and Dharmapala is that they set out to promote a global spirituality in many of their lectures and published thoughts but are mainly remembered for their inspiration they gave to Hindu nationalism and Sinhala Buddhist nationalism, respectively. Dharmapala was primarily interested in the development of World Buddhism for which he wanted to open up the major sites of early Buddhism in India like Bodh Gaya (where the Buddha had gained enlightenment) and Sarnath (where the Buddha began his teaching). He was not able to wrest control of the Bodh Gaya site from the Shaiva ascetics that had controlled it over centuries. However, Bodh Gaya has in the meantime, become a major pilgrimage centre for Buddhists from all over the world with a highway leading to it from the Patna airport and built by Japanese investors. Dharmapala travelled to Europe and started Buddhist monasteries in London.[8] His command over English (as in the case of Vivekananda) gave him a strategic advantage in linking Asian traditions to global spirituality. He truly became *anagarika,* meaning 'homeless' since he travelled almost all the time.

CHINESE SPIRITUALITY

Spirituality does not acquire centrality in the translation of Chinese traditions as it has in that of India's traditions. After the devastating Taiping and Boxer rebellions of the nineteenth century, Chinese nationalists decided that Chinese traditions were to be blamed for the backwardness of their society and that in order to progress, China had to adopt Western materialism based on science and secularism. In Chinese modern fiction of the first part of the twentieth century, there is a strong sense that China is a society not so much endowed with a spiritual heritage but afflicted with a spiritual disease.[9] Nevertheless, there were important currents of thought in China that attempted to resurrect some of the spiritual resources of the past, especially those of Buddhism and Confucianism. Liang Qichao, who was Rabindranath Tagore's host in the 1920s, was critical of the exclusive emphasis laid on science and rationality in the West, and argued that the East was spiritual and that science should have a moral foundation and purpose. In his foundational work for example in his Methods for the Study of Chinese History on Chinese historiography, he gradually replaced evolutionary history and chains of causality with the Buddhist notion of 'interdependence' (yinyuanjiebao, 因缘捷报).[10] While Liang rejected Confucianism as a model, others tried to develop a modern understanding of history as a sign of the nation by referring to Confucian social ethics as the 'spirit of the nation' (minzujingshen, 民族精神). This form of Neo-Confucianism as a kind of spiritual nationalism ultimately failed to take root in China since it turned out to be too difficult to separate Confucianism from the now-defunct imperial system and turn it into the civil religion of the modern nation state.[11]

Thus, we find the same kind of intellectual ferment in some circles in China as we find in India in, for example, the Brahmo Samaj; namely, attempts to understand and connect to Western thought without losing touch with indigenous intellectual traditions. The big difference is that they were not able to dominate nationalism to the extent that the circles around Mahatma Gandhi and Tagore could in India. Besides more or less 'secular' intellectuals like Yan Fu or Hu Shih, who are the subject of a massive intellectual historiography, we find new spiritual leaders in Buddhist and Daoist circles that have been brought to scholarly attention more recently.[12]

Probably the most important Chinese Buddhist reformer was the monk Taixu (1890-1947), whose significance for Chinese Buddhism can be compared to that of Vivekananda for Indian Hinduism and of Dharmapala, the Sri Lankan monk, for Theravada Buddhism.[13] Taixu was traditionally educated and given his tonsure initiation in the usual fashion. The head monk of the Yuhang temple near Yingbo gave him his name Taixu, meaning Supreme Emptiness. This emptiness was quickly filled with the reading of political pamphlets and radical philosophy, written or inspired by Western thinkers. An important period in Taixu's life was his stay at the Jetavana Hermitage (Zhihuan Jingshe) in Nanjing, founded by a layman called Yang Wenhui who had met Anagarika Dharmapala.[14] Dharmapala visited Japan and China after attending the World Parliament of Religions of 1893 in Chicago which, as we have mentioned, was also attended by Vivekananda. He wanted to gather support to revive Buddhism in the ancient sites of India.

Taixu primarily devoted himself to two major causes. First of all, he wanted to further the cause of monastic education to go beyond Buddhist studies to include modern subjects like history and psychology. He founded important monastic schools in Wuchang and Xiamen (the South Fujian Seminary). It is from these schools that his students spread his ideas throughout China and far beyond in the Chinese diaspora. Second, he wanted to promote the cause of Buddhism worldwide, especially in response to the challenge posed by the Christian missionary expansion. In 1924, he organized the first conference of the World Buddhist Association with a threefold purpose: 'first, to unite Buddhists from each province in China; second, to unite Buddhists from each country of East Asia; and, third, to transmit the truth and spirit of East Asian Buddhism to each country of Europe and to the United States so that the Federation could become in actual fact a World Buddhist federation. . . .'[15] These endeavours were hardly successful, primarily because of the dismal situation in which China found itself, torn between warlords, nationalists, communists and Japanese aggressors. Moreover, Taixu also received considerable opposition from major monastic leaders who thought that total renunciation and meditation would lead to the Pure Land (jingtu, 净土 净土).

During tours to Japan, the United States of America, France, and Germany, Taixu was able to gain substantial support for his endeavours. In this way, he can be visualized as a predecessor of Buddhist monks like the Dalai Lama and the Vietnamese Thith Nhat Hanh, who have used their transnational audience to further the cause of a socially and politically engaged Buddhism. The most significant difference between Taixu and someone like Vivekananda or Dharmapala (as also the Dalai Lama and Thith Nhat Hanh) is that these others were able to connect their spirituality to the spirit of the nation, to an emergent nationalism. In China, the nationalists were, in principle, not in favour of Buddhism but rather in favour of Christianity. The communists had even less space for a revitalized, socially active Buddhism which forced radical Buddhists like Taixu into the nationalist camp where they were only half-heartedly welcomed. After the victory of the communists and after Taixu's death, Buddhist leaders left for Taiwan where they staged a slow comeback following the relaxation of the Kuomintang rule in the 1980s. Some of the movements and leaders that have been instrumental in developing a civil society in Taiwan have been influenced by Taixu's ideas. With the opening up of Mainland China, these movements have also begun to actively revitalize Buddhism there.

In the context of the struggle for a Buddhist modernity that combined spirituality and nationalism, it is instructive to compare Chinese Buddhism with Daoism. In the period that Taixu tried to modernize Buddhism, Chen Yingning (1880-1969) tried to do the same with Daoism.[16] Both Taixu and Chen Yingning were deeply involved in the rise of a religious public sphere (newspapers, printing presses) in Shanghai. The process of the laicization of Daoism had already happened in the late nineteenth century and had led to the development of circles of learned lay practitioners of *neidan*, 'inner alchemy' in what came to be called *wenren Daojiao* (literati Daoism).[17] In the confrontation with Western imperialism, a new interest in the cultivation of the body as part of the reinvigoration of the Chinese national character (*guomin genxing*) emerged in ways that were very similar to the new interest in yoga and martial arts in India at the end of the nineteenth century. One finds here a widespread trope that the West had only been able to conquer the East because of the lack of masculine strength in the conquered nations. Pure Land Buddhism's ties with Japanese Buddhism prevented it from being regarded as nationalist, while Daoism had impeccable Chinese credentials. Moreover, there was a long history of polemics against Buddhism in the Daoist scriptures. The real issue now, however, was that of the national body that had to be strengthened in the struggle against Western and Japanese imperialists. It was of the 1980s and 1990s Qi Gong movement that both Buddhist and Daoist understandings of the body came to play a significant role.

CONCLUSION

There are some complex questions that are still partly unanswered in the study of the emergence of modern Buddhism. First of all, we need to have a better understanding of Buddhism in the century before the powerful impact of imperial modernity. In India, this question does not arise since Buddhism disappeared for all practical purposes but it does come up for the societies in which Buddhism has a continued 'living' presence. The research here has to grapple with the historical self-understanding in a tradition like the Buddhist. There is often a strong ideological denial of the significance of history in religious traditions which makes historical research of religion very difficult.[18]

Second, we need to gain a better understanding of the interaction between secularism (as an intellectual and state-supported project of modernity) and Buddhist tradition. It struck me in visits to Nanputuo in Xiamen (South-West China) that contemporary monks and nuns are much better versed in historical materialism than in Buddhist philosophy. At the level of religious practice, obviously, tourism is the frame in which pilgrimage takes place and again the question of the secular in relation to the religious comes up in such situations.

NOTES

1. Said (1978).
2. See for Buddhism, Almond (1988).
3. Van der Veer (1992): 173-87.
4. Masuzawa (2005).
5. Guha (2011): 12.
6. On this theory of 'historical stages' and its fallacies, see Thapar (1969).
7. Seager (2009).
8. Kemper (2009): 203-21.
9. Goldman (2002): 142.
10. Schneider (2001): 8.
11. Kuo (2008): 65-84.
12. Schwartz (1964). Levinson (1953).
13. Taixu has been the subject of a major biography: Pittman (2001).
14. Pittman (2001): 70.
15. Cited in Pitman (2001): 107.
16. His life and works are the subject of a recent monograph by Xun Liu (2009).
17. Goossaert (2007).
18. Van der Veer (2008): 633-41.

BIBLIOGRAPHY

Almond, P. 1988. *See for Buddhism: The British Discovery of Buddhism*. Cambridge: Cambridge University Press.

Goldman, M. and O.F. Lee, eds. 2002. *An Intellectual History of Modern China*, Cambridge: Cambridge University Press.

Goossaert, V. 2007. *The Taoists of Peking, 1800-1949*. Cambridge: Harvard University Press.

Guha, S. 2011. 'Material Truths and Religious Identities: The Archeological and Photographic Making of Banaras', in M.S. Dodson (ed.), *Banaras: Urban History, Architecture, Photography*. London: Routledge, pp. 42-76.

Hui, W. 2004. *Xiandai zhongguo sixiang de xingqi* 現代中國思想的興起 (The Rise of Modern Chinese Thought (4 vols). Beijing: SDX Joint Publishing Company.

Kemper, S. 2009. 'Dharmapala's Buddhisms', in H.L. Seneviratne (ed.), *The Anthropologist and the Native: Essays for Gananath Obeyesekere*. Florence: Societa Editrice Fiorentina, pp. 203-21.

Kuo, Y. 2008. 'Redeploying Confucius: The Imperial State Dreams of the Nation,

1902-1911', in Mayfair Yang (ed.), *Chinese Religiosities: Vicissitudes of Modernity and State Formation.* Berkeley: University of California Press, pp. 65-84.

Levinson, J. 1953. *Liang Ch'i-Ch'ao and the Mind of Modern China.* Cambridge: Harvard University Press.

Liu, X. 2009. *Daoist Modern.* Cambridge: Harvard University Press.

Masuzawa, T. 2005. *The Invention of World Religions.* Chicago: University of Chicago Press.

Pittman, D. 2001. *Toward a Modern Chinese Buddhism: Taixu's Reforms.* Honolulu: University of Hawai'i Press.

Said, E. 1978. *Orientalism.* New York: Pantheon Books.

Seager, R.H. 2009. *The World's Parliament of Religions: The East/West Encounter, 1893.* Bloomington: Indiana University Press.

Schneider, A. 2001. *China and the Crisis of Modernity, Inaugural Lecture.* Leiden: Leiden University.

Schwartz, B. 1964. *In Search of Wealth and Power: Yen Fu and the West.* Cambridge: Harvard University Press.

Thapar, R., H. Mukhia and B. Chandra. 1969. *Communalism and the Writing of Indian History.* Delhi: People's Publishing House

van der Veer, P. 1992. 'Religion in South Asia', *Annual Review of Anthropology,* 31: 173-87.

———. 2008. 'Does Sanskrit Knowledge Exist?', *Journal of Indian Philosophy,* 36: 633-41.

Contributors

Sonali Dhingra is pursuing a Ph.D. in History of Art and Architecture at Harvard University. Her dissertation research focuses onSouth Asian Buddhist architecture and sculpture and cultic practice at Buddhist sacred sites in South Asia. Previously, she studied ancient Indian history at the University of Delhi and at Jawaharlal Nehru University in New Delhi.

Weishan Huang is a Sociologist and an Assistant Professor in the Department of Cultural and Religious Studies, Chinese University of Hong Kong. Her work mainly focuses on transnational religious movements, the formation of immigrant community, and religious symbolizations of space in New York and Shanghai cities. One of her joint research projects was to inquire as to how culture and economics intertwined in urban re-structuring before and after the 1990 recession in New York city. She is the co-editor of the book, *Ecology of Faith in the New York City* (2013).

Meera Kosambi was a sociologist. Her several books include *Crossing Thresholds: Feminist Essays in Social History* (2007), *Women Writing Gender: Marathi Fiction Before Independence* (2012) and *Unsettling the Past: Unknown Aspects and Scholarly Assessments of D.D. Kosambi* (2013). She passed away on 26 February 2015 (before this book could be published).

Nayanjot Lahiri is Professor of History at Ashoka University. Previously, she taught at the Department of History, University of Delhi. She established her reputation as an accessible historian of Indian antiquity with *Finding Forgotten Cities: How the Indus Civilization was Discovered* (2005). Her books include *Marshalling the Past: Ancient India and Its Modern Histories* (2012) and *The Archaeology of Indian Trade Routes* (1993). Her most recent book is *Ashoka in Ancient India* (2015). She has written widely in the popular press as well, for publications such as the *Hindustan Times*, the

Telegraph, and *Times Higher Education*. Lahiri won the Infosys Prize 2013 in the Humanities-Archaeology. She is presently working on a history of Indian archaeology since Independence.

BILL M. MAK completed his Ph.D. in Indian Languages and Literature at Peking University in 2009. He is currently Associate Professor at Institute for Research in Humanities/Hakubi Center for Advanced Research, Kyoto University, Japan. His main fields of research include Sanskrit and Buddhist philology, Buddhism and society, and Indian astral science.

KITSIRI MALALGODA has had an abiding interest in the modern period of Buddhism in Sri Lanka. Following the publication of his monograph on *Buddhism in Sinhalese Society, 1750-1900* (1976), he has written a number of supplementary essays such as his contribution to the present volume. He has taught sociology at the University of Peradeniya and the University of Auckland.

SRAMAN MUKHERJEE is Assistant Professor in the School of Historical Studies at Nalanda University. Graduating from the Centre for Studies in Social Sciences, Calcutta and the University of Calcutta, he is trained as a historian of colonial and post-colonial South Asia. His interests include transnational geographies of heritage, modern biographies of sites, objects, and monuments, and histories of inter-Asian interconnections.

ANURUDHHA PRADEEP is a Senior Lecturer, attached to the Department of Political Science, Faculty of Humanities and Social Sciences, University of Sri Jayewardenepura, Sri Lanka. He earned his Bachelor of Arts Degree at the University of Peradeniya, Sri Lanka and Master of Arts from the University of Sri Jayewardenepura. His research interests include religion and politics. His work examines the complexities of the relationship between religion and politics.

TANSEN SEN is Associate Professor of Asian History and Religions at Baruch College. His publications include *Buddhism, Diplomacy, and Trade: The Realignment of Sino-Indian Relations, 600-1400* (2003), and, with Victor H. Mair, *Traditional China in Asian and World History* (2012). He is working on two book projects, one entitled *India, China, and the World: Networks of Exchange and Interactions,* and the other a study of cross-cultural trade in Asia during the fourteenth and fifteenth centuries.

H.L. SENEVIRATNE is Professor Emeritus of Anthropology at the University of Virginia, USA. He is the author of *Rituals of the Kandyan State* (1978), and *The Work of Kings* (1999); and the editor of *Identity, Consciousness and the Past* (1997) and *The Anthropologist and the Native: Essays for Gananath Obeyesekere* (2009).

UPINDER SINGH is Professor and Head, Department of History, University of Delhi. She is the author of *Kings, Brahmanas, and Temples in Orissa: An Epigraphic Study (AD 300-1147)* (1994); *Ancient Delhi* (1999); *The Discovery of Ancient India: Early Archaeologists and the Beginnings of Archaeology* (2004); and *A History of Ancient and Early Medieval India: From the Stone Age to the Twelfth Century* (2008). She has edited *Delhi: Ancient History* (2006) and *Rethinking Early Medieval India* (2011), and co-edited *Ancient India: New Research* (2009) and *Asian Encounters: Exploring Connected Histories* (2014). She received the Infosys Prize for Social Sciences – History in 2009.

PETER VAN DER VEER is Director at the Max Planck Institute for the Study of Religious and Ethnic Diversity as well as Distinguished University Professor at Utrecht University. He has published widely on Indian religion and is, more recently, engaged in comparative work on India and China. His latest book is *The Modern Spirit of Asia.*

DAN SMYER YU is Distinguished Professor and Founding Director of Center for Trans-Himalayan Studies at Yunnan Minzu University and a core member of the Transregional Research Network (CETREN) at University of Göttingen. Prior to this faculty appointment he was a Research Group Leader at Max Planck Institute for Religious and Ethnic Diversity and a New Millennium Scholar at Minzu University of China.He is the author of *The Spread of Tibetan Buddhism in China: Charisma, Money, Enlightenment* (2011) and *Mindscaping the Landscape of Tibet: Place, Memorability, Eco-aesthetics* (2015). His current research interests are religion and ecology, landscape and emotionality, transboundary state effects, hydraulic politics, climate change and heritage preservation, Buddhism and peacebuilding, and comparative studies of Eurasian secularisms.

Index